IRISH FOLK,
TRAD & BLUES

D1427938

First published in 2004 by The Collins Press
West Link Park, Doughcloyne, Wilton, Cork, Ireland

This paperback published in 2005

Published in Great Britain in 2005 by
Cherry Red Books (a division of Cherry Red Records Ltd.),
3a Long Island House, Warple Way, London W3 0RG.
ISBN 1 901447 40 5

British Library Cataloguing in Publication Data
Harper, Colin
Irish folk, trad and blues: a secret history
1. Folk musicians - Ireland 2. Folk music - Ireland -
History and criticism 3. Blues (Music) - Ireland -
History and criticism
I. Title II. Hodgett, Trevor
781.6'29162'00922

ISBN 1 903464 90 0

Design and layout: Dominic Carroll, Co. Cork
Cover design: Artmark, Cork
Printing: Creative Print and Design, UK

Front cover photographs
Main photograph, Rory Gallagher, courtesy Donal Gallagher;
from left, Rory Gallagher; Gary Moore, courtesy Liam
Quigley; Van Morrison, courtesy Colin Harper; Johnny
Moynihan (*left*), Terry Woods (*right*), courtesy Brian Shuel
Collections.

Back cover photographs
Main photograph, Altan, publicity photograph;
inset, Johnny Moynihan, courtesy Andy Irvine;
from left, Brush Shiels, courtesy Liam Quigley;
Henry McCullough, publicity photograph;
Charles O'Connor of Horslips, courtesy Liam Quigley;
Altan.

Frontispiece
Johnny Moynihan of Sweeney's Men

Irish Folk, Trad
& Blues

A Secret History

Colin Harper & Trevor Hodgett

The Collins Press

A browse in any music store reveals extensive collections of Irish folk, trad and blues. It is hard to imagine a time when it was otherwise, when musicians rarely had their work committed to any kind of disc. But great pioneers, groundbreakers, lived when the media and recording industry showed scant interest. Accounts of their lives and music survived through reminiscences and good fortune. This fascinating history reveals the frustrations and triumphs of trail-blazers before the Irish music industry, and acts like U2, existed. Forgotten heroes and latter-day legends inter-twine with honorary visitors, who took a bit of Ireland with them, like Bob Dylan and Arlo Guthrie.

But the main thrust of the book concerns the influence of homegrown pioneers from Sweeney's Men in the 1960s to Horslips, De Danann, Rory Gallagher and current groundbreakers like Martin Hayes. All are given their place in the sun. And, rescued from the shadow of Van, the further and long-lingering adventures of Them are finally revealed. Somewhere in between, the shadowy yet almost seminal influences of figures like Anne Briggs (Christy Moore's inspiration) are disclosed.

COLIN HARPER is a graduate of Queen's University Belfast. A professional writer from 1994–2001, he contributed regularly to *Q, Mojo, The Irish Times* and other UK and Irish news-papers and magazines, as well as writing CD sleevenotes and commissioned pieces. His first book, *Dazzling Stranger: Bert Jansch and the British Folk and Blues Revival*, was published to universal critical acclaim (London, 2000). Now a librarian, he continues to write prolifically.

TREVOR HODGETT is the blues and jazz critic of the *Irish News* and has contributed to the *New Musical Express, Sounds, Record Collector, Mojo, Jazzwise, Blues in Britain, Blueprint, Folk Roots* and other publications, and to reference works such as the *Guinness Rockopedia* and the *Mojo Collection*.

DEDICATION
For Heather and Trish

CONTENTS

continued over

FOREWORD
TOM DUNNE

This is a wonderful book – a loving and generous examination of a time when Irish music as we know it today was still in its infancy. Colin Harper and Trevor Hodgett have managed to shine a light on that time, to peer into the fog and put names and faces to bands that deserve to be better remembered and whose influence is still heard in the music of the many bands they inspired. And what a world they have chosen to illuminate – a world as far removed from today's record industry with its PR gurus, stylists, reality-TV shows, backing tapes and choreography. A world filled instead by long-haired types, alive with youth and creativity, armed with mandolins and guitars, and interested only in music and song in the era of Vietnam, the Summer of Love and Archbishop McQuaid.

Colin and Trevor succeed in bringing to life those early days, in re-animating the pubs, the sessions and the early recordings. They recreate the first meetings, the sense of adventure and excitement, the tours, the record-company interest and the personal and professional relationships as they blossomed and grew or all too often soured and died. It's a labour of love and it shows in the telling. What emerges is a view of an almost mythical time, peopled with musicians who were legends ('They were stars – they could walk down Grafton Street and be mobbed') and performances never to be forgotten by those who were there.

I got on the Irish music bus sometime after U2. The names we knew then were U2, Phil Lynott, Van Morrison, Rory Gallagher and Horslips, but as we travelled further we became aware of other names scratched into the seat-backs. Those names are rightfully restored here – names you might not know but should, such as Sweeney's Men, Anne Briggs, Davy Graham, Skid Row, Henry McCullough, Eric Bell, The Bothy Band, Jim Daly, John Wilson, Planxty, Gay and Terry Woods, Mellow Candle, Andy Irvine and many more.

Anyone who owns even one Irish record (*Joshua Tree*, perhaps) will greatly appreciate this book. Anyone who owns a lot of Irish records is likely to treasure it. It's a book that's long overdue, and Colin and Trevor will be rightly fêted for its completion.

Tom Dunne is a radio presenter and former singer/songwriter with Something Happens.

Sweeney's Men, 1969:
Terry Woods (left),
Johnny Moynihan

AN INTRODUCTION

Like Irish mythology, the popular music of the twentieth century has its own legends, heroes, kings and conquerors, and, like European history, its own Dark Ages – a time of great deeds made more wondrous still through the tantalising opacity and dearth of the written record. Though it barely covers a period of fifty years, some of the truest pioneers and ground-breakers in post-war popular music ploughed their lonely furrows at a time when there was little in the way of recording industry or media to document and acclaim their adventures – nowhere more so than the Ireland of the Sixties and Seventies.

Received wisdom would have it that before U2 and the exponential growth of the indigenous music industry that followed, Ireland's contribution to the worldwide history of rock comprised Van Morrison, Rory Gallagher and Thin Lizzy. Reverential doffs of the cap may have been reserved by more informed observers for Planxty or The Bothy Band, but that was folk music, so no matter how many units they shifted (and ex-Planxty man Andy Irvine believes the figure to currently reside in the millions) it didn't really count. As for Horslips – well, has anyone who wasn't Irish ever heard of them?

If a time traveller could zip back and communicate with the music world of 1970 or thereabouts – driven as it was by the rewards of the here and now and the thrill of finding musical limits and barriers that could still be leapt for the first time – would anyone from that period really believe that a generation down the line many thousands would be employed in the industry of musical retrospection? Magazines, reissues, compilations, books, digital remasterings, bottom-drawer ransackings of demos, rehearsal and dodgy live tapes by the momentarily famous along with websites dedicated to the causes of those who lived the dream testify to the power of the rock era in a popular-music world now regulated to within an inch of its life by accountants, marketeers and the transient wiles of multi-channel-television-format people.

In a business now geared towards homogenising, crushing or banishing to the margins those whose go-getting nous doesn't at least equal, if not outstrip, their creative worth, or whose face simply doesn't fit, there is no longer a place for the fragile artist or the raw talent which might take an album or two to realise its potential. Taking the example of traditional singer Cara Dillon's five years with Warners – wherein whole albums' worth of would-be pop recordings were created and not one note of it released to the public – the potential musical heroes of today are likelier to spend their time traversing the alternate universe of the 'development deal' (which could last just about as long as The

Beatles' entire career) than anywhere remotely adjacent to the public domain. Few mistakes are made in public anymore, and if they are you're probably finished.

The lost gods of Irish music are those free spirits who bucked the system, rode the lightning and paved their way long enough to leave some kind of legacy which merits acknowledgement and respect. Some have taken their place already in the rose-tinted annals of rock 'n' roll; others may yet need a leg-up. We hope this book will go some way towards doing that and that, cumulatively, the seemingly disparate tales we've brought together will combine as a patchwork history of sorts. It won't be definitive by any means, but we hope the whole will seem greater than the sum of the parts and that a sense of time, place and the joys of discovery may be found.

Some of those we celebrate, like Anne Briggs, Sweeney's Men and Davy Graham, can be viewed with hindsight as the shadowy foundation of much that would follow and find greater fame in the Seventies and beyond; some, like Henry McCullough, John Wilson, Eric Bell and Jim Daly would be sidemen at the courts of kings; the likes of Ottilie Patterson, an all but forgotten pioneer; and Horslips, like Something Happens years later, home-grown heroes whose magic was doomed to work only on the island. Others, like Shaun Davey and Martin Hayes, and even to some extent Paddy Keenan and Kevin Burke, remain maverick stylists whose now assured reputations could surely never have been predicted – and certainly not guaranteed.

From the phenomenal, sustained success of Rory Gallagher – who was, in his own phraseology, the 'last of the independents' – to the momentary brilliance of Mellow Candle and Skid Row, or the painfully long caterpillar roads to butterfly careers taken by Clannad or Cara Dillon, this is a book of outsiders who won. It matters not that Mellow Candle's one album has the simultaneous virtue and ignominy of being the rarest (least-bought) folk-rock album to have found release on a major label – all that matters, at this remove, is the quality of the work. Van Gogh, they say, sold only one painting in his lifetime.

On a purely technical level, the way we have chosen to present this book needs some explanation. It is not quite an anthology of two writers' previously published work, nor is it a straightforward work of thematic biography, and certainly not an attempted encyclopedia that somehow careered wildly off the rails. No, the bibliography of Irish music already has quite enough encyclopedias peddling potted histories, quite enough academic perusals on the hallowed tradition and quite enough coffee-table manuals on the genuinely famous. At the very least, let this claim the novelty of being a coffee-table book on the largely obscure!

Much of the work included here has been previously published in some form, although several pieces are entirely new to this volume. Of those pieces that have seen daylight before, every one – without seeking to disguise their original remits as stand-alone features – has been fine-tuned, generally shorn of purely ephemeral references, updated with postscripts or preambles and expanded by anywhere between a few lines and many thousand words. Several pieces are, indeed, several times their original length – bolstered either by material that wouldn't fit the available space first time around or, in some cases, by material gathered specifically for this book. For example, with regard to my essay on Davy Graham and Trevor's epic Them and post-Them sagas, the tales as presented here are composites of several previously published pieces on the subjects in question. The result, we hope, will be a patchwork history of Irish music woven of many fine tapestries.

But what of the added spice, gall or distraction of what can only be described as slabs of autobiography in the guise of prologues? Why have we dared to do this – opening ourselves up to accusations of giving the world an unasked-for sequel to the *Diary of a Nobody*? Well, as Roy Harper once put it to me, so simply and yet profoundly, any time we meet somebody we do so historically – we each of us influence, to a greater or lesser degree, the course and substance of others' lives. Were Trevor and I the sort of writers whose subjects were hugely successful, popular artistes of the world-conquering U2 variety, it would be highly unlikely that anything we could say to or about such people would have any lasting impact on either them or their audience. Published words on an artist of such stature will generally only serve as a long-winded advert to let people know that some product is out there, upon the sales of which the opinion of some little-known writer will have no meaningful effect either one way or the other. But the lower one sets one's sights down the scale of success, the more likely it is that a writer can, intentionally or otherwise, make a difference.

It would be inappropriate to list any examples of how my enthusiasms for this or that artist, translated into the written word, have had a tangible effect on the course of that artist's life or career. But there are several examples I *could* give, and perhaps many more that I'm as yet unaware of. And I'm sure that Trevor's position is just the same. In a way, the story of, say, Martin Hayes contains within it the story of Colin Harper writing *about* Martin Hayes; similarly, the story of all those (bar Van) who spent a few months of their lives in Them – and have consequently, for better or worse, been defined by it – contains the story of Trevor Hodgett writing *about* Them.

How and why did we come to embark upon these crusades – crusades which have, by now, spanned several years of our own lives? These are questions which I know that I, as a reader, would be fascinated to hear answered. Indeed, just before work on this book was completed I chanced upon a second-hand copy of Peter Guralnick's anthology of essays on early blues and rock 'n' roll, *Feel Like Going Home*. If I had been at all worried that the concept of using first-person introductions to largely third-person portraiture was an untried or unacceptable device, I should have known better – Guralnick's work, with its fascinating introductory essay on his own experience of growing up in the Fifties and Sixties, specifically given to provide the reader with a sense of where his biographical perspective was coming from, was first published in 1971 and deservedly received acclaim. If a literary device is good enough for Peter Guralnick, the master, it's good enough for us!

Insofar as the enthusiasms, aspirations and adventures of Trevor and myself have increased the public's knowledge about the people we've chosen to champion, to chronicle and to celebrate – initially in diverse newspapers and magazines, now revamped and presented in the relative immortality of book form – I hope that we've managed to share a little of how, in the first place, these people have had an impact on us. In simple terms, there are easier ways to make a living (and certainly more obvious ways to spend one's leisure time) than writing about the time Kevin Burke met Arlo Guthrie, the weekend Sweeney's Men rocked Cambridge or the day Muddy Waters came to Belfast. But there are surely few that can be spiritually so rewarding.

This book is, in short, a celebration of free spirits – musical priests who came from or to Ireland, and mostly did so during a loosely defined golden age of music where TV shows were not the making or breaking of careers but rather an occasional, transient diversion from the real business of touring, of taking music to the people. Even records took second place – airwave adverts for the live experience. And now all we have, in many cases, are the records. In some cases, not even those. So, in the terminology of rock, let us glorify these people as the lost gods of Erin, and find herein the reminiscence of how it all happened and where it all went to, in an Ireland long ago and faraway.

Kenny McDowell,
1968

Andy Irvine, 1967

SECTION 1
THE GATES
ARE OPENED

SWEENEY'S MEN
PROLOGUE

To a great extent this book came into being as a meaningful refuge for the story of Sweeney's Men. It was almost the last piece I would write in a seven-and-a-half-year career as a professional writer, but the yearning to delve this magical seam had been with me for yet longer than that.

Doffing their corporate coffers toward the onset of a new millennium, the arts and heritage office of Belfast City Council invited, during the year 2000, applications from creative types in the city for a dozen or so two-week bursaries at the Tyrone Guthrie Centre, a beautiful artists' retreat by Lake Annamakerrig in County Monaghan. Still recovering from a year's solid toil on *Dazzling Stranger: Bert Jansch and the British Folk and Blues Revival* (Bloomsbury, 2000) – a book that seemed in every sense to conclude my journey as a writer – I quite fancied the idea of getting some inspiration (or at the very least, a rest) down the country. I applied . . . and was rewarded for doing so. More or less resigned/resolved, for various reasons, to move into librarianship by this time, here was a little opportunity to prolong, with no deadline or obligation, the supposedly freewheeling life of a writer. My golden handshake. It was time to think of some achievable goal, and make the most of it. It was time to write the story of Sweeney's Men.

I would, I decided, take the first week in February 2001, by which time I had tracked down and interviewed for the purpose Gay Woods, Terry Woods, Ashley Hutchings and one-time Sweeney's manager Des Kelly. I already had – as shall be explained below – interview material from other relevant parties: Andy Irvine, Johnny Moynihan, Henry McCullough, Eamonn O'Doherty and Anne Briggs. Needless to say, when I finally met Terry he was delightful and co-operative, not at all as his reputation had painted him, while Gay was a bundle of free-spirited, mischievous wisdom and energy and Des more than happy to help with anything involving Andy Irvine. It had to be done. For some reason, a history of Sweeney's Men was something I had to get out of my system before I 'retired'. But when had the seed been planted?

I first became aware of Sweeney's Men, I think, in 1992. I was still two years away from being a professional writer but I had somehow inveigled my way into working with Demon Records on some Bert Jansch, John Renbourn and Pentangle compilations – projects dear to my heart at the time. Being, the label assumed (wrongly), an all-round expert on folk music of a certain vintage, I was offered the chance to compile and annotate a CD drawn from the two Sweeney's Men albums of 1968 and '69.

Demon had previously issued, during the Eighties, a vinyl compilation entitled *The Legend Of Sweeney's Men* which I vaguely recall seeing once, though I never owned a copy. Frankly, I hadn't a clue. Still, not wanting to turn down the handsome fee of £200, I took on the challenge and started scrabbling around for reference copies of the relevant recordings and anything in print from which I could draw. I found a slightly dodgy, but still just-about-playable, late-Seventies, cassette reissue of the first album and borrowed a copy of Mark Prendergast's wonderful book, *Irish Rock*, published by the O'Brien Press in 1987. Where I found any kind of copy of the rare second album I have now no idea, but the Prendergast book was to remain on long-term loan to me for many years and would prove the first port of call for many's an assignment. (Eventually my good friend Karen, its owner, gave up and said, 'It's yours!')

Using material from *Irish Rock* and other sources, together with an interview-by-post with Sweeney's associate, Anne Briggs, whom I'd met a year or two earlier in Lincolnshire, I completed a pretty respectable sleeve-note and sent it off to the label. During this time, they had also been trying to source photographs for the sleeve and had consequently come into contact with one-time Sweeney, Johnny Moynihan. Johnny, it seemed, was particularly keen to contribute to the notes and to refute, in print, a perfectly anodyne, if slightly pretentious, misquote that had been attributed to him in the Prendergast book. Happy to go the extra mile, and to meet someone whose voice and whose songs I found captivating, I agreed to meet Johnny in Belfast at the earliest opportunity. Arriving up from Dublin one sunny day with a package of photographs borrowed from Andy Irvine, we spent a long afternoon, tape recorder running, in various centre-of-town cafés. The following day, with my now furiously revised version of the sleeve-note (including refutation of *that* quote and rather carefully chosen words about Terry Woods) in hand, we met again. Johnny read through the document with meticulous care and, pointing out one or two further amendments to be made, signed it off.

Sometime later I had a phone call from Andy Irvine. Slightly piqued not to have been sought out himself for the notes, he was nevertheless complimentary of the end result. The whole time was a learning curve for me both as a writer and in terms of knowing how to interact with musicians of a certain era – prone to viewing their old recordings through a complex haze of affection, pride, denial, sadness for people and times that have passed, and resentment at the inevitable business rip-offs that took place at the time. With all those feelings fast becoming clear to me, particularly through the experience of trying to work, as an enthusiastic amateur, on a Pentangle biography (a family riven with the open wounds of blame), I was thrilled to have had the approval, albeit the slightly reserved approval, of both Irvine and Moynihan.

Of the other Sweeney's, Henry McCullough, I had heard, was a hard man and Terry Woods a 'bollox'. On this basis – outdated, simplistic or just wrong as each portrait transpired to be – I avoided both of these people for years. Irvine and Moynihan I returned to occasionally, as reviewer or interviewer.

Sweeney's Men, Cambridge Folk Festival, 1968:
(l–r) Terry Woods, Henry McCullough, Johnny Moynihan

When I came to write a long feature on Anne Briggs (a version of which appears below) during 1997, I reconvened with Johnny in Dublin, along with his friend and Sweeney's acolyte Eamonn O'Doherty. Through her time spent in Ireland, Anne's story mingled with that of Sweeney's Men. By stealth, I was getting closer and closer to a story the surface of which I had but scratched with that sleeve-note five years earlier. I had also, by now, met and become friendly with Henry McCullough – a gentleman, a survivor and the most astonishingly intense live performer, living an hour up the road from me in Coleraine at that time. He would also, gladly, contribute to that story on Anne.

Some years later, not long after I had finished work on *Dazzling Stranger*, I went with my wife Heather to see an Andy Irvine show in Mullaghbawn, a little village in south Armagh with an incongruously impressive arts centre. I realised during that show, if indeed I had really needed any further convincing, that Andy Irvine is an extraordinary man whose story deserved to be told. Andy, as it transpired during an interval chat, had been musing upon the idea of writing an autobiography while trying to write a potted (though rapidly expanding) version of his life for his official website. I had already glimpsed a tiny, though fascinating, part of his story during an interview the previous year for the Jansch book – Andy having lived in London and moved (with diary entries and admirable memory to confirm it) among its folk scenes during the late Fifties and again in the mid-Sixties.

We began exchanging e-mails. I interviewed Andy in Dublin for a short feature in *Record Collector*, reviewed another show, attended a fabulous semi-Sweeney's reunion in Galway with Johnny also on the bill, and then finally we met, at a large pub near his Donnybrook home, to begin work on what was planned as a Harper-assisted autobiography (a project which, given Andy's eleven-out-of-twelve-months round-the-world touring regime, remains ongoing!). After a few hours Johnny and Eamonn arrived as arranged – Johnny, somewhat stand-offishly, producing a dictaphone in order to avoid any more of those dastardly misquotes (one, apparently, having crept into the Anne Briggs feature). We managed, by e-mail, to craft the story in Andy's eminently quotable first-person right up to the gates of the Sweeney's Men era. And then, with Andy off touring the world as ever, I decided to attempt the Sweeney's Men story – as far as the Annamakerrig muse would take me – as third-person biographer.

I wrote the piece over four days in the happy ambience of Mr Guthrie's bequest, and sent it to *Mojo* editor Paul Trynka. Paul had expressed a tentative prior interest but the work had been entirely whimsical. There had been no commission, no certainty even that Andy would welcome the device of a third-party narrative in the midst of his autobiography. In the event, Andy loved the piece and after initially doubting it could be a part of his autobiography as it stood, given the approach, now (subsequent, I should explain, to the contract for *this* book being agreed!) feels it should be. He is, after all, Andy Irvine – and since when has Andy Irvine ever paid the slightest bit of notice to the conventions of life, the universe or the music business?

Paul Trynka was also generous in his response, agreeing to buy the piece just before handing over to new editor Pat Gilbert, to ensure its future publication by the magazine. Pat honoured that commitment, and repeated his predecessor's enthusiasm – as did his successor, Phil Alexander. At the time of writing, a 4,500-word edit was finally scheduled to appear in the magazine's June 2004 issue. By no coincidence, the complete recordings of Sweeney's Men were also scheduled to appear, on double CD, that same month, on the Sanctuary label. But here, at last, is the unexpurgated tale of troubadours and visionaries from an Ireland long ago and far away . . .

THE LEGEND OF SWEENEY'S MEN

They did not cease, either walking or eating, from the delights of colloquy and harmonized talk contrapuntal in character nor did Sweeny desist for long from stave-music or from the recital of his misery in verse . . . On occasion an owl or an awkward beetle or a small coterie of hedgehogs . . . would escort them for a part of the journey until the circumstances of their several destinations would divert them again into the wild treachery of the gloom. The travellers would sometimes tire of the drone of one another's talk and join together in the meter of an old-fashioned song, filling their lungs with fly-thickened air and raising their voices above the sleeping trees. They sang *Home On The Range* and the pick of the old cowboy airs, the evergreen favourites of the bunkhouse and the prairie; they joined together with a husky softness in the lilt of the old come-all-ye's, the ageless minstrelsy of the native land, a sob in their voice as the last note died . . . When they suddenly arrived to find mid-day in a clearing, they wildly reproached each other with bitter words and groundless allegations of bastardy and low birth as they collected berries and haws into the hollows of their hats against the incidence of a late breakfast . . .

Thus did Flann O'Brien describe the men of Sweeny, a mad king of Irish myth, in his 1939 oddball classic, *At Swim-Two-Birds*.

Somewhere in Galway in June 1966 a trio of singular individuals, collectively characterising something similar to the *mélange* of Joycean profundity and *Wind in the Willows* whimsy in Flann's tale, had decided to pick a name (his book being read at the time), pack up their troubles in an old Volkswagen van and spend the summer playing music around the wild west of Ireland. This was, in itself, an extremely odd thing to do in that time and place, but more seminal yet was to be the enduring influence of the group and its members – most notably Andy Irvine, Terry Woods, Johnny Moynihan, Paul Brady (for a day) and Henry McCullough. Largely unnoticed at the time, Sweeney's Men would become the wellspring of the entire British folk-rock movement and the Irish revival of the 1970s. Their story has never been told, but as it happens O'Brien's dream sequence on his travellers' oneness with nature, passions for cowboy songs and Irish music, and tendency to acrimonious absurdity provides a summary of remarkable prescience.

'There's a timeline between The Clancy Brothers and The Pogues,' says Bill Leader, who engineered the albums of both, 'and you could slap a lot of the Irish groups of that time somewhere along it. The Dubliners would be three-quarters of the way there. But Sweeney's Men didn't seem to fall along that line, they were off to one side.' Drawing uniquely from hillbilly music, the English folk revival and the then still cobwebbed Irish tradition, all glued together with bohemian zest, these were precisely the sort of people the conservative forces of Catholic Ireland were trying to hold at bay. So who were they? The originals were Andy Irvine, a frustrated actor from London with a Woody Guthrie fixation, Johnny Moynihan, a college drop-out from Dublin, and Joe Dolan, a left-wing freedom fighter cunningly disguised as a second-division showband guitarist from Galway. While Moynihan – ironically, as perhaps the most single-mindedly anti-commercial individual ever to remain tethered for longer than a weekend to a band of any description – would be the lone stalwart of every line-up, the tale really begins in 1959, at a union building in Soho, home to a virtual secret society known as the Ballads & Blues Club. Grand Wizard was an earnest, ear-fingering socialist called Ewan MacColl.

Andy Irvine, born in St John's Wood, London, to Scots/Irish parents in 1942, was a reticent but regular presence at the club – a veteran of guitar lessons with Julian Bream but turned on to a life in music through skiffle and already exploring its roots via Woody Guthrie (with whom he corresponded) and through Harry Smith's *Anthology Of American Folk Music*. Ramblin' Jack Elliott, living in Notting Hill at the time, became a friend and mentor but by 1960 Irvine had followed another calling and joined the BBC Repertory Company.

Irvine's mother and elder sister were both thespians, and Andy had worked in radio as a child actor. At the age of eight he had appeared in *A Tale of Five Cities* – a Gina Lollobrigida film which he's been trying vainly to find on video in recent years. But the BBC Rep was a backwater, a dead end: 'Any actor would have told you, "If you want to further your career, get out of the Rep." But it was a very easy job and I was making good money – maybe £150 to £175 a week.' An additional perk was hanging out in bars with poet and broadcaster Louis MacNeice and his cronies: 'Of course, I'd have no idea what they were talking about, but I'd be nodding my head, looking interested and I think Louis appreciated that!'

During the summer of 1962 Andy went on holiday to Dublin. An Irish actor friend brought Andy to a musical evening at the city's oldest pub, The Brazen Head. It was a revelation: 'A guy called Gerry Cairns took out his guitar and sang, and I took out my guitar and sang – and this is actually the very beginning of where I am today. A number of other people who would remain on my horizons for the next few years, like Pearse MacAuliffe, were also there, and we were drawn to each other. We were the same age, singing the same kind of music.' Andy returned to London, saw out his contract with the BBC and by March '63 was back in Dublin. Pearse MacAuliffe had meanwhile inaugurated a fairly unique scene at the Coffee Kitchen in Molesworth Street – seemingly the first venue in what might be described as the Dublin folk underground.

'I'll never forget the first time I saw him,' says Gay Woods (née Corcoran), a fifteen-year-old later to marry future Sweeney Terry Woods. 'He was sitting on the floor, actually in rags, playing a guitar or a mandolin, and he was so dark and handsome that he looked like the "dark eyed sailor" just returned from the sea.'

'I was down the back,' says Terry. 'It was very dark and here was this guy playing guitar and harmonica. I couldn't see anything but I could hear it – and weeks and weeks I spent after that trying to figure out how he did it, how he played the two at the same time! Was it balanced on a stick or something? I couldn't figure it out. But Andy became a hero to me.'

Far from being modelled on the rapidly growing English folk-club scene, the quietly creeping folkish activity in Dublin had, in Andy's recollection, 'more to do with people who went hill-walking – and architects'.

Two such architects were Johnny Moynihan and Eamonn O'Doherty, both crucial in the Sweeney saga and both regulars at O'Donoghue's – a pub in Baggot Street that was unwittingly becoming the city's fulcrum of folkish bohemia. Eamonn had just finished his degree, while Moynihan – reputedly the first person to play a note in O'Donoghue's, on a tin whistle that was swiftly trousered before the landlady could identify and eject the perpetrator – had repeated a year and still flunked it. Two years older than Andy, Johnny's family was relatively well off and he would come into rentable property by the end of the decade. Although music has been his professional activity for nearly 40 years, it's fair to say there has probably never been much of a financial imperative. Johnny Moynihan may be one of the most captivating and enigmatic musicians of his era, but he does what he wants to do and never does it in any one place for long. His mythical status is consequently in direct proportion to his availability and the paucity of his recordings. 'One of the main factors in my disappearing,' he once told me, 'which is not complete by the way, contrary to popular belief, is that I never wanted to be part of a system which requires that your diary is booked up six months in advance.' But in the Sixties, at least, he was somehow kept on the path of making records and playing gigs long enough to establish a lifetime's worth of reputation. Indeed, was there ever a time when Johnny Moynihan was *not* a legend?

'He had this aura,' says Andy. 'People thought he was kind of heroic – he was recognised as being one of his kind. I remember meeting him very vividly: myself and Pearse were returning from a *fleadh* in County Limerick in April '63. I was on my motorbike and somebody said, "Here's Johnny Moynihan," and Johnny was ushered up to me almost as if it was an epic encounter – "Mr Moynihan, I presume?" I don't know why that should have been! So Johnny introduced himself in this gruff, macho way that he always had and said, "Where you going now?" to which I explained that Pearse had to get back to Dublin for work the next day. It was freezing cold and I had no gloves. So he gave me a pair of socks.' Reminded of the incident, Moynihan's response was to wonder had the socks been on his feet. Apparently not.

The summers of '63 to '65 were routinely spent by Irvine, Moynihan,

Sweeney's Men, 1967:
(l–r) Joe Dolan, Andy Irvine, Johnny Moynihan

O'Doherty and their friends travelling to *fleadhs* up and down the country. Organised by an austere cultural institution called Comhaltas and occurring at weekends in places that one seemed to locate largely by word of mouth, the purpose of these events was to find winners at county, provincial and then national levels in competitions on traditional instruments. 'There always seemed to be people on bandstands giving speeches in Irish as well,' says Andy, 'but none of this was of any interest to us. We'd be on the streets busking or at pub sessions listening to the likes of Willie Clancy or Felix Doran – being in awe. You'd know you'd hit the motherlode. And there was a touch of the old Woody Guthrie about it. It wasn't easy to travel about in bohemian fashion in those days, and there weren't many tourists around. We were frowned upon – even by the very musicians we adored. They didn't know what to make of us: people wore suits, they had their dinner on the table when it was presented by their mothers or their wives and they went to Mass on Sunday. We didn't do any of these things. We slept in hay barns!'

During the summer of '63 Andy had been sharing a particularly happening pad in Mackie's Place, Dublin, with nascent Dubliners' main-man Ronnie Drew and various others. 'I shared a room there with a girl,' say Andy. 'This was a big deal: how much more bohemian could one get in Dublin in 1963 than sharing a room with a girl?' Around August '63 Ronnie got married, the after-wedding booze-up was back at the flat and the whole scene collapsed: 'Somebody pulled a knife and the police were called,' says Andy. 'The next day I went down to a *fleadh* in Kilrush, arriving back a few days later to find that we'd all been thrown out and my belongings had been floundering in the street ever since. Some of the stuff had been rescued but not, unfortunately, Woody's shirt which had been given to me by Jack Elliott. We all dispersed and I was very lucky to get a flat – directly opposite O'Donoghue's!'

With Luke Kelly bringing in political and contemporary material from Ewan MacColl's circle and Ronnie Drew fronting his unique brand of earthy Dublin street songs, The Dubliners were just beginning to come together – but almost didn't. Having saved a few quid from his BBC work, Andy was probably the only person Ronnie knew who could save him from skipping the country: 'Towards the end of 1963 he was bankrupt – penniless, in debt, serious romantic problems – I lent him £150 to clear his debts. I probably changed the entire course of Irish history there! The trouble was, pretty soon – pretty immediately – The Dubliners became popular, and there was a big rift between Moynihan and Ronnie for years. Johnny felt Ronnie was a good guy until Ronnie suddenly started making records and becoming famous. I remember being mistaken for Johnny once and being nearly beaten to a pulp by this man who was convinced I'd been going around badmouthing Ronnie. "You been saying things about Ronnie? I'll beat the shite out of you!" And I'm going, "What are you talking about? Ronnie's a friend of mine!" Ronnie came down the stairs, completely pissed, mumbling something about being stabbed in the back. Thankfully he was in a fit enough state to establish my credentials, but it was only later I managed to find out what on earth this was all about.'

Ironically, Ronnie had actually given Moynihan his first mandolin – one of two instruments, along with the Greek bouzouki (debuting in summer '66) which Moynihan effectively introduced to Irish traditional music – defining, along with Irvine (who had been playing mandolin since 1960), their styles and tunings: 'That was one of the things that either bound us together or set us apart,' says Andy. 'There was this very archaic form of accompaniment on early hillbilly records from the Harry Smith *Anthology Of American Folk Music*, which was one of our Bibles, where the singer would accompany himself merely on the fiddle, playing a break after each verse. We were much taken by that. I think Johnny and I might well have been the first people in terms of Irish music who accompanied themselves on mandolin, tuning it GDAD. It was Johnny's idea and it was entirely original in my experience.'

The interweaving of multi-stringed instruments would be just one of the factors that would make Sweeney's Men unprecedented, but curiously it was to be a guitarist, Joe Dolan, who was to bring the group together. Dolan, a brash, loud, pathologically unreliable, beer-swilling veteran of a second-division showband, The Swingtime Aces – from Galway – was another O'Donoghue's regular. By the end of the year, with ad hoc gigs at summer *fleadhs* already under their belts, Dolan, Irvine and yet another erstwhile architect, Kevin Carroll, became The Liffeysiders – a group that managed only a promotional photo-session-cum-booze-up at the Guinness brewery and a stillborn trip to Israel. Moynihan, reputedly 'chilled' at the involvement of Carroll – not a man of much musical integrity – was keeping his distance.

The Israel adventure began in January '65, the trio heading first to London with the intention of earning enough cash to proceed. In a manner which Irvine describes as exasperatingly typical of the man, Dolan simply made a few quid working at the Hudson's Bay Trading Company and went on without them. Kevin took a job with an architect while Andy signed on at Wandsworth Gasworks. Realising after one particularly wild night at the Troubadour with Anne Briggs – a stunningly enigmatic singer from Nottingham whom he had simply met on the street – that there was no shift suitable to his lifestyle, Andy quit and muddled through thereafter on odd BBC jobs and casual labouring, and with the support of a loyal girlfriend, Muriel Geraghty, who was gainfully employed as a temporary secretary. As Terry Woods would find with his own similarly temping girlfriend, Gay, this was a crucial sustaining element in the progress of Irish folk pioneers.

Appearing at a London concert with her in May '65, The Dubliners noticed a similarity in spirit between Anne Briggs and Johnny Moynihan – back in Dublin – and suggested she get in touch. Within a few weeks a freewheeling relationship that would last the course of the Sweeney adventure was set in motion. They were two of a kind. Meanwhile, Kevin Carroll had inconveniently met a woman he wanted to marry. Israel slipped out of view. Andy embraced the British folk scene, hanging out with the likes of The Watersons, Bert Jansch and The Young Tradition. Notwithstanding another bumbling foray around Europe with Dolan in September (or rather, trailing after Dolan only to find the crucial rendezvous appointment a blow-out), he was still in London a year later: 'By that time it seemed half of Dublin was living there – and all drinking at Finch's in Notting Hill Gate.'

Eamonn O'Doherty, however, had set up some gigs for himself and Andy in Copenhagen, beginning at Easter, 'with Eamonn on flute and a passable attempt at guitar,' says Andy. 'Looking back it feels like we were there for months, but it can only have been six weeks.' Mid-May, a letter arrived from Dolan: they had gigs for the whole summer in Galway, at the Enda Hotel. A third man, Jimmy English, would play fiddle and Johnny Moynihan – working for an architect in nearby Roscommon – would join them at weekends. Bliss seemed guaranteed; once again, Dolan cocked it up.

'Joe got into a row with the owner,' says Moynihan, 'I think it was immorality – overnighting with a girl, which was frowned upon. [Andy recalls that, true to form, Joe simply didn't turn up for the show one night.] So the whole gig collapsed and Andy was desolated. This great summer we were going to have was in ashes, but I said, "Well, it doesn't have to be – we could actually form a group and go on the road." And if we didn't get gigs we could busk and maybe the busking would get us some gigs and we could have Eamonn as the manager.'

It all came to pass. 'There's a time in your life when your innocence equals your needs and you're on top of the world,' says Andy. 'That was that summer.' Joe knew a bloke with a pub in Killarney called The Laurels who, in Eamonn's words, had the reputation of being a man 'who would put up with anything in his bar – and at that stage Sweeney's Men *were* anything'.

Back in Dublin Eamonn organised a photo-session with a uniform of waistcoats and black trousers and made calls to pubs and hotels. Gigs miraculously appeared – Annie Briggs turned up at some as did Gay and Terry, trying the same unmapped route as a duo. And already hangers-on had attached themselves to the bandwagon (literally – Johnny's ramshackle VW doubled as sleeping accommodation) including a German beatnik known as 'Troll' and one Séamus who, when once asked had he slept OK, replied, 'Fine thanks, but I had to get up once for a bit of a rest'.

'The speed at which they were able to get stuff together onstage astounded me,' says Eamonn, who recalls not one rehearsal. 'I knew Dolan's professional ability with chords and so on, but the other two were amazing.' By mid-August, however, at Puck Fair in Killorglin, the initial contacts were exhausted. 'Things were going so ropily there that everyone was busking,' says Eamonn, 'including myself and Barbara, my wife!' Joe Dolan had one more idea: an old friend from Galway called Des Kelly, who just happened to be leader of the second-biggest showband in the country – was playing in town that very night.

The showband craze was at its peak in 1966, with literally hundreds of mohair-suited, brass-sectioned ensembles of young men pumping out UK pop covers, Fifties rock 'n' roll and the entire Jim Reeves repertoire to packed, alcohol-free dance halls all over the country, six nights a week. A unique cultural phenomenon, which would lead ultimately to Daniel O'Donnell and a weird vestige of waltz-time accordion-and-drum-machine acts abounding in rural Ireland to this day, Des Kelly's Capitol Showband was second only to Brendan 'Hucklebuck' Bowyer's Royal and was making huge money. Kelly had a double share 'which only meant I spent twice as much as everyone else!' Perhaps he could use his contacts to manage Sweeney's Men? Checking out the boys during a midnight interval in his own band's set, Kelly was stunned. He'd been actively interested in Irish folk music since hearing The Clancy Brothers in America in '62, but this was something new: 'It hit me like a sledge-hammer,' he says, 'because everyone else was playing three-chord stuff – and out-of-tune three-chord stuff at that – but there was order in this, it was a breath of fresh air.'

Johnny and Andy's relationship, personal and musical, was the key to the Sweeney magic: 'It was a delicate balance of respect, rivalry and affection,' says Anne Briggs. 'It was a high-wire act based on precision and timing and only they knew the choreography. Offstage they seemed to form up into a sort of psychological safety net in case one or the other came tumbling down.'

In crude terms, Andy admired Johnny, Johnny admired Andy and Joe, while Des Kelly was a friend of Joe's 'and that,' says Johnny, inherently dubious about marketing the band or, heaven forbid, having a diary full of promotional commitments, 'was good enough for me.'

'I never thought, There's money in these guys, I'm going to get some of it,' says Kelly. 'It was just the music, and for some reason Andy and I became very close – I loved his integrity. Like the rest of them he probably had me down as a bourgeois bollox at the time – they were full of that kind of talk – but Andy could never work up enough venom to be annoyed about it!'

Back in Dublin, while the Sweeney's survived with odd gigs at the Neptune Rowing Club and a diet of free soup at O'Donoghue's, Kelly arranged for new photos, press coverage, a singles deal with Pye Records, and introduced striped shirts (and later polka-dot efforts straight from the States – one of which Moynihan was reputedly still wearing well into the Seventies) and moreover did his best to find out where they were actually living. 'The only place I could ever contact them was O'Donoghue's! But they were eventually all in a squat in Ellis Quay. I remember being there late at night with a load of drink and various substances going around, and there was no light in the place – bodies everywhere, music everywhere and a lot of strange noises coming from dark corners of the room. I remember bringing my wife there once. She thought she was in hell!'

Des kept the wolf from their door with a series of session fees for surreptitious work on three Capitol Showband singles. Their Eurovision-winning singer Butch Moore, having just left to go solo, a damage-limitation wheeze saw every

Terry Woods, 1967

other member of The Capitol Showband fronting a single a month, one of which, 'The Black Velvet Band', became one of the biggest sellers in Irish chart history – a number one for eight weeks. By May '67 it was rubbing shoulders with a bona fide Sweeney's Men single: out of nowhere, 'Old Maid In The Garret', a rumbustious old music-hall number reworked by Andy with Des adding electric bass, hit number six. Bizarrely, Sweeney's Men were now stars. There had already been a foray into Glasgow – memorable for Irvine unwittingly singing a Jack Elliott number set to the tune of a well-known Protestant song at a gig in the wrong part of town – and at least one Irish TV appearance, courtesy of Kelly's contacts.

But now, when the offers were rolling in, Dolan was rolling out. 'This was a group nobody had heard of and all of a sudden they were Top Ten,' says Kelly. 'It was unheard of. And of course I was all excited and rang Joe – at O'Donoghue's – and he said, "Hold on Des, we're a bit late." I said, "What the hell are you talking about?" "There's a war on – I've got to go to Israel." And I'm saying, "But Joe, you're in the charts – now's the time to go and make a few quid for yourselves." "Ah, Des," he said, "this thing is bigger than you or me or Sweeney's Men; I've gotta go." And on top of that, aside from Joe splitting the group up to go to Israel, I found myself having to buy various rubbishy paintings from him to finance it! But I suppose as far as I was concerned it was a love affair, both with the music and themselves. They were free spirits. I was strapped into the rules of the showband industry – these fellows were doing exactly what they liked, when they liked and I loved that. I'd have joined them myself if I thought it would make enough money – and if I was allowed!'

What became known as the Six Day War had just begun. Legend has it that Dolan, kingpin of the Galway Popular Front, arrived on the seventh day. Sweeney's Men were in crisis. There were only two possible candidates to fill the gap: Paul Brady or Terry Woods. Brady, on a scholarship to college in Dublin, had been keyboarding in various beat groups around town and scrupulously avoiding lectures for three years. He'd also been discovering first American and then Irish folk music via Leadbelly, and in June 1967 had just joined, as guitarist, The Johnstons – a clean-cut folk trio which had already enjoyed a couple of Irish chart singles. 'I always thought Sweeney's Men were extremely cool,' says Brady. 'They were unique – there was nothing like them in Ireland.' Brady, who would later work more fully with both Andy and Johnny in trad supergroup Planxty in 1975, pleaded loyalty to The Johnstons but stepped in for an immediate booking in Limerick. 'I had to wear the striped shirt and waistcoat!' he says. 'I was impressed with Andy Irvine from the word go, but Johnny was one of the most eccentric men I've ever met. There was an awful lot of tuning, and Johnny wouldn't be the best tuner in the world. It would take him forever.' (Stories about Moynihan's endless tuning become more surreal as time goes on: a stint with De Danann in 1976 included a live Irish TV appearance wherein Johnny spends the entirety of the song tuning his mandolin; Des

Kelly, running a pub years later, invited Johnny to play – he arrived at the advertised start time with twelve instruments, none of them tuned.)

Terry Woods was now the only option, but everyone had doubts: yes, he was on the same wavelength musically, evangelical about pre-war mountain music and someone they had often jammed with, but Terry was a driven individual. These days, having survived the ravages of The Pogues and various other career traumas before, Woods is an almost serene fellow, spending much of the Nineties managing rock bands in Dublin and only recently returning to playing music himself. As to his character in the Sixties, the fact that various Sweeney associates prefer to go off the record when his name is mentioned should suffice. Sensing more problems than rewards, even mild-mannered Des Kelly – coincidentally on the cusp of an illness which also spelt the end for his own performing career – quietly drifted away (albeit returning, on Andy's request, to manage Planxty in the Seventies). 'We were shotgunned into it,' says Johnny. '"Better the devil you know" was a phrase I remember being used at the time.' But the classic line-up was born.

Several years younger than Johnny and Andy, Terry was a product of the brutal Christian Brothers education regime: 'Their attitude was "All things Irish are wonderful and everything else is shit". And hillbilly music was my reaction against that. As a young kid I spent a great deal of time at the movies – and cowboy pictures were a favourite. When I picked up an instrument it was a very natural thing for me to play American music – and American old-time music.'

Somehow Terry – a shoe-salesman by trade – had built up a collection of Carter Family recordings, unavailable in Ireland at the time, and had been the driving force behind a duo with himself and his shy girlfriend Gay. By summer '66, as Gay recalls, 'Terry got it into his head that we could make a living at music.' Lots of people were taking to the road with similar dreams at that time but few had the focused ambition of Terry Woods. After a whirlwind of performing activity, including a period in Glasgow, partying with Billy Connolly and his crowd, Gay was emotionally drained and split from Terry – musically and otherwise.

Terry was thus free to join Sweeney's Men. As he admits now, he would have done so regardless: 'I wanted to play in a successful situation,' says Terry. 'I always loved Moynihan and Irvine's music, I loved the way they played together. But when Gay quit I couldn't understand it, frankly. She wasn't as fired up as I was. It's funny, when I meet Gay now – and I don't meet her very often – she *is* fired up about the music thing. It's such a pity that she wasn't as focused then because if ever a voice deserved success in those days it was hers.'

Incredibly, neither Gay – who was soon back with Terry as a couple – nor Anne Briggs, who both travelled with the group along with Andy's partner Muriel, never sang with them. As far as Gay is concerned, 'I was never asked!'

'Initially Johnny wanted me to play exactly like Joe,' says Terry. 'But I wasn't interested in playing like Joe Dolan; I wanted to play like me. I brought a twelve-string into the group so we all had double-stringed instruments. It was a very interesting sound.'

A tour of London-Irish ballrooms coincided with the release of The Beatles' 'All You Need Is Love', and in November a second Sweeney's Men single – 'The Waxies Dargle' – was recorded, at Eamonn Andrews' studios in Dublin. Another Top Ten hit, this one was notable in having a call-and-response chorus added to traditional verses, with a surreal 'Lazy Sunday'-esque play-out of authentic bar-room chatter, while the B-side, 'Old Woman In Cotton', was a Pat Carroll poem with an Andy Irvine tune – his first composition. Things were progressing. (In 1970 Dublin's answer to the Incredible String Band, Dr Strangely Strange, doffed a cap by slipping 'The Waxie's Dargle' chorus into their even more whimsical 'Donnybrook Fair', taking homage a stage further on their 1971 album, *Heavy Petting*, in having both Moynihan and Irvine play on it. Woods, curiously, did not record with the Strangelies but did briefly join up, along with Gay, as a touring member around that time.) By now, as Gay recalls, 'They were stars – they could walk down Grafton Street and be mobbed. And there were all these groupie types, these country 'n' western tarts, they met down the country. I learned a lot about women.'

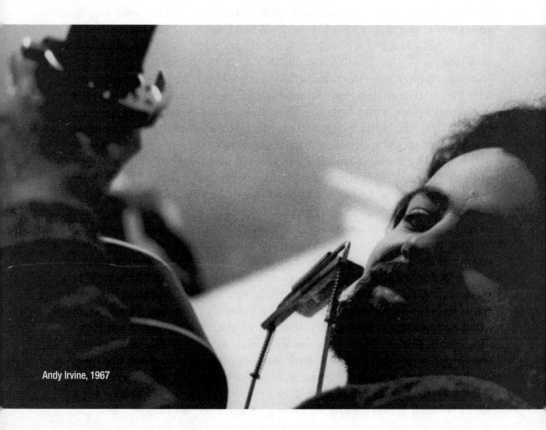

Andy Irvine, 1967

Aside from hotels and lounges, the group was also playing lucrative but hellish interval spots at showband gigs in ballrooms holding literally thousands of people, often roaring and shouting; The Johnstons were doing likewise, recalls Paul Brady: 'Sweeney's Men and The Johnstons went through a period where we would do even two spots a night – twenty minutes at a dance in Limerick, then drive on to Ennis and do another. Having a record in the charts we'd probably get paid more than the bloody band that was playing all night. But the sound was appalling. I mean, more often than not we just stepped up in front of two open-head Shure microphones. No monitors and no mikes for the instruments, we just held them up as high as we could – which is where that whole folk style of playing guitar up around your neck comes from! How the people in the hall heard us I've no idea.'

Sometimes even the group couldn't hear themselves: 'I sang "Old Maid In The Garrett" in all twelve keys down in Wexford one night,' says Andy. 'It sends me into a cold sweat just thinking about it.'

By now Sweeney's Men were also regularly selling out headlining concerts at Dublin's Liberty Hall. An album was the next step. Brit-folk mover and shaker Anthea Joseph – whose boyfriend frequented O'Donoghue's – oiled the wheels with Nat Joseph (no relation) at Transatlantic, who had already broken The Dubliners in the UK, if ill-advisedly allowing them to slip to a rival label for their 1967 UK hit single 'Seven Drunken Nights'. Sweeney's Men, and indeed The Johnstons (who both signed to Transatlantic in early '68), were now being managed by Roddy Hickson and Gerry McDonagh – two hipsters who had apparently met through being the only people in Dublin with Levi jeans and who had simply fancied the idea of managing bands. 'We thought we could have a bit of *craic* with them,' says Johnny, and he was right.

'Pye didn't want to let us go,' says Terry. 'They wanted us to keep doing singles. I'll always remember sitting in [MD] John Woods' office and he rang down to his secretary and said, "Can you bring up Sweeney's Men's contract?" We were all there I think. The secretary rang back, "I can't find it, I'll keep looking." Twenty minutes of small talk later and he rings down again, pretty agitated. She still can't find it. And Roddy says, "John, let's stop shilly-shallying – the reason she can't find the contract is because it's here." He pulls it out of his inside pocket – and it had never been signed.'

With Bill Leader producing, the legendary *Sweeney's Men* LP was cut at Livingstone Studios in Barnet, with the group fitting in a concert at Croydon's Fairfield Halls and their first BBC radio session (for *My Kind Of Folk*) before-hand: 'It was made on pint bottles of stout and, God help us,' says Terry, 'Johnny's father [a doctor] gave Johnny a load of Dexedrine to keep us awake – and we did it in 36 hours straight. I came back with Andy on the Wednesday and I remember the two of us were sitting in an air terminal – and Andy couldn't shut up, his eyes wouldn't close and his mouth wouldn't stop! And we sat there for hours waiting for the plane to come home, because I was getting married on the Saturday – 18 May 1968.'

Andy was best man and the wedding, of course, was a riot. Days later Andy played his farewell gig at Liberty Hall – a symbolic event, with one line-up playing the first half in uniforms and another coming on in far-out threads for the second. Andy, prompted by a childhood fascination with Magyar postage stamps and The Beatles' recent India trip – but also determined not to jump on anyone else's bandwagon – was off to the Balkans with Muriel: 'Sweeney's Men were successful enough that I had saved some astonishing figure like £383 and that was, believe it or not, enough for us to live in Eastern Europe for eighteen months.' They would return briefly in early '69 for Joe Dolan's wedding and their own, but this was a seminal period in Andy's artistic journey: he would return with four songs of striking, quasi-mystical character, inspired by the experience, which would eventually trickle out onto the three Planxty albums and his duo album with Paul Brady in the early Seventies, while the time-signatures and modes of the region continue to inform his work. Unwittingly, and unrewarded, he would prove a crucial source of ideas for Bill Whelan's financially phenomenal *Riverdance* empire in the 1990s.

Andy's replacement was Ireland's hottest electric guitarist, Henry McCullough: 'I'll never forget it,' says Gay Woods – 'I didn't quite know what was happening but I just thought it was the most exciting thing ever. I saw one man walk off and Henry McCullough walking on, with his long hair, his fringed jacket and his red guitar – it was great. And then I was at the Cambridge Folk Festival gig as well, when they were booed off for "going electric". Thank goodness I witnessed those two moments. They were brilliant.'

Lasting just over two months, this is the most enigmatic of all the line-ups: Henry, a Northern showband veteran who had stormed Dublin in '67 with his psychedelic soul group The People – subsequently taken on and renamed Eire Apparent by Chas Chandler – had just been booted off a US Jimi Hendrix tour for drug possession. Having previously enjoyed a mutual appreciation vibe with Moynihan (the latter being remarkably catholic in his musical activities, even appearing the following year on the first Skid Row single, 'New Faces, Old Places', with Phil Lynott and Gary Moore), Henry somehow slipped into Sweeney's Men. Nobody recalls quite how, but the time for fusion was right – it was just the group's audience who didn't know it: 'I remember one gig in Mayo where they practically threw us out of the town,' says Henry, 'throwing coins and shouting "sell-out". But the electric guitar would only have been used on certain numbers – mostly as a drone, creating an undercurrent like the uilleann pipes, with a bit of a blues feel, while somebody else was playing the melody, which was most likely traditional. It was to try and intertwine the whole lot. It wasn't gratuitous – there was certainly work put into it. There was a lot of songwriting going on as well. It was incredibly exciting. By this time even people's style of dress – particularly Johnny's – had changed. It was becoming very hippy-ish.'

'He had a flat off Pembroke Street by then,' says Terry, 'and you'd go to rehearse and Johnny would be there in a loin cloth with a ferret skin hanging down from his belt. He'd run over this ferret and had actually got out of the car, put the ferret in the boot, taken it home – and probably eaten it for all I know – and had made the ferret skin into a tin-whistle case, like something you'd keep arrows in!'

The biggest frustration for this potentially awesome fusion direction was the primitive nature of the amplification available, but the legend lives on in its tantalising unattainability: a BBC radio session (*Country Meets Folk*) and an Irish TV show (*Twenty Minutes Of Sweeney's Men*) were the only recordings – both erased. Eamon Carr, future brains behind Seventies Celtic rock gods Horslips, and already a McCullough disciple, witnessed the latter: 'I remember at the time being astonished,' he says, 'and wishing I had a tape recorder. It became a bit of a legend, and I never met an awful lot of people who actually saw it. There had always been this suggestion of possibilities with Sweeney's Men. When Terry stepped in they began to look a bit more interesting. But McCullough was just astonishing. I ranked Henry then on a par with Clapton, Page and Beck. Rory Gallagher was around, too, but at that stage he wasn't holding a candle to McCullough. I still believe he was never given his due.'

Certainly, he was given short shrift by a strangely unsympathetic audience (who had no problems in welcoming the new English-centric fusions of The Pentangle on the same bill) at what became his swansong at the Cambridge Folk Festival in July '68. Bill Leader remembers it well: 'They shuffled onto the stage and somebody went, "One, two, three, four, five," and they all started with magic cohesion. Why five and why in such an a-rhythmic way? It was quite brilliant.'

Other musicians on the bill, like Roy Harper – whose band McCullough would join in the Seventies – were full of praise. Paul Brady was also there: 'I still feel disappointed that nothing more happened with that line-up because it was a genuine, bold attempt to do something that was new and hadn't been done before out of a series of influences. It was in keeping with the hippy mood of the times – in the direction of The Incredible String Band. But I just didn't see that it had what might have been necessary from a commercial point of view.'

Yet, as McCullough recalls, 'We were beginning to get a handle on what we'd set out to do.' The group, perhaps unfortunately, was staying at London's Madison Hotel, along with various other acts including Joe Cocker. Someone told Henry that Joe needed a guitarist and feet became itchy: 'I think it was the attraction of playing in a band again with a drummer and a bass player,' says Henry. 'I suppose it was selfish on my part. Sweeney's Men hadn't got to that stage – with time I think it would have done.'

There was no ill feeling: 'I'd never heard of Joe Cocker,' says Moynihan, 'but when I heard "With A Little Help From My Friends" [just released, with Jimmy Page on guitar] I thought anyone would be mad not to take a job with him if they had the chance.'

Roddy Hickson panicked and told *Melody Maker* Sweeney's Men were finished. Sweeney's Men disagreed, (too) swiftly recruiting one Al O'Donnell – a popular Dublin-based solo artiste with a sweet tenor voice and a penchant for lengthy Scottish ballads – in other words, wholly unsuitable. 'It was a non-event,' says Terry, to whose chagrin Al insisted on billing the new act 'Sweeney's Men *and* Al O'Donnell'.

Moynihan, never one to willingly deprecate a fellow artiste, could not circumnavigate the word 'bland' in his recollection of the man they call 'the forgotten Sweeney'. As Gay Woods puts it, 'Al had a very organised home life and that wasn't a thing to have in Sweeney's Men.' And she would know.

Amidst all this uncertainty, the LP – trailered by a single, 'Sullivan's John', which did nothing – had finally slipped out. Capturing the dust-bowl-Celtic-hillbilly magic of the classic line-up it would be a blueprint for every British and Irish progressive folk act of note for years to come. 'Willie O'Winsbury' alone, the source of Fairport Convention's 'Farewell Farewell' and now a standard in itself, had been serendipitously created by Irvine through accidentally cross-referring unrelated words and tune in a folksong manuscript, while other songs and tunes on the album would be subsequently plundered and revamped by the likes of Pentangle and Horslips. By the time the next UK tour arrived, in November '68, Sweeney's Men were a doomed-from-day-one duo of Woods and Moynihan. 'Terry and Johnny are both eccentrics,' says Gay, 'but they are two opposites – it was impossible for them to co-operate.'

There were nevertheless gigs looming, now mostly in England: 'I think it was becoming too queer for Ireland,' says Gay.

The left-field shift was matched by gigs in increasingly progressive venues like Mothers in Birmingham and Les Cousins in Soho, supported by the likes of John Martyn and Bridget St John: 'We did a gig with Al Stewart and David Bowie in Les Cousins,' says Terry, 'and I always remember Bowie and Stewart up the back talking about which of them was the better guitar player – such a load of bullshit!'

Roddy Hickson had by now emigrated to Sweden, but Gerry McDonagh continued nominal management from Dublin, with NEMS and then Blackhill Enterprises handling bookings in England. It was a well-oiled machine, of sorts, which rumbled on a year longer than it had any right to. Johnny was now living in a caravan with Anne Briggs in Sussex while Terry – not knowing where on earth Johnny was between gigs – was sharing a flat with *Melody Maker* writer Tony Wilson in London. There was another LP to deliver, and this time the sessions dragged on, periodically, over six months. Andy, observing one in March '69 on his way back to the forests of Romania, recalls the lack of empathy as painfully obvious. 'We had decided, I think,' says Moynihan, 'to make a "contemporary" album. If I had had more songs then it wouldn't have seemed unbalanced but Terry was writing a lot. Some of his stuff I hadn't learnt and was unlikely to so he ended up doing it solo.'

By summer '69, an album finally in the can, Terry and Johnny could stand each other no longer. Terry drifted back to Dublin, playing in Phil Lynott's pre-Thin Lizzy band, Orphanage, and protecting sixteen-year-old guitar hero Gary Moore from his Skid Row führer Brush Shiels: 'Terry was very, very good to me,' says Moore. 'Brush used to be a bit of a bastard sometimes but Terry would always give him such a bollocking if he upset me. He always stood up for me, and not many people did with Brush. I used to hang around with Sweeney's Men, when it was Terry and Johnny, and played with them, separately I think, in Slattery's pub in Dublin. Henry had left by the time I got to Dublin but people kept talking about him and he became this kind of legend to me – I didn't actually meet him until he was in Wings.'

Johnny, meanwhile, was making his way to Ljubljana to visit Andy. 'When I came back,' says Johnny, 'I hadn't met Terry Woods for a long time. For some reason we decided to meet up and play a few numbers to see would we take up where we left off. Because I hadn't seen him for such a long time or played in that way the novelty of it was so pleasing that we decided to go on together – which was a bad mistake.'

A tour was booked for October–November. By September Andy Irvine had arrived in London, joining Sweeney's Men at the Peelers folk club on 11 October for one last hurrah, aware that anything more permanent was not an option: 'I remember the very phrase,' says Andy. 'I said, "Johnny, what are the chances of getting back into the band?" and Johnny said, "Well Andy, even if Beethoven wanted to join the band it wouldn't work – there *isn't* any band!"'

The Tracks Of Sweeney, issued to little fanfare in December 1969, was still the fascinating afterglow of a great experiment. Some tracks were indeed solo but Moynihan's dreamlike 'Standing On The Shore' – a dope-sozzled folkish equivalent to 'Strawberry Fields Forever' – and triple-tracked, polyrhythmic trad arrangement 'The Pipe On The Hob' were extraordinary, as were Terry's achingly evocative 'Dreams' and thoroughly cosmic 'Brain Jam'. These, and two songs actually written by Henry McCullough (a third from this period later appearing on Anne Briggs' 1971 LP *The Time Has Come*), reveal in glowing embers the lost fire of the mythic McCullough era. Johnny is less sentimental: 'When we heard the thing we wanted to remix it and they wouldn't let us. I remember a particularly crushing phone call from a call box somewhere in England, myself and Terry, talking to Nat Joseph and getting nowhere: "We have this tape, now fuck off."'

Bowing out a fortnight before its release, once again at the Peelers, on 22 November, must have seemed a suitable revenge. But the tale has a truly bizarre coda: Ashley Hutchings, godfather of British folk-rock, had just left the critically and commercially successful Fairport Convention. His plan? To join Sweeney's Men.

Returning to London from a gig in Birmingham in the early hours of 12 May 1969, Fairport Convention's van had crashed on the M1 leaving their drummer, Martin Lamble, and lead guitarist Richard Thompson's girlfriend, Jeannie Franklin, dead and others in varying states of physical and emotional trauma. Recuperating through swiftly filling the drum vacancy and retreating

Sweeney's Men, 1969:
Johnny Moynihan (left), Terry Woods

to a country house to work on their next album, *Liege & Lief* – a ground-breaking and thoroughly fulfilled fusion of rock with English traditional music – the driving force was bass player Ashley 'Tyger' Hutchings.

During the same period Hutchings was meeting up regularly with Terry Woods for Sunday football matches behind the Prince of Wales' Feathers in London. One thing would lead to another: 'Terry I liked enormously,' says Ashley. 'He became a good friend and he was a different kind of friend to the Fairport people. He was a bit of a "scamping blade", a breath of fresh air. Andy and Johnny I hardly knew but admired them both, and Andy in particular.'

The *Liege & Lief* material was debuted in style with a Festival Hall concert on 24 September 1969, notable for Nick Drake being the warm-up act. A couple of weeks later, having in the interim finally met Ashley Hutchings and judged him (immortalised in a diary entry, along with Hutchings' ravings on the genius of The Band's second album) 'a good straight bloke – a bit shy, but dead honest'. Andy attended another Fairport event, at Croydon's Fairfield Halls: 'I went with Paul Brady and we sat next to [noted folklorist] Bert Lloyd,' says Andy. And therein lies a tale: somehow Andy had received word in the deep forests of Romania that he was being sought out to join Fairport Convention. If that initial mooting was unpursued, by whichever party, it was but a preamble to the kind of bizarrely convoluted situation the resolving (or ruthlessly clipped summation) of which now earns Pete Frame his reputation.

Having clearly tapped into a potentially rich seam with *Liege & Lief*,

Ashley wanted to pursue that direction, while Fairport's recently added vocalist Sandy Denny had only just escaped from the folk clubs and wanted less, not more, of that repertoire, electric arrangements or otherwise. Sandy left during November, with Hutchings departing only days later.

'So much of that period is a haze for me,' says Hutchings. 'I had a delayed reaction to the crash which eventually caused a kind of nervous breakdown, towards the end of the year. The crash happened; we never discussed it, we gritted our teeth and got on with re-forming – and we never grieved together. Some people have told me, and they're probably right, that Richard's still grieving. It was a very strange few months: getting out of hospital, re-forming Fairport, *Liege & Lief*, mixing with the Irish guys, getting Steeleye together . . .'

The name Steeleye Span would be suggested to Ashley by Martin Carthy (who had himself turned down an offer to join Fairport Convention prior to *Liege & Lief*), drawn from an unpleasant character in a particularly obscure traditional song. But the concept of a new band had been floating around through conversations with Terry Woods for sometime, certainly before Sweeney's Men finally expired. 'Our ideas were very similar,' says Terry. 'We anticipated a band from Ireland and England that would have a similar feel to The Byrds and would use traditional elements and bring it forward – because nobody was doing that at that point in time – nobody.'

In truth it was the first album line-up of Sweeney's Men that Ashley wanted to reconstitute as the core of such a group: Irvine, Woods and Moynihan. Tantalising mention of a 'three-week rehearsal group' in Pete Frame's 'Fairport Family Tree' is a masterful précis of a deeply complex, compact period. Only one full meeting/rehearsal is generally recalled by those involved but there were seemingly three. An initial get-together at Hutchings' parents' house with Ashley, Johnny and Terry – presumably before Irvine's return from Europe – was marked by Gay's arrival from Dublin. Soon after (as Irvine was apparently still not present) was a meeting with Nat Joseph at Transatlantic; 'Ashley, Terry and myself were in there and Gay was outside,' says Moynihan, revealing Mrs Woods to be perhaps not yet entirely embraced into the new project (indeed, he also recalls another female singer being mooted at the meeting). Irvine's diary reveals Transatlantic to have offered a £2,000 advance, Harvest countering with £3,000.

A full-scale rehearsal was arranged – with Gay seemingly now on board – though a misunderstanding meant Hutchings failed to show. The date was rescheduled to 10 November but by now Moynihan was experiencing what he describes as 'heebeegeebees at the prospect of spending any more time with Terry Woods'. Irvine's diary records 'some nice music' but 'an air of gloom' around the Moynihan/Woods issue. 'As my diary puts it,' says Irvine, '"Tyger and Terry tried hard to push us in with their enthusiasm." I was definitely "on" for it but only if Johnny agreed. Apparently I played "Autumn Gold" which Tyger said was "a minor masterpiece"!'

The song, one of Andy's exquisite 'Balkan quartet', would finally surface on his LP with Paul Brady in 1976 and Hutchings' judgement was not wrong – even if he was hopelessly biased: 'To be honest, Andy could have sung the alphabet and I would have drooled. I thought he was wonderful.'

A couple of days later Moynihan confirmed to first Andy then Tyger that he was out – citing publicly (not wishing to air his antipathy to Woods) that he simply wasn't convinced by electric folk. Loyal to his friend, though disappointed, Andy also confirmed his withdrawal. Things now became a little desperate: 'Tyger was upset,' says Andy, 'and talked about going back into Fairport Convention with Terry and Gay. He wasn't able to do this in the end because Fairport considered seven people too many. He said that my name had been suggested as a replacement for Sandy and asked if I would join. I said, "More or less certainly, no." I felt I couldn't walk into a well-established group, let alone into Sandy's shoes.' Intriguingly, Irvine's diary reports that the folk-club duo Tim Hart and Maddy Prior – who were coincidentally living in the same building as Irvine (who was dossing at a friend's place) while all this was going on – were following developments with more than casual interest.

'All of a sudden we were a trio,' says Gay. 'I thought that would be it but Ashley wanted to get someone else in – still trying to replace Johnny and Andy, instead of just saying, Well, maybe this is sufficient.' Hutchings' bridges with Fairport now certainly burnt, Robin and Barry Dransfield, on the cusp of releasing their career-defining *Rout Of The Blues*, were approached for the ever-changing new group and came down to jam, as did Bob and Carole Pegg – future mainstays of electric trad oddities Mr Fox – but none committed to joining. 'A lot of people had a really healthy income from folk clubs in those days,' says Gay. 'So then Tim Hart and Maddy Prior were approached.'

'They said yes,' says Terry, 'but the proviso was that they had x amount of gigs themselves and they wanted to continue to do those gigs while we were rehearsing. We were naive enough to say yes. In retrospect we should have copped that Tim is very much a manipulator and he was never going to do anything that didn't create a winning situation for him and/or Maddy – I don't know whether she was as strong a part of that as he was.'

A further problem was where Terry and Gay would live: 'I signed on to an agency to start temping because otherwise where was the money going to come from?' says Gay. 'But we were staying at various people's houses, sleeping on floors. I blame Terry for that still, though we were all still very young.' Sometimes hard to picture in these epic tales, but all the participants were indeed only in their early twenties. The housing crisis was solved, in an ultimately disastrous step, by Gay and Terry moving into a spare room at a house in Archway where Tim and Maddy were renting a flat. With Irvine having presumably left the soap opera for Dublin, it was Johnny Moynihan who was now staying with the friend in the same building. He consequently became involved in just about the only non-controversial aspect of the whole period:

'We had a great football match,' says Terry – 'Steeleye Span versus Fairport Convention, near where they lived – near Braintree. We got our team together at the Whittington Arms in Archway and drove out in this beautiful Steeleye van with the Irish flag flying out. I remember Dave Swarbrick got the ball and he was coming down towards me – I stopped the ball with my foot, Swarbrick's foot was behind it and he shot past and came down on his nose! We hammered them: six-nil.'

None of which made any impact on the familial strife back at Archway: 'I should just have gone home immediately,' says Gay, 'and I'm sorry I didn't because from then on I was treated like a serf, by everybody, and it was horrible and my health suffered. But then eventually this nice couple downstairs who had a bungalow in Wiltshire [at Winterbourne Stoke] offered that to us to rehearse. So we moved down there – it was January [1970] – it was snowing. But this became another hell. The bitterness started immediately – lines being drawn as to where everyone's food began and ended and so on. And to this day that kind of spirit has not left that band. I think the moment they called it that name there was some psychic evil going around! It was awful, I hated every moment of it.'

'I was aware of a division,' says Ashley. 'I'll never know how deep it went because people didn't open up to me. I remember niggly feelings and I remember, funnily enough – it makes me laugh – clashes in the kitchen with each couple cooking separately, with one oven. It was like two families trying to coexist – totally different styles of attitude and living.'

'Ashley wasn't well enough to take a stronger stance,' says Terry. 'He spent a lot of time in his room. We'd go for walks, play a little football round the back – but he was having all the legal stuff coming in to do with the crash, and he was suffering mentally with that.'

'If I was presented with that situation now,' says Hutchings, 'I would handle it absolutely totally differently. Things would get nipped in the bud before they festered, but I was on medication at that time – in a little cocoon. Far from being me who was leader, it was Terry who was the driving force. The repertoire came together quickly, from three sources: from me, from Terry and Gay and from Tim and Maddy. If pushed, I'd say most came from the Woodses.'

Colm O'Lochlain's book of Irish street songs was a key source, with several songs from it being tried out that weren't ultimately recorded. One song that would be recorded was 'Dark-eyed Sailor', deriving from Andy Irvine and hinting at what might have been: 'You could say that it was a mistake,' says Hutchings, on Irvine's declining to join. 'Because if Andy and Terry and I had formed a band together I think it would have been a monster band, and with Andy's temperament – not as volatile as some of these other people – it could have settled down and been great.'

As it was, Terry's customary drive was powering himself and the project along on creative energy alone. The mooted deal with Transatlantic somehow fell through, and he recalls endlessly traipsing the streets of London with Ashley looking for a record deal and being routinely turned down. Ashley, who recalls none of this, does put it in perspective: 'Some people have to struggle to get deals over a period of years. We're talking only four or five months here – from conception to destruction!'

A chance meeting with an old acquaintance of Ashley's, Sandy Roberton, finally led to a deal with RCA. Roberton would produce the album, entitled *Hark! The Village Wait*. 'I remember getting a phone call one day,' says Gay, 'saying "You can give up the job, we have a deal." I said, "Oh, great." It wasn't great at all!'

A BBC radio session was recorded in March 1970, just prior to the album sessions. Things were going downhill fast: 'It was during the sessions that it became impossible to work with Tim and Maddy,' says Terry. 'It got beyond music. It was exceptionally nasty – *he* was particularly nasty. After the falling out in the studio we – Gay and myself – went up to my sister who lived in Nottingham. We had an agreement that if any one or two of the five left that the name Steeleye Span would cease. But I think a week later we heard that Martin Carthy had joined the band. Worse than that, there were threats, legal threats, issued to us – we wouldn't get this, they'd take that – and we ended up signing stuff that we should never have signed. Not to the publishing, however – though, funny enough, I've never *received* any publishing royalties. Which they will be hearing about shortly anyway because I won't be letting it rest – it's long enough. But it was such a nasty way for such a great thing to end.'

As Maddy Prior views it all now: 'The five of us rehearsed in the country for three months, made *Hark! The Village Wait* and promptly split – which is what happens if total strangers spend that amount of time together.'

Yet Steeleye Span did indeed continue, making two further albums with Hutchings on board and then becoming, as members came and went, to all intents and purposes Maddy Prior's band. (A truly surreal coda, however, transpired in 1994 when Maddy had voice problems and Gay Woods was tempted out of retirement to save the day. Three albums later, early in 2001, she quit – once again citing acrimony and one-upmanship.) Gay and Terry licked their wounds for a while, working with ex-members of King Crimson and Dr Strangely Strange before forming The Woods Band and recording a sole, eponymous album for Decca in 1971 – a natural successor to *Hark! The Village Wait* and at last the realisation of Terry Woods' musical vision for fusing the Irish tradition with ethnic American music and the power of rock. By the following year The Woods Band were floundering through business problems, with Gay and Terry retreating to rural Ireland (renting a cottage from Johnny Moynihan of all people). At the same time Andy Irvine had just found his niche with Planxty – another approach to bringing Irish music to a youth market, which would see both Paul Brady and Johnny Moynihan joining in due course to make their mark on a band that continues to act as the revered template for the ongoing Celtic-music explosion.

Sweeney's Men never entered the consciousness of these later generations, but they were the start of it all. Some deference was given, though, by The

An impromptu reunion, Galway 2000: Andy Irvine (left), Johnny Moynihan

Pogues, who recruited Terry Woods in the mid-Eighties for a decade of life in the fast lane, while a smattering of full or partial Sweeney reunions have taken place over the years: a disastrous Irish festival gig by Terry, Andy and Johnny in 1982 (though a fabulous tape of a warm-up show in a nearby pub testifies to the original magic); a chaotic live RTÉ-radio session and interview in 1986 with the legendary Terry, Johnny and Henry line-up, organised by former Led Zeppelin publicist and Sweeney's devotee B.P. Fallon; Andy and Henry, uniquely, in Cork in 1990; Andy and Johnny in Galway in 2000 (forced into it through being on the same bill and national newspapers erroneously trumpeting a Sweeney reunion – but magical in its spontaneity, with Joe Dolan tantalisingly in the audience). Earlier that same year Henry and Johnny played a gig together in Ballycastle; it may prove to have been the final straw for Henry when Moynihan – in between interminable tuning-up – took a mobile phone call during the show. But of such things are legends made.

AFTERWORD: JOHNNY'S ADVENTURES 1970–77

You disappeared for a while around 1970?
Er, yeah. I have a favourite phrase about recording studios. I describe them as places I'm dragged screaming into and led weeping out of. It doesn't bother me not to have made more recordings. I never had any luck in recording studios: when I played well, machinery broke down; when the machinery worked I didn't play well. But what I was doing was living with Annie in

England and we were doing a few gigs. Basically, we were living on the cheap in the countryside. I was having to go back and forth to Ireland for various family reasons, and unfortunately Annie had a dog and there was some law at the time that you couldn't bring a dog into Ireland without six months' quarantine, so she couldn't come with me. So the combination of her having this dog and me having these reasons to go to Ireland is probably responsible for us not staying together in the long term.

Yet you did contribute to her Topic *album.*

But, again, I wasn't happy with what I did. I decided to make an honest living for a while, as an architectural draughtsman, in the early Seventies, in Ireland. I'd been doing a few gigs, though, and when Donal Lunny left Planxty I was asked to join. And I did. Until they split up.

And were you happy with the Planxty experience?

Well, no. I felt I didn't contribute very much to the band. I think the band probably had its troubles before I joined but I definitely wasn't happy with the album [*Cold Blow And The Rainy Night*, 1974]. 'P Stands For Paddy' was OK but the two polkas that I was responsible for were appalling. There *had* been a good performance of it done in the studio but the tape machine broke down, inexplicably. I suppose because I'd been drafted in – that it wasn't organic, a band that I'd been part of – I didn't contribute much to that band. I'm sorry. Apologies to all concerned. But then a couple of months later De Danann wanted me to go to the States with them for the bicentennial celebrations. Andy had been playing with them but he didn't want to go to the States unless it was on his terms – because it was the Smithsonian Institution [*sic*] that was bringing us out and giving us something like $10 a day pocket money, and he didn't want to do that. I happened to be in his house when Frankie [Gavin] phoned to talk about the States thing, and he said, 'Do you want to join a good band?' 'If it's going to the States I do!' So that's how I joined De Danann. Alec Finn was playing bouzouki so I had to play mandolin, which was a pity, but basically they needed a singer. A lot of traditional musicians regard songs almost as a necessary evil, and it was difficult to get arrangements on songs to work well, which was a bit frustrating. But we managed OK. I did a lot of unaccompanied singing. I like unaccompanied singing.

ANNE BRIGGS
PROLOGUE

'The first folk club I ever encountered in my life was the Scot's Hoose [in Cambridge Circus, London],' says Christy Moore, 'and Annie Briggs was the guest. It was a very interesting experience hearing this woman singing unaccompanied to a quiet room. It was quite a turn-on. I think that night was the only time I ever encountered her and I didn't actually get to speak to her. At that time I was playing in Irish pubs in London and it was difficult. People didn't listen. Really, you sang a few songs when those who played the jigs and reels wanted a break. You were the filler and, in the main, the people who went to hear Irish music weren't that good at listening to songs. And then I went to this folk club and the order, the atmosphere . . . I said, I want some of this! I never actually worked at the Scot's Hoose myself, but shortly after that I went

Colin Harper · Previously unpublished

Anne Briggs, Bert Jansch, London, c. 1965

up to Manchester and really started my career working on the folk-club scene there. But the Scot's Hoose – I went there one night, Anne Briggs was playing, I proceeded to get drunk and I was chucked out. I've no doubt it was entirely my own fault!'

I first met Anne Briggs in the relatively tame wilds of Lincolnshire in 1991, during the first phase of working on what would eventually see the light of day, ten years later, as a biography of Bert Jansch. How I managed to locate such an elusive figure, known to me only from a handful of song credits on Bert Jansch albums from the Sixties and from a then recent, and captivating, reissue of her own recordings from that decade, I no longer remember. But reputation can be deceptive. The restless, solitary young woman of old with a voice of such personal vulnerability yet age-old power had become a self-contained, rough-hewn but contented individual who was ready and willing to welcome, and be interviewed by, an awestruck novice.

I met Anne twice after that: in Edinburgh during the early spring of 1992, for the filming of a documentary sequence with Bert which I wouldn't have missed for the world; and in 1997, on an island off Scotland, for a many-paged retrospective in *Mojo*. In between times Anne had helped me by phone and by letter with a Sweeney's Men sleeve-note and with a *Mojo* feature on Led Zeppelin's folk influences of which she, to her complete lack of interest, was one. David Suff's Fledg'ling label had recently unearthed – if licensing something from Jo Lustig (Isle of Man) Ltd can ever be termed thus – Anne's previously unissued third album, *Sing A Song For You*. Its lack of daylight had been entirely at her own insistence but, somehow, David had convinced the lost goddess of trad that what in 1973 may have seemed a travesty was, at this remove, a flawed-gem remnant of a better age.

Having allowed David to release the album it was largely for him and I believe at least partly for me that the request for a comprehensive interview on her own life, and the consequently unavoidable overnight stay on her own island, was granted. Mentioning that most musicians would probably sell their granny for a few thousand words in the magazine in question was greeted, over glasses of wine, with a mischievous grin and the raising of an eyebrow. Living on an island with no television, a rarely used mobile phone and unspoiled nature as far as the eye could see, the flimsy accolades of the music business were literally worthless to this born survivor. Personally, she really couldn't care less, and probably never had.

For my own career, though, this was a big deal – my first major feature in *Mojo*, an upwardly mobile publication with class, cred and status – and I think Anne knew that. I remain grateful for her time, her friendship and her hospitality. Anne's husband Pat – a retired forester dedicated to their shared pursuit of Tom & Barbara-like self-sufficiency on this barren edge of the British Isles – was far from keen, but put up pretty well with this rare intrusion from a past life. Taking two days to get there from Belfast by car, I stopped over in Glasgow with my friend Kate, a would-be actress and rather-not-be barmaid who would eventually give in to 'the Man' (aka the Edinburgh Civil Service), and went to a Martin Hayes concert. The inevitable review (reprinted below) kind of covered the travel.

I let Anne see and approve, by post, various drafts of the piece up to almost the final one. Alas, when it appeared, after sub-editing and with the admittedly over-zealous addendum that I was hoping to pursue a full-scale Briggs biography, she was not happy. It grieved me then, and still does, that something had happened to annul our association. Sadly, I have never heard from her again. It was some comfort to hear a little later from Ken Hunt, an enormously knowledgeable and dedicated polymath of non-mainstream music writing, that this kind of severing of ties was not unusual with Anne; something similar had happened after his own superb retrospective on the singer in *Swing 51* a few years earlier. Trevor Hodgett's experience with Ottilie Patterson, as we'll see, is another case in point.

Mojo published the piece in March 1998, and I was delighted to find through correspondence from other writers and from readers, the like of which I have never since experienced with any journalistic work, that it had struck some kind of chord. (The version given here is, for what it's worth, as close to the last Briggs-approved draft as I can recall, with a few corrections of detail in the light of subsequent work.) Later that year Sony reissued her impossibly rare second album, *The Time Has Come*. The following year Topic released *Anne Briggs: A Collection*, a beautifully remastered chronicle of all the Topic recordings plus two stray 1963 live tracks, licensed from Decca. Both releases included sleeve-notes from myself – Topic MD Tony Engle generously agreeing to push the physics of CD booklets to allow an 11,000-word history and appreciation, loosely based on the *Mojo* piece but rearranging its bones with the flesh of detail and wider quote-age. With all this activity, with glowing reviews and with Topic's PR operator Harriet Sims treating her task as a labour of love, there were several significant interview requests, some at national newspaper level. As I understand it, all went unanswered. Likewise, extra-mile communiqués from Tony concerning the improvement of her royalty arrangements have yielded only silence.

In recent years I've become friendly with Steve Ashley, a lovably stoic, self-deprecating survivor from the second division of Seventies folk-rock. He remains justly proud of his own association with Anne Briggs, immortalised on the long-lost (if not forever) third album, *Sing A Song For You*. During 2002 Steve and his wife Liz visited Anne on her island. It was good to know that the circle was not yet entirely broken. It was also strange to hear that such an icon of self-containment was now, of all things, running a tearoom. Perhaps we all get lonely sometimes.

Anne Briggs, 1963,
at the recording of
Decca's *Edinburgh Folk
Festival* albums

ANNE BRIGGS
THE SINGER AT THE GATES OF DAWN

In a hole in the ground lived a hobbit. Or so the story goes. And off to the west of Scotland, on the farthest shore of an island whose name shall remain discreet is a solitary, ancient and once ruinous cottage in a place which translates from Gaelic as 'the pass of the hobgoblin'. Its new resident is not impressed: 'I'm not really into hobgoblins,' she says. 'Not my scene at all.'

'No – more Renbourn's sort of thing,' I suggest, dismounting with no small degree of discomfort from the back of the all-terrain vehicle that has brought us thus far, over the few roadless miles from the populated (26) side of the island to the home of Britain's greatest and most adored traditional singer of the modern era (retired).

'I'll tell him you said that!' she says, softening the mischievous jibe at once with a famously rakish grin, and manfully unpacking a trailer full of groceries, firewood and her visitor's rain-racked belongings.

Anne Briggs: hard as the weather, soft as the sound of the ocean; the wandering siren of the British folksong revival, shunning company for months on end and intermittently making a handful of records that every other woman singer then and after would cherish as god-like inspiration. The first new-age traveller in history – but no fool for all this hippy claptrap.

Possessed of a voice that could take the listener into the world of the old songs themselves, the Anne Briggs of folk mythology was no fey romantic living out a fairytale. She was a born survivor, with no one and nothing to fall back on. Her young age, her strange attraction to what was then a certainly dying oral tradition and her singular personality meant that Anne Briggs was for so many others – Bert Jansch, Sandy Denny, June Tabor, Christy Moore, Richard Thompson, Dick Gaughan among them – the bridge. She made the whole thing credible and attainable. Not to put too fine a point on it she was, as was the best of the music itself, sexy, wild, mysterious, otherworldly and vulnerable all at the same time. '*She was a rare thing/ Fine as a beeswing*' sang Richard Thompson, many years later in 'Beeswing', with its thinly veiled if romanticised story of a strange girl with a wolfhound triumphing over the confines of conventional living. This is the thing – rock 'n' roll people wrote songs about her, but her own role models had absolutely nothing to do with rock 'n' roll. 'I had no interest in it,' she says. 'None whatsoever. My heroes were the nameless people who were recorded "in the field". Their singing struck a deep chord within me and I immediately felt, That's my music, that's what I should be singing.'

Colin Harper · Originally published in *Mojo* (March 1998); plus additional material

The whole British folk revival, shadowy and peripheral as it seems today, is probably as much a contributor to the very *sound* of British rock as the earliest American blues and rock 'n' roll, perhaps the classic lineage demonstration being the well-travelled story of 'Black Mountain Side' from the first Led Zeppelin album. Anybody who cares knows Jimmy Page got the thing from Bert Jansch's take on the traditional 'Blackwater Side'; Page once claimed he got it directly from seeing Anne in a folk club; Bert certainly got it from Anne – either way it all comes back to the same place. The analogy won't stand too much scrutiny, but if British folk needs one single Robert Johnson figure, this defiantly reclusive woman who hasn't seen a recording studio for 30 years is the closest it's got. 'There's no neighbours for two miles in any direction,' she says, 'which is great. Suits me.'

A long time ago Sandy Denny also wrote a song about Anne, 'The Pond And The Stream'. And true to the lyric there's something about the way she has lived, and still does, that's enviable. Anne's own song 'Living By The Water', both childlike and vaguely unsettling as the best of her writing, says it all: *'Voices from the empty moor/ They call me past the stranger's door/ Because I keep no company/ I'll make no enemies'.* It's not some con, some 'elusive artist' hype, and yet neither is she unsociable nor especially eccentric – no more so than the rest of us. She doesn't dislike people, but can live without them. And, likewise, without music. Her own children, Sarah and Colin, born in '71 and '73 respectively, only became aware in the late Eighties that their mother was some kind of legend. Eliza Carthy showed Colin an old photo in a magazine and he was stunned. As you would be. Even in her prime Anne Briggs recorded precious little: a handful of odd tracks in the early Sixties; two albums, *Anne Briggs* (Topic) and *The Time Has Come* (CBS), in 1971; an aborted third in 1973; and a lot of living in between.

'If you want a reason why I stopped singing it's 'cos I met my husband,' she says, typically matter-of-fact, 'which meant I got better feeding and I got a roof over my head. And I think that was responsible for me having kids, which stopped me singing. We moved up to a very remote area of Sutherland. You can't just clear off and leave them. There were no babysitters, basically.'

Born in Toton on 29 September 1944, her mother (herself adopted) was from Northern Ireland, her father from Nottinghamshire. Both died when Anne was young and she was raised in Nottinghamshire by an elderly aunt old enough to be her grandmother, whose maiden name had been Briggs. Anne was a difficult child 'but it was really awful for her when I suddenly went off with Centre 42. She had no concept of where I was at or what I was doing. But she came to terms with it eventually. Actually, there was one occasion when I was on television and somebody told her, "We saw your girl on the telly." She was thrilled to bits, it was OK then – it was a level of achievement that was acceptable and understandable to her! But I'd really enjoyed my secondary education. I'd got a bunch of O levels and I was going to try and get into Durham University to do fine art but after a year in sixth form Centre

42 came along and I thought, Yeah, a bird in the hand's worth two in the bush. Go for it.'

Centre 42 was an attempt by the Trades Union Congress to devolve culture and art from London to the provinces with a touring package show throughout 1962. It was a grand ideal, with the playwright Arnold Wesker at its helm and the two great 'architects' of the folk revival, Ewan MacColl and A.L. 'Bert' Lloyd, looking after the musical programme. Part of the brief was to involve singers from the areas the tour stopped in, and the second night was in Nottingham. Anne was among half a dozen locals auditioned for the concert by Ewan MacColl. He was suitably impressed and gave her a slot. She sang at least two songs, 'Let No Man Steal Your Thyme' and 'She Moves Through The Fair' – two songs that she would record live in Edinburgh later that year.

Her whole recording career, or perhaps more accurately 'series of sporadic recording incidents', and likewise the beatnik lifestyle, happened as a result of Centre 42 – not only playing that one festival, but joining up for the rest: 'My family disowned me,' she says. 'I left home a runaway. They threatened to put a court order on me to keep me at home but, as I pointed out, it was only four weeks to my eighteenth birthday. But for a couple of years I was out on my own. After the festivals, the Centre 42 movement felt a bit guilty about all this and offered me a job in their offices in London and I had a very interesting six months as a "gofer", nipping about all over London to theatres and galleries and suchlike. And I was getting gigs there on the back of it.'

The skiffle and rock 'n' roll eras, centred on coffee houses in Soho, had died away by this stage in late '62, and the venues that would form the centre of the wild acoustic scene that would soon find its heroes in people like Bert Jansch and John Renbourn had mostly yet to emerge. But it was starting to happen. Davy Graham and Wizz Jones, both in their own ways left-field individuals and the godfathers of the guitar movement, were certainly around, and the Troubadour, in Earl's Court, was already plying its trade as a venue for the exotic. Anne was staying with Gill Cook, an assistant at Collett's record shop – which would remain Anne's postal address for some years – and was spending her free time exploring the capital's thriving Irish-music scene. By winter she had the company, on their first trip to the bright lights, of a bunch of ragamuffins from Edinburgh: Bert Jansch and, founders of The Incredible String Band, Robin Williamson and Clive Palmer.

Bert and Anne were as uncannily alike as they were gifted. They'd met once before, in the summer of 1959. Anne had hitchhiked to Edinburgh in the school holidays with a friend who knew Archie Fisher. Bert was staying at Archie's at the time, having just quit his job as a gardener for Glasgow Corporation and taken up guitar. As remote as each other, they hit it off immediately: 'I'd never met anyone playing that sort of music before,' remembers Anne. 'I'd never heard anything like it. He hadn't been playing very long but he was obviously a born guitarist, plus he was starting to write one or two of his own songs. He was interested in the sort of stuff that I was doing, but no more than an acknowledgement of its worth. There was no way he was going to play it himself.'

At least not for a while. They were coming at music from completely different yet highly personalised directions. It was to be the one abiding focus in their lives and, solitary to extremes as they both were, their paths would cross time and again over the next number of years – writing songs together, travelling together, living together. And then the pivotal if little-known matter of Anne convincing freelance sound recordist Bill Leader, firstly, into making a record of this introverted, commercially unacceptable genius and, secondly and perhaps more remarkably, talking Nathan Joseph of Transatlantic Records into putting it out. But that was a couple of years down the line.

'Everybody used to think we were brother and sister,' she says, 'because we looked very alike at that stage. We were on the road together, going to each other's gigs, just literally dossing side by side. For me, it was great to be in Bert's company because he was a companion. Yes, he was a boyfriend but he was a very loose sort of boyfriend. We were just very, very close – in music and in lifestyle.'

They shared a squat in Earl's Court for a while and much later, at the height of Bert's fame, *circa* 1965, a house on London's Somali Road with Annie, The Young Tradition and any number of itinerant folkies downstairs, and the relatively well-off (by then) guitar heroes Jansch and Renbourn upstairs: 'They got all the gigs, we got all the visitors,' she says. 'In fact I suspect they paid our rent quite a lot of the time!' The remarkable canon of songs that Bert and Anne wrote together date from the early weeks of 1965, when Anne was staying at Gill Cook's flat – a perfect time and place, in the downtime of daylight, to create: 'Writing songs was just a thing we did for pleasure when there was nothing else to do,' says Anne. 'We'd found that my traditional songs and his dramatic guitar playing could really gel together. As far as I'm aware now, nobody had done it before and it was stimulating to the extent that we started writing songs together. It was a very creative period. A lot of it drifted away, but some of them survived.'

Davy Graham and Shirley Collins were the first to get a mad-guitarist/traditional girl-singer record on the market in *Folk Roots, New Routes* (February 1965), and although Bert tapped Annie for the traditional songs – including the notorious 'Blackwater Side' that featured on his ground-breaking, genre-defining *Jack Orion* (1966) album and later on as repertoire with The Pentangle – they never did perform or record together at the time. It's virtually impossible now to believe that the dark, weird songs they'd written – like 'Wishing Well', 'Go Your Way My Love' or even Anne's own hymnally ethereal 'The Time Has Come' – were of a time before even The Beatles had truly broken free of songwriting convention.

Accompanying songs with instruments and writing more songs of her own would be some way off. All the early period Anne Briggs recordings were unaccompanied voice, and yet so arresting, so perfect they lack nothing. In the wake

Anne Briggs,
onstage in
the mid-Sixties

of Centre 42, she recorded on two projects for Topic in fairly quick succession: two tracks for *The Iron Muse*, a themed album of British industrial songs overseen by Bert Lloyd; and her own four-song EP, *The Hazards Of Love*. In between the Topic sessions she was recorded live in glorious mono at a multi-artist bash in Edinburgh by erstwhile Topic producer Bill Leader and his new associate Nathan Joseph – a Cambridge cabaret artiste turned entrepreneur who had, in effect, convinced the good folks at Decca that folk music was the next big thing and why didn't he go off and record some for them. Two monstrously uncommercial albums entitled *Edinburgh Folk Festival 1963* and one large cheque later, Joseph had the wherewithal to kick start his own label, Transatlantic, conveniently signing many of the acts he'd met up in Edinburgh – Ian Campbell, The Dubliners, Hamish Imlach. Anne Briggs wasn't so easy: 'I turned him down,' she says. 'He was flashing money about but I felt a certain loyalty to Topic and, quite honestly, although they never had any money I felt they had discretion.'

The Hazards Of Love, recorded in '63, took the better part of a year to appear. By the time it did, Annie was experiencing something of that very nature. She wouldn't record again until 1966, and the intervening years were dark ones: 'It was two years of hell,' she says, still unsettled by the memory. 'I was in Scotland those two years. Surviving. Really on the edge. Ran with a very wild guy, very violent guy. A really, really bad time and I don't wish to talk about it. I wasn't singing, I wasn't in contact with anyone on the folk scene – except this one time I met Hamish Henderson on the street in Edinburgh . . .'

Like Bert Lloyd in England and Séamus Ennis in Ireland, Hamish Henderson – as a catalyst, an encourager, a field recorder of those nameless individuals whose music Anne adored – was a primal figure in preserving his own nation's heritage, active since the Forties. When he chanced upon Anne he invited her to a gathering of many of the great names in Scottish music of the day. She didn't need to be asked twice: 'It was a ray of golden sunshine in a really bad time,' she says, with the relief still evident all these years later. 'I was asked to do *The Bird In The Bush* shortly after that and I decided to break out of the life I was in. It took some doing.'

Another of Bert Lloyd's projects, *The Bird In The Bush* was a themed album of erotic English folk songs. It was released in July 1966 – around the same time as *Jack Orion*, Bert Jansch's open-tuned guitar assault on the tradition and a flowering of the Briggs influence. Lloyd himself contributed in rakish fashion, along with Lou Killen, future Fairporter Dave Swarbrick and Frankie Armstrong, between them creating a work, now available on CD, that remains conceptually robust and influential. Annie, at the time, 'wasn't physically in very good shape', had a cold and didn't enjoy the recording process. But, four decades on, her four simple, unaccompanied songs for the project shine like diamonds. And, true to form, they'd be her last for nearly five years.

Annie Briggs is always referred to, in the books where she is referred to at all, as an English singer but in every sense bar accent she could be considered

Irish. Some weeks after our meeting, the Hebridean mud just about absent from my shoes, I'm spending a pleasant afternoon in a Dublin pub with Johnny Moynihan and Eamonn O'Doherty, recalling the unwritten past. These people, Briggs included, are at the foundations of what Irish music has become today – living, breathing and commercially viable. It's a far cry from the cultural doldrums of the Sixties. Yet Irish musicians and singers, with a few exceptions, have become very narrow in their sense of history. 'In a way,' says Johnny, 'I don't think anybody in Irish music needs to remember her, as such, because I hear an awful lot of Annie Briggs in the singing of women today – not enough of them, but a good few. And yet when I mention her name they've never heard of her.'

Moynihan, like Annie, is himself something of a lost legend today, and that's exactly how he likes it. A modest, professorial demeanour and periodic allusions to a near-pathological dislike of the recording process belie the fact that here is one of the key figures in the story of modern Irish music and, like Bert Jansch before him, a kindred spirit and sometime partner in the Anne Briggs story. Along with Andy Irvine and Terry Woods, with Eamonn O'Doherty as court photographer, Moynihan was a member of Sweeney's Men. They were the very first of the 'modern' Irish folk groups and for a few months in the summer of '68, culminating in an incendiary performance at the Cambridge Folk Festival with Northern Irish rock guitarist Henry McCullough on the team, they were the very first of the 'British' folk-rock bands. Between them, the men of Sweeney went on to found or join acts like Planxty, De Danann, Steeleye Span, The Pogues, Wings and The Grease Band, and influence trail-blazers in Irish rock like Horslips and Thin Lizzy. As with Anne, you've never heard of them but they can't be underestimated.

The death of the showbands that had dominated Irish culture for years and the birth of a real, modern Irish music is a story for another day, but for a brief period in time, when there was no real money around and everyone was experimenting with styles (and substances), the Dublin folk and rock scenes were equal in outsidership, with musical interaction as creatively exhilarating as it was a neighbourly gesture. Moynihan himself guested on Phil Lynott's very first single, 'New Faces, Old Places', with Skid Row, in 1969. But the long-lost Irish episodes of the Anne Briggs story begin a little earlier than that.

'It was The Dubliners,' says Johnny – 'They'd met Annie at some festival across the water, and they were struck by a certain similarity – this girl who sang like me, looked like me – so it was a sort of arranged match. On a subsequent occasion she came over with them and we felt almost obliged to be in each other's company. And very nice it was, too. She was wilder than I was, a tomboy with a rakish grin but stunningly beautiful. The first night she spent in Dublin we were going along Clare Street and there was scaffolding outside this building, about five storeys high, and she climbed up all the way to the top and with a great whoop of delight discovered there was a rope on a pulley. But there was nothing on the other end and she came down like a fucking stone! The whoop got louder very fast – but there must have been some kind of drag on the rope 'cos she emerged unscathed. I was quite impressed.'

It was the summer of 1965, and it would be the first of four that Anne would spend in Ireland. The fact that there already existed in England a commercial folk scene proved useful. Anne would return there every so often to play some gigs and earn enough money to sustain her in Ireland for a while. The freedoms she found there, for singing without stages, for travelling on sunny summer roads in the west in the days when horse-power was still a living means of transport, for disappearing off into the blue, made it feel like a spiritual home. Her live performances were always erratic, dependent on circumstance, but they were most likely to touch the sun in Ireland.

'She had a direct line to the muse,' says Eamonn O'Doherty, 'and if the moment was right it was magnificent. My memories are of her singing informally in pubs. You'd arrive in these country pubs with these bullock-like men standing around not taking very much interest in life and maybe after a pint or two and a bit of conversation Annie would launch into something and it would transform the moment, transform existence, transform everybody's life and probably the way they looked at their history. It was remarkable. At one stage, just before the Troubles, I was going to the North and she asked to come along because she said her mother had come from Moneymore, in South Derry. We eventually got there and that's one place where the magic happened. She sang a few songs and by the time we left people were whooping and whacking each other on the backs with bonhomie. Perhaps because she sang things that people in that area would have recognised it brought their minds back to better days and the good things in life. We headed on to Malin Head, in Donegal, and one thing that will remain visually with me is seeing Annie jumping into the deep, dark waters of a cove without warning and swimming out towards these seals – swimming like a dog swims, without even thinking about it. I remember it because she borrowed my shirt when she came out and I froze for the rest of the day!'

There was always a curious attraction to water. Johnny recalls one occasion, in Dublin, when he was drunk and trying to start an argument. Anne simply dived into a canal. Johnny, believing in his altered state that he had precipitated a suicide, leapt to her rescue only remembering, mid-air, that he couldn't swim. One of them rescued the other. Anne Briggs may not be well-known, but she has continued to exist almost as a 'rural myth' through stories of sleeping in the woods, of being followed around by a cat for six months, of pushing Johnny and Andy Irvine out of a hay loft 'in a spirit of fun' twenty feet above the ground, of running out of money and almost joining a circus. At one point she did disappear, for weeks on end, to live on the shores of an island off Kerry: 'Very profound time that,' she says. 'Focuses the mind wonderfully on priorities. I've always felt totally at one with the natural environment – the landscape, the wildlife. What is. It's only people that make life difficult.'

Her most resonant song, 'Living By The Water', was written on bouzouki during her solitude on the island. She'd been introduced to the curious Greek instrument by Moynihan, who pioneered its use in Irish music. Like the D-modal guitar tuning she'd already been taught by Jansch (also now a permanent feature in Irish trad) it gave her music a wholly unique sound and, with lyrics to match, a singularly otherworldly feel. 'Living By The Water' was the first self-written piece she would record herself, on her eventual album debut in 1971, and typifies a strain of nature-driven writing, with about as much regard for accepted compositional technique as Van Morrison's *Astral Weeks*, that would become a recurring feature of her work.

'My life has always been seasonally based,' she says, 'even before I got into music. I worked from the age of seven in my uncle's market garden, after school and weekends. I was an odd child in that my life revolved around wildlife. I was really involved in birdwatching, badger-watching, otter-watching. That was my life. And the sea as well – I love the concept of the edge of the land, and the beginning of the unknown. It's like a mystical thing.'

Unwittingly, the mystic fascination would place her music very much within the parameters of the vaguely psychedelic, hippy world-view of the later Sixties. For her second album, when the relationship with Moynihan was finally over, Anne would record his own 'Standing On The Shore' – a dope-haze recollection, originally featured on the final Sweeney's Men album, *The Tracks Of Sweeney* (1969), and incorrectly credited as 'traditional' on both records. The meeting of styles, musical and lifestyle – traditional and contemporary, ancient gypsy and modern beatnik – had blended into one.

The Irish adventure couldn't last forever. Sweeney's Men were formally constituted as a unit in Galway, summer of '66: 'We used to travel around in Johnny's beat-up old VW van,' says Anne – 'Three guys and three girlfriends. Initially it was great fun. Then they got a manager and the next thing I know they all wanted irons, 'cos the manager had got them these striped shirts they had to wear for the gigs. I refused point blank to iron their bloody shirts! That's when things started to change. It wasn't so much fun after that.'

One change that *was* welcome, indeed revolutionary, was the arrival of Henry McCullough. A showband veteran, he'd been storming the Dublin scene in 1967 with his psychedelic soul band, The People. Dave Robinson, subsequent founder of Stiff Records, was the roadie and they'd done the trekking-off-to-London thing in search of fame. And almost found it. Blowing off Procol Harum at the Middle Earth club, with Hendrix managers Chas Chandler and Mike Jeffries (who subsequently changed the group's name to Eire Apparent for reasons nobody understood) in attendance provided the ticket. Getting busted for dope in Canada, on a Hendrix tour, provided Henry the ticket for an early bath.

When the guitarist arrived demoralised back in Dublin, early in '68, Sweeney's Men had just recorded their first album and Andy Irvine had developed itchy feet to go and explore the music of Eastern Europe. It sounded

Johnny Moynihan, Anne Briggs,
Puck Fair, Killorglin, County Kerry, 1967

a weird diversion at the time, but proved enormously influential to Irish music later on, not least in the *Riverdance* phenomenon. But at the time Sweeney's needed a new man. Henry and Johnny had been mutually knocked out by each other's gigs before the Canadian debacle and it seemed right. But, with Terry Woods a man of singular temperament, the chemistry was fragile: 'It wasn't achieving what it could, because it wasn't an ideal collection of people, and Henry knew it,' says Johnny. Nevertheless, the trio, along with Anne – now living with Johnny in Dublin – survived long enough to create a stir. Their final gig, at the 1968 Cambridge Folk Festival, sent the English music press ecstatic and set Ashley Hutchings, subsequent godfather of English folk-rock, a-thinking.

But Irish audiences hadn't been so visionary. 'I seen us getting almost killed in the car parks,' says Henry, 'pennies being thrown at us – "Sweeney's Men selling out," and all this sort of thing, 'cos the live thing was nothing to do with the record at all. It worked in the house, but when you took it onto a stage the whole thing just didn't connect. If we'd had another six months at it . . . We just didn't know what we were doing 'cos we were the first to do it and, consequently, it's a case of having an idea in your head and not being sure how to put it into practice. But it was a very experimental time, and it got us all writing as well.'

As if to keep the legend safe, no recordings of this line-up remain, though Henry's legacy left two songs to turn up on *The Tracks Of Sweeney* (1969) – a hit-and-miss experimental affair recorded with only Johnny and Terry – and one other, 'Step Right Up' which turned up on Anne's *The Time Has Come* (1971). If the music had been a revelation to Henry, so had this strange young woman: 'She was part of our little team for a period,' he says, with lingering affection, 'and I found her fascinating really. She was beautiful, absolutely beautiful – so gentle in her voice and yet she had all this depth. Her and Johnny, I suppose you could call them the first hippies, just travelling when the notion took them. It was a great eye-opener for me, an introduction to an earthier way of life. But then Annie had been into it for years.'

Immediately after Cambridge Henry auditioned, successfully, for Joe Cocker's Grease Band, just after Cocker's breakthrough hit, 'With A Little Help From My Friends', had appeared, and went off into the sunset. That summer of '68 was the end of an era in other ways, too. Anne had got a dog, a great lurcher hound called Clea which she took everywhere. With a foot-and-mouth scare at the time, it meant she couldn't bring the dog to Ireland: 'I suddenly thought, My God, I'm responsible, I've got to put a roof over this dog's head. After a few weeks living at Gill Cook's house I knew it was no life for a dog, or me. I had these friends in Suffolk, and they had a caravan so I took over the tenancy. Johnny would come over and stay, or I'd leave the dog with friends and go to Ireland – but I wouldn't leave her long. Johnny and I were drawing apart then anyway, so it was a natural separation.'

Anne kept her tenancy in Suffolk until the early Seventies, and this increased availability in England made a marked difference to her public profile. She started appearing with some regularity in the now thriving folk clubs of London and in the pages of *Melody Maker*. For a while, too, she allowed herself to be managed by Roy Guest, a promoter and agent who'd cut his teeth on the Edinburgh scene of the early Sixties and had since been taking folk music onto grand new platforms. 'I remember one great occasion at the Albert Hall,' says Johnny. 'To get onstage you walked through a tunnel under the back seating. It should be pointed out that Annie was always extremely shy and nervous about performing in public – that's why she used to drink a lot. She finished singing, looked right and left and couldn't see any wings – she'd completely forgotten how she'd got there. So she just jumped off the stage, crossed the footlights, jumped down into the aisle and walked out the front door! She had to go round the streets till she found the stage door to get back in.'

In the big commercial world Annie Briggs was still a fish out of water, but during those later years of her career she was at least trying to play the game. In August '69 she was tracked down by the BBC to come in and record the first of two sessions for John Peel's *Nightride* (sessions which, sadly, no longer exist, though BBC Transcriptions does retain three thus-far unreleased live performances from a 1966 programme). One of the four songs broadcast was the old Jansch–Briggs co-write 'Go Your Way My Love'. Anne would finally release it commercially on her Topic album in early 1971 but, in the meantime, Jansch had been keeping her songs in the public eye. 'The Time Has Come' had turned up, fairly raggedly, on *Bert And John* (1966), 'Go Your Way' on *Nicola* (1967), 'Wishing Well' on *Birthday Blues* (1969) and a splendid live recording of 'The Time Has Come' on *Sweet Child* (1968), the second and most critically acclaimed album from Jansch and Renbourn's new fusion band, The Pentangle. The song was also covered joyously as a single B-side, in 1968, by former Animal, Alan Price. 'Can't imagine why it was so popular,' she muses. 'I was nineteen when I wrote that, first song I ever wrote. It was unbelievably simple. Maybe that simplicity is all you need. Maybe you lose it when you grow up.'

Californian singer Dorris Henderson recorded one further Briggs song, 'Mosaic Patterns', in 1967 which the writer would never commit to tape herself. Given that Anne hadn't herself actually recorded *any* of these songs yet, it was an extraordinary situation. At the time, she was unaware of all this vinyl flattery. She was also unaware of how much she was causing her friend Sandy Denny to muse upon the price of fame. 'The Pond And The Stream', Sandy's song from *Fotheringay* (1970), was the clearest indication: *'Annie wanders on the land, she loves the freedom of the air/ She finds a friend in every place she goes/ There's always a face she knows/ I wish that I was there'*.

By that stage even Bert Jansch, now married and living within occasional visiting distance of Anne, was caught up in the treadmill of international concert tours. 'I assumed they were all having a great time,' says Anne, 'making a great deal of money and travelling all over the world. There was me, happy to wander around and live in my Suffolk caravan. I was very content. Sandy made her choice and I made mine, and I'm very happy for her if that's what she wanted. She was a great lass, a smashing girl and it's very sad that she had to miss out on some things to achieve that fame. I didn't realise what those songs were about for years until other people told me. I'd no idea at the time.'

'To hear the elusive Anne Briggs on her first solo album is an opportunity not to be missed,' opined *Melody Maker*, on its release in early '71. Bert Lloyd, still the most capable force in actually getting her into a studio, wrote a sleeve-note, and an evocative silhouette of the loping young lass and her faithful hound adorned the cover. Eight traditional songs – mostly unaccompanied and stunning as ever – and two originals were featured, with Moynihan remaining long enough in the studio to guest on 'Willy O'Winsbury', a much-recorded song of the period that had been inadvertently 'created' by Andy Irvine for *Sweeney's Men* by cross-referring the wrong tune to a set of words in a folksong manuscript. Other songs included further sparse renderings of folk-rock staples like 'Reynardine', 'Blackwater Side' and a variation of 'Tam Lin'.

Folk-rock was becoming the big currency of the day but while *Anne Briggs* would, like the first Sweeney's Men album, be a virtual source book of material for the Fairport generation, its author had little time for it herself. Musical purity had always been the Anne Briggs trademark. Rock music as rock music, fine – but don't mess with a music that's lasted this long without need of electricity. Ironically, then, the final two records she made would fall utterly within the parameters of rock.

Jo Lustig was a brash, larger than life character who'd originally come to England from New York as press agent for Nat 'King' Cole. His earliest claims were to have 'discovered' Nico and to have turned a not-especially talented folk singer called Julie Felix into a British television celebrity. His acts didn't always like him but they all knew he was the best PR guy in the business. He was, in manner, reputation and results – up to a point – the Peter Grant of the folk-rock crowd. 'I'm not out to make friends with my bands,' he once told me. 'Bert Jansch once said to me, "Jo, you never hang out." I don't like hanging out, that's not my scene. I get a group of musicians who know their own way artistically; I handle their business.'

Early in 1968 he signed Bert Jansch's exciting new group, The Pentangle, to a management deal, bullied Nathan Joseph into bankrolling an album and within six months had transformed them from a London-club attraction to an international concert act. In subsequent years he would take on the affairs of Mary O'Hara, The Chieftains, Roy Harper, Ralph McTell, Steeleye Span, Richard Thompson and Jethro Tull – and they would all benefit as a result. He also took on Anne Briggs: the most naturally gifted, least manageable and certainly least successful of the lot.

CBS believed the 'next big thing' was going to come from the folk world. They didn't know anything about it and reasonably assumed that Jo Lustig, manager of a critically acclaimed folk/jazz fusion act at their commercial peak, could come up with the names. Jo knew nothing about music but knew some people who did: John Renbourn recommended his old mentor Wizz Jones, Ralph McTell championed Clive Palmer's new band, COB, and Bert Jansch suggested Anne Briggs. An act from Northern Ireland called Therapy (I kid you not) were also in the frame. They all got to make horrendously unsuccessful records for CBS and, at the end of May 1971, two of them – COB and Anne – got to play the Royal Festival Hall supporting the first Bert Jansch solo concert in years. Heavily reviewed in the music press, words like 'beautiful', 'uncompromising', 'compelling' and 'impossible' were lavished on the typically nervous goddess of trad, although the *Melody Maker* reviewer struck a more quizzical poise: 'Dressed in a pink trouser suit she was the subject of some astonishment when presented with a bouquet. Had Anne Briggs sold out, one wondered. More so than Bert, her music taxed the patience of the uninitiated, balanced between monotony and fascination.'

Anne remembers it well: 'I was stone-cold sober when I did that gig. I was pregnant and I didn't have anything I could actually wear and Jo's wife Dee gave me this bloody awful pink maternity thing. I think Jo was so gobsmacked he sent somebody out to give me a bunch of flowers. He didn't know what else to do and I didn't know what to do with the flowers. I was so embarrassed.'

The Time Has Come, Anne's first and last CBS album, was out by the end of the year. Swathed in reverb, enshrouding the Lewis Carroll-esque dreamscape its delicate songs presented, it featured thirteen tracks – eight originals and five covers – all accompanied, on guitar and bouzouki, by herself alone. The covers included work from Moynihan, Henry McCullough, Steve Ashley and Lal Waterson. Lal was the most mysterious of the famous Hull singing family, The Watersons, with whom Anne had often sung – garnering a long-lasting cachet as 'the fifth Waterson' (making a cameo appearance in their 1966 BBC TV documentary *Travelling for a Living*), while Ashley was a young songwriter who lived just down the road from Anne's caravan.

The record was quirky, off-the-wall, highly individual and a combination of dark dreams and childlike visions. It didn't sell, and until relatively recently was available on CD only in Japan, and probably illegally. Anne didn't much care for it and, even at the time, told interviewers as much. But it remains an essential piece of the jigsaw. The final piece, a lost album called *Sing A Song For You* – released in 1996 for the first time – was recorded in 1973 with Steve Ashley, Barry Dransfield and Ragged Robin: a full-blown folk-rock band.

'My relationship with Jo Lustig was quite remote,' she says. 'He'd asked me if I'd make five LPs in five years for CBS. I said, "OK, I'll have a go." I wouldn't see him from one year to the next except when it was time to do a record. I always had the impression he had far more important things to do and bigger fish to fry than me. We lived in two different worlds, and it was becoming increasingly obvious to me that I lived in a different world to most of the people involved in folk music by then, too. I wasn't happy with where I was going commercially – in fact, I never had a bloody clue where I was going commercially. I began to feel I was losing control and I didn't like that. I jumped off the merry-go-round.'

To most people's minds she just slipped away on another trip somewhere and this time didn't come back. By the time her second CBS record was due, in early '73, Clea – her dog – had died, she already had a young daughter and was eight months pregnant. 'I should never have been recording,' she told me back in 1991. 'The singing wasn't easy. My confidence and my material was constantly being undermined by people who didn't want to listen unless there was a band involved. Yes, there were a few vaguely interesting things happening on it but I don't want it released because I don't think it's good enough – it's as simple as that.'

But attitudes mellow, even Anne's, and five years later she was persuaded by the Fledg'ling label to let it be unearthed. Even to diehards it was a revelation – not at all the half-hearted travesty of rumour, but a powerful, multi-textured and sparkling recording of a long-distant figure who had only ever existed to posterity in grainy monochrome, now – at long last – going out in a blaze of colour, playing through amplifiers with the sterling support of young Steve Ashley and his band and showing history that she could have played the folk-rockers at their own game had she been so inclined. She was still the best. Astonishingly, the whole thing was rehearsed and recorded in two days. Twenty-five years on, it can be revealed as a lost gem – not vocally her best, for sure, but featuring some wonderful traditional and original songs and, in the title track, perhaps her best. At the time, though, Anne was at her lowest ebb: 'I was just dismayed at the state of folk music, dismayed with myself at having produced this album. And by then I was very remote, living 600 miles from London. I had two kids and my priorities just changed.'

With almost no exceptions, she didn't sing again for over fifteen years. By the late Eighties her family had moved down to Lincolnshire and Anne was market-gardening. When Bert Lloyd died, in 1990, she was persuaded to appear at a memorial concert hosted by Martin Carthy and Dave Swarbrick. BBC Radio 2 salvaged a wonderful performance of 'Martinmas Time', a track originally from *The Bird In The Bush*, for broadcast while Carthy and Swarbrick began a process of coaxing her back on the road. As with The Beatles, the *idea* of an Anne Briggs resurrection was always going to be better than the real thing. First-hand reports from a handful of festival and club dates she undertook in 1991–92 suggest her nerves were against her all the way. It was a mistake: 'Martin and Dave made me feel guilty for not doing it so I gave it a try. But I was so unhappy. I was nervous travelling about in the cities and I hadn't been on the Underground in London for twenty years. It was a difficult time.'

I first met Anne, in Lincolnshire, in 1991 and had just that year heard her voice for the first time on a cassette issue of Fellside's *Classic Anne Briggs* – an essential compilation of her Topic recordings. I remember exactly where I was when I heard it: in Edinburgh. And I was in Edinburgh again in March the following year for the recording of Anne's sequence with Bert Jansch, Archie

Anne Briggs, at home in the Hebrides, 1997

Fisher and the late Hamish Imlach in Jan Leman's wonderful BBC film homage to the British folk scene of the Sixties, *Acoustic Routes*. Sitting mere feet away from Bert Jansch and Anne Briggs playing 'Blackwater Side' and 'Go Your Way' together for the first time in public, for the first time in decades, in the shell of Roy Guest's old Howff folk club on the Royal Mile, is an experience I'll never forget. Far from being remote, Anne was almost the life and soul of the party: 'It wasn't so alarming,' she says. 'I had my friends around me.' Yes, she was nervous; yes, in the cold light of day her performance was ragged but Leman spliced together two takes of 'Go Your Way', and the magic lived. Included on the soundtrack album, it remains the last recorded work of Anne Briggs.

Today, she lives on the island with her husband Pat, putting in long hours renovating their new home and planting a garden. Their daughter Sarah has a lovely cottage on the island, too, and hopes to live there more permanently herself one day. She has a photograph of her mother singing in 1962 pinned to a noticeboard with the shopping lists and memos, and it all seems like a lifetime away. Anne listens to Archie Fisher's BBC Scotland programme on the radio and Jim Lloyd's *Folk on Two*. She tells me she bumped into Bert Jansch's old sparring partner John Renbourn last year and he's kept in touch, telling her of a good studio in Fortwilliam, encouraging her to record again. Johnny Moynihan and Henry McCullough tell me they'd gladly be there if she needed them. She feels it might be nearing the time again, if only for herself. But most of all she delights in hearing about young girl singers – in a now stable, accepted traditional scene – like Eliza Carthy, Kate Rusby or Mairéad Ní Mhaonaigh from Altan citing her influence and singing her songs, just as June Tabor and Maddy Prior did in the Seventies and Eighties.

'I feel honoured,' she says. 'I felt it was important to keep the songs alive, like a cog in a wheel of respect back to the tradition. Now there's all these young lasses doing it and doing it really well and I'm so pleased because it's like a confirmation to me of my singing career. Songs are reaching them like they reached me. I feel what I've done is really and truly worth it.'

Long after midnight, cross-legged by the embers of the fire, drinking hot whiskey with the awesome silence of this corner of the world around us, Anne Briggs sings 'The Recruited Collier', just for me, 35 years after that first-ever recording for Topic. My tape machine is running, and if she never records again I'm privileged to have saved the last evidence of such a truly wonderful voice. In the last verse it wavers, she laughs and there is no more.

DAVY GRAHAM
PROLOGUE

At one time seemingly doomed to be an occupier of lonely footnotes in the history of music, Davy Graham has gained in recent years some degree of belated recognition through the combined efforts of various documentary-makers, a close-knit body of fans and the writers of suitably venerating books and magazine profiles – all of whom, like myself, begin from the standpoint that nobody in the world has ever heard of Davy Graham but that all who care at all about music certainly *should*.

Paraphraseable as a musical polymath whose infamous drug use in the Sixties flew him too close to the sun, it's true that a Davy Graham performance these days – and they remain rare, if ongoing, events – can be an erratic experience. But to see the man play at all, and to see him receive the adulation of those who know that the musical world would surely be a different place without him, is a thing that should be treasured. And just occasionally he will

Davy Graham (left), Martin Carthy, recording for a Nadia Cattouse album, mid-Sixties

reclaim the dextrous heights of yore. Though I chose not to interview him for *Dazzling Stranger* – for reasons stated in the opening paragraphs below – using instead previously published sources, I was persuaded to do so for a compare-and-contrast piece on both Graham and Jansch commissioned by *Mojo* in 2000.

Davy's fans are a fiercely protective lot. One of the very few letters of complaint I ever received for a published review (in this case, in *Q*) came from someone deploring my opinion of Davy's low-key 1995 release *Playing In Traffic*. One man's incoherent mish-mash is another's joyous 'eclection'. Desperately wanting to champion Davy to the *Q* generation, I could not in all honesty recommend that particular release, which was sad indeed. A decent budget and a lot of care and attention may yet produce a new Davy record of worth; certainly, I was surprised and delighted when, at the end of our interview at his home in Camden, Davy took up a guitar and played a new piece, happy for me to record it on mini-disc. It was very much better than anything that had been glimpsed in the admirable, if painfully low-budget, Channel 4 documentary the previous year. I said as much at the end of the resulting feature, but there remain those who still nourish the belief that the whole piece was a castigation rather than a celebration of the man. Not so. The idea of contrasting and trying to explain Bert's commercial success in the Sixties with Davy's incontestable lack of it came from the magazine's editor, Paul Trynka – having already read but rejected a purely Graham-based piece which I had offered him. It involved a lot more work on my part (and a plane ticket to London), but it was a good judgement call on Paul's part, and I defend it as valid.

A few months after meeting Davy in London, and after this apparently controversial piece had been published, I was invited to present a lifetime achievement award to the man at the annual Ards Guitar Festival, held in Newtownards, County Down. I was privileged, proud and excited to do so and, though a modest gesture in the wider world of awards, Davy, I believe, was touched to receive it and was applauded with great warmth by his audience. None will have left that building unaware that here indeed was the very architect of the instrumental guitar music without which such festivals, and their myriad professional participants, would not exist.

The piece below, while featuring the opening paragraphs and some of the interview material from that *Mojo* feature, has been crafted specifically for this volume – based around a sleeve-note commissioned by Universal Records in 1999 for an aborted Davy Graham compilation (a piece which was neverthe-less subsequently published in Kay Thomson's inspirational Davy Graham fan magazine *Midnight Man*) along with additional material adapted from *Dazzling Stranger* – and focuses more sharply on Graham and on his small but defining contribution to Irish music.

DAVY GRAHAM
THE FIRST WORLD MUSICIAN

'I *am* living in the past,' says Davy Graham, quite out of the blue. 'I *am* sitting on my laurels – because that's what they're for. God, if you've got to go out and do bloody auditions at my age, nearly 60, then life is a bowl of weevils, isn't it? If I've got anything happening for me now, it's because I worked hard when I was young. It's the same for anyone, isn't it? And I can't play as fast as I used to.'

Viewers of the 1999 Channel 4 documentary on Graham, *Blame It On My Youth* – and, screened at 3 a.m., their number will be few – may be forgiven for wondering if the godfather of British folk guitar can really play much at all these days. For that reason (that prospect of disappointment in meeting a fallen hero) and in deference to a man who is often said to be in ill health, and frankly also in fear of a man reputed to rage at the very name of Jansch, I have long avoided meeting Davy Graham. I am, and cannot deny being, Bert Jansch's biographer.

Davy's name has been linked to Bert's for decades. Their styles of playing are superficially similar, but while Davy was the first – the first acoustic-guitar hero Britain ever had, the first herald of fusion and world music – Bert was simply, and by far, the successful one. As Davy disappeared at the dawn of the Seventies, sporadically to reappear thereafter, Bert never stopped. However much he drifted out of fashion, Bert was always *there*. Davy was a figure from the past. It seems strange, thinking about it, to have met such a man *in colour*, in the twenty-first century, striding the streets of Camden in search of hyacinths and a cheery thought for the day. Now, with his studio work finally re-emerging on CD and a steady stream of vintage amateur live recordings retrieving his true magnificence from oblivion, a modest Davy Graham revival is underway. He is once again playing in public, content to be the semi-active curator of his own museum, and working on an autobiography.

'I'll never be rich,' he says. 'A man who loves pleasure will never be rich – but I've no illusions. I've travelled a lot and I've seen starvation and death and all kinds of things. I'm very lucky. If other people think I'm unlucky they can think I'm unlucky. The biography can deal with why I was unlucky.'

Davy Graham was born in Leicester on 22 November 1940. His father Hamish hailed from Skye, his mother Winifred from Guyana. He was brought up in the Notting Hill area of London. At various times, the ages of ten and twelve have been given as the starting point in Davy's guitar-playing adventures, but either way he was sixteen before he owned one, at which point the individual and the instrument became inseparable: 'I started not doing homework and playing "My Baby Left Me", "Mystery Train" and Lonnie Donegan hits,' he says. 'I couldn't concentrate at school thinking of Lonnie Donegan.'

The skiffle explosion, heralded by the million-selling success of Lonnie Donegan's spirited cover of Leadbelly's 'Rock Island Line' in January 1956, inspired thousands of British youngsters to take up the guitar over the next couple of years. The craze had been initially fostered by band leader Chris Barber in particular and the booming trad-jazz scene in general, and it would subsequently feed into what passed for British rock 'n' roll, British blues, the Merseybeat phenomenon and the British folk revival. In London alone, the skiffle-into-folk/blues transformation at the end of the Fifties gave platforms to a vast array of talent which would flower in the next decade and beyond: Martin Carthy, Wizz Jones, Alexis Korner, Long John Baldry, Clive Palmer, Robin Hall & Jimmy MacGregor, Steve Benbow and many others.

Davy Graham was there pretty much at the start, leaving school in 1958 and becoming one of the first to follow in the footsteps of Alex Campbell – a melancholy Scot, and Britain's first real troubadour of the modern age – and go busking in the streets of Paris. Wizz Jones, a young man from Croydon who shared Davy's aspiration to short-circuit the drudgeries of post-war life by simply playing guitar and travelling, followed the same path and has compelling memories of Davy from the period: 'I knew someone who knew him at school in the Fifties and they said he had this guitar with him in the lessons – he used to carry it around with him at school, which, if you think about it, at that time was pretty far out. Skiffle hadn't even really got off the ground . . . I knew Davy from London and I'd spent a bit of time with him, on and off, but I hadn't seen him for a while. When I hit Paris [in 1959] it was late at night and he suddenly came round the corner. I remember seeing this vision of this tall, blond-haired, statuesque, deep-tanned, god-type of person as he was walking towards me. I thought, That's what I wanna be! And he said, "I've just come up from Greece, man." He was so cool.'

There can be no doubt that, certainly by the time he was making records in the Sixties, Davy Graham exuded a mean and moody persona that complemented perfectly his brilliance and exoticism as an instrumentalist. But at least a degree of this was a studied cool, an affectation which he maintained and very probably grew into. It was, one could conjecture, a necessary part of coping with the rigours of life from an unusual background. Duffy Power, a sensitive individual himself, one of Britain's early rock 'n' roll recording artists and subsequently among its greatest and most underrated blues and jazz singers, moved in the same circles as Davy Graham and jammed with him at the guitarist's home a couple of times: 'He had a fine line in home-made copper jewellery,' he says. 'He lived on Westbourne Grove but he chose to go to a school on the south side of the river, miles from where he lived. This is just speculation, but I get the feeling this might have been to keep his mixed-race background private. There were race riots around Notting Hill at that time,

Davy Graham,
late Sixties

plus he'd damaged his eye with a pencil as a kid and he was slightly withdrawn anyway, so you don't know what kind of trials he had in the Fifties.'

Others who recall Davy Graham from his pre-performing days in the Fifties affirm this picture of a shy, bookish and withdrawn individual – but one nevertheless on a mission to become the master of his instrument. Steve Benbow was arguably the first guitarist to accompany English folksong on guitar, performing in the skiffle cellars of Soho and recording traditional material as early as 1957. He was also a veteran of north-African and Middle-eastern army service, where he had collected at least one song, 'Miserlou', which Graham would adapt to his own repertoire for live performance during the Sixties, though he did not record it. In 1959, Benbow was part of a folk group thrown together by a BBC producer to record specifically for *Saturday Club*. 'We were called The Wanderers,' he says, 'and we rehearsed in Old Brompton Road, near the Troubadour. Davy, this kid, used to sit in the corner and watch and every so often he'd say, "Could you show me that chord?" And, of course, we did. We had no idea he'd become so good. It was unbelievable what happened. He went away to Morocco, came back and blew a hole through everyone. Terrific player.'

'I'd [already] met Alex Campbell, the street singer,' says Davy. 'He was the embodiment of the outdoor life with a denim suit and cowboy boots – a rumbustious type. Steve was much cooler. He was one of the first that I heard who was any good. He stretched me. But I suppose there weren't all that many other people around then. The scene was wide open if you applied yourself. I was just in the right place at the right time.'

Andy Irvine, who would make his own considerable reputation firmly in the Irish traditional-music bracket – not least as the man who introduced East European influences into the picture – was also born and raised in London and, by the late Fifties, was fascinated with the American folk tradition of Woody Guthrie and his acolytes. One such, Ramblin' Jack Elliott, was actually living in London at the time: 'I used to hang out with Jack and his wife June in 1959, 1960,' says Andy. 'I would arrive at Jack's bedsit and sit at the end of the bed till they woke up. But then Davy would arrive, at 11 or 12 a.m., and Jack and June and myself would go out – while Davy would stay in the flat and play Jack's guitar. And when we came home Davy would quickly go. It was as if he could not be in the same space as the rest of us. The strings would be dead and Jack would say, "Oh, I don't know why I let that guy play my guitar." But he'd be there every day. Jack or June might say, "Come on Davy, let's go for a drink or a meal or something," and he'd go home to his mother. He lived with his mother at the time and had a job pushing a broom somewhere. He was an odd kind of guy, always a very strange man. But I know him, and he's aware of it, which is strange because you'd think that Davy wouldn't remember things. But he would remember that he met me when he was very young. I met him subsequently. He was a friend of some people I know who'd got married in the west of Ireland, some years ago, and that's where he said, "Oh yeah, I remember you – you were in Jack Elliott's house."

But yeah, he was kind of scary – you thought of him and needles. He had this mystery about him that you didn't want to get into. I thought he was very shy when I first met him but the fact that he practised guitar six hours a day showed where his outlets lay.'

Over the next couple of years the combination of natural shyness and dedicated effort at his instrument were apparent to anyone who cared to wander into any one of a number of coffee bars and restaurants in and around London's Soho district. Wizz Jones recalls telling episodes from an all-night coffee-bar called the Gyre & Gimble near Charing Cross: 'He would be sitting in the corner, playing down there through the night,' says Wizz, 'and just be totally ignored by more or less all the punters that would come in. Then Long John Baldry would come down, start singing in a really loud voice, get halfway through, say, "Oh, to hell with it!" and stop! It was years before I heard him finish a song. Davy and Long John didn't used to speak to each other. They had a feud going but everyone used to say, "Wouldn't it be wonderful to see them play together?" 'cos John had such a great voice and Davy was such a brilliant player – a true innovator, the first guy in England to use open tunings and write his own instrumentals.'

Long John and Davy did work together on television once but never on record. While Davy was undoubtedly a gifted and innovative instrumentalist it could never be said that his vocal ability was much more than adequate – although on some of his recorded material, where the melodies are undemanding, the combination of mannered English diction and the dextrous, angular patterns of his guitar work with pounding American blues rhythms are compelling. The real beginning of Davy Graham as a guitar legend, as an astonishingly advanced technician amongst a peer group of guitar pickers still happy to master the basic licks on Big Bill Broonzy and Leadbelly records, was an appearance in Ken Russell's film for the BBC's *Monitor* series in 1959 called *Hound Dogs and Bach Addicts: The Guitar Craze*. Budding guitarists the length and breadth of Britain watched the broadcast, with Davy performing a complex blues-and-fingerstyle arrangement of 'Cry Me A River' alongside contributions from Julian Bream, Bert Weedon and Lonnie Donegan. Perhaps enhancing his reputation just a touch, a couple of years later Davy told one admirer up in Scotland that he had only been playing six months at the time. Either way, Martin Carthy was certainly impressed: 'The twelve-bar blues he played seemed to have about three parts going at the same time. Contrapuntal blues! It was outrageously brilliant.'

Davy was later seen and heard – in 1963 – in the background of scenes shot in Nick's Diner in Joseph Losey's film *The Servant*. Davy Graham's first album, *The Guitar Player*, released on Pye's budget label, Golden Guinea, that same year, was representative of the repertoire he was using at such engagements. An odd record and to a great extent 'of its time' – though still rated by Wizz Jones as Graham's best album – it was nonetheless an impressive exercise in adapting easy-listening material for solo guitar and drums. It showed Davy to be both imaginative and accomplished. The calling card that more truly fore-shadowed the style, techniques and repertoire that would be explored more fully on his Decca recordings had been released on the tiny Topic label around March the previous year and titled, intriguingly, *3/4 AD*. The numerals cunningly reflected the time signature of the title track while the letters denoted Davy and his accomplice on this one-off EP, Alexis Korner, the godfather of British blues. Karl Dallas was not wrong when he noted in *Melody Maker*, the most influential music paper of the period, that 'it could mark as important a stage in the development of instrumental folk music in Britain as Pete Seeger's Nonesuch [label] album has in the States'.

Featuring an original Graham instrumental called 'Angi' – later popularised on record by both Bert Jansch and Paul Simon – it was indeed a pivotal moment for anyone aspiring to be a guitarist within the then broad spectrum of the rapidly expanding British folk scene. Being able to play it became almost a test for anyone calling themselves a guitarist and seeking bookings in a folk club for years thereafter. Up in Edinburgh, Davy's sister Jill had been passing around an advance tape of 'Angi' to the whiz-kids on that particular scene, among them Bert Jansch and Robin Williamson. It was a revelation: 'Davy was the first person I ever heard play more than one line of music at once on the guitar, in that baroque manner,' says Robin. 'He'd kind of done a Big Bill Broonzy/baroque thing. Big Bill would go thump, thump, thump on the bass string but that was as far as it went. Davy took the notion of making a baroque bass line, moving slightly. The classic example of that was "Angi" – a simple moving bass line, which Bert Jansch developed further. Davy was the man really. The first man to have a go at it in Britain.'

Curiously, although introduced to Davy, in passing, at Edinburgh's Waverley Bar, Jansch never witnessed the master playing in the flesh until late '64 and in London. But on one occasion, Davy had brought his girlfriend Angi, who had inspired the tune, to The Howff. The regulars were tickled pink to meet her but the young lady's immortaliser was a different prospect entirely: 'Extraordinarily intense,' is Scots traditional singer Dolina MacLennan's recollection. 'I wouldn't have spoken to him.'

'I got to know Davy really only later,' says Bert. 'But I already knew his brother Nick and his sister Jill – in fact, I seemed to know all his family except him. He was much more enigmatic than anyone else, and still is exactly the same. You still can't have a conversation with him.'

From a distance of nearly forty years, Graham's view of Jansch is similarly pithy: 'He's just as bloody-minded as I was,' he says. 'He sat in the corner and played all day. But I didn't have the same formation as Bert. I was southern, where Tennyson observed people to be capricious and fickle, while the north-erner is the true romantic. Bert's a romantic undoubtedly and this James Dean image he had with women is something that was alien to me. I thought that a bit juvenile. I read *On the Road* and formed the impression that Jack Kerouac might be the same sort of person!'

Karl Dallas later coined the phrase 'folk-baroque' to describe Davy Graham's music and the school of guitarists – most notably in Britain Bert Jansch and John Renbourn – who followed in his wake and developed the potential of fusing jazz, blues, classical and various ethnic styles together using the folkish idiom of the steel-strung acoustic guitar. Davy was already listening to the likes of Miles Davis, Eric Dolphy, Charles Mingus and Ornette Coleman. (Appropriately enough 'Angi' itself would, in Bert Jansch's subsequent recording, incorporate a snatch of Cannonball Adderley's 'Worksong' as its middle-eight.) It is perhaps ironic and to some extent regrettable that Davy Graham was widely perceived then and certainly now to be primarily a folk artist for, though he did perform and record traditional and singer-songwriter material, very few of his recordings of such repertoire are as robust or as impressive as his blues and jazz recordings. Regarding blues, Snooks Eaglin was a particular favourite, although Davy never recorded any of his songs: 'I never played slide guitar,' he says, 'so I never knew what all the fuss was about Robert Johnson. I liked Robert Johnson but I think I liked Muddy Waters more. It was lovely and rich and oily. Very sensual. And being part Negro myself, part black, I feel that.'

Davy recorded several songs associated with Muddy Waters and the Chicago blues sound generally – 'Hoochie Coochie Man' and 'I'm Ready' among them – while an extant folk-club recording made at St Andrew's in May 1966 adds the otherwise unrecorded 'Sweet Home Chicago' to the canon. But while Alexis Korner had been the motivating factor in getting Davy into a recording studio, and while Davy worked with Alexis on at least three TV dates backing Australian artiste Shirley Abicair in July 1961 and was briefly involved in Alexis' band Blues Incorporated, Alexis was not ultimately convinced that Davy was a bluesman at heart. 'Alexis told me he didn't think Davy had a good *feel* for the blues,' says Duffy Power.

For Davy, his admiration for Alexis was as much to do with the latter's loveable roguish tendencies: 'He was a terrific hustler,' says Davy. 'He once asked me to do a gig for him that he couldn't do. I did it and got £12 for it and he got the other twenty!'

It was nevertheless Alexis who had realised the importance of getting 'Angi' on record, and who had arranged the session with Bill Leader. Alexis' patronage within British blues has long been recognised, but his patronage of Davy Graham would prove no less crucial to British folk. 'Folk-baroque' may have been a controversial phrase, but in describing a music that blended folk, baroque, blues, jazz and other exotica together on an acoustic guitar, it would come as close as anything to putting a label on Davy Graham. Whether playing blues, jazz, traditional music, baroque themes or the various adaptations of Indian ragas and Arabic tunes that pepper, in particular, his six albums for Decca, Davy had a very distinctive, idiosyncratic style. It can sound awkward at times, somewhere between slippery and angular, and more to do with his right-hand playing technique than choice of notes, but at its best it empowers the feeling of musical brinkmanship and invention that he would bring to whatever the material was. At the time, slotting himself into an easily identi-fiable category of music was clearly of no concern although it is certainly true to say that as the British folk-club scene exploded in the mid-Sixties, that – as opposed to jazz, blues or rock venues – was where Davy ploughed his furrow.

Contributing two solo tracks to a live EP, *From A London Hootenanny*, shared with the Thameside Four (featuring Martin Carthy), Graham's Decca debut was every bit as innovative as 'Angi'. Recorded in July 1963 and released in September, the key track was a jazz/Eastern-influenced reworking of the Irish air 'She Moved Through The Fair'. The 1997 Rollercoaster release of *After Hours*, a reel-to-reel recording made at Hull University in 1967, illustrates how Davy would develop this particular theme into a full-blown, meandering but massively impressive fusion exercise. But for 1963, in three-minute form, it was still mind-blowing. It was certainly the first time anyone in Britain had recorded using the now commonplace DADGAD guitar tuning, which Davy had invented with particular regard to playing the music he had heard on a trip to Morocco and which, again, would later be popularised amongst folkies by Bert Jansch and elsewhere by Jimmy Page. Page would often feature a tune in the Led Zeppelin live repertoire entitled 'White Summer', earlier recorded on The Yardbirds' 1968 album *Little Games*, which could be said to bear an extraordinary similarity to Davy's DADGAD debut.

Alongside trying to grasp Davy's outrageous concept of multiple parts on one-stringed instrument the exploration of alternate tunings was also becoming a valid pastime for the more intrepid among his protégés. Martin Carthy was still working mainly in standard tuning, but he had begun the process of groping in the uncharted dark for any useable alternatives. By the end of the decade he had found by process of elimination the tuning that would most easily adapt to the demands of accompanying English traditional song and thus effectively create the distinctive Martin Carthy sound: CGCDGA. That tuning would remain largely exclusive to Carthy's vision. But before Davy he had almost stumbled upon the tuning that would become a Technicolor revelation in the hands of Bert Jansch (who has employed it much less frequently than many assume) and something integral to the subsequent careers of Archie Fisher, Dick Gaughan, Stephen Stills, Jimmy Page and virtually every future accompanist of Scottish and Irish traditional music: DADGAD. 'I met this old-timey band from Harvard University, The Charles River Holy Boys, in 1961–62,' says Carthy, 'and I worked out this tuning that was one step away from DADGAD: DGDGAD, a G9th tuning. I was trying to accompany a particular song of theirs and it did the job, but it wasn't very adaptable. I remember showing it to Davy and later Davy came up with DADGAD. I'm not trying to take credit. I don't know if what I showed him had anything to do with it at all. But he was the man. When he invented DADGAD that was the moment life got interesting.'

'People were nice enough to say I was something unusual,' says Davy. 'But

Julian Bream and Ali Akbar Khan had already done a duet on "Greensleeves" for sarode and guitar, so I certainly wasn't the first "fusion" event. Anyway, Sandy Bull in the States arrived at the same thing, on the other side of the world.'

In lay terms, Graham's discovery opened up hitherto impossible chord sequences, new melodic possibilities (albeit within a limited range of keys) and created a bigger, richer voicing on the instrument – its modal, droning nature perfectly suited to Celtic and Eastern music. The idea of Eastern-influenced guitar accompanying traditional music from the British Isles was taken further the following year. In July 1964 both *Melody Maker* and the *Observer* previewed an unprecedented and 'not to be missed' concert on the twenty-ninth of that month at London's Mercury Theatre. The performance marked the debut of an experimental partnership between Graham, described in *Melody Maker* as an avant-garde musician, and Sussex traditional singer Shirley Collins, with an aim to merge traditional song with modern jazz. 'The concert will have an Eastern flavour,' noted *Melody Maker* writer Jeff Smith. 'For two years Davy's interest in Oriental forms has led him to experiment with different tunings, themes and rhythms (he recently spent three months in the Arab quarter of Tangier, sitting in with the local groups).' The following week, Smith declared the concert both musically successful and profitable, announcing a further concert date for the duo at Hampstead in September and suggesting that Ember were likely to take up the option of recording the partnership.

In the event, it would seem that Davy and Shirley recorded the eventual *Folk Roots, New Routes* later that year with freelance engineer Bill Leader – who had a makeshift studio in his Camden home and was simultaneously recording a debut album for Bert Jansch – and sold it on to Decca. Graham was now living nearby to Bill Leader in Camden: 'He'd be walking round like a young retired colonel,' says Leader. 'Brisk walk, short haircut – which was out of keeping at that time and very out of keeping with the idea you had of him.'

Bert Jansch would be a spectator at a Collins/Graham session. It was his first opportunity to watch Graham playing although he was already familiar with his techniques, mostly through Martin Carthy: 'Martin was forever coming up to me and saying, "Hey, have you heard this one yet?", and he'd show me something he'd picked up from Davy. I'd be learning all his licks second-hand!'

Midway through the sessions for both the Jansch and Collins/Graham albums, Leader enlisted both guitarists to accompany the Chicago blues legend Little Walter Jacobs on alternate nights at his – Leader's – Broadside folk club, at that particular moment located at an out-of-the-way Irish pub in London's Willesden Green. Incongruous and tantalising in equal measure, Davy himself remembers nothing whatsoever about it.

The Collins/Graham project, as it was known, racked up at least nine concerts between July '64 and May '65 – four at the Mercury Theatre, one at Cecil Sharp House, one at the Flamingo of all places (hub of all-nighter mod sessions) and a handful of others, concluding a show at the New Lyric Theatre

Davy Graham,
late Sixties

where the duo were billed with the New Jazz Orchestra. Shirley, a mother of two young children at the time and already pursuing a heavy schedule as a solo folk-club singer, had had enough: 'It was really masterminded by my then husband, John Marshall,' she says, 'and I sort of went along with it because obviously Davy was a wonderfully talented guitarist and I enjoyed a great deal of it. I didn't think it was ever quite right, but I think it was a brave experiment. It became very difficult working with Davy because he was talented but moody, and a late train-catcher. It was a really interesting episode of my life, I must say, but when John wanted to push it a bit further, into working with a jazz orchestra, I sort of opted out.'

A keenly anticipated album at the time of its release, the idea of *Folk Roots, New Routes* was nevertheless welcomed more than the actuality and it provided plenty of food for thought for others on the folk scene. Ashley Hutchings, founder member of folk-rock pioneers Fairport Convention, for instance, acknowledges Graham's arrangement of 'Nottamun Town' on the album as being the blueprint for the later Fairport version. Featuring a couple of Graham solo pieces, including his take on Thelonious Monk's piano classic 'Blue Monk', the album was released in February 1965. It was only a month after Graham's *magnum opus*, the legendary *Folk, Blues & Beyond*.

Seemingly around this time, probably after *Folk, Blues & Beyond* had been recorded, Graham's lifestyle took a notorious turn. 'He lived with danger all the time,' says Martin Carthy, one of Davy's greatest admirers then and now and a man whose own work is the very apogee of how guitar with traditional music can truly succeed. 'He decided to become a junkie. He did that quite deliberately because his heroes – people like Sonny Rollins, Charlie Parker, Bud Powell, Art Pepper, Gerry Mulligan, Chet Baker, all those guys – were heroin addicts. It was like part of the furniture: you were supposed to become a junkie to be a serious musician and Davy took all that in. At the time it was legal and you got it on prescription. I remember when it happened because I did a session with him at Lansdowne Studios in Holland Park the very day after he first took it. It was 1964. I think it was a session for a Nadia Cattouse album. We were walking down the road and he told me, "I had my first fix yesterday." It was a deliberate act. He was a good man, but he was always a very strange man. I remember meeting Alexis Korner three weeks later and his opening remark to me was, "Do you know what that stupid bastard has done?" And it was basically bye-bye Davy for four years. Actually, four years after that my first wife Dorothy ran into him in the street in Soho and he just flung his arms around her saying, "Thank Christ! Somebody I know!" Because he'd just cleaned himself up and it was like he'd been asleep for four years. All these people had been coming up and talking to him and he'd no idea who they were.'

Those four years – 1964–68 – cover the greater part of Davy's association with Decca and, however one may judge the wisdom of Graham's decision, he somehow held himself together for long enough periods to produce a string of albums that may each be patchy in their sheer eclecticism and, in truth, in terms of the suitability of some of the material, but which always contained their fair share of quality and adventure. 'Drugs aren't something that I like discussing,' he told one interviewer much later. 'I survived but it took me several years to get over them.' He countered another questioner, on the same topic, with a more philosophical perspective: 'The trouble is artists are self-indulgent,' he said. 'It never occurred to me that art was self-indulgent. I always thought art was the product of self-denial. It seems to me you deny yourself something to acquire a technique over an instrument. When you've got the technique it's as if you've got a dog. The neighbours don't understand you.'

Folk, Blues & Beyond arrived in January 1965 at the very dawn of the singer-songwriter-guitarist boom in British folk music and similarly at the dawn of 'swinging London's' thriving, bohemian, late-night folk-club scene centred around venues like Les Cousins and the Scot's Hoose in Soho. It epitomised the sense of adventure abroad in all forms of popular music at the time, crystallised a lot of ideas that other guitarists would explore for years to come and established itself as a benchmark for others to live up to. Regarded widely as Davy's most important release, its impact was something of a slow-burner – there were few reviews, for instance, and it would seem that writers in the handful of specialist folk publications of the period could either not grasp where he was coming from or would prefer to regard him only, and begrudgingly, as an experimental accompanist for Shirley Collins. *Melody Maker* didn't carry a review at all, while an unaccredited critique in the journal *Folk Music* (edited by Karl Dallas) had this to say: 'The level of instrumental technique amongst revival folk guitarists is low enough for us to be impressed when one of them can play tunes by Bobby Timmons, Thelonious Monk and Charlie Mingus, but this still doesn't explain why he should want to do so. For after stating the theme, musically he doesn't have a great deal to say. He doesn't compare, for instance, with a Jim Hall or a Charlie Byrd, although he seems to be applying to join them. Vocally, he's a lightweight, a sort of mid-Atlantic Mel Torme without the depth to his voice (and experience?) that the blues tracks on this record demand. Some of his blues accompaniments are a bit too pretty and in time he will probably drop the tiresome raga bits he keeps inter-posing, like a six stringed Errol Garner, in front of and in the middle of some of the numbers.'

Some of the points made were valid to a degree – Davy's obsession with Eastern modes worked best in moderation, and his treatment of blues material would toughen up on later albums in parallel with his jazz interpretations loosening up. The same journal carried a similarly damning review of *Folk Roots, New Routes*, but within eighteen months, in September 1966, Karl Dallas, in *Melody Maker*, was addressing all the earlier doubts in a review of a show at Les Cousins: 'The big question is: Why isn't Davy Graham booked into Ronnie Scott's jazz club?' he wrote. 'He has as much to say as his fellow guitarist and admirer Jim Hall, and a decidedly original way of saying it. His roots seem to be more in jazz than folk, though it's in folk clubs that he gets his work. Of course, the folk world is more tolerant of original sounds than the jazz world (despite legends to the contrary) which is why a big audience at Les Cousins sat enthralled by Davy's exotic playing . . . His singing lacks power, although in the flesh it appeals more than the light-textured disembodied voice of his records . . . Though he is often lumped together with Jansch and Renbourn, Davy Graham is not only the guv'nor of the field within which all three work, but he is also quite distinct from the other two . . .'

Out among the cognoscenti Davy was fast becoming a legend and an inspi-ration. The other two-thirds of that era's great trio of acoustic-guitar gods, Bert Jansch and John Renbourn, both held Davy Graham in awe and still do to this day. Indeed, Jansch – who at that time would have regarded Davy as only one of many influences – would not hesitate in acknowledging Davy as the biggest single factor in how he sounds today. At the time, though, there was minimal contact, and some would say rivalry. Bert and Davy played very few shows together in the Sixties: there was one all-nighter at Les Cousins in June '65; a double-billing of Davy with Bert and John as a duo at the White Swan, Romford in March '66; and a six-hour jam at the London Hilton in March '68, involving Davy, Bert, Roy Harper, John Renbourn and Paul Simon in cele-bration of Simon's US chart success with 'The Sounds Of Silence'. At some point Simon actually asked Davy to become a member of his band. Davy declined.

In July 1965, at a time when hindsight reveals his status to have reached its zenith in terms of influence and popularity, Davy had disappeared, off on one of his prolonged adventures, this time to the Middle East. While no one was thinking in such terms at the time, as a career move this was suicidal. It may have grieved him in the past, but from the vantage point of the present Graham has no regrets: 'You can't blame anybody for wanting to live like an iguana – a nice simple life where you just sunbathed and played the guitar and travelled the world. Everybody wants it simple. But I don't think you can escape. Some people have sunny dispositions. Not me. I yearned for new experiences. I sometimes travelled to get away from the drugs scene – that was part of it. But I don't think men are prime movers in their fates – I think planets are. People born between 1940 and '42 had Neptune in Virgo – a very bad place for that planet to be.'

During November 1965 Danny Kyle, an old friend of Bert's from Glasgow, was in town and was invited to a party at 30 Somali Road, a now legendary flat shared by Jansch and Renbourn: 'I had my guitar with me,' said Danny. 'A three-chord merchant, playing my wee Scottish songs, and there was Bert, Davy Graham and all that crowd. They started chopping up this black stuff, cooking it and smoking it, and I had a go of that. Then the guitar work started and I just quietly put my guitar away.'

Roy Harper, who lived only a few streets away, was also present. It was something of a rare contact, either socially or professionally, between Davy (just returned from his four months in the Middle East) and Bert and John who were, at the same time, both his devotees and his rivals: 'Suffice to say I didn't even pick my guitar up,' says Roy. 'Bert put his down after about five minutes and five minutes later so did John. Davy never managed to turn his talent into a brand that people could go out and buy and enjoy, but in those days he was just amazing. He would turn up and play the entirety of Ravel's *Bolero*, which is a pretty strange thing to do, but you could tell where each instrument came in – the clarinet, the trombones, the bassoons – all on one guitar.'

'We only kicked in in 1956,' says Duffy Power, 'into what you could call rock 'n' roll, and that includes the folkies. And the first one to pop up who was decent, who was quite bright and inspirational, using world ideas, was Davy Graham. But then along comes another bloke who's better. He may not have had Davy's original fashions but he had much more of it in the fingers – and that was Bert. And then up comes another one and another one. I think for Davy that must have been a bit of a blow.'

Ashley Hutchings, then simply another awe-struck member of the audience, has a similar view: 'To be honest, if you were a casual listener you were hardly aware of Davy. Regular club-goers in London obviously knew Davy well but the casual listener would have known Bert Jansch, and Davy hardly at all, because Bert was the man on the road. That was my impression. As a guy in the audience I was *told* I should go and listen to Davy. Bert was the one you went to see because you wanted to see him. He was a romantic figure, a figure-head. Insofar as the audiences were concerned, Davy was a shadowy character and Bert was a hero – and that is a very big difference.'

Nevertheless, throughout 1965–67 especially, Davy Graham remained a revered and prolific figure on the London folk scene. Every time he played Les Cousins, in Greek Street, there would be queues up the street and that wouldn't happen for anyone else. During the early weeks of 1966 Davy consented to do a Friday-night residency at the venue but it wouldn't last – he was not that easily to be tied down. He had gone off travelling to the Middle East between July and November 1965 and shortly after what was undoubtedly a routine but sensational performance at St Andrew's folk club in May '66 – captured on tape and revealing a performer adept at communication and more consistently convincing as a live artist than on record – he was off once more. In the same issue as it announced the formation of a band for underground poet and future Cream lyricist Pete Brown, including 'for larger concerts' Davy Graham, *Melody Maker* carried the news that the guitarist had been 'ordered to Greece by his doctor for a rest'. Two weeks later, in any case, Cream was formed and Pete Brown's creative future secured.

The sleeve-notes to *Midnight Man*, released in July '66, put a certain gloss on these latest travels 'to Ibiza, through the Aegean and then on to Constantinople, listening carefully to all the musical sounds en route'. The album itself was a punchier, bluesier effort than before, declared by Karl Dallas in *Melody Maker* to be a real grower. 'Partly this may be because with the sitars and all being played around now, Davy's Eastern overtones have lost their novelty,' he wrote. 'His voice has not gained in strength – it is completely incapable of coping with the emotional demands of a powerful song like Oscar Brown's "Rags And Old Iron" for instance. But there is some lovely guitar playing on the record, coupled with some fabulous bass playing by Tony Reeves . . . Now that Davy's innovations have become an accepted category of music – "folk baroque" – and other artists in the school are forging their independent ways, his records can't have the same effect they had at first. But there's still a lot of interesting music going on here.'

The next time a Davy Graham record appeared it was, of all things, a single: a cover of Joni Mitchell's 'Both Sides Now' with a suicidal, non-commercial intro of some length and a recklessly ambitious vocal astride a vibrant full-band arrangement. Released in October 1968, it pointed the direction of his next two albums: *Large As Life And Twice As Natural* – released in three formats in January 1969 – and *Hat*, released in October 1969. Comprising folk, blues, ragas, singer-songwriter material (a particular, though rarely successful, penchant for Paul Simon and Lennon/McCartney) and jazz, featuring top rhythm players like Danny Thompson and Jon Hiseman, and produced as ever by Ray Horricks, these were Decca's clearest attempts to push Davy Graham as a commercial proposition to the new 'underground' progressive rock audience. The Pentangle, the jazz/folk fusion ensemble formed by Jansch, Renbourn and Danny Thompson, were already doing great business with a sound very similar to that on these albums – reaching the UK top five with their own *Basket Of Light* album that very year. Davy, indeed, had depped for The Pentangle on one of their early club gigs in 1967, while the group were

Davy Graham at an Alexis Korner
memorial concert, Buxton, 1994

enjoying a booking at the prestigious Windsor Jazz & Blues Festival. But by 1969 Davy was becoming something of a yesterday's man.

The preamble to a rare interview for *Melody Maker* in March 1970 said it all: 'It's an uncomfortable thing being a pioneer. The man at the front of the parade gets seen by a few snotty-nosed kids at most. The crowds don't start gathering till he's long past, and it's the followers-on who get the cheers.' By that stage Davy was somewhat resigned to making his living, at least in part, as a guitar teacher, operating from a flat in Camden Town, but also thinking seriously of giving up altogether. Karl Dallas had called round to enquire what he was up to and what he planned for his next LP, *Holly Kaleidoscope* – recorded a couple of months after the interview and released to virtually no fanfare in November. 'I'm not doing anything new especially,' he said. 'There's no reason for getting into new things just for the sake of it. I'm still working out things I started doing years ago. That's the reason I work mainly with other people's material, because it gives me a wider choice. I can't understand this insistence that people have got to sit down and write a dozen new songs before they can make a record. It takes time for a song to become worth singing. They've got to mature.'

Davy went on in a noticeably morbid frame of mind about life in general, and in a curiously holistic sense about his career in particular. *Holly Kaleidoscope*, when it subsequently appeared, was a much more upbeat affair, recorded with his partner Holly Gwyn taking some vocals. It was as wilfully eclectic as ever, with a handful of excellent tracks – including a shaky but appealing stab at Duffy Power's 'Mary Open The Door' – but on the whole it was still a patchy and unsatisfying collection. Ironically for an artist whose career can be seen in hindsight to have been drifting towards something of a limp conclusion, Graham received the accolade of another *Melody Maker* interview in July 1970. He was in more positive but still reflective form. 'Maturity can only be achieved by being dearly bought. Young and brilliant people do not exist in my world,' he said, going on to lavish praise on Andrés Segovia and Julian Bream, to declare that the new breed of folk-rockers like Fairport Convention and Steeleye Span were natural successors to The Beatles, and to admit that while he found The Pentangle indifferent he held one or two things by Jansch and Renbourn as solo artistes in high regard. In retrospect, it was a positive note to go out on. *Holly Kaleidoscope* duly appeared and *Godington Boundary* – another up-and-down collection – came out on President the following year: mostly featuring jazz tunes on electric guitar, the opening number was a somewhat atonal vocal crack at The Johnstons' 1967 Irish hit single 'I'm A Freeborn Man Of The Travelling People'. And that, for a while, was that.

After a gap of four years, a very pleasing new offering entitled *All That Moody* (now reissued in expanded form on Rollercoaster) slipped out on the tiny Eron label in 1976 and featured strong reworkings of 'Angi' and some of his Decca-period album tracks. A couple more all-instrumental albums, *The*

Complete Guitarist and *Dance For Two People*, appeared on the American Kicking Mule label before the Seventies were out, and the former at least proved that Graham could make a consistent-sounding album when he wanted to – in this case embracing Irish traditional themes and hymn tunes as the bulk of his material. Released with a booklet of tablature – regarded by comedian and erstwhile folk singer Billy Connolly, given a copy by Graham, as being as impenetrable as 'the stuff written on the sides of Pyramids' – *The Complete Guitarist* was essentially Graham's resurrection as a professional musician and probably, given the obscurity and/or limited sales of his previous releases, his introduction to a new generation and, indeed, genre of music fans. The innovations of the British fingerstylists of the Sixties had spawned, by the mid-Seventies, a viable international market for dextrous acoustic instrumentalists. Graham's revival was, if anything, a little overdue but, quoted by Robin Denselow on the album's sleeve-notes, the man himself was unconcerned: 'I'd rather do less work and be a better musician. The more often I turn on TV or listen to the radio, the better I think I am. People seem to have such low standards.' As to the strong showing for Irish tunes – 'Lord Mayo', 'Frieze Britches', 'Hardiman The Fiddler' and suchlike – 'they are mostly pipe and fiddle tunes and I've been working on them for sometime. I take a great interest in the Irish scene and I'm learning the language.'

While the aspirational ceilings associated with previous albums may have appeared lowered, this was, at least partly as a result, a satisfyingly consistent release and superbly executed. Denselow noted the absence of north African and Indian pieces but revealed that this was because Davy was 'currently mastering their authentic instruments, i.e. the Moroccan lute, Indian sarode and even the Greek bouzouki. He will only use these professionally "when I'm at a professional standard".'

True to his word, no doubt, and dressed in the white garb of some foreign culture, Davy brought all these exotic instruments (and a friend with a tin whistle) along to the atmospherically lit studios of BBC Bristol in 1980 for a superb half-hour recital in the station's *A Little Night Music* series. In retrospect it was to be the swansong of his late-Seventies revival.

Another lengthy sabbatical from recording since then has been broken only by a couple of performances on the 1992 soundtrack to the BBC documentary, *Acoustic Routes* (a film celebrating the British acoustic players of the Sixties and centred, ignominiously perhaps for Graham, on Bert Jansch), and a disappointing new album, *Playing In Traffic* – erratic in both repertoire and recording quality – in 1995. Still living in Camden, Davy Graham reappears only periodically in live performance but over the past two or three years has enjoyed something of a resurgence in profile through the good fortune of a coincidental slew of CD reissues from various quarters and the good auspices of Kay Thomson, whose biannual fan magazine *Midnight Man* provides a lovingly produced focal point for the faithful. Kay is also involved in helping Davy with his autobiography.

Ken Hunt, chronicling Graham's career in *Folk Roots* in May 1997, made the profound observation that Graham, for all his brilliance, made great tracks and poor albums. But the abiding influence of those great tracks and the relative lack of product since have all helped fuel his myth: 'Davy Graham is now a better enigma than he ever was in his period of greatest influence,' wrote Hunt, 'when journalists would come away with "eccentric" doodled in their notepads.' Eccentric yes, but whether or not Davy Graham was a genius or simply a brilliant, unprecedented burst of colour in a monochrome age is a subject for endless, ultimately irresolvable debate. At the very least Davy Graham can be said to have single-handedly introduced Britain to the concept of the folk guitar instrumental. It is often said that over in America John Fahey, in releasing a private pressing of his bizarre all-instrumental blues pastiche *The Transfiguration Of Blind Joe Death* in 1959, invented both steel-strung guitar music and the industry to support it, but Davy Graham could hardly have known what was going on in the curious world of John Fahey. In Britain, Davy Graham can claim the mantle of inventor.

'He was an inspiration of his time,' says Duffy Power. 'He was inspired, but not a genius. Then again it's maybe a kind of genius once, when it's your moment. There are lots of things like that in life, when there's somebody who for a certain moment will fly, will burst into flame. He was ahead of his time.'

Ashley Hutchings takes a harder line: 'I don't think hard work makes you a genius – ever,' he concludes. 'It just makes you very, very accomplished.'

Even those who met Graham only briefly retain invariably strong impressions of the man. Christy Moore would certainly be one: 'I met Davy Graham once or twice,' he says. 'I met him one night at a Planxty concert at the Hammersmith Odeon sometime in the Seventies. He came backstage and I shook hands with him – and to this day I believe he was trying to break my hand. He didn't like my guitar playing I suppose! I love his music though.'

The final word goes to Chris Barber, one of the founders of skiffle and British jazz: 'I enjoyed his music but he was always out of his head in those days. I hadn't seen him for years and we did an Alexis Korner tribute show in Buxton a couple of years ago and there was Davy sober – totally sober, brewing tea. I couldn't believe I'd ever have seen Davy Graham brewing tea!'

EPILOGUE: INTO IRELAND

While Davy Graham's career seemed to be proceeding irrevocably through the early Seventies towards what theoretical physicists might term a singularity, his protégés and – in the parlance, at least, of the commentators of the day – his one-time rivals, Bert Jansch and John Renbourn, were scaling undreamed of international heights as members of The Pentangle. Still friends as well as colleagues, Bert and John would go off together adventuring around Ireland during their free time at least twice during the Pentangle era. On one occasion during the summer of 1971 they went with Sue Draheim, a recently arrived American old-timey fiddler with whom John would return and set up home in the woods of Devon. For Bert, the Irish trips were remarkable in that seemingly every pub they ventured into, there would be Luke Kelly from The Dubliners. Bert's hope for the summer '71 trip was to seek out the celebrated uilleann piper Willie Clancy. The first step was to make for his home village, Milltown Malbay in County Clare: 'We went to the pub that we knew he always played in,' says Bert. 'A pub-cum-post-office-cum-grocer's-shop – and they said, "Oh, he doesn't come in till eleven o'clock, but if you want to talk to him here's where he lives . . ." So we went round to his place and knocked on the door. His wife came out and told us exactly the same thing: "He won't be back till eleven o'clock." So I think we just wandered about until half past ten and went back to the pub. Quite a few people were gathering – quite a few Americans, people with tape recorders and all that! – and come eleven o'clock they shut the pub, closed it up. Willie arrived with his mate and that was it – we were there till dawn. He sang and he played and then somebody else played and then Sue played, and they were all knocked out because she knew all the tunes. It was a great night. In fact, we became Willie's roadies for about a week after that – went to about three or four gigs with him. And the funny thing is, money didn't seem to be involved – food, drink and general hospitality seemed to be the system.'

Later on in that holiday, the three adventurers made it to the Cliffs of Moher, on the western shore – among the highest sea cliffs in Europe. Taken by the experience, Bert came back with a most curiously titled song for the next Pentangle record: 'Jump Baby Jump'.

Milltown Malbay now hosts the annual 'Willie Clancy week' – a summer tuition school and jamboree for trad buffs and revellers. Several years before Bert and John's trip Christy Moore had worked at a bank in Milltown for a couple of months and would often go to the same pub, Hennessey's, to hear Willie Clancy: 'Money wouldn't have changed hands,' he recalls. 'Willie was a carpenter who loved to play music. I don't know if he ever did any "gigs" in his life.'

The one record that would confirm the existence of a commercial context to allow for a 'revival' of Irish music to compare with the English and Scottish experience of the Sixties – or, perhaps more accurately, to allow for the development of an Irish folk scene where money would finally start changing hands – was Christy Moore's *Prosperous* (1971). Having effectively served his apprenticeship on the English club scene since 1966, Moore had returned to Ireland in 1970 with repertoire and ideas and mastery of the performer's craft. Accompanied by a band of now legendary musicians – among them Andy Irvine – Moore was recorded for Bill Leader's own label, Trailer. The resulting album, *Prosperous*, was initially released only in Britain but demand began to grow in Ireland. As Mark Prendergast notes in *Irish Rock* (O'Brien, 1986), though it was not a fusion of folk and rock in the same manner as Steeleye Span, whose influence was now spreading rapidly across the water, it was progressive in spirit: 'It had a spontaneity, a certain youthful exuberance and enough original ideas on presentation to make people realise that Irish traditional music had to change . . . The time was right to give the dusty native Irish scene a taste of what was happening in the UK.'

The Pentangle did perform a handful of concerts in Belfast and Dublin, but the influence of Bert, John and/or the group – and, in a sense, the influence of Davy Graham by proxy – was largely via recordings. They had been heard by many of the people who would go on to play key roles in Irish music's renaissance within its own borders and internationally: Rory Gallagher, Johnny Fean, guitarist with Horslips (1972-plus), the future members of Clannad (1970-plus) and Micheál Ó Domhnaill of Skara Brae (1970–71), subsequently of the extremely influential Bothy Band (1975–78).

While Archie Fisher – who has himself always cited an anonymous intermediary as the 'thief of DADGAD' – is largely responsible for the tuning entering the Scottish traditional world, Micheál Ó Domhnaill appears to have been its source within Irish music. Standard tuning has made a resurgence in recent years, but Graham's invention was probably dominant among accompanists of the instrumental tradition during the Eighties and early Nineties and still remains the obvious tuning for any solo guitarist wishing to play jigs and reels. Ó Domhnaill discovered the tuning in 1970 on the back of a Bert Jansch record (undoubtedly 1966's *Jack Orion*), when sharing a flat in Dublin with fellow Skara Brae member, Daithí Sproule, while at college: 'It's amazing the way it all comes together,' says Micheál. 'You're not aware of it at the time – you're just absorbing what you find and what you like. We started experimenting with this tuning and it became an obsession. It was through Bert's records that I found out about Davy Graham but I never really checked him out. I stayed in the Jansch/Renbourn camp and became infatuated with them. I later recorded [English traditional song] 'Lord Franklin' myself which was completely plagiarised from the Renbourn version and I used to do [Irish traditional song] 'Blackwater Side', too, straight from Bert's recording – a great guitar track. I remember taking Pentangle records up to Ciarán Brennan from Clannad, which of course blew our minds, but I wasn't aware of other people on the Irish scene who shared our enthusiasms.'

'We used to play in our father's pub,' says Clannad singer Máire Brennan. 'It was basically a stage for us to get up on when we got home from school or college. There was one Pentangle album we used to do *all* the songs off – not all at once, maybe two a night! But being in Donegal the only chance of hearing anything at all like that was either on the radio or getting the albums in Derry [50 miles away] – and the albums would have been rare. To be able to get a Pentangle album we'd have to order it. It was a long process!'

SECTION 2
THE STORY OF THEM

Them, 1965: (l–r) Ray Elliott, Van Morrison,
John Wilson, Alan Henderson, Jim Armstrong

THEM
PROLOGUE

Two blonde girls are dancing on the bench-table in front of the stage, their bodies writhing and gyrating to the music, their hands caressing each other's breasts and hips. A swarthy, curly-haired lad has climbed on stage – not much of a feat, for the stage is only a foot high – and is beaming, totally blissed out, one arm round the singer, the other waving ecstatically in the air. This is Geordie Mann and he's the barman, so don't expect to get served any time soon. Standing right in front of the stage another lad is gazing spellbound. This is Les, the other barman, so definitely don't expect to get served any time soon.

An army patrol has just marched through the bar in full camouflage, rifles at the ready, the tail-end Charlie walking backwards, covering his colleagues. They're from the UDR (Ulster Defence Regiment), a part-time reserve regiment of the British Army. But don't worry – they're really just slipping in out of the cold and if you can tear yourself away from the band and go down to the far bar you'll see them sinking a few pints and grooving to the music before they drag themselves back out again.

An intense, staring dude is dancing alone, jumping high into the air and jack-knifing; a girl, in ecstasy, is bending so far backwards, like a limbo dancer, her hair is brushing the floor; a few nutters are hanging by their legs from the rafters. Everyone else is standing on the long tables or on their stools for there's not enough floor space on which to dance.

On stage Spike are playing, fronted by singer Kenny McDowell and guitarist Jim Armstrong, and they're the best band I've ever heard.

Two old people – in their forties if they're a day – have come in. They look worried sick and appalled by what they are seeing as they scan the room despairingly, for they fear their teenage child has come to this infamous den of iniquity. Because this is the Pound music club in Belfast's Townhall Street, thronged every Saturday afternoon with those of the city's youth who are desperate to hear hip music. And the parents are wrong to be worried – for this is the most civilised place in Belfast. Because this is 1974 and outside the Pound the city is in flames. Hundreds of people die this year because of inter-communal hatred. Sometimes in the quiet between songs or in the break the rumble of a distant or a not-so-distant bomb can be heard – but there is never any trouble in the Pound. There is no sectarianism. There is no fighting. There is no hate. Everybody is united by the magic of a music that truly frees one's soul. The Pound doesn't even have a bouncer. Once a gang of thugs descend on the venue intent on trouble. 'Where's the bouncer?' they demand.

'We don't have one,' mildly answers George, the gentle, middle-aged man who collects the door money. It takes a while to convince the thugs but when they realise that this is indeed a club without a bouncer, and that there's nobody to fight with, they visibly sag and trudge off, with their tails between their legs.

The Pound had originally been a pound for runaway horses and 'basic' is probably too fancy a word to describe it. The rough, wooden bench-tables are all painted black. The place is dirty. Virtually the only heat is body heat. The urinals have no plumbing – you simply piss in or around a concrete gutter. Regularly the urine on the floor is deep enough to lap over your shoes. There is no sink in the toilets. Eventually the club is busted and heavily fined for breaching pretty well every health regulation that applies to licensed premises. The judge seems to particularly disapprove of the rats living amongst the boxes of crisp packets. The punters aren't deterred but sales of crisps are less brisk for a while.

Once I ask for some water in my glass of whiskey. 'Sure it's watered already,' laughs Dermot Moffett, the laid-back manager, a charming guy who presides benignly over proceedings. I don't think he's joking. Another time, faint with flu – but I wasn't going to miss a Saturday afternoon for that – I order a medicinal hot whiskey. I get handed a glass with whiskey and hot water in it. 'Could I have a slice of lemon with that?' I ask. 'What do you think this is? The fucking Europa Hotel?' ripostes the barman snappily. I decide I won't ask for cloves.

Leaving the Pound at teatime on Saturday is like sliding from the best dream of your life into the worst nightmare of your life. The streets are deserted. A lot of city-centre bars are shutting their doors for the night – it's the only way to safeguard their staff, never mind their customers, for barmen going home late at night have been targeted by sectarian murder gangs. It sure as hell doesn't feel safe walking through the streets but there are no buses. The buses stop at teatime because the drivers have been targeted by sectarian murder gangs. Luckily I'm only attacked once and I survive with a broken nose and a few bruises.

There are few other entertainment options in Belfast. Places of entertainment are regarded by terrorists as legitimate economic targets. This means that if they're blown up the government will have to pay the owners compensation and the economic cost of this might encourage the British government to wash their hands of the whole benighted province. Places of entertainment are also good to blow up because not only will you inflict economic damage but there's a good chance that you'll be able to kill and maim a lot of people into the bargain. Most other clubs and ballrooms and restaurants and cinemas have gone out of business. Maybe they've been bombed or firebombed or maybe the owners just feel they can't take the chance that they may be the next target.

I'm a student but most of my friends at Queen's University won't go to the Pound. They're simply way too scared: scared that the place will be blown up – and since the club is basically a rectangular box with only one way in or out

Spike, at the Pound, Belfast, mid-Seventies: Alan Hunter (left), Jim Armstrong

the carnage would be horrendous – scared about how they could get safely back to student land afterwards; and scared of the clientele, which is, shall we say, unpretentious and, often enough, pretty damn-hard looking. I go down the Pound every week, and often I have to go on my own and join my friends in the student bars of south Belfast afterwards.

But the miracle of the Pound is that not only is it one of the few entertainment options available but that the entertainment on offer is of world class. Spike are a phenomenal band and would be regarded as a phenomenal band if they were playing in a club in London or New York or LA. Kenny McDowell sings with a power and a passion that is staggering; Jim Armstrong is a thrillingly virtuosic guitarist of apparently limitless imagination; Gerry McIlduff, who later moves to London and becomes an early member of The Pretenders, is a drummer of formidable technical prowess and extraordinary subtlety; Alan Hunter is a fluent, swinging bassist and an accomplished harmony singer; and Barry McCrudden is equally talented as a tenor saxophonist and keyboard player who also sings fine harmony. Together the band, with their repertoire of blues songs, current or recent material by The Allman Brothers and Steely Dan, and original songs, send me – and everybody else – to Thrillsville, Arizona every time.

And they get me to thinking as well. The rock orthodoxy is that Them, the first Northern Irish band of the rock era to make it in England, with hits like 'Baby Please Don't Go' and 'Here Comes The Night', had consisted of Van Morrison plus a bunch of losers who had got lucky by meeting Van before being dispatched to the scrap heap. But Jim Armstrong had played in Them and every week in the Pound his playing has me gasping in disbelief. And Kenny McDowell had actually replaced Van in a later version of Them and he is a mind-blowing singer. Could it be that rock orthodoxy is wrong?

I begin to check it out. I track down copies of the two Them albums that Armstrong and McDowell had made in the States and they are terrific. I track the careers of other ex-members of Them and find albums by people like Jackie McAuley, The Belfast Gypsies and Stud. None of them has been a big seller but pretty well all of them are great. In interviews Van Morrison never says anything positive about his old Them colleagues but it is now apparent that this can only be because Van is working to his own agenda: the less credit he gives to his old mates the more credit accrues to himself.

And so, somehow or other, I become a Them expert. My first profession-ally published piece of writing is an unsolicited review of Spike in the Pound, which is published in the NME (*New Musical Express*); my career as a freelance journalist has begun. And listening to the repertoire of Spike – and Bronco, the band, also led by McDowell and Armstrong and featuring another ex-Them man, drummer John Wilson, who play the Pound on Wednesday to Saturday nights – my own listening tastes develop and are educated. I buy dozens of albums by bands like The Amazing Rhythm Aces, Firefall and Orleans because I'm turned on to them in the Pound. But rarely do the originals sound as good as the covers by Spike and Bronco. When I say this to the guys in Spike and Bronco they point out that I'm probably sober when I listen to the records and that I'm certainly not sober when I listen to their cover versions. This is certainly true, but I still maintain that Kenny and Jim and the guys do most of those songs better.

Armstrong and McDowell have a falling out and in the reshuffle McDowell brings in Ronnie Greer, another phenomenal guitarist who I subsequently listen to hundreds of times both with Kenny in Bronco and in the Jim Daly Blues Band.

So I owe my journalistic career to the Pound. I owe my critical standards to the Pound because every band I listen to now I can compare to the bands I saw there. I owe my musical tastes to the Pound because I was turned on to such good music there by listening to the cover versions played. And I owe my now decades-long love of the music of Kenny McDowell, Jim Armstrong and Ronnie Greer to the Pound for I first heard them play there and I have never tired of their musicianship.

I'll never forget the Pound. I'll never forget the fabulous music I heard there and I'll never forget the vibe of the place for in those frightening, dangerous, nightmarish years people really were transported to a better place by that music. Even today, a quarter of a century later, occasionally, someone will come up to me in a bar and smile and say, 'I know you – you used to go down the Pound,' and I will truly feel that they are my friend.

THE STORY OF THEM

In September 1964 a single was released that flopped miserably – and yet changed the course of Irish popular music. The single, a version of Louisiana bluesman Slim Harpo's 'Don't Start Crying Now', was by Them, five Belfast rhythm-and-blues fanatics fronted by Van Morrison, who attacks the song with a wild ferocity that still shocks today, and it began a blues boom in Ireland that signalled the end of the line for the unoriginal, besuited showbands which had until then dominated the scene.

Them's second single, a version of Big Joe Williams' 'Baby Please Don't Go', with Morrison's classic composition 'Gloria' on the B-side, was released in November and became a worldwide hit, providing Van with the momentum that enabled him, by and by, to become the superstar that he remains today.

The extraordinary story of Them is a story of success and failure, of betrayal and bitterness and exploitation – and of wonderful, imperishable music.

The saga begins with a small-time, no-hope band, The Gamblers. Band

Trevor Hodgett · Includes material previously published in *Record Collector* (January 1987), *Mojo* (December 2000) and *Causeway* (Spring 1998); plus additional material

Them, 1965: (l–r) Ray Elliott, Alan Henderson, John Wilson, Van Morrison, Jim Armstrong

leader Billy Harrison explains: 'We were Ronnie Millings on drums, Alan Henderson on bass and myself on guitar and vocals, gigging round Scout halls and Legion halls and wee functions. Then wee Eric Wrixon came along, playing keyboards. We were playing rhythm and blues, leaning towards rock 'n' roll – the original "Hippy Hippy Shake" before the Swinging Blue Jeans got their hands on it, Little Willie John's "Fever" – that sort of thing. And we were heavy into early Presley.

'Then we brought in Van Morrison, who had left The Monarchs Showband, to play saxophone. I never knew him as a singer, but he knew a lot more blues songs than me, so he began to sing a few songs, then gradually more and more, which allowed me to concentrate on guitar, so it just came about that Van became lead singer. I was into R&B like Chuck Berry, but Van was into Howlin' Wolf and Muddy Waters, so he introduced more blues into the band. His father had a phenomenal blues collection and that's where that influence came from.

'We used to rehearse above Dougie Knight's cycle shop in Shaftesbury Square, and Eric Wrixon came up with the name Them, when we were sitting in the rehearsal rooms. And we decided to let the hair grow, which was "el freako" for Belfast, and not wear uniforms. That was our kick against the establishment. Every band then did Shadows steps and dressed the same. We were a group – but individuals at the same time.

'Then the "Three Js" – Jerry, Jerry and Jimmy – took over the Maritime Hotel, a trad-jazz gig in College Square North, and approached us to play blues there.'

Eric Wrixon continues: 'The Three Js ran a very good advertising campaign in the *Belfast Telegraph*: "Who Is Them? What Is Them?", and the first time we played the Maritime there were 50 people; the second night 180; the third night we sold out – and we sold out as long as Them were there. There was a time, a place, an atmosphere and a band and it all fitted together and it was all totally right. We were the first band in Ireland not to wear band suits, the first to have long hair, the first to play rhythm and blues. And we weren't lagging behind England – Them were more extreme than The Rolling Stones and musically in advance of them. [Bobby Bland's] "Turn On Your Lovelight" was Them's biggest number. It was fifteen minutes long, which was unheard of, starting as practically a dirge and building to a frenzy. Van had this incredible act of tearing off his clothes, falling on his back and singing very well at the same time.'

Harrison agrees. 'We were nutters onstage. We did whatever we felt like doing and that as much as the music got across to the crowd. They would clap time, stomp, dance, shout and yell. The crowd was feeding off us and we were feeding off them. When it came to the end of the night you didn't really want to stop. It was an unbelievable period. It wasn't big money, of course, but we were playing for the love of playing. There were no breadheads.'

'The way of making money,' explains Wrixon, 'was to play as many places as possible in one night. In those days bands, even people coming from England, played short sets – in fact once there was a nasty rumour that Georgie Fame was coming to Romano's Ballroom and in his contract he refused to play less than two hours! I think the Musicians' Union here had an enquiry about it! So Them would play half an hour in the Dance Studio, then half an hour in the Plaza, then half an hour in the Fiesta, then an hour in the Maritime. Also we were on the door in the Maritime – which was sold out by seven o'clock, with 250 people paying ten shillings each.

'A few months later the band started to play provincial Northern Ireland – about six months before provincial Northern Ireland was ready. People just stood with mouths open. And we got bottles thrown in one or two places, notably Cookstown.'

'There was a disastrous incident there,' agrees Harrison. 'They threw pennies at us and we collected the money off the stage, which annoyed people even more. They got incensed, things were said on both sides, and the police had to escort us out of town.

'But we reckoned the band sounded as good as The Rolling Stones. There wasn't another white man in Britain could phrase like Van. He was always good at ad libbing. He could just conjure words. My recollection is that Van didn't write songs – he wrote ideas and then the song came as he was performing. He never had a song written down – maybe words here and there on cigarette packets – but you'd diddle about with some riff and he'd put something on top of it and gradually it evolved. Everything was refined on the road.

'My memory of "Gloria" was us sitting down in me mum's house playing riffs and different chord sequences and "Gloria" popped up out of it. So did "Philosophy".'

'Van was superb,' enthuses Wrixon. 'He had presence, he was a songwriter, a great singer and showman, fun, one of the boys, uncomplicated. But the band was talented as a unit. It wasn't Van plus band. Billy Harrison, as a guitar player, wasn't the man with the most technical ability that I've ever heard but he sounded right. He was rough – which was his charm.

'I was terrified of him. He was a hard man and I just did what I was told. When people offered not to pay us, Billy changed their thinking very quickly. He would not have been physically intimidated by a lot of people. He was the brass-necked organiser that Van never was. Van was the very artistic, laid-back, "Ach, it doesn't matter, man" sort of person. Billy Harrison was, "No, he owes us another 20p, let's have it." To me both inputs were part of what made Them work.

'One of the most important things for Them was to arrive in London with the usual inferiority complex coming from Northern Ireland, to play with The Pretty Things – who became good friends of Them – on live shows and say, "Fuck, we're better than that. We're not looking up at them – they're looking up at us."'

The Melotones, early Sixties:
(back row, l–r) Ken Cowan (trumpet),
Bobby Sinclair (sax), Jim Armstrong
(guitar), unknown;
(front row, l–r) Billy McCandless (bass),
Walter Davison (piano), Belle Crowe
(vocals), Tommy Smith (drums),
Albert Quigley (guitar)

The band, now managed by Philip Solomon, signed to Decca, having recorded a demo tape for electronics whiz-kid Peter Lloyd in Belfast. 'I still have a copy of the demo,' declares Harrison. 'It's very, very raw. You can hear all the mistakes. But Peter Lloyd opened the door with that, because he knew people in Decca. He knew Dick Rowe, so Dick Rowe arrived one night at the Maritime, when we were in a wild phase of "Turn On Your Lovelight", which worked at winding up the crowd and winding up the band as well. The wee man used to pace the stage during it like a wild animal. It really used to lift things up and get things going.'

Suitably impressed, Rowe signed the band, their first Decca session, on 5 July 1964, producing 'Gloria' and several other tracks. But for Harrison this session, produced by Rowe himself, and subsequent sessions produced by in-house producer Tommy Scott, were unsatisfying. 'You got people trying to refine things and telling you what to do and we were naive. You say, "They know more than I do," and you think you have to do what you're told. A certain amount of spontaneity goes out of it.'

Them's reputation has been sabotaged by stories that they were replaced by session men on their records. In particular, it is said that Jimmy Page – later of Led Zeppelin – plays the immortal guitar lick on 'Baby Please Don't Go'.

Harrison is adamant: 'I can stand with my hand on my heart and say I played lead, not Jimmy Page. I wrote the lick and I'm playing it. Page was there, but he played the solid chunk in the background. And a session drummer, Bobby Graham, played, but Ronnie Millings was playing as well.' The rumour is, however, that Millings was unmiked and only Graham was recorded. 'I don't know. They were both being recorded, as far as I'm concerned. Another guitarist, Dave, sometimes used to augment, but there was no one else.'

Wrixon supports Harrison: 'There are plenty of witnesses who can testify that Billy Harrison had been playing "Baby Please Don't Go" live exactly the way it later turned out on record. Billy Harrison plays like Billy Harrison. He played it before, during and after the session the way you would expect Billy Harrison to play it.'

A few Them tracks, including 'I Gave My Love A Diamond', were produced by American producer Bert Berns, who had written 'Twist And Shout' and other classics. 'Brilliant. Unbelievable guy,' enthuses Harrison. 'I remember him coming out of the console: he walked over to the drum kit, grabbed a stick and started beating on a cymbal and saying, "Let's get this thing cooking," and created an atmosphere. Suddenly everybody went, "Yeah, we're not sitting here tied to these seats, we're allowed to express ourselves." Berns just created a whole freedom of atmosphere within the studio. Helluva producer. The guy was magic.'

The band stayed at the same London hotel as blues harmonica legend Little Walter. 'We used to have sessions with him and John Lee Hooker in the lounge. We ended up getting thrown out because they brought amplifiers into the bloody place! Little Walter was an unbelievable player, an unbelievable bluesman. We were acting what that guy had lived. That's really the size of it.

'Van, Alan and myself went to see Walter at a club one night and he called us up on stage to play with him. He and Van both sang and blew harp, Alan played bass and I played guitar. I'll not forget that. He thought highly of the Wee Man, too. Everybody did.

'And we played as Jimmy Reed's backing band at a couple of gigs. He was easy enough to play with but you couldn't hear anybody else but Jimmy Reed, he turned the amplifier up so loud. A guy came up to me between numbers saying, "Would you mind turning down – we came here to hear Jimmy Reed," and I said, "Who the fuck do you think you're hearing, man? It's not me." The next song started – and I took my hands off the guitar and shrugged!'

Them were notoriously unco-operative with journalists, and top Sixties writer Keith Altham famously tells a story about being intimidated by a sullen Harrison cleaning his nails with a knife during an interview. 'Quite possible,' concedes Harrison. 'But no one was threatening him with it! What created the thing about Them being bad to interview was you got journalists who came in with their standard, prissy, stupid, bloody dickhead questions, with no real relevance, and we didn't have any time for it. "What's your favourite colour?" Who gives a monkey's? We were playing for love of music and enjoying playing, but no one was asking about the music. We were walking, talking, eating, sleeping, playing, working music, all the bloody time. The one big release was we all loved the cartoons. We all used to go to the cartoon cinema, if we got to a town early for a gig, and let off steam. Pure escapism.'

The Bert Berns-produced 'Here Comes The Night', released in March 1965, became another international success, reaching number two in the British charts, but by then Wrixon was long gone. 'I had A levels to do and Solomon said, "Either you're in the band or leave." I said, "Surely this ultimatum can be waived for six weeks and I'll get these A levels out of the way?" It couldn't be, so I left. If management had supported, instead of exploiting, Them could have been on a level with the Stones.'

Drummer Ronnie Millings, a family man, was another early defector, resigning to find a steadier income. John Patrick (Patsy) McAuley came in on keyboards to replace Wrixon, then moved to drums, replacing Millings, with his brother Jackie joining on keyboards.

Jackie McAuley played on several tracks on the band's first, self-titled album – subtitled *The Angry Young Them* – released on Decca in June 1965. 'There's no session men on those tracks at all,' asserts McAuley. 'In those days, in Belfast, an original band couldn't get arrested. They were all showbands. Brilliant musicians, but all doing covers. We done some really bad gigs in ballrooms, where people wanted to hear the Top Ten. "Do you know any Cliff Richard numbers?" Van wouldn't answer them, just give them a look: "This is it and fuck you." We had our lives threatened loads of times, but it was a terrific thing Van did. He stood his ground and never went into covers when he was under pressure to do it.

'We were doing eight gigs a week, all over the country. I was popping pills to stay awake and we were all living on top of each other. There were all these disputes. "You did this, you did that." When it came to my turn I said, "Fuck it, I'm going." When I left the disputes carried on. Because if something's wrong, it can't be the manager's fault, or the agent's fault, it's got to be one of your friends. That's the naivety of it.'

McAuley was replaced by Peter Bardens, his brother Pat leaving soon afterwards to be briefly replaced by Terry Noone, and the band began to disintegrate, dissatisfied with their management's handling of finances. Harrison tried to resolve matters. 'The band agreed things weren't right, but when I broached the subject and created a big row I was left standing on my own – the union rep with no members! Management used the principle of divide and conquer. There were threats like, "I'll see you guys never work again." The threats got across and I heard certain ones had whispered about finding another guitarist, so I copped the needle. One day they arrived at my house to go to a show and I said, "Bye – I'm not going." I think now I was too hasty, but I still think I held that damn band together, 'cos it collapsed after I left.'

Joe Boni briefly replaced Harrison before the band fell apart and the only survivors, Morrison and Alan Henderson, limped back to Belfast where they

recruited guitarist Jim Armstrong, drummer John Wilson and keyboard/sax/
vibes player Ray Elliott.

Armstrong was a local phenomenon who, while still a schoolboy, had
played in Belfast's top showband, The Melotones, who were resident in the
city's Romano's Ballroom. 'The summer holidays were great,' recalls Jim. 'I
could do eight hours a day in Romano's, just practising on my own.'

The Melotones were veterans, a generation older than Armstrong, but a
tribute record to Jim Reeves, 'Jim Forget Them Not', sung by Billy McCandless,
had nearly led to a record deal. 'Decca wanted to sign us. They wrote, "Great
record, send us details of lead singer: colour of hair, age, etc.". When we wrote
back, "White; 56", they didn't want to know!

'But with The Mels I developed my ear, playing all those old standards like
"Lullaby Of Broadway". I was into Barney Kessel and Joe Pass, then I went
back into the R&B and blues that it all came from – Howlin' Wolf, Muddy
Waters, B.B. King . . .'

Another of the new recruits, John Wilson, only seventeen when he joined
the band, had already lived out some serious rock 'n' roll fantasies with Belfast

Them on TV in the US, late Sixties:
Kenny McDowell (left), Alan Henderson (centre),
with Eric Burdon (right) of The Animals

band The Misfits. 'The Misfits were into covers of American hits and we had mohair suits and all the right gear,' he explains. 'We went out to Hamburg in '64 and for young boys from east Belfast to arrive in "Sin City" in the mid-Sixties, with sex 24 hours a day in the Reeperbahn, was mind-blowing. It took us two weeks just to calm down! The Top Ten club would have been our main gig and we would have worked from seven o'clock at night to four o'clock in the morning, an hour on, an hour off.'

Wilson understood the appeal of the original Them. 'Musically the original Them wouldn't have been good, but as entertainment it was excellent. They had an in-built insanity and at gigs it seemed like these guys could self-explode at any minute. There was a madness there and not much discipline, but they were exciting and this madness made them stand out.'

The new Them went to work. 'We rehearsed for two weeks at the Maritime,' recollects Armstrong. 'Then did the Top Hat in Lisburn, the Flamingo in Ballymena – "The best hot dogs in the world" [the club's proud boast] – and then on the road. Up and down the motorway. We had Selmer gear which was clapped out, a minibus that was clapped out . . . *we* were clapped out! We didn't even have seats to sit on – we sat on speakers. We drove overnight from Wales once, were in London at 8 a.m. to record some TV show, then drove to Edinburgh for a gig that night.

'We were playing on the strength of Top Ten poppy records like "Here Comes The Night" and there wasn't enough publicity saying it was a blues band. Scotland used to be good 'cos they were into a bit of gut music and some of the universities were great, but other gigs were awful, like the Top Rank ballrooms where they were wanting to hear "Here Comes The Night". We were doing "Stormy Monday", with the nice chords in it – not the twelve-bar, all the substitutions – and they were going, "What's that?" It was bad management – you have to tell people what to expect.

'But there were times Van came off raving 'cos we were doing Jimmy Witherspoon's "Times Are Getting Tougher Than Tough" and he liked the jazzy feel to it, with vibes and sax.

'One night in St Mary's College, though, they pulled the plug. Ray and Van were playing "The Train And The River" on two saxophones, which was originally a jazz thing by Jimmy Giuffre with Jim Hall on guitar, where the music gives the sounds of a train and then the river weaving through. The crowd were going, "What's going on here?" and the caretaker came on and switched off the power!

'But the most embarrassing gig was once when Van came wandering on with a drink in one hand and a joint in the other, downed the drink, ran forward and leapt over the speaker, slid on his ass across the stage and spread-eagled into the mike stand.'

Even worse, the debacle was witnessed by Billy Harrison. 'It was horrific,' he sneers. 'And very amusing. Van came leaping in over an amplifier and fell on his face. I went with Phil May and Viv Prince out of The Pretty Things and

I suppose we were going to do a bit of piss-taking but we didn't have to – they did it for themselves.'

Returning from Scotland once, Them's career nearly came to a grim end. Armstrong: 'The roads were caked with snow – it wasn't gritted or anything. You couldn't see a thing. The van did one of those slow-motion turns and I was sitting with my suitcase on my knee going, "Arrrgggghhhh . . ." I can remember sliding down, thinking, This is it, goodnight. There was a drop at the side, but the van spun right round and went straight. The snow cleared and we thought, Only another six hours and we'll be in London! The next thing . . . CRUNCH – we had skidded on black ice and hit a traffic island. I thought I was sent for.'

Armstrong, who had given up a steady job in a bank to join Them, wasn't enamoured of the rock 'n' roll lifestyle. 'Every time I had two days off I went home. I was saving to buy my own bank! Ray Elliott and Alan Henderson were great looners. They would lose all their money gambling and drinking and hanging out with The Pretty Things. I was only a small-sherry-at-Christmas man at that stage. I was a clean-cut kid fresh from Sunday School.'

The new Them recorded the *Them Again* album, released in January 1966. 'Tommy Scott produced and Tommy would come in and say, "Here's the tunes you're doing,"' remembers Wilson. 'If my memory serves me well there were a few tunes that I was sure I'd heard before by people like Nina Simone, and I suddenly found out, no, this was one of Tommy's tunes! They realised the power of copyright and the money to be made through publishing.'

Five of the songs on the album are Morrison compositions. 'Probably he'd have cornered somebody on their own like Ray Elliott and they would have fiddled about with the song and then come to the band and said, "Let's have a blow over this," but it was very haphazard. If management had've had their act together they'd have seen the potential Van had and they'd have nurtured it and never let it disintegrate through greed.'

'There were a few tracks left over from before, but everything after I joined was played by the band,' asserts Armstrong. 'We're on twelve of the sixteen tracks – no session men. They weren't going to put "I Put A Spell On You" on the album – "It's too jazzy" – and what happens? Alan Price does it and has a smash. Plus we were getting ripped off – the album went gold, but I didn't get any money.'

John Wilson fared no better. 'I never got any money from Them recordings,' he declares. 'At a later stage in my career I signed a piece of paper 'cos The Misfits were stuck in London and needed money to get somewhere and I got a cheque and I signed over all my rights to anything I did with Them. Real business sense! But joining Them was good experience for me. It got me into the major leagues doing recordings and one-nighters and TV – things you wouldn't have got the chance to do back in Belfast.

'When I think back I was probably the weakest link in the band, because the other guys were extremely talented, experienced players. They used to make

Them on TV in the US, late Sixties:
(l–r) Alan Henderson, Jim Armstrong, Dave Harvey, Kenny McDowell, Ray Elliott

fun of me 'cos I was so young and I was influenced by buying clothes in Carnaby Street and all this sort of stuff. They used to say, "Don't worry, Junior, you might meet a pop star tonight." They used to make fun of the fact that I was actually into that. In fact I was so young I couldn't get a permit to do European gigs, so they had to get a stand-in drummer any time they played in Europe.'

Like Armstrong, Wilson remembers life on the road with Them as gruelling. 'We crashed the truck in Preston once. Van got us a taxi and the driver says, "Where to?" and Van says, "Oxford Street." We arrived in London, said our goodnights and I went straight in, loaded everything and went to the airport to fly home to Belfast. And there were all the other guys already in the airport! Everybody had had the same idea!

'Looking back, mostly the band didn't work well live because there was too much drink and whatever else. It had the potential to be good, but it was never nurtured. No one cared. But there was a definite charisma when Van performed. He was always creative but in those days he was just a commodity, like a tin of beans. I left two weeks before they went to America in 1966. I'd had enough of the madness, the drinking and the uncertainty and it was just awful – just loads of pressures.'

Them's American tour has gone down in rock 'n' roll legend. 'We were met in New York and got the Riot Act read about do's and don'ts,' remembers Armstrong. 'No drugs, no under-age women. Then we flew to San Francisco and the guy who read us the Riot Act woke up with a fifteen-year-old! Then we flew to Phoenix and we stepped off the plane in 110-degree heat. I was wearing a tweed double-breasted jacket which near killed me – I didn't know what to expect.'

The band's first American gig, with Wilson replaced by English drummer David Harvey, was in a football field. 'They drove us on in an open-topped Cadillac,' recalls Armstrong. 'Masses of screaming kids, a PA with two little speakers and I had a little Fender amp, not miked – to fill this huge outdoor arena.'

Them played at the Whisky A-Go-Go in LA for two weeks, with The Doors and Captain Beefheart supporting. 'They were all heavily into drugs and we were all heavily into drink. Everyone wanted to know what we were on! I didn't identify with the drug culture. That first time I was over there I didn't take anything. I came from this little staid upbringing. I had this Mr Sensible on my shoulder. But our drink tab in the Whisky – beer was free and spirits half-price – was $2,600 in two weeks.'

Jim Morrison of the then little-known Doors, fell under Them's drunken influence. 'The guys introduced him to alcohol and he couldn't handle it. He wrecked rooms and stuff like that. Him and Van were thrown out of the Whisky one night for shouting, "Johnny Rivers is a wanker." The Doors did all the things that went on to be hits – and they sounded just like the records did. Jim Morrison did a lot of Van tricks, like turning round and crouching into the bass drum and then turning round. Van did that – but then Van stopped doing anything, except cartwheels now and again.' On the last night of the residency Jim Morrison joined Them onstage. 'We did the big "Gloria" jam.'

Frank Zappa also befriended the band. 'Ray [Elliott] being a typical looner woke up in bed with this girl. Frank walked in with his ponytail and Mexican bandit moustache and the girl said, "That's my old man." Ray near shit, but yer man just says, "Come on out and hear this album [*Freak Out*] I've just recorded." Ray came back stoned out of his lid and thought it was great. That was his introduction to Frank. And then Frank came down and played with us a few times. He got onstage and played blues and we swapped choruses on the likes of "Stormy Monday". It was great fun. And we talked guitar and influences and stuff we liked.'

The band, however, often felt misunderstood. 'We played Waikiki Shell once absolutely sober and played, we thought, a respectable set, very musical. And the promoter was raging, saying we were all drunk, 'cos we just stood there and played. So next night we all got drunk, Van fell into the drums, we did an awful set, and the promoter said, "That's brilliant; that's what I wanted!"'

Another gig ended ingloriously. 'Van went funny. He went over to Ray Elliott, lifted a mike stand and went to hit him with it – took a swing at him. It just missed him. He came over to me and I said, "You come near me and I'll wrap this guitar round your head." The promoter pulled the curtains 'cos there was going to be a fight on stage.

'I thought Van was a great singer. Very creative. He couldn't play guitar – still can't – but he can say enough with those few bits he can do. Same as saxophone. The feeling was there. But he wasn't doing his job 100 per cent a lot of the time, because he didn't want to be doing what he was doing. He didn't want to play to screaming kids. But he couldn't communicate that to anyone else. But a lot of stuff we rehearsed was the guts of [Morrison's 1968 solo breakthrough album] *Astral Weeks*, like "Ballerina". Alan, Ray and I sat acoustically with flutes and stuff playing that into a tape recorder. And we used to do "Ballerina" on the tour, so the band was creative.

'And there's a track on that second album which is very creative – "Hey Girl", which is very poetic. The G6-C6 feel – very pastoral, with flutes, which was "things to come".

'But we didn't have a manager who was half-way sympathetic to what we were doing and nurtured the talent. Plus we were getting ripped off. We did four months knocking our bollocks in and I finished with nothing. I had to borrow money to get home.'

Back in Ireland Them petered out. 'We played Derry Embassy Ballroom with Van's cousin Sammy Stitt, who played harmonica with the Jim Daly Blues Band, depping on drums. The band was awful. There was still bad feeling from the tour and the drummer was all over the place so I said, "Forget it."'

Morrison began gigging with Them Again, with future Thin Lizzy guitarist Eric Bell, who had previously played in local bands like The Atlantics and The Deltones. 'The Atlantics was the first band I played with,' reminisces Bell. 'We did Shadows numbers, then Beatles numbers, then the Stones came out, so we went from instrumentals to The Beatles to the blues. After that I was in about twelve groups. Every band I left [future blues rock superstar] Gary Moore would take my place!

'The Deltones had their own van which was unheard of. And a Vox AC 30 amp – I used to dream about owning a Vox AC 30! We played Betty Staff's and Clarke's, but weren't allowed into Sammy Houston's 'cos we were a pop group and wore suits! We played a lot of showband supports, like for The Freshmen and The Royal, so we would be playing to 2,000 people, which was very frightening, 'cos we were just fifteen or sixteen, but an incredible experience.

'Then I was in Crymble's Music Shop one day and Van introduced himself and gave me his address in Hyndford Street. I went up and he had this tape recorder and a few songs. He plugged me into an amplifier and said, "Play along." He liked what I did so we formed a band, and he got these two guys that were in The Alleykatz: Joe Hanratty, a drummer, and Mike Brown on bass. We played around Ireland for two or three months – Van Morrison and Them Again.

'The first gig was the Square One club in [Belfast's] Royal Avenue. I had the list of numbers but Van just said, "Start a blues in E." I said, "What about the list?" and he said, "To hell with it! Start a blues in E." The stage was quite small, so I was standing six inches from the front, and these two girls tied my shoelaces together. I seen them doing it, but I couldn't stop playing!

'Van was quite intense and a perfectionist. He wanted to give his best but in some places, they didn't understand what he was doing. But he was a professional. You can't force people to like you.

'We played Queen's University rag ball one night. Everybody was smashed – the audience and the band. I was pissed as a newt and Van said to the bassist, "Tell Eric to turn down," so I turned down. Then Van turned his guitar up, so I said, "To hell with this!" and I turned up again. I got a really bad write-up in *City Week* from Donal Corvin: "Last night Eric Bell tried to outshine Van Morrison with sheer volume." I left the band that night because there was bad feeling.'

Morrison soon emigrated to America and rock stardom, while his former Them colleagues – Henderson, Armstrong, Elliott and Harvey – regrouped, with Morrison being replaced by Kenny McDowell who had sung with The Mad Lads, the regular support group to the original Them in the Maritime.

'In the Sixties Belfast was the hub of the music industry in Ireland,' explains McDowell. 'The whole of Belfast was buzzing. The first time The Mad Lads played the Maritime was the second gig Them had done in the place. We used to play the break for them every week. They were a really good band. We never got together with them onstage – we in The Mad Lads were in awe of them, watching them play and Van was always, even then, that bit aloof from it all.

'We played a mixture of R&B, like Don Covay, and blues, like Howlin' Wolf and Muddy Waters, and I even remember doing a few of Otis Redding's early things and the more middle-of-the-road Chuck Berry sort of thing. And the guys who ran the Maritime were these blues enthusiasts and so you were always being fed this music in the interval on the old reel-to-reel tape recorder.

'There was no beer sold in the Maritime, though it didn't stop people coming in stoned on scrumpy or whatever, but it was a great atmosphere and people like Joe Harper [later immortalised in Morrison's song "Joe Harper Saturday Morning"] made it. Joe was the caretaker. He took a great interest in the kids and if they had too much to drink, made sure they got home. And he gave musicians great encouragement. If we had a gig in Dublin, Joe would hire the minibus 'cos we didn't have licences, and drive us down. When I first started writing Joe actually bought me this fabulous tape recorder to encourage me. And he would go guarantor for guys who wanted guitars. A super guy. Everybody told Joe their troubles and he would sort them out.'

The Mad Lads had signed to the same record company as Them – Decca – and like Them had been assigned Bert Berns as producer. 'Bert had just produced Them's "Here Comes The Night". He had brought a few tunes over from America and I guess The Mad Lads got the lesser of them, but having said that, it was still a privilege for somebody who was just starting out in their career to be working with someone who had written such classic songs as "Piece Of My Heart".

'"Out With My Baby" was the first single we had out, with a tune I had written, called "So Long", on the other side. The other track we did was "Answer Your Phone". I was the only one of The Mad Lads who actually played on them. Andy White was the drummer and Phil Coulter was the keyboard player, who took me under his wing and looked after me because this was the first time I'd done anything this grand, so I was in awe of the whole thing. It was just "Sing!" and that was it: it was all out of my control.

'And on "Answer Your Phone", when I went back to London a second time to do a bit more singing, Berns had written down the wrong chords for four bars. He'd actually recorded it, but had by now gone back to the States and I didn't have the heart to say, "This is wrong!" so I sang my part straight through, struggling to sing the melody over the wrong chords. So my part was right and Bert Berns' part was wrong!

'The manager put the single out as Moses K & The Prophets. He sacked the band and was going to form a backing band for me, with me as Moses K, but the whole thing collapsed and I was left without a band. I'd been happily playing with The Mad Lads, with guys I'd grown up with, and suddenly they're axed, I've no band and I can't play. I didn't play at all for maybe a year and a half. Then I got a phone call from Joe Harper, so I met him and we went to Jim Armstrong's house and Jim's first words were, "Do you want to go to America?" Sure I want to go to America!

'Carol Deck, who worked in a teen magazine *Flip*, had become a friend of the band when they were there before and she was instrumental in getting Them back over again. Through Carol Deck Ray Ruff was chosen to put the money up and he brought the band over and managed us. He had been a minor musician years before, a Buddy Holly impersonator at one point.

'"Dirty Old Man", on Sully, was our first single and that was a tune I absolutely hated. The idea was, "Let's do another 'Gloria'" and it certainly was no way another "Gloria". But touring was the greatest bulk of what we did. We started off with 65 days straight touring, then a day off, and then 38 days. We started off on the Mexican border and worked the whole way up into Canada. Then across Canada and down to LA with some of the hops between gigs being 700 miles, so you were driving through the night to the next one. It was gruelling.

'You start off, it's great, everybody has plenty to talk about, but when you live in a small, confined space, with five or six blokes, and you've talked about everything there is to talk about, the tension builds and builds. The strain of living two or three in a room and the roadie on the floor and not knowing anybody, anywhere, is very hard. You can get quite ill. I know I was totally run down.

'And I was never a great fan of our music. We were getting away from what Them was about which was R&B/blues and getting into psychedelia which I was never a fan of. I was more into the O.V. Wrights and Otis Reddings of this world. But I was the kid in the band, the new recruit, so I went along with it. But we were a good gigging band – we still had the rawness.

'Probably the ultimate was playing three nights with Frank Zappa and the Mothers of Invention at the Electric Theatre in Chicago – that was probably the highlight of my career. The guys had met them before so there was a good bit of *craic* going on. Frank was a great guy and he and Ray Elliott got on really, really well because Ray was a quite off-the-wall guy. The Mothers were absolutely superb. The quality of their musicianship was tremendous. I remember the last night they played they were rushing off for a plane to fly to New York, so the last tune they played they called "Packing Up" and they packed the gear as they played! They packed the whole gear, the snare drum was the last thing to go in and that was it, the lights went down and end of the show!

'And I remember we played the Baton Rouge Festival with [blues legend] Freddie King and a tornado blew up and it just went black. They had to tie all the gear down. You stood into the wind: the crowd were out this-a-way but the sound all went that-a-way. When you took your glasses off afterwards your face was totally black but for the white eyes.

'And we played with [jazz legend] Joe Pass. We were doing the *Merv Griffiths* TV show and the tune we were doing was "Nobody Knows You When You're Down And Out" and Joe Pass was in the house band. We were playing live and they just joined in which was a nice gesture so I can always say I played with Joe Pass.'

Armstrong, who was voted third-best guitarist in an *LA Free Press* poll, behind Hendrix and Zappa, remembers a misadventure in Perrytown. 'A little redneck town. We did four numbers, with lots of rednecks flicking cigarettes – "Urgghh, long-haired weirdos" – then the power went off and these rednecks followed us into the band room. The promoter just didn't want to pay us, so he got his friends to cause trouble. When we left they drove after us and rammed us. At the red lights they got out and put in the windows. We got out of town and there were twelve cars across the road so we couldn't get past. We turned back and went into a garage to call the police and the man says, "Get the fuck out of here" and pulled a gun. We went to the police station and the guys came in. They knew the police – you know, good old boys. All this "Hey Jethro, how's your dad?" And we're sitting picking glass out of ourselves! We sued the town for one million dollars. We never got anything. Maybe our manager got one million dollars. Perrytown. Wonderful place.'

In LA, while gigging at the Whiskey, all the band's passports were stolen – except Armstrong's – but temporary passports enabled them to fulfil gigs in Canada. After gigging in Winnipeg the band drove to the border but were stopped because their temporary passports didn't contain work permits, and told to go back to Winnipeg. Armstrong takes up the tale: 'Everybody thought it would be a jolly good idea to sneak over the border. *Boys' Own*! Five go Tramping Over the Border! We drove 200 miles along the border through the night. At dawn we picked this lonely crossing . . .'

The roadie dropped the band on the Canadian border and drove the Cadillac across. 'I was legal, I had a visa, but I wanted to join in the excitement. We were sneaking through the wheat fields. Ray Elliott was heavy on the drink the night before. He started to feel it. "Oh Jesus, the heat, slow down, fellas." We cut back into America . . . the Cadillac draws up . . . into the car . . . drive on. Next thing we heard this siren. It was the border patrol, guns and all. They thought we were drug smugglers and brought us back to the customs post where Ray threw up all over the floor. They gave him a bucket and mop: "Hey, long-haired bastard. Wipe it up." We got the fingerprints bit. Then they realised we were harmless and said, "You'll have to go back to Winnipeg." Here we go again – we'd just driven 200 miles away from Winnipeg!'

After Winnipeg it was back across the border, legally this time, to Sioux Falls for a flight. The band were told their flight had left, even though for the next half-hour they could see it on the runway. 'The guy didn't want to put us on 'cos we'd long hair. We thought we'd show him. So we chartered a wee six-seater plane. A horrendous experience. The lights went off – the pilot's flying over Route 66 with a map and a torch. We stopped for refuelling and he couldn't turn the engine off 'cos it wouldn't restart. Kenny and I had fallen asleep in the back while the others got off for a Coke but the plane lurched into gear and started lumbering down the runway. Kenny and I were staring out at the guys and the wee pilot was running along beside the plane. He just managed to hop in and stop it!'

Three days after the journey began the band reached their home base, Amarillo. 'There was no radio contact. "Fuck it," the pilot said – "We'll just go in." If anything else had come in we were dead. We had three days' growth, we were stinking, and people were saying, "What kept you?!"'

In January 1968 the band released *Now And Them*, on Tower, an uneasy mixture of the R&B for which they were famous (for example, a storming version of John Mayall's 'I'm Your Witch Doctor'), commercial pop (like Goffin and King's 'You're Just What I Was Looking For Today') and psychedelia – notably a ten-minute group composition 'Square Room', on which Elliott, with a spellbinding flute solo and Armstrong with a guitar solo featuring an exotic, Eastern-sounding tuning, play scintillatingly.

One track, 'Walking In The Queen's Garden', had been left behind by Morrison. 'Van had had a few lines and it was something that they had been jamming about with and then Alan Henderson took it up and wrote more lyrics for it,' explains McDowell.

'We used to do it with Van. It's based on an old Howlin' Wolf lick,' adds Armstrong.

In keeping with the times the band are photographed in beads and kaftans on the front of the sleeve but are described in teenybopper prose by Carol Deck in the liner notes. McDowell, we are informed, is 'charming in that delightful Irish way,' and 'you can't help but love Kenny'. Armstrong 'likes to like and is easy to like'. However, there are a few hints of the strong feelings of bitterness and resentment felt by the group, as a result of their bruising experiences in the music biz. Of Henderson it is written, 'It's a little difficult to earn Alan's respect, as it is with all of Them,' and of Elliott, 'Ray doesn't trust people, but maybe he has a reason.' Elliott is further described as being 'the world's largest leprechaun not necessarily in captivity . . . impossible to understand . . . capable of talking for hours without making sense to anyone other than himself'. And Harvey, we are told, is 'quiet, easygoing and slow at everything' – a rather unfortunate choice of phrase, as the drummer's time-keeping was regarded as being suspect.

Released as a single, 'Walking In The Queen's Garden' became a heavily requested item on Californian radio stations – for example, it made the KFXN Top 40 – but neither Tower nor manager Ray Ruff had the clout to push the band to stardom.

Increasingly the strain began to tell on the band and Ray Elliott cracked first. 'It really is difficult on the road,' sighs McDowell, 'and he'd just had enough. We were in New York and he just flipped and decided he was going home to Belfast and that was it.'

Despite the chaos the band, now a quartet, somehow recorded *Time Out! Time In*, released in November 1968, an acid-rock classic, with stunning singing and musicianship. The (near) title track, 'Time Out For Time In', is mesmerising raga rock with Armstrong on sitar and McDowell handling the long melodic lines with masterful control. But drummer Dave Harvey was out of his depth. 'It's in 11/8, a funny tempo,' muses Armstrong. 'We were into all that. We used Johnny Guerin, who was Joni Mitchell's old man, on most tracks, because Dave wasn't a good drummer.'

Many of the songs, it must be said, have misogynistic lyrics, typical of the

Them, 1968: (l–r)
Kenny McDowell,
Ray Elliott,
Jim Armstrong,
Dave Harvey,
Alan Henderson

era: '*She got a sweet love potion to blow your mind/ You've fallen under that strange girl's spell*' sings McDowell venomously on 'She Put A Hex On You', his voice filled with contempt, as Armstrong's vicious-sounding guitar freaks out in the background. And on 'Bent Over You' – on which Armstrong unleashes a dramatic, savage solo – McDowell accusingly declares, '*You've twisted my mind*'.

All but two songs were written by obscure hippy songwriters Tom Lane and Sharon Pulley. On one track in particular Armstrong was in his element. 'On "The Moth" I play seven guitars: an acoustic; four guitars like a string section; then two twelve-strings detuned to sound like balalaikas.' Indeed, throughout the album Armstrong's playing is audacious, imaginative and wildly exciting.

The only band composition is the raga rock 'Just One Conception', with McDowell in hippy prophet mode, pontificating on the meaning of life: '*There's no deception*,' he advises. '*Only one conception*'.

Again the album didn't sell and the band lost heart. 'We were getting ripped off and it's hard when you're out there playing every night and all the money's going elsewhere and everybody's getting rich except you,' explains McDowell. 'It had got to the stage where we were living on $5 a day. I tried to fight Ray Ruff but I'd been away two years and I was physically and mentally gone and the idea of coming home appealed to me.'

Armstrong, too, had had enough. 'We were drawing minimum money and sending money back to pay our publicity agent and so on. Suddenly we were contacted saying bills hadn't been paid. It turned out the money we were sending back wasn't going to who it should have. I had to contact home: "Send me the money for a ticket. This is another fiasco." That was me home again, with the proverbial tail between my legs.'

Alan Henderson kept Them's name alive using American musicians and the production talents of Ray Ruff for two further, weak albums. *Them*, on Happy Tiger, was a collaboration with Jerry Cole, a respected LA session man who had been in the resident band on the *Shindig* TV show, had recorded with The Beach Boys and Johnny Cash, and had played on The Byrds' version of 'Mr Tambourine Man'. *In Reality*, for the same label, featured Jim Parker (guitar) and John Stark (drums) of The Kitchen Cinq, an Amarillo band whose album *Everything But . . .* had been produced by Lee Hazlewood. The remakes of 'Gloria' and 'Baby Please Don't Go' included on this sixth Them album can safely be called unnecessary.

The albums inevitably flopped, although Henderson remained with Ray Ruff for a grandiose Jesus rock-opera project, *Truth Of Truth*, released on Oak Records in 1971, featuring the talents of top session musicians like Larry Carlton, Jerry Scheff, Hal Blaine, John Guerin, Joe Osborne and, again, Jerry Cole. The double-LP was lavishly packaged with a twenty-page booklet, but despite the presence of so many illustrious contributors the music was truly appalling. Henderson wrote or co-wrote eight of the songs, but lyrics like

'*Awake, awake, O Israel, God is sending you a Messiah*' are not the stuff of which rock 'n' roll classics are made.

Ruff went on, by his own count, to produce 254 records that entered the *Billboard* charts, working with Commander Cody, Phil Everly, Hank Williams jnr. and others and being called by top producer/arranger Jimmy Bowen 'a promotional genius and the best promotions man ever', but Henderson drifted out of music. Which should be the end of our saga – except, amazingly, a Them re-formation took place in 1979.

Eric Wrixon explains: 'A film called *The Rocker* came out in Germany with Them's "It's All Over Now Baby Blue" on the soundtrack, which, released as a single, went to number one, whereupon Them re-formed.'

Harrison clarifies: 'It was going to be John Wilson on drums, Jackie Flavelle from the Chris Barber Band on bass, Eric Wrixon on keyboards and Mel Austin as chanter. Mel and I were putting some songs together between us and I'd written some songs. Jackie and Wilsey opted out and the whole thing fell through which put me into an almost mental-breakdown state, so not wanting to let it go I got in touch with Alan Henderson in the States and he was all for it. We got another drummer, Billy Bell, and that was the line-up that went and made *Shut Your Mouth* [on Teldec] under the name of Them.

'It could have been a lot better. My playing wasn't as good as it could have been. Pure rustiness 'cos I hadn't been playing at all. That would apply to a certain extent to the rest of the band as well. And a weakness was we weren't actually a working band, nor were we session men who could just come together. That was a weakness but at the same time it lent a certain rawness

The aftermath of Them, Germany, late Nineties

to it – the end result sounded very much like where Them had left off, sound-wise. There was no great musical ability but there was an honesty about it, which was a good thing.

'Another weakness would have been in the songs that I had written myself. When you get someone else to sing them it doesn't quite work the same way. I think if you listen to the songs that Mel and I wrote together, Mel sounds a hell of a lot better than when he sings the songs that I wrote on my own – he had a better feel for them. I think I should have sung a couple of my own songs myself.'

'Billy wasn't into playing current-day solos,' argues Wrixon. 'All the solos on the LP are either organ, piano or mouth organ, which I had to go back after-wards and do. So although Billy wrote every song on the album, certain people in the band got paranoid about how it was going to sound live and Billy was replaced by Jim Armstrong.'

'Yes, for a change!' grimaces Harrison, who still seethes about being ousted. '*Et tu,* Brute. I was looking forward to going. There were 21 gigs over a 30-day period and we were going into the studio to put down some more tracks which I had a lot of material written for. We were going to come back with three grand each in our pockets which I reckoned was good bread for a band that was only trying to get their foot in the door again. I think they ended up doing five gigs – they talked themselves out of it and made a Horlicks of it. Funnily enough and cheekily enough – and they had no chance – they asked me before they went if I had any songs that they could take with them for when they went into the studios and I said, "No, you gotta be joking. You ain't getting anything."'

Wrixon merely says, 'The band toured Germany, but without the promised record-company support.'

Jim Armstrong is blunter: 'The tour was a shambles.'

And so the mighty name of Them was finally – perhaps mercifully – laid to rest. Nearly twenty musicians played in Them between 1964 and 1979 with only Van Morrison achieving lasting stardom. But history has unfairly neglected some terrific musicians who, with Van, put Northern Ireland on the musical map and made some unforgettable music. Let us then salute, not only Van, but also all the others – Irish rock heroes to a man – who helped create the undying legend of Them.

LIFE AFTER THEM
SPIKE, POUND MUSIC CLUB, BELFAST

Bombs and bullets may have deterred most English bands from crossing the sea to Ireland, but local rock fans are not completely deprived of entertainment, for every Saturday afternoon in Belfast's Pound music club Spike play a set that is of world class.

Spike's repertoire is basically that of a late-Sixties British blues band, but they play with an instrumental flair and sophistication undreamed of by their predecessors. Main-man is lead guitarist Jim Armstrong, who played with Them during their heyday. Armstrong's solos on songs like B.B. King's 'Everyday I Have The Blues' and Sonny Boy Williamson's 'Help Me' are nothing short of phenomenal, characterised by almost limitless imagination and an immaculate sense of timing and rhythm.

Belfast rock fans characteristically dress in dull, safe anonymity, wearing denims rather than attention-grabbing satin and glitter. Nevertheless, the atmosphere is one of joyous celebration as Spike tear into a ten-minute version of the old Them favourite 'Mystic Eyes' or the Irish rock national anthem 'Gloria' which is sung superbly by Kenny McDowell (who once actually replaced Van Morrison in Them). McDowell also plays magnificent mouth harp, most notably on their featured jam 'It's Not How Long You Make It, It's How You Make It Long'.

For those who find it hard to believe that a group of any real talent could be playing in a Belfast club, it is worth remembering that in the late Sixties Armstrong was voted third, behind only Hendrix and Zappa, in a guitarists' poll organised by the *LA Free Press*.

Spike and the pop hype machine may never get together but the rock-starved people of Belfast already have more than one reason for thinking they're a great band.

Trevor Hodgett · Concert review originally published in *New Musical Express* (20 December 1975)

LIFE AFTER THEM
BILLY HARRISON

Billy Harrison was the man who founded Them, the man who led the band in its earliest days and the man who played the immortal guitar lick that drove the band's most successful record, 'Baby Please Don't Go'. And yet, having walked out of the band, bitter at mismanagement and bitter at his colleagues for not supporting him, Harrison's subsequent career was virtually a non-event.

'If you've played once it's like a drug. It's in your blood and you can't get rid of it,' he sighs. 'You can put it behind you but you can never get rid of it. I actually went back to Them when Jim Armstrong's appendix burst and played a few gigs in England and went to France and Scandinavia with them. I suppose I was the obvious replacement when Jim went ill – but I also heard that there was nobody else around who would play with them.

'And I toured all Scandinavia with The Pretty Things, in Dick Taylor's place, when he went walkabout. That was an experience. The Pretty Things were very good friends, all smashing blokes – real nice, genuine guys. Phil May, the singer, was a super showman. I remember him saying, "If I could sing like Morrison I could blow the rest of you buggers away," which was probably true because he was as good a showman as Mick Jagger.

'I did recordings with The Pretty Things and I did session work with [maverick independent producer] Joe Meek before he blew his brains out. I did overdubs – there was nobody else there. He was a nice guy, easy to work with. He played the tracks and I put my ideas over the top of them and I never knew what I was playing over. I think some of the overdubs were for Heinz & The Tornados but I couldn't tell you the tracks. I got paid and came away. I remember two years later my wife and I were sitting in the cinema and I heard this song over the ads: "I know that. Shit! That's me playing." I don't know who the hell it was – I just recognised myself.

'I suppose I jacked in music about April/May '66 'cos I went into the GPO in the telephones in March '66. The weekend before I started work I was playing in the Isle of Wight with The Pretty Things, so coming back from that on the Sunday night and going to work on the Monday morning was a bit of a downer.

'I still had all the gear, I was still doing the odd wee bit of demo sessions and things like that and I suddenly just made the decision: no grey areas; it's black or white. In retrospect I should have come back to Belfast and formed another band while I still had a reputation here because I still had all my contacts in England – but I made a different decision. I was married, I had a

Trevor Hodgett · Originally published in *Wavelength* (December 1994); plus additional material

Billy Harrison, at the time of his solo album, *Billy Who?*

wife to keep and responsibilities and I just decided – Cut. And not long after making the decision I took all the gear and sold it because I knew while I had it there was going to be that temptation and it'd drag me back, which leaves you very unsettled.

'I never touched a guitar for seven years and then I took the urge to have something about me to fiddle and play with so I bought an old beat-up acoustic and I used to beat that about. Now I've got a houseful of guitars again.

'And I also got heavily into martial arts when I came home to Northern Ireland in 1975. I was a karate black belt at one time. It would have done me a lot more good ten or fifteen years earlier – not the black belt but the self-discipline.'

The 1979 Them reunion for the *Shut Your Mouth* album gave Harrison hope again but the catastrophe of his sacking by his mates devastated him. 'I was still with BT [British Telecom] so I had a good steady job. I was willing to kick it all over for the music but I wasn't going to kick it all over for a wild promise, so I was wheeling and dealing with Germany, putting it across that, yes, we'd like to come to tour, but we're not doing it for nothing. And it reached the stage where the other guys felt that I didn't want to go – it was put to me, "Bill, you don't really care whether you go or not because you've got a good job and you're going to get the royalties off the songwriting anyway." So there was a meeting up in Alan Henderson's mum's house on the Cregagh Road and the animosities arose and I was accused of not really being interested in going and it turned out that they didn't really want to go with me, whether I wanted to go or not, so I said, "Well, fuck it, go. Goodbye." It was very sad because I didn't want that to happen.'

Harrison had an ally, however, in Frank Dostal, producer of *Shut Your Mouth*. 'Frank said, "I believe you're not coming, Billy." They had told him I didn't want to leave my job but I told him what had really happened and he said, "Well, that's bloody stupid of them. Do they not realise that apart from Morrison you really are Them?" So Frank said, "Come and make your own album," and I took a week's leave, went over and did the album *Billy Who?* [Vagabound, 1980] which again I can say, yes, I know, in hindsight, there's bits I could improve and there are bits that don't sound that great, but I still think it's quite good and I had the time of my life doing it. I thoroughly enjoyed it.'

One of the tracks has the same title as Them's first hit, 'Baby Please Don't Go'. 'Funny, isn't it? That just happened when I was there. It was a riff I had and I was trying to think of words and the only thing that came out of my mouth sitting in the studio was "Baby please don't go", and I went back to the hotel and I wrote the song that night 'cos it was hot in my mind. It just all fell in place. I like that song very much.'

Another song, 'Orangefield', evokes the Belfast of Harrison's youth. 'Those are my actual memories of Belfast when I was a kid. We played in Orangefield, we used to go up to the Cregagh Glens and I remember the steam organ at Bellevue and the trams.'

It looked promising for Harrison but effectively that was the end of his career. 'I was still writing songs because I was keen to make another album, which Frank wanted me to do, but something seemed to go wrong every time I got the incentive. The last time I had a big incentive I got my skull shattered doing a yacht delivery to a yacht club – that's where my business is now; I'm a marine electrician – and the boom came round and whacked me and I woke up in the neurological ward of Southern General in Glasgow, shattered from top to bottom. I'm semi-paralysed in the right side of the face, deaf in the right ear, I can't close the right eye unless I close the left eye – all wee things like that. You can't change it so you live with what you've got.'

Jackie McAuley, 1970

LIFE AFTER THEM
JACKIE McAULEY

Of all the fine players who served their blues apprenticeship in Them, the band's one-time organist Jackie McAuley is – apart from Van himself – surely the least nostalgic. 'It's all years ago. I was young, naive and stupid, and I'm fed up talking about it,' he laments. 'Things I've done in my life are far, far more important, but even to this day I get "Jackie McAuley, ex-Them".'

After his disillusioned departure from Them McAuley licked his wounds in Dublin. 'I met the Dubliners, who sang in O'Donoghue's pub. There was no after-hours in those days so we'd go to this little café where loads of musicians hung around and sang. Of course there was no keyboards so I learned guitar and picked up loads of songs.'

But McAuley's rock career began to move again. 'My brother [ex-Them drummer Pat, aka John, McAuley] had met Ken McLeod [guitar] from Belfast and Mark Scott [bass] from London. They rang from London and said, "We can work as Them, because Van has left and gone solo and people want some of the original band to do some gigs." I wasn't really into it – I hate going backwards – but I was desperate so I went over and we got gigs under the name Them.

Ken McLeod recalls: 'We were getting good gigs, like £100 for half an hour, as Them, until Van's management brought a court case against us and the judge said the name should go with the singer – Van. We were allowed to use the name only in conjunction with another name, so we did five or six gigs as The Other Them. But then we went to Denmark where the ruling didn't apply, so we went back to being Them.'

McAuley's recollection is different. 'When we heard Van was continuing Them, [producer] Kim Fowley came up with the idea of The Belfast Gypsies.'

McLeod is adamant. 'We were never, ever billed as The Belfast Gypsies. We never even heard the name Belfast Gypsies until a year after the band broke up.'

Kim Fowley was a legendary music biz mover and shaker, who had created novelty hits like 'Alley Oop' by the Hollywood Argyles. 'He was a head case – but generous,' reminisces McLeod. 'We went through very hard times after that court case when it was hard to book The Other Them and gigs dried up. Sometimes we had nothing to eat for a day or two. More than once we'd walk three miles to Kim's and beg a few shillings to buy something to eat, and on occasions Kim paid the rent on this awful bedsit Jackie and I shared. He was good like that.'

'Fowley was a complete nutcase,' agrees Jackie, 'and a real hustler. One day

Trevor Hodgett - includes material previously published in *Mojo* (March 1999), the *Irish News* (14 April 1995), *Wavelength* (March 1996), *Blueprint* (August 1996) and *Rock'n'Reel* (summer 1991; January 2002); plus additional material

he introduced me to Mohammed Ali. He says, "Come and meet a buddy of mine." We went to this hotel and there was yer man.'

Fowley produced several tracks for the band. 'He was hard in the studio,' reflects McLeod. 'I wasn't being aggressive enough for him. "Stuff these namby-pamby-type guitar solos – go gggggggrrrrr!" So I got annoyed and went "Gggggggrrrrr!" Playing nothing, just strumming chords fast. I hated a lot of what Fowley was doing.'

To the band's horror Fowley retitled one song 'Gloria's Dream'. 'I wrote a song called "Round And Round",' insists McAuley, 'and Fowley says, "Can we change those chords a bit?" So the chord sequence was almost the same as [Them's classic] "Gloria". So I said, "All right," thinking, What can I do? And he thought up the title. When I got the album that's what was written on it: "Gloria's Dream". Very, very embarrassing.'

McLeod was similarly appalled although he remembers the song differently. 'It was an obvious rip-off but Fowley pushed so hard, telling us to come up with something with the "Gloria" riff. We came up with a stoned thing we called "Levitation", but that wouldn't do for Fowley – it had to be "Gloria's Dream".

The band escaped England when they were booked to play Copenhagen with The Pretty Things. McLeod recalls: 'We played for 10,000 people and it was bloody wonderful. We went down a bomb and the money was ten times what we were making at home. We went there again in June '66 and never came back. We played as Them but it wasn't as if people felt conned. We were there and they liked us. Maybe if Van's band had gone there they'd have liked them better – I don't know. But they liked us – except once at a jazz festival in Belgium. The crowd started throwing bottles so we all gave them the finger and walked off.'

The band's demise was muddled. 'We had a week and a half in Sweden working our way up to almost the Arctic Circle and back. In Stockholm we had three gigs on the last night and we had lots of money,' recalls McLeod. 'In the hotel we were throwing it in the air and watching it rain down. It was near Christmas and John and I went to Copenhagen. Then we got a message from the roadie that Jackie and Ray Henderson, our manager, were going home with the gear. Jackie and Ray must have made the decision it wasn't going on. It had not been discussed and I was left to scratch my head for a month saying, "Is this going on or not?" It was the end of January when I finally got Mark on the phone and he said, "Yeah, the band has split up." I never saw John or Mark again. And Mark died last year [2002] and John in '84. And I didn't see Jackie again until 1985.'

McAuley remembers the band's demise more pithily. 'It was bound to split. I didn't want to carry on.'

The band's album slipped out the following year, comprising the tracks recorded in London with Fowley and others recorded in Denmark. McLeod only found out when he saw the album in a shop. 'There it was – *Them Belfast Gypsies*. I had never heard of Belfast Gypsies till then. It was Fowley's way of getting around the name problem; was it *Belfast Gypsies* by Them? Or *Them* by The Belfast Gypsies?'

'They put "Them" on the sleeve instead of "The" – *Them Belfast Gypsies*,' muses McAuley bitterly. 'You'd have to pay me to play that album.'

Confusingly, one track – 'People Let's Freak Out' – had already been released as a single under the name Freaks of Nature. 'Fowley denies all knowledge and so do we,' asserts McLeod. 'I think they couldn't use the name Them in the UK, so had to come up with something else, and the LP hadn't been released so nobody had seen the name Belfast Gypsies.' In fact McLeod isn't quite right, for 'Gloria's Dream' had, unbeknownst to the band, previously appeared as a UK single, on Island, under the name Belfast Gipsies (*sic*). 'I never knew that until recently,' grimaces McLeod.

McLeod continued to work in Denmark and Finland as a guitarist and drummer, mainly with Eero and Jussi and the Boys, before returning to Northern Ireland in 1972. 'I never played the guitar or drums again,' he explains. 'But I took up the Irish pipes and I've been playing them ever since, just for friends. I'd had enough of the music business – but not of playing music and that's why I wanted to play something that had no connection with making money.'

McAuley, meanwhile, returned to Dublin and formed The Cult with future folk superstar Paul Brady. 'Paul played very good guitar and very good piano at the time. It was back to the old R&B roots, but then, hanging around with all the Luke Kellys and Ronnie Drews, I'd picked up that folk thing and I wanted to merge that.'

However, in 1969 he diverted to Beirut with the League of Gentlemen – 'I almost got killed; some Arab pulled a gun on me in a club' – before returning to the UK where he formed the duo Trader Horne, the line-up of which must, at the time, have seemed truly bizarre. McAuley was a Belfast blueser, battered and battle-scarred after his bruising experiences in Them and The Belfast Gypsies. His new partner, Judy Dyble, a singer and electric autoharp player, was, frankly, posh looking and sang with a refined south-of-England accent that was somewhat upmarket of the average BBC newsreader. Yet, the unlikely combination of such apparently incompatible talents created a small miracle in *Morning Way*, a glorious album whose strange, ethereal beauty is compelling.

Pre-Trader Horne Dyble had sung with Fairport Convention and Giles, Giles & Fripp, the prototype King Crimson. 'Fairport decided they weren't happy and wanted a different singer,' explains Dyble of her replacement by Sandy Denny. 'Giles, Giles & Fripp was fun, but I keep leaving bands before they do anything! Then I met Jackie.'

'The problem was the press saw it as a boy/girl thing,' recalls McAuley. 'It wasn't: we were just two musicians in a band. We done photo sessions where they were pushing us together: "Put your arm around her." I couldn't handle the phoniness. In those days I was very weak. I could be persuaded to do anything. I never could stand by my convictions like Van always did. I was always very envious of him, that he had the strength to do that. No matter what anybody says about him, there's nobody can knock him for that.'

On the almost totally acoustic *Morning Way* both McAuley and Dyble variously sing lead and harmony, and play a dizzying array of instruments – in McAuley's case guitar, harpsichord, organ, piano, flute, congas and celeste; in Dyble's, electric autoharp and piano. Superficially the album is a gentle, flower-power artefact, and yet the blend of instruments and voices creates an unsettling, hallucinatory effect, with instruments dropping in and out of the mix and with each song linked by the same insistently catchy but faintly creepy and rather ominous musical motif.

'The original concept was to do children's songs, like "Jenny May" and "Luke That Never Was", but the concept broadened,' explains McAuley, who wrote ten of the thirteen songs.

'The songs were fairly children-orientated,' agrees Dyble. 'That was fine by me: they were good tunes, nice harmonies, played well.'

Dyble herself wrote two songs and also sings crisply enunciated lead on the album's only non-original track, 'Down And Out Blues', which features a striking alto-flute solo from Ray Elliott, who had joined Them after McAuley's departure. 'A fabulous musician,' enthuses McAuley. 'He also plays bass clarinet – there's a great collection of different instruments on the album.' But the standout track is McAuley's wonderfully stirring, exuberant 'Sheena'. 'Everything was very flowery then and it was about the kind of girl you'd see at parties, dancing away to herself, in total outer space,' explains McAuley.

Disappointingly the band only released one other single, 'Here Comes The Rain'/'Goodbye Mercy Kelly', before splitting. 'My fault,' admits Dyble. 'I left in a tantrum. It wasn't Jackie's fault.'

McAuley briefly replaced Dyble with Saffron Summerfield. 'She was a folk singer picked up by the management. That was another engineered thing: "Keep it going, earn some money," and all this kind of shit. But my heart wasn't in it and once something's gone, it's gone.

'I started picking up electric guitar. I was so into Buddy Guy. I loved that sound – it could sing for me where I couldn't really sing myself, and I joined One with Rosko Gee, who later joined Traffic, and Adam Marsh. They got me a Telecaster and I worked really, really hard to get it together.'

In 1971 McAuley released a superb, self-titled solo album, accompanied by outstanding British jazzers such as flugelhorn player Henry Lowther and bassist Roy Babbington. 'I never gigged any of the album. I never considered myself a solo artist. I always wanted to be part of a band. I could never talk to an audience or look at an audience. In fact in those days when I was playing guitar I'd turn my back if there was a solo.'

Thereafter McAuley played in Mackerel Sky, with Rod Demick (ex-People, Wheels) and with Christian rocker Bryn Haworth. 'Fabulous band – Bruce Rowland [Grease Band, Fairport Convention] on drums, Rabbit [Free, The Who] on keyboards – but nobody wanted to share a room with Bryn. He's a

Bible-basher. God is everywhere but you don't want him in your hotel room when you want to sleep.'

McAuley also put in four years with Lonnie Donegan. 'I've the greatest respect for him. He was like a dad to me. A hard man to work for at times but very funny. I loved the guy.'

McAuley worked extensively as a session man. 'I done two albums with Rick Wakeman. Very, very hard going. The charts were phenomenal – pages and pages, like the Bible.' And in 1982 he wrote a hit, 'Dear John', for Status Quo. 'That was written with [ex-Merseybeats, Roxy Music bassist] Johnny Gustafson. It got to number ten.'

For most of the Eighties and into the Nineties McAuley concentrated on Celtic rockers Poor Mouth, recording albums like *Gael Force* in 1990. But a catastrophe nearly wrecked his career. 'I fell onto a plate and it cracked and the corner went into my hand and I cut three tendons. I had therapy for nine months.'

In the Nineties McAuley released further solo albums, such as *Headspin* in 1994, and *Shadowboxing* in 1998. The latter includes a strikingly original version of blues legend Robert Johnson's 'Come On In My Kitchen'. 'I was kicking around a wee idea for a little ethereal tune with pipes. I liked 'Come On In My Kitchen' and I got the idea to tie the two up and go from a raw blues/slide thing into this pipey Irish tune and then into a light restaurant-jazzy thing and it turned out very interesting. And I think Robert's very happy with it, the last time I spoke to him!'

McAuley, however, reckons that 2000's *Bad Day At Black Rock* is his finest achievement. 'Of all my albums it's the only one I would play,' he declares.

The album is virtually a true solo album for, apart from Esther Hackett's accordion on a few tracks, McAuley sings and plays everything himself, multi-tracking assorted acoustic guitars, dobros and mandolas. 'It was rushed and low budget and there are clangers here and there but I like it very much.'

The album's opening track is 'Dynamite Town', a place which in the lyrics is also referred to as Dodge City. 'It's a light-hearted country-rock thing about Belfast, and it's typical Belfast humour from the bad old days: Dodge City means dodging the bullets.'

A highlight is a sinister-sounding reinvention of Robert Johnson's classic 'Crossroads Blues'. 'The music is my own but I put his lyric to it. There are a lot of guys playing Robert Johnson songs just like Robert Johnson. That doesn't appeal to me. It's very clever but I haven't time to learn to play like someone else – because at the end of the day you can put the other person's record on.'

Nearly 40 years after his troubled times in Them, McAuley remains a highly creative musician whose early albums have reappeared on CD to acclaim and whose newer albums – including a surprise return to electric blues with the Harbour Band's 2003 album *Live In The Spirit Store* – are released to excellent reviews. 'I'm happier now than I've ever been,' he asserts, 'but every so often the ghost of Them comes back to haunt me!'

Truth, 1970: (clockwise from left)
Curt Bachman,
Jim Armstrong,
Reno Smith,
Kenny McDowell

LIFE AFTER THEM
JIM ARMSTRONG & KENNY McDOWELL

Jim Armstrong's career in the Van Morrison-fronted Them had collapsed igno-
miniously, in bitterness, disillusionment and financial mayhem; his career in
the Kenny McDowell-fronted Them had collapsed similarly. Both times he had
had to send an SOS to his parents to send him the money for his fare home
from America.

But after a short interlude back in Belfast with Sk'boo, again with Kenny
McDowell on vocals, Armstrong felt ready once more to do battle with the
rock 'n' roll bizness. 'I got phone calls from a guy called Scott Doneen in
Chicago – they had wanted me to join Rotary Connection [with Minnie
Ripperton] when I was over there. Now they wanted me to go back out and I
said, "Well, Kenny's in the band." And they said, "OK, we need a singer." So
we scrubbed Sk'boo and went to Chicago and they set us up in apartments and
we drew a wage every week.'

The two ex-pats formed Truth with bassist Curt Bachman (ex-
Buckinghams) and drummer Reno Smith (ex-Baby Huey & The Babysitters).
'Curt goes – typical Yank – "What sign are you all?" We were all fire signs. He
was a Leo and I was a Leo. "Hey, wow!" And Reno and I hit it off right away.
He was going, "Hey, give me five!" We were just locked in. It was good fun.'

McDowell takes up the story. 'We parted from the management guys who'd
brought us over and we finished up with a guy called Aaron Russo who has
since made himself famous managing Bette Midler and has produced movies.
It was an article in *Billboard* that started things off with him. This writer had
come to see the band unbeknownst to us on more than one occasion and
obviously liked it and he wrote this absolutely cracking article in *Billboard*,
which is the Bible of the industry, so that started a little flutter of excitement
and Aaron Russo was one of those ones who flew in to Chicago to see us play.

'I remember him saying he liked the band but he didn't like me. So the band
had a meeting about this and decided, "No, Kenny's got to be part of it because
he's involved writing some of the tunes and so on," so he said he would come
back and have another look. The next night I thought, Fuck that, and I got
into it and it was enough to change his mind. I think maybe the first night I'd
smoked too much drugs and I was probably a wee bit too laid back for him.

'We always knew we wanted [ex-Them colleague] Ray Elliott to join the
band so we sent for Ray as well and he came over. When you go to the States
you need to have a few bob in your pocket to make sure you can look after
yourself when you're there so Aaron Russo had sent him $1,000 so that he

Trevor Hodgett · Includes material previously published in *Wavelength* (March 1997; September 1999), *Belfast Magazine* (October 1989), *Rock'n'Reel* (spring 1990), *Irish News* (26 May 1995); plus additional material

would have $1,000 in his pocket when he came in – which he would then give back to Aaron. But Ray thought it was for him and went on the binge in London and bought himself this, that and the other, so he didn't have any money left when he arrived. So they turned him round at the airport and put him on the next plane back home. So we had to send him another $1,000 and another ticket to get him back over again!

'Obviously when Ray had left the States before, when he left Them, he left under great strain and with very little money, so when he got a chance to come back over again he swore he was going to play it dead straight – he was only there for the money. But by the end of the first night he had pills down his neck and he had smoked drugs and drunk lots of booze so his good intentions just went by the way.'

The band gigged regularly. 'We were playing all the Chicago gigs and were the house band in Beavers,' recalls Armstrong.

'That was our regular,' agrees McDowell. 'It was quite a small, intimate place but I saw people like The Allman Brothers, Rod Stewart, Tim Hardin and Buddy Rich play there. One night they needed a band at short notice. Reno and Curt and I, who used to share a house together, had taken acid and Jim, who was living with his wife Anna up in the other side of the city, had settled down for the night with his bottle of Scotch, so by the time we rang each other and got it organised we were flying. It was a strange night but obviously we managed it because they let us come back to the club and play again after that!'

The band recorded a film soundtrack, *Cum Laude Fraud*. 'We finished up appearing in it, playing in the background,' laughs Armstrong. 'We saw it in the Playboy Theatre in Chicago. Most embarrassing. Totally fuckedable movie. But the band was shit hot. We would practise for hours and hours. Pick a tempo: "OK, 12/8." Jam for three hours in 12/8. Then stop and put your finger in an iced beer! Without a doubt that was the best band I ever played in. There was no pulling in opposite directions. We were all plugged into one little box.'

One gig in the Aragon Ballroom in Chicago proved unforgettable. 'Some looner gets on stage starkers, totally out of his head on acid,' recalls Armstrong. 'Afterwards we were sitting in the band room upstairs. The looner comes in starkers, walks past, just about dick height, walks to the open window, "Hey, looks good," and leaps out. We thought he was on a ledge. We went over: he had bounced off a car and was lying on the road all crumpled up. We thought we were going to be done for illegal immigrancy, so we all did a runner. He broke two ankles and his wrist.'

The band signed to Epic, who arranged for them to record in London. McDowell explains: 'We'd been over there eighteen months and we decided there's three of the guys from the British Isles and since British bands are very big over there we'd try and use this to our own advantage. We decided we'd go back home and have a rest and see the family and then record in London. And then we'd go back to the States again having a British album, as opposed to an American album. But communication collapsed between New York and

London and we never did get recording the album.'

Armstrong adds his perspective on the disaster. 'We were home in February – then heads rolled in Epic. By the time Epic sent for the band in September to go and record, it was too late. Reno had moved off into Europe and Curt had gone off with a stripper from the 77 Sunset Strip club and was finally deported. I just got totally fed up with the whole thing. Kenny said, "Let's do it, let's do it," and I was saying, "I can't hack this; this is awful. This is the third time. I hate the scene."'

Decades later the release of *Of Them And Other Tales*, which comprised demos and soundtrack music from *Cum Laude Fraud* (Epilogue Records, 1994), confirmed what a tragedy the demise of Truth was, for the originality, adventurousness and virtuosity thrillingly demonstrated on the album provide compelling evidence that Truth had the talent to become massively successful.

With his musical dreams in shreds Armstrong joined the Civil Service. A shattering experience? 'It was. I said, "I'm going to have to get a job." I'd walked out of a nice secure job in 1965 and here I was in 1971, six years later, having had my fare paid home twice by other people. I still had nothing. Just a guitar and a suitcase. You want a bit of comfort. You want to have a house, a car, a stereo. I didn't have that.'

A part-time musician again, Jim played with cabaret singer Roly Stewart, who was resident in the Trocadero club – 'I just switched off,' – and then rejoined Kenny McDowell, who had been singing with a showband, The College Boys. 'The Troc was in Cromac Street and it was quite hairy – they'd be shooting up and down the street. Then The College Boys' guitar player left and Kenny rang me and said, "Do you fancy joining?" My first gig was the Stardust in the Bogside in Derry after the army opened the Bogside [no-go area]. All these wee girls saying, "Are you from Belfast? What religion are you?"'

The collapse of Truth had left McDowell devastated. 'It knocks you sideways and you begin to think, Why? I stopped playing. I didn't really get any offers until the guys from The College Boys contacted me and even then I had to do an audition. I had to actually go down and sing a few tunes with them.'

McDowell and Armstrong transformed the band, as McDowell explains. 'It's weird when you think of the name, College Boys, and you think of the showband thing but we finished up playing stuff like Sons Of Champlin and Blood, Sweat & Tears and playing the blues and, typical me, trying to pick tunes that are good tunes that nobody has ever heard of before rather than take the easy road.

'But because we were playing this strange music the gigs dwindled, so Jim and I then went to play in Reunion – all of a sudden we were playing a club circuit and we were a club band playing things that were in the chart. But we also changed that band round as well because we finished up playing stuff like Sonny Curtis and Dobie Gray and Tim Hardin and even the blues when we should have been playing "Crystal Chandeliers".'

In the mid-Seventies the glorious Pound-music-club era began with Armstrong and McDowell playing five times a week in two bands – Spike and first Reunion and then Bronco. But finally an onstage disagreement occurred. 'I packed my guitar and walked off,' admits Armstrong.

'We had to finish the gig without him,' declares McDowell.

Armstrong formed Light, while McDowell continued with Bronco, who brought in ace blues guitarist Ronnie Greer. 'On paper Bronco would have ate us. But we had more energy,' asserts Armstrong. Light recorded a self-titled album. 'That was one of the first rock albums cut here but we lost a lot when it was cut. The LP sold very well and I got royalties for it although not much.'

Armstrong next joined the reformed Them for the shambolic 1979 German tour. Another stint with Light followed and then another reunion with McDowell in Sk'boo. McDowell explains: 'I guess I was maybe putting a lot of pressure on Ronnie to give up his time and he just didn't have the time, with his day job. So I finished up ringing Jim again.'

The band recorded an EP comprising old Truth tracks. 'The sound was awful,' laments Armstrong.

'Horrendous,' groans McDowell. 'Not that the playing was bad – it was all down to the mix and downloading it from tape to vinyl was the big problem. It came out like a tin can and going at 100 miles per hour. I didn't rate it at all.'

But after several successful years, resident at the Pound and then the Errigle Inn, another rift occurred. 'The whole thing for the band was that Kenny sang well and I played lots of guitar,' argues Armstrong. 'But it got that if I played a solo Kenny went and sat in a corner and scowled, which annoyed me, so then I wouldn't play. But Kenny is a great singer – the best I've ever played with.'

'I guess it had run its course,' sighs McDowell. 'We'd done the Errigle every Saturday night for eight years. At the time I thought, What the fuck's going down here? But I guess relationships had strained slightly and I guess Jim felt he wanted to do something different.'

Thereafter Armstrong led various line-ups of his own band, The Jim Armstrong Blues Band, and seemed terminally trapped in the nightmare situation of being a world-class guitarist doomed to a life in the Civil Service and poorly paid gigs in Belfast bars. The lack of fulfilment must have been almost unbearable. 'OK, I could say, "Yes,"' he acknowledged at the time. 'I can listen to most guitar players and say, "I can do that." It's frustrating, yeah. It's probably what messes me up a bit. But I had the opportunities to do all that. I turned down good jobs because I wanted to play with people I got on with – I turned down The James Gang, with Joe Walsh, and Minnie Ripperton. You have to be a total bastard to get on in the business. You've got to walk all over people. I didn't feel like doing that.'

And yet, miraculously, in the Nineties Armstrong found himself able to ditch the Civil Service and once more become a full-time player, on the international circuit, by joining forces with Them founder member Eric Wrixon in

Sk'boo, 1969: (l–r) Kenny McDowell, Ricky McCutcheon, Jim Armstrong, Colm Connolly

The Belfast Blues Band, who have carved out a niche for themselves on the lucrative European club circuit. In 2002 he was able to say, 'I've played in more countries in the last year than I've ever worked in – Denmark, Norway, Sweden, Germany – East and West – Austria, Switzerland, Liechtenstein, Italy. I'm doing 200 gigs abroad a year – I'm only home for a week or ten days at a time – and the reception from audiences is amazing.'

Meanwhile McDowell has continued as a stalwart of the local scene playing in various line-ups of Sk'boo, leading the western-swing-style Hens' Teeth, and, currently, co-leading The Kenny McDowell/Ronnie Greer Band who released *Live At The Island* in 2003.

'My voice has improved,' asserts McDowell, 'There's more character to it because of getting older and more experienced and hearing other things. Having tried all the different styles of music I can bring a bit of the blues to a country tune and vice versa. Having tried them all I can pull wee bits and pieces out and add them together, which maybe makes up the sound of Kenny McDowell.'

Postscript: In 2003 Armstrong left the Belfast Blues Band and re-formed his own band.

John Wilson at the Limelight, Belfast,
mid-Nineties

LIFE AFTER THEM
JOHN WILSON

The mighty Van aside, few indeed are the ex-members of Them who have gone on to bigger and better things. But John Wilson, who drummed on 1965's *Them Again*, can truly claim that his sojourn with the Belfast legends was but a stepping stone. For after restoring his post-Them spirits with local bands Derek & The Sounds and Cheese, Wilson played with Rory Gallagher in Taste, one of the most acclaimed and successful bands in Europe in the late Sixties, and subsequently worked with the highly respected Stud, as well as appearing on hit records by Medicine Head, Jive Bunny and others.

Wilson recalls how he joined forces with Gallagher. 'Rory was playing with Norman D'Amery and Eric Kitteringham in the original Taste at that time and, as you do if you dig somebody, you always say, "There's my number. If you ever need anybody, give us a ring." The story goes that they were set to sign with Polydor, who said Rory'd need to get a different drummer and bass player if Taste were going to go on and do things. I've a sneaking suspicion that there were other reasons involved, but anyway, Charlie McCracken and myself were asked to join.

'It was on a Tuesday and Taste were playing Romano's Ballroom in Belfast on the Wednesday, so we went down to the gig. Rory and Eric and Norman played and then said their farewells and then Rory and Charlie and I went off to Scotland on the Thursday and did the first gig, and there we were, on the road with Rory.

'The music would have been blues-based, but anything went, with lots of improvising, and the more inventive you could be the better. Rory's inventiveness at that time was endless and he was always open to rhythmic interpretations. I might play something, or Charlie, and Rory would be on to it. Or he might play something and we'd be off like a rat up a spout after it. Taste could easily have played one tune for a whole show, if we'd have wanted to.

'Most musicians would strive for a situation whereby when you play you actually leave the planet. Time stands still and nothing matters, just the playing. It's hard to get to that point, but playing with Rory and Charlie you got to that point every night. Every night! I can remember many occasions when we came off stage in the early days, that we'd have spent a lot of time just staring at each other or hugging, simply because we were just gone.'

Taste rapidly became one of the most popular club and festival acts on the circuit in the late Sixties. 'It was exciting in as much as you were reaching a bigger audience, but we never felt anything from a financial point of view. We

Trevor Hodgett · Includes material previously published in *Blueprint* (August 1995), the *Irish News* (10 February 1996) and *Wavelength* (September 1995); plus additional material

didn't have Rolls Royces or anything like that and we were still living in stinking bedsits. Obviously somebody was doing all right out of it all – but we certainly weren't. But we were young and naive and all we were interested in was the music.'

The band recorded two albums on Polydor: *Taste* and *On The Boards* with *Live* following soon after the band's split. 'I was never satisfied with any Taste recordings. There was no thought put into them. It was straight in and straight out. No overdubbing, no mixing or nothing. Just go in and throw a few tunes together. I certainly have no great fondness for any of them.'

Few remember now that in Taste's early days Gallagher doubled on sax. 'Rory had a vast record collection of all sorts of music and we both had a love for the sax, especially alto, and one of the many things that Rory would have done for me at the time musically was to turn me on to Ornette Coleman. So, yeah, Rory played a bit of sax, and we did gigs where he produced it, much to the amazement of the masses. I'm sure he could have been good, but he didn't pursue it.'

Taste memorably toured America with the Eric Clapton/Ginger Baker/Stevie Winwood/Rick Grech supergroup Blind Faith, along with Delaney & Bonnie. 'Blind Faith were supposed to travel on their own and stay in a big hotel, Delaney & Bonnie were supposed to travel on their own and stay in a medium hotel and we were supposed to travel on our own and stay in a small hotel. But it ended up everybody just travelled on the same bus and stayed together 'cos it was good fun. It was awe-inspiring to play in baseball stadiums and ice rinks, but daunting inasmuch as we were always following in the footsteps of other famous trios, particularly Cream. We worked from the same office, Robert Stigwood's office, as Cream, and we were always referred to as the new Cream, although we were nothing like them.

'One of the things that was difficult for us was that we didn't go in for loads of gear. We just went on stage with a tiny little jazz drum kit, an AC30 amp and a tiny bass amp, and that was it, whereas other bands had Marshall stacks and everything. In those days the opening band on a tour were used to test out the PA rig and the punters would be still trying to get their seats, but we didn't mind. Our attitude was, it doesn't matter whether it's Comber Orange Hall or Shea Stadium, a gig's a gig. You always do your bit, whether it's a small place or a big place.

'We socialised with everybody on the tour and I remember once we all crammed into some club in Chicago to see Muddy Waters: Eric Clapton's there, Rory, Stevie Winwood, everybody. It makes for an exciting evening! Clapton and Winwood and all would have jammed with Muddy, but, unfortunately, Rory, for whatever reasons, basically kept himself to himself on a musical level, at that time.'

Disastrously, relationships in the band began to fracture. 'It was a case of gross mismanagement to let it all go the way it did. The manager Eddie Kennedy's dead now and it's all past history, but it wasn't pleasant for everyone concerned. A lot of things were said at the time which I regretted in hindsight when I found out things, and apologies were later made.'

At the time it was claimed that Rory wanted to take over the band and put his colleagues on a wage. 'It would appear Rory had been led to believe that that's the way the deal had been done all along, whereas Charlie and myself were led to believe all along that it was not like that, so it was a typical case of management divide and conquer. It showed a lack of foresight 'cos if the people concerned had really realised the potential, they'd have sorted things out and made it work. At that time Charlie and I couldn't believe that our manager, who we'd known from Belfast, could do that sort of thing, but Rory realised all was not well and something did not smell right and he felt that the rest of us were all in the same bed together. There was a lot of non-communication which was unfortunate and Rory took it all very bitter.'

The tensions in the band near the end became apparent on stage. Once, legend has it, an irate Wilson lashed out with a drumstick and broke Gallagher's guitar strings. 'Well, no, I wouldn't have broken any strings, but the guitar may have gone out of tune – which meant that me and Charlie would have had to play on our own! Guys in bands can be juvenile at times and near the end we were like that, but bearing in mind we were being fed misinformation by people, which led us to think certain things, it's understandable.'

Another time, in Glasgow, Wilson refused to go back on stage for an encore. 'Rory just went out and did it on his own. I made a complete asshole of myself. It was a dumb thing to do. And the point it highlighted was that, although I was the drummer in the band, the main musical movement in the band was Rory.'

As the band neared collapse they played a highly rated gig at the 1970 Isle of Wight Festival. 'Unfortunately the band was going through a really bad spell. It was near the end and there wasn't a lot of communication between us. A couple of days prior to that we'd had all our equipment stolen, when we were playing the Lyceum in the Strand, so we went to the Isle of Wight with borrowed gear. I'd somebody's bass drum and somebody's tom-tom and it was awful, so although it was a monstrous event it was overshadowed by the vibe we were having with each other, which was unfortunate. So I don't have fond memories of the Isle of Wight.'

Taste, surely on the brink of superstardom, spectacularly self-destructed, with Gallagher estranged from his colleagues and with all three musicians penniless. 'I never got a penny from any Taste recordings in any way, shape or form, not even when they were reissued on CD,' asserts Wilson. 'In Taste we were on a weekly retainer of £30 or something. It paid your rent and bought you food. That's about it. Supposedly money was being invested, but I never got a penny. Nothing. But Taste was the most creative time of my life musically and nothing can take away from the beauty of what we created. The fact that we created great music together transcends everything.'

Gallagher, of course, rebuilt his career with his own band, working successfully through the Seventies and Eighties until ill health undermined him in the

Nineties. Wilson and McCracken stayed together – and catastrophically stayed with the same manager – in Stud, along with future Rod Stewart guitarist/producer Jim Cregan and ex-Animal John Weider, and recorded three highly acclaimed albums. 'We wanted a band that could do everything. We would start a gig with just two acoustic guitars, which would then be joined by a string quartet and went from that to semi-folk-type music to bluegrass to rock to avant-garde jazz – in two hours! It was weird, obscure music that we wanted to play and nobody wanted to listen to!

'But eventually things became blatantly obvious about the management and the band fell apart. Jim joined Cockney Rebel, John Weider went off to the States, Charlie played with Spencer Davis, Kevin Ayers and later Fastway and I kept Stud together with various people, the most famous of whom would be Snowy White. Snowy had roadied with us and then he played with the band while we finished out some gigs and he went on to have a good active career as a session player [for Pink Floyd and others].'

Wilson himself became involved in sessions, playing on Medicine Head's hit 'One And One Is One' and for Leo Sayer and Spencer Davis, and played with the band Brush (sometimes referred to as The Bell/Brush Band) with ex-Skid Row bassist Brush Shiels, before returning to Northern Ireland where he played with a re-formed Skid Row and The Freshmen – Tiger Taylor was the guitar player – before briefly taking a day job. 'It was good financially because I've never made money out of music and now I could get credit and a mortgage. But it was pretending to be somebody else I couldn't cope with so I gave it up.'

He resolved to do the impossible and make a living as a pro drummer in Belfast. 'It's been a hard struggle but I got involved with Ulster Television and BBC shows and I branched out into theatre work and shows like *Jesus Christ Superstar* and *West Side Story* and, good grief, pantos. I was a house player at Hyde Park and Outlet Studios, playing on loads of recordings and I've worked with everybody from Roger Whittaker to Dr John to Jive Bunny to Andy Stewart and with Northern Irish bands like the Jim Armstrong Band, Sk'boo, the Belfast Blues Band, the John Anderson Big Band and the Apex Jazz Band.

'But I couldn't have survived without my wife working and if I have any regrets it's that I didn't do enough for her and the girls. I could've been less selfish. I've always had my way. It's always been "Let John do what he wants." But the first moment I ever held a pair of drumsticks in my hand, as a schoolboy, I knew that that was what I was supposed to be doing and when I'm drumming I'm happy, whether I'm playing at the Isle of Wight Festival in front of hundreds of thousands or at a wee wedding reception.'

Postscript: Owing to the efforts of Donal Gallagher, Rory's brother and long-term manager, Wilson (and Charlie McCracken) finally, three decades late, received a fair settlement for their Taste recordings. They then re-formed Taste, with Sam Davidson replacing Gallagher, and toured Europe and America before the reunion fizzled out.

LIFE AFTER THEM
ERIC WRIXON

To leave one band, Them, when they stood poised on the brink of international stardom, may be regarded as a misfortune. To leave a second band, Thin Lizzy, when they stood similarly poised, looks like carelessness. Keyboard player Eric Wrixon is just such a person – an unfortunate soul who twice had eight score draws on the football pools of life, but on each occasion forgot to mail his coupon. Yet now, with the Belfast Blues Band, Wrixon is at last sampling significant success internationally.

Wrixon still laments the crass management that sabotaged Them. 'There was an in-house producer [Tommy Scott] who foisted a lot of his own third-rate songs onto Them – if he'd allowed Van to develop as a songwriter, then Them could have been on a level with the Stones.'

As we have seen, Wrixon left Them to take his A levels, on successful completion of which he joined The Kings Showband. 'It wasn't really me. What we played was worse than the top twenty. You were allowed a few top-twenty numbers but the rest was country. Basically crap. The next realistic thing that cropped up that was worth doing was Tony & The Telstars, the top group in Belfast. Basically The Telstars started at the age of thirteen and grew up getting ever better until they were eighteen, at which stage I met them. They were incredible: very professional, very slick. The guitarist was Rod Demick, rhythm guitarist was Ernie Graham, bassist was Chrissie Stewart. The drummer left and was replaced by Davy Lutton, later of T-Rex fame, and the singer Tony Ford left, so Ernie and myself started singing a bit. Then the band became The People and became a rhythm-and-blues, Rolling Stones kind of band and was one of the bands that filled the gap that was left in Belfast by Them.'

The band contributed two numbers, 'Well . . . All Right' and 'I'm With You', to *Ireland's Greatest Sounds: Five Top Groups From Belfast's Maritime Club*. 'Those were the two current numbers that got the best crowd reaction and which Ernie felt most comfortable singing. Then Demick was poached by The Wheels who were doing very well in Lancashire, in the northern-soul scene, and for a while we played with [guitarist] Tiger Taylor but Tiger was fairly unreliable. Then Demick and [singer] Brian Rossi from Wheels said, "Why don't you come over to England – we can fix it for you," so The People packed up and went to England. We played Bolton Palais, Preston Locarno, all the Mecca stuff in the north of England, all the northern-soul all-nighter, amphetamine scene, trotting around behind The Wheels. We weren't actually playing soul music – we were playing a mixture of rhythm and blues, folk, rock and soul music.'

Trevor Hodgett: Includes material previously published in *Irish News* (24 March 1995), *Wavelength* (March 1995) and *Ugly Things* (1995); plus additional material

In fact Wrixon soon transferred to The Wheels, with whom he recorded two singles. 'I got a better offer financially. The People at this stage were on £25 a night and The Wheels were on £100 a night and were a very high-profile band. So I joined Wheels and The People got [guitarist] Henry McCullough in to replace me. Wheels were a successful band live, but it was never taken across on record. They were less significant musically but a better live act than Them. They had an incredibly dynamic stage act – the most phenomenal stage act ever to come out of Ireland.'

Wrixon then decamped for Germany with The Never Never Band. 'We were an agency band – everybody's favourite soul backing group in Germany. We played with Sam & Dave and a whole string of Atlantic artists.'

The band were regulars in Hamburg's legendary Star club, where The Beatles had served their apprenticeship. 'Fantastic venue,' enthuses Wrixon. 'All the illegal attractions that nowhere in the UK had. A magical, seedy atmosphere. You were surrounded by 24-hour-licences and prostitution and gangsters. The ultimate experience. We played seven nights a week, eleven hours a night – an hour on, an hour off – with matinées on weekends.'

Returning to Ireland Wrixon joined The Trixons showband, who were managed by Albert Reynolds, who was later, in the Nineties, to become the prime minister of the Irish Republic. 'He was a very down-to-earth guy and I have loads of respect for him. He was a fair man and after some of the early experiences I went through in my career I was prepared to fall over backwards for a man who was fair. I had had years of playing R&B and you were always overdrawn in the bank, always struggling, you owed people money. Then you went into a showband and got £200 a week, you cleared debts, you could live like a human being for a change and take pride that you were making money. We had four Irish top-ten records, but it reached the stage where I thought, This isn't really me – and I've always tried to be true to myself.'

Determined to find musical satisfaction Wrixon left The Trixons and joined forces with guitarist Eric Bell, who, after his early break with Van Morrison and Them Again, had been languishing in showband limbo, and set about forming Thin Lizzy. 'We chanced upon a disaster which was Phil Lynott, who'd just been sacked as Skid Row's singer. They'd finally got themselves a TV show: they took one listen afterwards and said, "Fuck, we're never going to do a TV show like that again," and sacked Phil, because the vocals were so awful.

'Phil was screwed-up completely. He had a chip on his shoulder about being black in Ireland and not knowing who his father was, and the next greatest trauma in his life was getting sacked from Skid Row. He then decided to learn bass – but he never in his life became a good bass player. I was eight years into my career and I didn't have the patience. I didn't want to spend my life waiting for Phil to learn to play bass. I know there are stories in *Irish Rock* [Mark Prendergast, O'Brien Press] saying I used one hand to play and the other one to drink. The hard fact of the matter is Lynott was confused enough if I played with one hand: if I'd used two, he'd have been fucked completely.

'Eric and myself would say, "Have you heard this thing by Deep Purple?". We'd spend an hour and a half learning the keyboard and guitar parts. It would then take five days to get the bass player to play it. After six months of this crap somebody said, "There's not enough money to keep four of us," and I said, "I'll leave!"'

Wrixon returned to Germany. 'I played with Junior Walker, Junior Wells, Buddy Guy . . . I survived as a journeyman pro musician.'

Such a career was of course interrupted by Them's ill-fated 1979 re-formation. 'After that tour life degenerated into playing local gigs and basically bringing the name of Them down, and I left and joined Rob Strong who was steaming ahead at the time. Rob became the father of Andrew Strong of The Commitments, and he was twice as good as Andrew. He's a superb singer; the man is incredible.'

But by the early Eighties Wrixon had become disenchanted with life as a muso. 'No matter how recognised you are as a musician a little voice inside you always says, "How can I measure up in real life with all these people I meet like bank managers and salesmen?" During my years in Germany I'd become bilingual so I did a degree in business studies and marketing and became a certified translator and became European marketing director with a Japanese company. But in 1989 I realised I should be back in music, because you have to wake up in the morning and look in the mirror and say, "That's me, that's not me pretending to be someone else."'

Re-energised, Wrixon formed The Belfast Blues Band, with drummer John

Wilson [ex-Them and Taste], bassist Jackie Flavelle [ex-Chris Barber Band] and guitarist Sam Davidson. 'We want to target the blues circuit in Europe and become established players on that circuit,' he said at the time. 'The idea is to earn your money where earnings are high and have your overheads where it's cheap. We've 120 years of cumulative blues experience and there's more fun as a musician in this band than anything I have ever done. This is the band I would love to have played in since I was sixteen. It's the best band I have ever played in.'

Postscript: The personnel of The Belfast Blues Band evolved, with Wrixon's masterstroke being the recruitment of ex-Them guitar genius Jim Armstrong, but the dream became a reality. Improbably, miraculously, from a base in Northern Ireland, The Belfast Blues Band have made a name for themselves on the European circuit, where they now work for several months a year – but no longer with Armstrong on guitar. 'I had to let Jim go to refresh the band,' claimed Wrixon, early in 2003.

'Eric owed me money and I got fed up asking for it,' alleged Armstrong, who subsequently formed his own band, with Jim Gilchrist on vocals.

LIFE AFTER THEM
ERIC BELL

The immortal guitar lick on Thin Lizzy's 'Whiskey In The Jar' is one of the most beloved in Seventies rock. And the man who played it is none other than Eric Bell, who had left Van Morrison's Them Again band so ignominiously after a drunken, shambolic gig at Queen's University rag ball.

Between his inglorious exit from Them Again and his emergence as a groovy pop star with Lizzy, Bell paid his dues in showbands, first turning pro with The Bluebeats in Glasgow. 'We lived all in one room – eight of us – for nearly two years,' he recalls. 'We came back in the same shirts we went in. I think I had a shirt and a tie and a guitar strap in my case and that was it. Then I went to Leeds for two years with another Irish showband – Ray Elliott, the sax player out of Them, was in that band.'

Returning home Bell replaced Gary Moore in Shades Of Blue, regulars in the legendary Maritime Hotel. 'It was a real dive, but it had an absolutely amazing atmosphere. Whatever it takes, it had it. The ironic thing was they shut it for a few weeks and did it all up, and nobody went back 'cos it lost all its atmosphere!'

Next came the Dublin-based Dreams Showband. 'Like being in the army. You weren't supposed to do this and that. You had to smile on stage. The manager used to stand in the balcony and if you weren't smiling he'd go . . . [And here Eric puts his fingers in his mouth and stretches his lips into a rictus smile.] You'd get a drop in your wages. I couldn't come to terms with it.

'Around that time I was listening to blues albums and Hendrix, and I went one night to see Skid Row in this club. I was in my showband suit and I had really short hair, so everybody was looking at me, and I was really stoned as well. I'd never heard anything like it. Gary Moore was playing guitar and they were absolutely ridiculous, absolutely unbelievable. And I said, "What am I fucking doing in a showband?"

'So I went to the Dreams manager and said, "I'm leaving." He says, "What are you going to do?" and I says, "I'm going to form a group," and he says, "Have you any musicians?" "No." "Have you a van?" "No." "What numbers are you going to do?" "Don't know." "Have you an amp?" "No." So he said, "You're making a big mistake!"

'But I had an idea and it was becoming too strong, so I threw away the suit and I started wearing hippy clothes and letting my hair grow. Then I met Eric Wrixon who was the original organist with Them. He had left The Trixons showband and was doing the same thing as me. So we struck up an acquaintance

Trevor Hodgett · Includes material previously published in *British Blues Review* (June 1990), *Blueprint* (March 1996), *Wavelength* (October 1997) and the *Irish News* (1 September 1995; 5 September 1998); plus additional material

Eric Bell,
onstage in Dublin,
mid-Seventies

and we went to the Countdown club one night and we took half a tab of acid each. This band Orphanage came on with Phil Lynott singing and Brian Downey was the drummer. Afterwards I went into the changing room and I said, "My name's Eric Bell. I used to be with The Dreams showband" – they looked at me with great disapproval when I mentioned showbands – "but I'm into blues and I'm trying to form a band. Do you know any bass players or drummers?" So Phil said, "If we hear of anybody we'll let you know. What pub do you drink in?" And at that point I looked at him – on acid – and I seen his face melting and I went, "Yeah!" That's all I said: "Yeah!" They asked me what was wrong and I said, "It's my first trip on acid," and immediately I said that they seemed to change towards me. So Phil said, "We'll form a band on two conditions: if I can start playing bass – I'm taking lessons from [Skid Row's] Brush Shiels – and if we do some of my songs."'

Bell and Wrixon convened with Lynott and Downey for a jam a few days later. 'It was in this cellar which was totally covered in water – we had to walk over planks to get over – and there was a little alcove you couldn't stand up in. Phil didn't know where he was on bass. We were playing a blues in C and he went off somewhere in F sharp.'

Nevertheless, Thin Lizzy was born. 'But one day the manager said, "There's not too much money around. I think we're going to have to go three-piece." So Eric Wrixon goes, "When do you want me to leave?" Because the bass player couldn't leave, the drummer couldn't leave, the guitar player couldn't leave.'

The band began to take off. 'After four months there were people queuing up outside everywhere we played. I used to say to Phil, "I wonder who we're on with tonight?"! [thinking the queues were for the other band.] I just couldn't believe what had happened.'

The band recorded their first LP, *Thin Lizzy*, in London. 'We recorded in the same studio where John Mayall had recorded the *Bluesbreakers* album with Eric Clapton, so it was a big deal for us. The producer was Scott English, who wrote "Hi Ho Silver Lining", and he had a bag of grass about the size of a pillow case!'

Lizzy began gigging in England. 'It was desperate. Embarrassing, really. English audiences all sat down in the lotus position, smoked dope and watched every note you played, whereas Irish audiences got pissed and jumped up and down. All the English players had great clothes and the guitar players would be out front, throwing all these shapes, going, "Whoooaaah!" with the foot up on the monitor, so we were a bit overawed. We thought the English musicians were better but they weren't – they just looked better. Once we came to terms with that we started building a steady following.

'Our first album was very Irish, and like every band on your first album you've got maybe eight or nine of your best songs and you've played them and played them. Your second album creeps up very quickly and you haven't got the material, so you have to rush, so the second album [*Shades Of A Blue Orphanage*] had a few fillers.'

The band's breakthrough came in 1973 with 'Whiskey In The Jar', which emerged from a rehearsal-hall jam. 'Our manager Ted Carroll says, "Play that again, I think you have a hit." I went, "Come on, man – we left Ireland to get away from 'Whiskey In The Jar'!'

The manager's judgement prevailed and the song was recorded and released. 'For three months it didn't do a thing. We had to go to Germany on this horrible tour to stay alive. We were playing wine bars full volume. A guy would be looking into his girlfriend's eyes, with a bottle of wine, and the wine would be jumping up and down on the table. Me and Phil had a fist fight on that tour – the only fight we ever had. Then we got a telegram saying, "Congratulations! Whiskey number 20. Come home."'

After Lizzy's third album, *Vagabonds Of The Western World*, in 1973, Bell packed it in. 'It was ill health – too much drink – and also we weren't allowed to jam on stage anymore. We had to play the same every night and I said, "I might as well have stayed in the showbands."'

Bell returned to guest with Lizzy on their 1983 tour. 'I felt like a stranger, to be honest, 'cos I hadn't that much in common with them any longer.'

On 4 January 1986 Phil Lynott died, aged 34. 'Brian Downey phoned me and said, "Eric, I've got some bad news for you. Philip's just died." It was the heroin,' sighs Eric, grimly miming plunging a needle into his arm.

How does Eric remember Lynott? 'He was extremely romantic and incredibly, unbelievably determined. If he wanted to do something there was nothing stood in his way. He loved fame and fortune. From the early days people used to ask him in interviews, "What do you want?" – "I want to be rich and famous!" That's all he said.'

Since leaving Lizzy Eric has toured and recorded extensively, firstly with ex-Jimi Hendrix bassist Noel Redding, with whom he occasionally reunited until Noel's death in 2003, and subsequently with his own blues band, who are regulars on the European blues circuit. He has also toured Europe with Bo Diddley, a mean, embittered dude by all accounts. 'No! He's not bitter at all! I used to go to sleep in the van with my head on his shoulder!'

Bell has also released an excellent album, *Live At Ronnie Scott's*, with Main Squeeze. 'That was the band that backed Bo Diddley. [Ex-John Mayall drummer] Keef Hartley was in it and [ex-Alexis Korner keyboard player] Victor Brox and [ex-Colosseum saxophonist] Dick Heckstall-Smith.'

In 1996 he released *Live Tonite!* recorded in Gothenburg and Helsingborg, on the Swedish label BMA Records. The album, on which Bell is accompanied by bass and drums, includes long-time staples of his live shows such as Them's 'Baby Please Don't Go', Van Morrison's 'Madame George', Thin Lizzy's 'Whiskey In The Jar' and Freddie King's 'The Stumble'. The totally self-written 1998 album, *Irish Boy*, a departure from Bell's normal blues idiom, is dedicated to his great contemporary and friend Rory Gallagher, whose death affected him deeply. 'It was terrible,' he sighs.

Bell has continued to gig and record into the twenty-first century, returning

to blues and to live albums with 2002's *A Blues Night In Dublin*, which was described in a *Record Collector* review as 'a damn fine live album' – which, of course, is no less than we'd expect from this great Belfast bluesman, whose position on the contemporary European blues scene is as secure and unassailable as his position in Irish rock history.

John McLaughlin,
Cork Opera House,
October 1995

THE MAHAVISHNU
& THE MAN (UNCORKED)

When the quietly admired Cork Jazz Festival announced the elusive John McLaughlin as one of its two headline attractions for its October 1995 event, there was much excitement. Its other 'big name' was Van Morrison, much less elusive and in the middle of his (still continuing) monochrome period – black suit, black hat, shades and an understandably dour-looking Georgie Fame on the (presumably thankless) task of cheerleading from his organ stool.

Strangely, the Morrison and McLaughlin shows were to happen in succession at the same venue, but not on the same bill. Audiences would have to file out and file in again – even those with tickets for both events. Somebody should have realised this was a disaster waiting to happen, as indeed turned out to be the case. I was lucky enough to secure review commissions for each show, and to secure a photographer's pass from the festival – an accreditation that Van and his flunkies, proactively patrolling the aisles, held no regard for on the night. Not that they seemed to hold that much regard for McLaughlin either. 'We were ripped off!' he'd roared, right after the show – '*Ripped off!*' – memorably lapsing from mid-Atlantic into some vestige of a Yorkshire accent and instantaneously combusting any notion of 'Mahavishnu John McLaughlin', beacon of otherworldly bliss and serenity, scattering to the cognoscenti the secrets of Truth encrypted in billion-mile-an-hour flurries of modal scales and complex rhythms (characteristically delivered during onstage situations involving garments of white cheesecloth, double-necked guitars and blistering volume). Clearly, times had changed.

This was McLaughlin's first appearance in Ireland for 30 years, but he was only an hour and a bit into his incendiary performance (albeit with no sign of the cheesecloth) when it became apparent that somebody, from the side of the stage, was trying to interrupt his locked-in state of bliss. The stage manager, one presumes, was more concerned with clearing one audience, wheeling another in and shifting the onstage pot plants around for the midnight arrival of The Man (in Black). The earthly presence of the God of Fusion was plainly of no interest to this individual, and – possibly for the first time ever – the stage manager of an international jazz festival pulled the plug on John McLaughlin. And John McLaughlin was not happy.

His dressing room door was, I recall, wide open; Van's, one couldn't help but notice, lay somewhere behind a squad of burly individuals stopping people getting anywhere near it. (Frankly, I wondered, why would anyone want to?) John McLaughlin doesn't give interviews at the best of times, and this wasn't

Colin Harper

even close. 'No chance,' the festival's PR had said.

'He's only done one in the last three years,' said the record company, 'and that was on the phone.'

Here then, seething with bile after an inglorious ejection from the stage, was the man who had turned down *The Irish Times*, a national newspaper, only a day or two earlier. 'So, John, hi . . . sorry to hear about the Van stuff, too bad ... great show. Er, can we do an interview sometime?'

Remarkably, the answer was yes. 'You set it up,' he'd said. Two months later we were locked in journalistic combat over cups of tea (virtuosi-tea?) at London's Langham Hilton. But that's a story for another day.

So what, then, of Van? What indeed. Intriguing as the fellow's whole 'boorish genius' enigma may be, I have yet to encounter for myself the transcendental concert experience that his apologists (what a fine word that is!) go on about. And, as time goes on, I find myself increasingly less interested in parting with any more of my time or money in pursuit of that fabled goal. Better, perhaps, to just stay at home and stick on a CD of *Common One*. Or perhaps something by John McLaughlin . . .

VAN MORRISON
CORK JAZZ FESTIVAL

It's midnight Saturday at Cork Opera House and it's a vintage night for Van watchers. The Man has a new band, it's their debut performance, it's being filmed for TV, there's an album in the can and only the fearsome reputation of one man in Ireland could have prompted the stage manager of an international jazz festival to pull the plug on John McLaughlin ten minutes before the end of his set.

McLaughlin – the real coup for the festival – was playing his own show in the same venue prior to Van, and he wasn't amused. Neither, one imagines, were the TV crew, as Van repeatedly insisted on lowering the lights to something approaching the visual quality of a nocturnal wildlife documentary. Photographers with legitimate passes who still felt they weren't wasting their time had to contend with somebody Van was sending round to tell them they were. Regardless of the music, this was Van doing what Van does best, and for once he actually seemed to be enjoying himself.

Musically, though, the bottom line is that Morrison likes jazz but with the best will in the world he's not a jazz singer. He may have the impenetrable life-darkness of a pre-war blues man, the mystical, metaphysical predilections of the literary greats and the techniques of a soul singer but he simply doesn't have the diction, range or emotional breadth to be a great jazz vocalist.

That said, his music has always lent itself to improvisation and the new band do feature some of the best players around – Guy Barker on trumpet and Alan Skidmore on tenor sax in particular. Robin Aspland (piano), Alec Dankworth (bass), Leo Green (tenor), Ralph Salwins (drums) and Georgie Fame – sole survivor of The Man's last outfit – on Hammond completed the line-up.

Green's outrageous, swaggering persona and F.R. Leavis shirt-and-pin-stripe situation provided a potentially explosive counterpoint to Van's serious-artist obsession, while The Man himself was happy to grind through a mixed bag of standards including, most successfully, a disciplined stab at Ray Charles' 'You Don't Know Me', and revealing selections from his own enviable oeuvre. For all the beauty and warmth of 'No Guru, No Method, No Teacher' and 'Did Ye Get Healed?', the refrain of 'Raincheck' (*Don't let the bastards grind me down . . . I don't fade away unless I choose*) pretty much set the tone for the night's material, borrowed or otherwise.

Georgie Fame, the dutiful deputy, warmed up the crowd at the start and managed to whip up the encores at the end with a set-piece routine of

Colin Harper · Concert review originally published in the *Independent* (2 November 1995)

Van Morrison,
1990s

hyperbole-repetition of the '*Let's hear it for The Man/ He fills your heart with gladness/ Takes away your sadness*' variety. There were five encores and they were the best performances of the night – most particularly an exhilarating, endless medley of 'Tupelo Honey' and 'Why Must I Always Explain?' with spirited soloing all round and what, if the film surfaces, will probably end up being labelled in the world of Van fandom as the 'laughing version' of 'Have I Told You Lately?'. They were making a film all right, and it'll certainly have its moments – but I don't think they should call it *The Jazz Singer*.

JOHN McLAUGHLIN & THE FREE SPIRITS
CORK JAZZ FESTIVAL

Another year, another McLaughlin group with metaphysical nomenclature. Given that Ireland missed out on The Mahavishnu Orchestra, Shakti and The One Truth Band, the anticipation for the fusion god's first visit to the Emerald Isle in 30 years was second to none. The fact that Van Morrison was debuting his own less esoterically titled 'Jazz Set' in the same venue later that evening was of no concern to anyone but the stage manager.

Featuring Dennis Chambers on drums and 'rising star' Joey DeFrancesco on Hammond B3, the reborn electric guitarist's new ensemble are a power trio in musicianship alone. The high-speed multi-layered motif/riff/solo discipline and volume of the early Mahavishnu recordings – still unrivalled in the largely excruciating pantheon of fusion – and the high-speed, multi-layered solo/solo/more-solo feel of some of his more frenetic acoustic projects of the past fifteen years have given way to a kind of proud but graceful middle age in which the 53-year-old McLaughlin can draw on the fiery, otherworldly energy of his own work within the context of the wider history of modern jazz.

Space, both physical and musical, was the key tonight. With Chambers and DeFrancesco necessarily seated and instinctively responsive to the music, McLaughlin was free to lurch around in archetypal axe-hero agitation, arching backwards in a way that is, to him alone, an apparently genuine aid to expressive musicianship. Soberly attired in black and white, and literally blowing on his fingers after every billion-note flurry like some cartoon gunslinger, McLaughlin still cuts a unique figure on the blurred edges of musical genres. His very sound and style retain the hint of danger that remains his own: the eerie colourings of quarter-tone bends and those choppy, almost Townshend-reminiscent, suspended inversions which bleed into the songs like some dense liquid. The stage manager pulled the plug ten minutes early. Another Irish concert by Van was obviously cutting more ice backstage than a once-in-three-decades experience from one of the greatest living musicians of his generation.

Colin Harper · Concert review originally published in *Mojo* (February 1996)

A PLAQUE FOR VAN MORRISON

Mick Jagger, we all know, was a profound influence on Muddy Waters. And B.B. King, of course, rethought his whole approach to guitar playing after hearing Eric Clapton. Now it can also be revealed that one of Buddy Guy's major influences was Van Morrison.

The revelation came on 26 November, when Guy unveiled a plaque on the redbrick wall of Van Morrison's childhood home, 125 Hyndford Street, Belfast. 'This is easier than playing,' joked a cheery Guy outside the small terraced house before the heavy questioning began from the massed ranks of the Northern Irish media.

'Was Van Morrison an influence on you?' asked one earnest hack.

The truth had to come out. 'Yeahhh,' admitted Guy. 'Yeah.' And after a momentary, enigmatic smile he paid this tribute to east Belfast's favourite son: 'He's tops in my book and this is a great day for me. He's a great guy. People like that don't come every day.'

The silver plaque was inscribed 'Van Morrison Songwriter Lived Here 1945–1961', and was the brainchild of the Belfast Blues Appreciation Society. Founder Rab Braniff explained: 'It's to recognise Van for what he is: a genius.' The genius himself was not present at the ceremony, but Braniff was undeterred. 'Apparently he was very emotional when he heard. He was very pleased to get it.'

To seasoned Morrison observers it seemed too good to be true – and it was. Three days later a letter was published in the *Belfast Telegraph* from solicitors Cleaver, Fulton and Rankin, 'on behalf of Ivan Morrison (Van Morrison)'. The letter, in no uncertain terms, points out that '. . . our client was not consulted nor asked for permission . . . is not associated with "The Belfast Blues Appreciation Society" . . . and does not desire that his name be used in or in connection with promotional activities'.

'No comment,' sighed a sadder and wiser Rab Braniff, 'except that it was meant sincerely and we're sorry if it caused any offence or embarrassment to Van.'

Trevor Hodgett · Originally published in *Blueprint* (February 1992)

Jim Armstrong,
onstage in Germany, 2003

EPILOGUE JIM ARMSTRONG & JIM GILCHRIST, SPINNERS BAR, BELFAST

Ireland's greatest blues duo, Jim Armstrong and Jim Gilchrist, scintillated in Spinners Bar, on 'Diving Duck Blues' ('*If the Lagan was Guinness . . .*'), 'Take This Hammer', 'Stormy Monday Blues' and others. Gilchrist's raw vocals and effective harp and second-guitar playing (and let's not forget his foot percussion device, constructed from a lump of wood and bottle caps – no high-tech samplers for these guys) were impressive and satisfyingly complemented Armstrong's wild virtuosity on electric guitar.

So when the bar manageress approached our heroes during their break, was it to offer a bonus? Or to sign them up for a residency? Or just to congratulate them on their excellence? Well no, actually: instead the manageress told our local legends that if they didn't drop all this boring blues stuff and instead play middle-of-the-road songs in the second half, they were sacked.

'We play what we play,' riposted the two Jims, before being ingloriously given their marching orders, as their fans in the audience looked on aghast.

So, can I suggest the 1995 *Blueprint* readers' poll introduce a new category, for the Worst Venue in the UK? And can I save myself a stamp and register now my vote for Spinners Bar in Belfast's Plaza Hotel?

Trevor Hodgett · Concert review originally published in *Blueprint* (February 1995)

Muddy Waters, 1971

SECTION 3
BELFAST BLUES

MUDDY WATERS
IN BELFAST

I was a schoolboy living with my mum and dad in Bangor, twelve miles from Belfast, when I heard that Muddy Waters was booked to play the following week at Queen's University in Belfast. This was exciting news. I was only sixteen but I knew how important Muddy Waters was. I had, after all, been reading two music papers a week since I was ten and I'd been regularly listening to Mike Raven's blues programme on Radio 1 and Kid Jensen's blues programme broadcast in the early hours of the morning on Radio Luxembourg. In fact, so seriously did I take this passion that I used to take notes during the programmes and make long lists of must-buy records – which in the cold light of day I could never actually afford on my pound-a-week pocket money.

I'd never been to a gig. A few years previously hip bands like Jethro Tull and Fleetwood Mac were regular visitors to Belfast but I was a little too young to go. Now I was just about old enough to go to gigs but the Troubles had hit and few bands wanted to play in the province. But I knew I had to see Muddy Waters.

My friend and I took the train to Belfast and walked a couple of miles to the Whitla Hall at Queen's. In my recollection there were only a couple of hundred punters in the audience, in a hall that holds 1,200 people, although years later the promoter insisted to me that 400 tickets had been sold.

The support act was the Jim Daly Blues Band. Admittedly, as a kid at my first gig, I didn't have anything to compare it to, but I thought Jim's piano playing was staggeringly good. I was right, too – subsequently I was to hear Jim play hundreds of times and he really was a staggeringly good piano player and in later years, when I became a friend as well as a fan, it used to please me that the first blues band I ever heard was the Jim Daly Blues Band. I could have done a lot worse – in truth, I could hardly have done much better.

After Jim's set there was a hiatus. It was a dirty, foggy night and it transpired that the Muddy Waters Blues Band's flight had been delayed. Some of the audience decamped to the nearest pub but my friend and I stayed put. I was a young-looking sixteen-year-old and although there were a few dodgy bars in Bangor who turned a blind eye to my baby face I didn't want to risk the public humiliation of going to a strange bar and being told to bugger off. In any case I had no money, the train fare and ticket having seen to my pocket money. So we sat and waited . . . and waited . . . and waited. Eventually I happened to look around and I saw a bunch of hapless old black men, muffled up in coats and scarves and carrying their own instrument cases, trudging

Trevor Hodgett

miserably through the main entrance of the Whitla and on through the length of the hall to the dressing room. Obviously this was the band and I've no idea why they didn't use the stage entrance.

Shortly afterwards the band, minus coats and scarves, straggled on stage. I don't remember what the first number was but I can still remember my emotions at the sight of the great man standing in front of my very eyes, singing and playing. My friend and I were beside ourselves with excitement, elbowing each other in the ribs. And after the song he announced, 'Ladies and gentlemen – Muddy Waters' – and someone came on from the wings, on crutches, and limped over to a chair, centre-stage. And we realised that the great man we'd been drooling over was in fact the band's second-guitarist and that Muddy was only now coming on stage. Clearly we were hip enough to go to a Muddy Waters concert but we weren't hip enough to actually recognise him or his playing.

I thought the gig was great although in retrospect, given the exhausting hassles the band had endured and the small crowd and the consequent lack of atmosphere, I would assume that they could hardly have been in very inspired form.

Either way, we were then faced with the problem of getting back to Bangor, for the last train had long gone. So we walked miles through town to the dual carriageway and stuck the old thumbs out. But this was 1970, sectarian murders were at their height and no driver in his right mind was going to stop and invite a couple of scruffy-looking youths into his car. We began walking, calculating that this would suggest our good intentions to any driver. It didn't. We continued walking, mile after mile after mile. Eventually we reached Holywood, eight miles from the Whitla Hall – and my friend cracked. We went to a Chinese takeaway and begged them to allow us to use their phone and he rang his dad, who came and collected us and drove us home.

So the evening ended ignominiously – but there are very few people who can say that they saw Muddy Waters in Belfast, and I am one of them. And my friend Colin Mercer, who himself became a blues critic with *Blueprint* magazine, is another.

MUDDY WATERS
WHITLA HALL, BELFAST

The most thrilling night in the history of blues music in Northern Ireland occurred on 9 December 1970. For on that never-to-be-forgotten date Muddy Waters, the music's greatest hero and most influential figure – even The Rolling Stones named themselves after one of his songs and recorded several others – made his first and last appearance here, performing in Queen's University's 1,200-seater Whitla Hall.

'They must have had to turn thousands away!' I hear you cry. 'Queues must have stretched halfway down University Road.'

Well, strangely enough, it wasn't like that at all. But let entrepreneur Dougie Knight, who promoted the gig in conjunction with the Queen's Esoteric Music Society, explain: 'We only sold 400 tickets – and not everybody who bought a ticket turned up. We had only been offered the gig at two weeks' notice because Muddy and his band were due to fly home after a European tour from Shannon Airport, so they wanted to fit in an Irish gig. That meant we didn't have to pay their airfares and we got them for £300. But there was no time for posters or press. It was just word of mouth.'

While the few hundred fanatics who had found out about the gig and had managed to buy tickets were positively vibrating with anticipation, Dougie unwittingly found himself cast in the starring role in a farce. 'There was an electricity strike that day but I found a standby generator. The janitor said that it would either work – or explode. Luckily it worked, but it wasn't really sufficient to drive a seven-piece band. When Muddy's tour manager found out he went berserk and threatened to kill me, so I had to lock myself in a room in the Whitla until the storm passed. Then there was fog at the airport and the band's flight was delayed and they didn't get started until 10.45, so lots of people had to leave early for the last bus. Because of the power situation the band played semi-acoustically. I'm told the gig was very good but there was so much tension that I was shattered and I can't remember enjoying it.'

Belfast pianist Jim Daly, whose trio was the support act, has happier memories of the night. 'It was a beautiful gig and Muddy was a lovely person. Very nice to talk to and very informative.' Jim even had the thrill of playing with Muddy and his band. 'I sat in on "Blues Before Sunrise". Muddy's great pianist Otis Spann had died in April 1970 and Pinetop Perkins was playing piano with him. I said to Pinetop, "What key is he singing in?" and he just said, "Watch his fingers, man!" Afterwards Muddy said to me, "You play more like Otis Spann than Otis did!" It was a marvellous experience and a nice memory.'

Trevor Hodgett · Originally published in the *Irish News* (8 December 1995); plus additional material

Despite the poor crowd, delayed start and power problems, the band played impressive versions of 'Hoochie Coochie Man', 'Five Long Years', 'Honey Bee' and others, for the couple of hundred diehards who stayed till the end. Harmonica player Carey Bell, guitarists Sammy Lawhorn and Pee Wee Madison, pianist Pinetop Perkins, drummer Willie Smith, bassist Little Sonny Wimberley and Muddy himself all played memorably, although Muddy, on crutches after a near-fatal car crash, had to play sitting down.

So, what became of the participants in this legendary night? Jim Daly still plays wonderfully authentic blues piano in Belfast and Dougie Knight still runs his record shop in Botanic Avenue and promotes jazz and blues gigs. Pinetop Perkins tours as a solo artist, as does Carey Bell, who has twice since played in the Errigle Inn, Belfast and Pee Wee Madison and Little Sonny Wimberley are also still musically active. Sammy Lawhorn tragically descended into alcoholism and died in 1990, of cancer. And Muddy Waters died in 1983, aged 68, a revered legend, internationally recognised and acclaimed as a giant of twentieth-century popular music, but a giant who, thirteen years earlier, could only sell a third of the seats at his one-and-only Belfast gig.

Oh, and the schoolboy sitting agog in the front row, at his first ever gig? Well, he became the blues critic of the *Irish News*!

Postscript: Jim Daly died in 1997.

JIM DALY
PROLOGUE

It might just have been the most disappointing moment of his career. After playing world-class blues piano in Belfast for a phenomenal 30 years Jim Daly was finally, in 1984, in Chicago, in a real Chicago blues club and sitting in with a real hotshot blues band, Big Daddy Kinsey & The Kinsey Report. And as he played and sang with his characteristic authenticity, conviction and panache, and as the audience roared with delight and as the band beamed with pleasure at this visiting stranger's unexpected and stunning prowess, Jim looked into the audience. And, in what I still fear might have been a dismal anticlimax, who should he see dancing exuberantly in front of the stage but – and I blush to admit it – none other than myself, just as he had done a hundred times before at innumerable, nondescript gigs in innumerable, nondescript Belfast

Jim Daly,
1995

Trevor Hodgett

Jim Daly,
at home
in Belfast,
late
Seventies

bars and clubs. But gentleman that he was, Jim never thereafter so much as hinted that my prosaic presence had marred the magic of the moment for him.

Of course, I wasn't there as a Jim Daly stalker or by some unfathomable coincidence. Jim and I were friends and when he discovered that I was planning a holiday in the States the same year that he was, he synchronised his schedule with mine. He wanted my company because he had never been out of the British Isles before and he knew I was an experienced traveller and I was delighted to have his company because, well, bloody hell, he was the mighty Jim Daly, Ireland's greatest ever bluesman.

Watching my home-town hero blow away a Chicago blues-club audience and band is one of my most cherished musical memories. I can still hear, in my imagination, Big Daddy Kinsey announce, 'Brother Jim Daly from Eye-er-land.' And I can still vividly recall Jim clambering on stage, settling himself behind the keyboards, calling out a key to the band, and creating twelve-bar magic. And I can still, equally vividly, recall the stunned expressions on the faces of the band as they realised what a profound bluesman their unknown guest was.

Almost as vivid in my memory is the sight of Jim, in the audience, before he inveigled an invitation on stage, looking like he had died and gone to heaven, so thrilled was he to finally hear the music to which he had devoted so much of his life, at source. Indeed, so obviously transfixed was he by the music and by the experience that I wouldn't have been surprised if a tear had started to trickle down his face.

We were only in Chicago for a few weeks but even in that short period of time Jim began to be recognised and regarded as part of the local scene, and several times, as we walked between clubs, we would be stopped by musicians and blues buffs who would greet him delightedly and say that they had seen him playing in one club or another.

Jim rarely played outside Ireland – although a 1991 appearance at the prestigious Burnley Blues Festival was hugely acclaimed in the British blues press. But in 1984 musicians and audiences in Chicago learnt what musicians and audiences in Ireland had long known – that Jim Daly was a true bluesman who understood and played the music with all his heart and with all his soul.

JIM DALY

The Northern Irish blues community has been devastated by the death, after an illness, of pianist Jim Daly, a decades-long friend of Van Morrison's and a legend in the province, both for his own profound musicianship and for the consistent generosity with which he shared his massive knowledge and love of the blues.

Almost unbelievably, Jim had been playing blues in Belfast since the Fifties and it is no exaggeration to say that countless local blues musicians were as influenced by Jim as they were by the pioneering legends of the music such as Muddy Waters and Howlin' Wolf. Van Morrison, early in his career, happily sat in with Jim's band and the two men remained friends right up until Jim's death. In a comment that one has heard repeated by many local musicians, harmonica player Bill Miskimmin, who now tours internationally with the highly rated English band Nine Below Zero, said, 'Jim's was the first blues band I ever saw, and the first time I ever got on stage to play blues was with Jim – I cried my eyes out when I heard the news.'

Daly's career began inauspiciously with The Jimmy Compton Jazz Band. 'I was so young and shy that I refused to do it by myself, so I got a friend of mine and he played the left hand and I played the right,' recalled Jim before his death. 'Jimmy was part of the showband era. He drove around town in a big pink Cadillac. He used to take the band down to Cork and they'd all have to sleep in the pink car – Jimmy wouldn't pay the money to put them up for the night!'

Daly's skills developed with fondly remembered jazz bands such as The Saints, The Crescent City, The Oriole and The White Eagles. 'We played at Ophir Tennis Club, Belfast Tech, Belfast Boat Club, the Drill Hall at Queen's and so on. As far back as the Fifties I remember playing the Saturday night hops at Belfast Tech, doing solo spots as part of The White Eagles and doing Brownie McGhee numbers. And George Hays – the banjo player – and I used to do a little blues spot. George played a National Steel and I remember us playing "Dust My Blues".

'The White Eagles had offers to tour England, but we never took them up because we all had day jobs. Even now I don't think I would want to be a professional musician. I enjoy it as a hobby, but I think if I did it full time it would be too much like work.'

In the Fifties blues records were almost impossible to obtain. 'You couldn't get them in Belfast. I got them from a guy in France, a famous collector called

Trevor Hodgett · Includes material previously published in the *Irish News* (17 October 1997) and *Wavelength* (June 1998); plus additional material

Bert Bradfield. Locally Gerry McQueen was the king of collectors – it was a great thing if you got to hear his collection.'

Jim's own blues heroes first began to tour Europe in the late Fifties, often on package tours. 'I was crafty. I would find out what London hotel they were staying in and book into the same hotel. There were people like Skip James, Bukka White, John Lee Hooker, Son House . . . They were all great, all great guys.

'I remember sitting talking to Otis Spann, who was sharing a room with Sonny Boy Williamson, who was lying drunk, and Victoria Spivey came in and wanted to get him awake – she had a packed lunch prepared. And Otis Spann was saying, "Oh, leave him, he's all right the way he is." Then Big Joe Williams came in and we all went to the Crawdaddy club with Lonnie Johnson,' reminisced Jim, casually dropping five of the most legendary names in the history of blues.

Jim also met Sonny Terry and Brownie McGhee. 'They said, "You from Ireland? We played a gig with guys from Ireland." I was racking my brain for all the names I could think of. It turned out it was The Clancy Brothers!

'And Muddy Waters was a great guy. He became like an old friend. When I first met him he could hardly believe that I had a Library of Congress 78 record by him. He wanted to buy it off me!'

For Jim these experiences were invaluable. 'It was laying a foundation – trying to get close to the music's roots. Meeting the legends. And most of them were happy enough to talk. Son House was a great old gentleman. So was Bukka White. And Skip James. Sonny Terry and Brownie McGhee would talk the leg off a stool. They were great *craic*. I later played with them many times.'

On his visits to London Jim got to know Alexis Korner, known as the father of British blues for the encouragement he gave in the early Sixties to young musicians who went on to form bands such as The Rolling Stones, Led Zeppelin and Free. 'Alexis and I became quite good friends. We would sit talking blues till four in the morning and I sat in with his band at the Marquee club, with [saxophonist] Dick Heckstall-Smith. And once in Belfast I took him to the Maritime to see Them.'

Enthusiasts like record-shop owner Dougie Knight began to bring legends such as Mississippi Fred McDowell, Memphis Slim, Jesse Fuller, Champion Jack Dupree and Juke Boy Bonner to Belfast. 'Did you know there was a blues outfit called "The Belfast Blues"? *When I first got to Belfast, boy was I surprised/ To see all those happy people and those big laughing Irish eyes.* Juke Boy wrote and recorded that after his visit.

'And Mississippi Fred McDowell was an absolute gentleman. He said the best night's sleep he had on his tour was in my bed in Alliance Avenue.

'Curtis Jones was another one. He played the Marquee in Belfast. They had a regular dance as well and when he saw the queues of people – who were actually queueing up to get into the dance – he thought they were queueing for him and he complained he wasn't getting enough money! He stayed with me afterwards and we'd just about reached the house after the gig when he started peeing up against my neighbour's car, much to my horror.'

Another visitor was Arthur Crudup, whose 'That's All Right Mama' had been covered by Elvis Presley. 'His voice was great. He played everything in one key – G. He used to refer to Elvis Preston – I didn't know who he was talking about!'

The great pianist Little Brother Montgomery unfortunately came to grief on his visit. 'Somebody had taken him out that afternoon and fed him Bushmills whiskey and he could hardly see the piano. I had to sit beside him and hold him on his stool, otherwise he'd have fallen off. I remember Tom Cusack, a local collector, telling him he was a disgrace to music and to his race. And Little Brother said, "Aw, fuck off!" But the next day – when he was sober – he sat down at Gerry McQueen's piano and played the most lovely piano.'

By the early Sixties Jim was running a blues club in the Jubilee Bar in Cromac Street and Belfast's own blues superstar-in-waiting Van Morrison inevitably befriended him. 'Van used to ring me at work and play John Lee Hooker records over the phone, and his mother, who was a good singer and a very lively woman – she used to jump on the tables and dance – used to sing with my band in the Jubilee. Later Van wanted us to record with her, but we never got around to it. Van sang with my band in the Jubilee. I was doing a bit of singing – because I was the only one who knew the words of the bloody songs. But when Van came up, without any alteration to the mike, his voice just came through loud and strong. He always was a great singer.

'One night we went together to hear [Eric Clapton/Jack Bruce/Ginger Baker's supergroup] Cream in Queen's student-union snack bar. Good times. And I remember once in London [harmonica genius] Little Walter coming over to me. "Hey, Belfast, I remember a little guy from there with long hair did a tour with me." It was Van Morrison he was talking about!'

The highlight of Jim's career came on 9 December 1970 with the visit of Muddy Waters to Belfast, when blues music's greatest legend invited Jim to sit in with him, on 'Blues Before Sunrise', and afterwards enthused about his playing. 'But one thing I've always regretted is he asked me to go with him to Dublin for his next gig, but I said no, because I had to go to work the next day.'

A lifelong dream came true for Jim in 1984 when he visited Chicago and, at last, heard in its natural habitat the music that had been inspiring him since his youth. On his first night in town Jim jammed with the critically acclaimed Big Daddy Kinsey & The Kinsey Report. 'It was great to be a white face in a Chicago club, playing with a black band. The thrill was terrific. Magic Slim sat in . . . and Big Time Sara . . . and B.B. Jones . . . and Sugar Blue. I heard all these people play in one night, which was incredible.'

Sugar Blue had recorded with The Rolling Stones after reportedly being discovered by Mick Jagger busking in the Paris Subway. 'Sugar Blue said that was a load of . . . "What would Mick Jagger be doing in the Subway?"'

In Chicago Jim also met the incomparable pianist Sunnyland Slim. 'I asked him to listen to me and give me some tips. Afterwards he said, "Man, you don't need any tips – you play good down-home piano."'

Daly's bands have included some of Northern Ireland's greatest musicians including ex-Chris Barber Band bassist Jackie Flavelle and ex-Them and Taste drummer John Wilson, but the two musicians most associated with him have been guitarist Ronnie Greer and singer Patsy Melarkey. 'I'm a great fan of Ronnie's guitar playing. He is an excellent guitar player and very devoted to the blues. And Patsy is one of the very few female singers who can create blues – one of the very few in Ireland, outside Ottilie Patterson. Ronnie could stand up to most of the guitar players in Chicago and the same with Patsy singing blues because they've been listening to it, they're steeped in it.'

For years Jim Daly backed all the American blues performers who visited Belfast, including Lowell Fulson, Fenton Robinson, Mojo Buford, Dr John, Byther Smith and Phil Guy. 'There's never time to rehearse with any of these guys. Frequently we never see them till they come on the bandstand. You just have to cross your fingers and hope it's all right. But I've never known any of them to be difficult to work with. And I can say without reservation that the most thrilling one to play with – outside Muddy – was Carey Bell. He gave my band the feeling of being a Chicago band. I could see him playing in Maxwell Street market in Chicago, with a hole in his pants, for nickels and dimes. The guy is completely unpretentious. He lifted me off the seat of the piano. He was great.'

As indeed was Jim himself, for he played Chicago blues with a feel matched by very few musicians in the British Isles. He was a colossal figure on the local scene and Irish blues lovers will surely never see his equal again. Like Bill Miskimmin, quoted earlier, Jim's was the first blues band I ever heard live and I was privileged to hear him play literally hundreds of times afterwards. It is truly heartbreaking to think I will never hear him play again.

Ottilie Patterson (left),
Sister Rosetta Tharpe, 1958

OTTILIE PATTERSON
PROLOGUE

I was eighteen years old when I first heard Ottilie Patterson sing, in 1972, when she guested with the Chris Barber Band, in Queen's University's Whitla Hall. From the mid-Fifties until the mid-Sixties Ottilie had been a regular member of the band, a pioneer of blues singing in Britain and something of a star, but by this stage her appearances had become rare. I enjoyed her singing and I enjoyed the exuberance of her performance but what really staggered me was the audience, which seemed to mainly consist of old guys in their forties, who sat beaming in delight throughout the performance and who were clearly, to a man, madly in love with Ottilie.

And the rapport between Ottilie and her fans was such that it was obvious that they loved her so much because they saw her as a down-to-earth, unpretentious Ulster lass, who had gone across the water and taken the English scene by storm and yet had remained unchanged by the fame – who was the same uncomplicated, fun-loving girl she had always been.

I saw her again, maybe ten years later, backed by the Jim Daly Blues Band, which featured Ronnie Greer on guitar, Jackie Flavelle on bass – who had been a member of Chris Barber's Band at the Whitla Hall gig – and ex-Them drummer John Wilson. Again I enjoyed the singing and the performance – although I remember feeling unconvinced that a blues version of 'The Mountains of Mourne' was a good idea – and again I was struck by the number of old guys, now in their fifties, who were clearly still madly in love with Ottilie.

In 1998 Greer, who had over the years become her friend, told me that Ottilie was coming over to Northern Ireland for a visit from her home in Scotland and would be agreeable to doing an interview with me. I was full of admiration for Ottilie's achievements and delighted at the opportunity.

But it turned into an embarrassing, mutually unsatisfactory fiasco. Not the interview itself – with Ronnie, we spent three pleasant hours in a bar talking and drinking and doing the interview and I liked Ottilie very much, although it was pretty obvious that she was not, in fact, the happy-go-lucky, uncomplicated Ulster lass of myth. She was instead a troubled, fragile woman, who had never really recovered from some of the bitter blows life had dealt her, and at times she had become weepy as she reminisced.

No, the interview was fine and in my *Irish News* piece I enthused about Ottilie's talents and achievements. I was very pleased with what I had written and felt sure that it would make an unhappy woman very, very happy. It didn't.

Trevor Hodgett

James Cotton,
Ottilie Patterson,
late Fifties

She wrote a letter to the editor complaining about what I'd written about her and implying she'd been misquoted. The letter was duly published. She also wrote to me saying how hurt she'd been by my article.

I was flabbergasted. I still am flabbergasted. I couldn't – and can't – understand why she didn't love the article, which praised her to the skies and which quoted her accurately and which, I maintain, was entirely faithful to the spirit of what she had told me. I wrote back and told her so and we exchanged a few further letters and she even sent me a tape pouring out her thoughts on the matter and, decently enough, lamenting the fact that our relationship, which had begun so pleasantly, was now strained. But somehow I never really understood what her problem with the article was. Eventually our communication petered out in mutual embarrassment and confusion. Ottilie remained hurt by what I had written; I remained hurt that she had publicly accused me of misrepresenting what she had said. After a few months I never heard from her or contacted her again.

But I still think Ottilie deserves enormous credit for somehow, miraculously, emerging from the Northern Ireland of the Fifties to become an internationally respected blues singer – long before the British blues boom of the Sixties that brought blues into the popular music mainstream. And I still think my article gives her the credit that is her due and I'm proud to have written it and given her that due.

OTTILIE PATTERSON

The greatest British blues singer of them all? Van Morrison, perhaps. Or how about the young Stevie Winwood? Or Paul Rodgers. Or Eric Burdon? Well, according to George Melly, who might be expected to know about such things – and who to this day plays a couple of Bessie Smith records every morning – the greatest British blues singer of them all is none of the above, but is in fact Ottilie Patterson, from Comber, County Down, a major star with the Chris Barber Jazz Band in the Fifties and early Sixties, but now a somewhat forgotten figure.

Nowadays, when blues music has long been part of the fabric of popular music and so ubiquitous that it is even used as the soundtrack for innumerable TV commercials, it is hard to recall that there was a time when to even hear the music was a formidable achievement. Patterson explains her own initiation: 'I was at the College of Art in the Belfast Tech and a fellow student, who was completely saturated in blues, lent me records of Bessie Smith, Jelly Roll Morton and Meade Lux Lewis.

'We only had a wind-up gramophone at home and if you put a twelve-inch 78 rpm record on it you had to wind it up again 'cos it wouldn't last twelve inches. But I stuck on Bessie Smith's "Reckless Blues" and I just nearly melted on the spot.'

A Belfast record collector helped Patterson's blues education. 'The legendary Gerry McQueen. I first went to McQueen's when I was nineteen in 1951. When you went up to his house you had to pass his test – we heard him turning someone away one night and the wee fellow went home all upset. He didn't even let him over the doorstep because he hadn't the right attitude. McQueen was the gateway but he had this infuriating habit – he would just put on a record and look at you but he never gave you titles and you didn't dare interrupt him and say, "What was that?" You just had to pick it up as you went along.'

Patterson began singing locally with Jimmy Compton's Jazz Band – there being no blues bands in Northern Ireland or, indeed, probably anywhere else in the British Isles at the time. 'If you wanted to sing the blues in the Forties or the Fifties where could you go but a jazz band? But at one rehearsal Jimmy said, "Right, Ottilie, I want you to do this wee song." It was [sings] "*Anytime you're feeling lonely . . .*" I said, "That's not blues; I'm a blues singer." He said, "Listen dear, I want my 30 bob in my pocket every Saturday night. If you don't want to sing it you know what you can do." And I walked out! I maybe didn't

Trevor Hodgett · Includes material previously published in the *Irish News* (27 March 1998) and *Blueprint* (December 1999); plus additional material

sound like a blues singer, but I felt like one! I was just freaked out on blues.'

By 1954 Patterson was teaching part time in Ballymena Tech. In her summer holidays she went to London and visited a club where the Chris Barber Band was playing. 'I kept going up to the band between numbers asking for a sing, saying, "How about 'Basin Street' in A flat? Or 'Careless Love' in E flat?" – just to show I wasn't some star-struck child! – and they would mumble, "Yeah, yeah." And the whole evening went down and I hadn't sung yet. The pianist Johnny Parker was hanging around afterwards and I said, "Play 'Careless Love' for me," so John played and I started to sing. The guys in the band were all packing up their instruments when I started to sing and they immediately unpacked and all joined in. It was like Hollywood! It was such a cliché, but it was true.'

Immediately hired by the band, Ottilie was invited to their next rehearsal. 'It was in an upstairs room in Greek Street in Soho. The room was bare and cobwebby, with a grimy window with a big hole in it and I'm singing "Make Me A Pallet On The Floor" and outside the streetwalkers were out in force, and I thought, This is like Storyville in New Orleans. I'm living the blues! I was a wee Comber girl with imagination!'

Patterson played her first batch of gigs with the band, including one at the Royal Festival Hall. 'Then I had to go back to Ballymena Tech, but in November I got a letter from Chris asking would I come back to the band and they would guarantee me £10 a week. I thought that was great 'cos I was only getting £5 a week in the Tech and no holiday pay 'cos I was part time. My answer was brilliant. From Newtownards I sent a telegram: "Coming if I have to ride the rods." I'm telling you, I was living it! I didn't even know what riding the rods was, but I knew it was a real blues thing and I knew it meant hard times. Riding the rods!

'So I told Mr McClelland in Ballymena Tech, "Thank you, but I'm off," I borrowed a fiver from my sister, and my last words were, "Well, mummy, I've burnt my boats."'

Patterson, one of the first British singers ever to make a career singing blues, won enormous acclaim touring and recording with the Barber band, with a repertoire that was simply astonishing for the era. 'In 1955 I was doing Memphis Minnie numbers, Leroy Carr songs, songs by Big Maceo, Tommy McClennan, Muddy Waters, St Louis Jimmy, Champion Jack Dupree, Sonny Boy Williamson, Ma Rainey . . . I was singing "House Of The Rising Sun" unaccompanied in 1955 but somebody laughed one night and I didn't perform it again. I was a bit hypersensitive!'

Patterson, in fact, soon married Barber, but at first found the lifestyle tough. 'It was horrible. I hated it. I was unhappy, I was homesick, I was like a fish out of water and I didn't feel welcomed by the musicians.'

Nevertheless, Patterson now had a chance to meet some of blues music's greatest-ever legends, including Big Bill Broonzy, Sonny Boy Williamson, Howlin' Wolf and Muddy Waters, who all worked with the Barber band on their earliest visits to the United Kingdom. 'Big Bill Broonzy was this big, black Mississippi negro and I was this wee skinny Ulster girl and he took me to the Great Wall Chinese restaurant in Oxford Street and walking along the street I couldn't have been more proud. And he turned and he said to me, "You don't mind being seen with me, do you?"' recalls Patterson, choking with emotion at the memory.

On his 1955 tour Broonzy stayed with Alexis Korner, the guitarist later known as the father of British blues because of the help he gave to the young musicians who formed bands like The Rolling Stones. 'After a gig he invited us back to Alexis' house, and he sat down and we thought, Oh good, he's getting out the guitar, and all of a sudden there was this vision on the stairs and it was Alexis' wife and she kicked us all out! We were most embarrassed 'cos we were at the foot of the great singer, and nobody was misbehaving! But Bill was the most beautiful man. He had charm and intelligence. A great brain. He was the sort of guy [who] was completely disarming. He could have flirted with some guy's wife and the guy wouldn't have minded! He was just wonderful. When Big Bill died Chris and I couldn't bear to listen to one of his records for eighteen months, 'cos we just sat and cried.

'Bill was very articulate, whereas Muddy was quite incoherent. But he played so wonderfully. He had that erotic earthiness. I think he'd just one thing on his mind – which was hoochie coochie. He was the hoochie-coochie man!

'I remember Sonny Boy Williamson came to our house and got drunk and was walking about saying he was going to kill people. He was a real evil-looking old devil. And Howlin' Wolf came up and I was ladling out Irish stew for him and I looked up and he was saying grace! And I stood there with the ladle. Oh, I was so ashamed! We had all the gospel singers come up to see us – they would have drunk you out of house and home. But Wolf came with the bottle and presented it to you. He was a gentleman, in our house anyway.'

In 1957 Sister Rosetta Tharpe toured with the Barber band. 'At Birmingham Town Hall, before she went on, she said, "You're going to sing 'The Saints' with me." I said, "No!" She says, "Yes you are." And that was that and she went on stage and I was sitting there for the next 25 minutes being petrified. She announced me and on I trots and she was very unselfish because she loved duetting – she left all the right spaces and gave all the right leads. Then we did a slow one, "When I Move To The Sky". It would make the shivers come on you.'

On the back of a hit record with 'Petite Fleur', the Barber band with Ottilie toured the States. 'One night we did a 200-mile detour to see Muddy Waters in his home club, Smitty's Corner, in Chicago. As we went in all the heads turned and looked at us. Oh, we felt very white! But then Muddy saw us and came down and got us a front table. I was so excited. We were out of our heads with the sounds that were hitting us. This was it, at source. Then he suddenly announces, "There's a little girl here from the state of England and she knows how to sing the blues," and I had to walk up and sing, with no run-through.

Crumbs! It was so exciting, but I was petrified. Afterwards I got a good hand and this lady said, "Hey lady, you sing real pretty. How come you sing like one of us?" So I always remember how in the cradle of the blues they accepted me and complimented me.

'The next time Chris and me stayed with Muddy at his house in South Lake Park, where [pianist] Otis Spann had a room in the basement and [pianist] St Louis Jimmy – James Oden – lived just along the street. We were in with him as well and he said to me [drawling], "You have a real blues voice."

'On a later tour, in 1962, we played at President Kennedy's Washington Jazz Festival in front of 8,000 people, with Duke Ellington, Dave Brubeck, Slide Hampton and George Shearing. I had never been able to get these Englishmen in the band to join in with anything. I'd be singing [loudly], "*I've got my mojo working*" and they'd go [weedily], "*I've got my mojo working*". So, this time I'm into the mojo thing and I thought, I hope the boys back me tonight, and I got to the bit, "*I've got my mojo working*" and all of a sudden there's this great roar – "*Mojo working*" – from the audience and I'm tambouring away and my bracelet flies off into the audience and the joint's jumping and it's a terrific reception. Duke Ellington actually had to wait – he couldn't get his guys onstage 'cos I got such a great reception. And one of the black stagehands afterwards said to me, "Well done, Bessie Smith!" It can't be bad.'

By the mid-Sixties though, Patterson's career and life were unravelling. 'One of my vocal cords was roughened and they said, "You've got to keep quiet for three months," and then I never seemed to get back in again, although I wanted to.'

Patterson thereafter only sang sporadically with Barber and their marriage broke up, although she did release a terrific solo album, *Spring Song*, in 1969 and another, *Madame Blues And Dr Jazz*, recorded live, in 1984. 'I've had very hard times. The life and the music were all jumbled up and they were causing the misery, but also the performances were the escape from the misery, so it was a vicious circle. I was trapped. I thought, Where do I go? What do I do?

'It's on that song ["Please Accept My Apologies, Mrs Pankhurst"] I wrote on *Spring Song*: "*Don't emancipate me/ I'd rather have my chains/ They hurt far less than brains/ And in this day and age/ I'd rather have my cage*". That's what I was writing about.

'I didn't know what to do so I just kept on and in the end it was decided for me. He decided for me. I'd been acquired, hired, married and fired. After that often I couldn't even listen to blues because I was heartsore.

'When I was young I wanted to be still singing, but life didn't turn out like that, and I haven't sung now for seven years. I try at home very occasionally, but I wouldn't want to go back onstage and do less than a full whack. Unless I can still belt it, I don't want to give half measures.

'I've come through a very difficult life and now I'm near the end of it. That's why I'm agreeing to this interview because all I want is to be appreciated and recognised.'

RONNIE GREER & JACKIE FLAVELLE

Imagine, if you will, a blues band whose four members have variously played with everyone from Sonny Boy Williamson to Paul McCartney; from Sonny Terry to Rod Stewart; from Dr John to Phil Coulter; from Lefty Dizz to The Doors; and from Deep Purple to Rosetta Stone. Such a band is Northern Ireland's Blues Experience, who recently sold out Belfast's 400-seater Lyric Theatre and who were acclaimed for their performance last year at the Edinburgh Festival.

The band was formed in 1993 by fretless bassist Jackie Flavelle, whose professional career had begun in 1959 with the massively popular Dave Glover Band. 'We all sat down with music stands and read music and had orchestrations,' recalls Flavelle. 'Then the showband thing broke and we moved towards that. We used to get the top-ten records in Smithfield Market and learn them. But Dave and I fell out over rock 'n' roll. I used to sing "Shakin' All Over" and one night Dave said, "You're too loud," and I says, "You bastards can't play rock 'n' roll anyway." There was a shouting match onstage. We got to my house afterwards and Dave threw my gear out of the back of the van and said, "Goodbye!"'

Trevor Hodgett • Includes material originally published in *Blueprint* (May 1996), the *Irish News* (10 March 1995; 4 May 1996) and *The Avenue* (12 November 1999); plus additional material

Recording session for the Chris Barber Band's 'Catcall', 1967: Jackie Flavelle (second left), Brian Auger (third left), Paul McCartney (far right)

A youthful martyr to rock 'n' roll, Jackie spent the next three years based in Derry with The Johnny Quigley Band ('One of the most popular bands in the country – we did the really big ballrooms which held from 1,000 to 2,500'), in Birmingham, leading the band in an Irish club, and Galway, with The Swing-time Aces. In 1963 he returned to Glover. 'We were on a wage, playing five or six nights a week. We did all right – and Dave probably made a fortune!'

By now blues was becoming popular in Belfast. 'That was totally taboo in showbands. But we used to hire the room above Dougie Knight's shop in Great Victoria Street for blows. Van Morrison lived on the top floor adjacent to showband drummer Tommy Thomas, so he was in and out. Also Peter Lloyd's studio was going strong at the time. He has a tape of Van and myself playing together. The first time I heard Them was in the Maritime and I was totally amazed. People would say now that the band was rough or whatever but it wasn't. It was at least the quality of, if not better than, any of the bands who were coming out of London.'

Them once performed as special guests with the Glover Band at the Astor Ballroom. 'The crowd went absolutely bananas. Rock 'n' roll idolatry! Van had stage presence and he was the first one I heard locally who could sing blues. I always believed in him, from the first time I saw him as a squirt to the superstar he deservedly is now. I thought he was terrific. Always.'

In 1966 Jackie was headhunted by top English jazzman Chris Barber, who had become a star in the trad boom of the late Fifties/early Sixties. 'Needless to say I nearly broke his arm! I was really pleased to get out of the showband scene, much fun as it was, because there was no musical satisfaction. The trad boom was in the doldrums so Chris hired me and [guitarist] John Slaughter and the band started to go in the blues/R&B direction. We were basically playing clubs but Chris had been very big in Europe and hung on to that, so the European work sustained us. We were the first British group in East Berlin since the Cold War. We played in a 15,000-seater for three nights and it was sold out. We arrived like The Beatles in New York and were followed every-where by photographers. Good fun!'

Ottilie Patterson sang with the band. 'A brilliant singer. Inspiring. Ottilie could turn you on. You'd go, "Arrrgggghhh!" She was Bessie Smith from Comber. She threw the odd head stagger but basically she's a very warm-hearted person and her IQ is amazing. Ottilie joined this Russian society in London: she could speak the language fluently in a month, she was into the literature in three months and she was giving lectures on it within six months. She's an absolute genius. She knows all about painting, all about literature. Amazing woman.'

The Barber band toured with Sonny Terry & Brownie McGhee. Sonny Boy Williamson also worked with Barber. 'He kept disappearing. We were playing the Marquee and we couldn't find him – he was in Leicester Square playing the harmonica to taxi drivers. Going from cab to cab saying, "I'm Sonny Boy Williamson, man, very pleased to see you. I play the blues you know . . ."'

Paul McCartney wrote and produced a single, 'Catcall', for the band. 'It took three days, a phenomenal time for a single for a jazz/blues band. It was a perfectly produced pop single and for an instrumental it did quite well. [Actress and McCartney girlfriend] Jane Asher was the chief go-out-and-fetch-food person. She would take a pound off everyone. Paul didn't carry any money, so when we had a whip-round [drummer] Graham Burbridge used to put the pound in for him.'

Was McCartney overbearing? 'With us he wasn't. He was absolutely fine. In fact he couldn't have been better to me. He spent at least two hours getting the bass sound right and at the end of the day it sounded like him. When the single came out people said to me, "That's not you; it's McCartney," because he has a very distinctive bass-playing sound and I sound a bit like it on this record.'

In the late Sixties Barber nearly hired a new singer. 'Rod Stewart used to come down to the Marquee where we were resident and sit in with the band, during the time he was out of work just before The Faces. He actually asked for the gig. We had a meeting to decide whether we would let him join the band and we decided against because he wasn't a good blues singer. But we were always very pally with Rod. Absolutely and entirely one of the boys. When Rod made it he wrote a track on the *Smiler* album with the Barber band in mind – "Dixie Toot" – so we recorded it with him and he made a video of it. There I am in the video with the boul' Rod!'

In 1972 Jackie released a solo album of his own compositions on York Records. 'Nobody more amazed than me. It was the sort of stuff I was listening to at the time – sort of Neil Young-ish, James Taylor-y. It got good reviews in *Melody Maker* and *NME* but York went bust shortly after. I sold about 2,000 which would have been the first run. I also released [James Taylor's] "Fire And Rain" as a single, before anybody else. It was in the charts but Blood, Sweat & Tears arrived about three weeks after me, split the airplay and neither of us made it.'

The magic began to fade for Jackie. 'That era when it was really exciting around the London scene, and kicking around with pop stars, all finished. A new scene came in with bands like Queen. The old R&B, mates-together scene died on its feet. If they weren't already rich they weren't going to be. It was over. And to be frank I got bored out of my tree.'

While pondering his future Jackie dabbled in session work. 'Those Liverpool kids like the Jackson 5 [possibly Five Star] – I played on five or six top-ten records for them but I forget what they were called. And I did quite a few sessions with Deep Purple. Me with the fretless bass: maybe [Purple keyboard player] Jon Lord would have a song and he would want a different style and we'd go and do that.'

In 1973 Jackie, bizarrely, almost became one of The Doors following the death of Jim Morrison. 'We rehearsed for about three months. Nice guys. The only thing [keyboard player] Ray Manzarek ever said to me was either, "Yeah," or "No." We were trying ambitious things like funny time signatures but it didn't really work 'cos the only musician in The Doors who could blow was Ray Manzarek – and he didn't talk. Robbie Krieger, though sounding fine, learnt everything off on guitar. He would go away for three days and come back with something to play and that wouldn't have changed till the end of time.

'It was all mega – "Come over and we'll give you a ranch in California." I enjoyed it but if I'd been living on a ranch in California I wouldn't have wanted to do it with those guys.'

Instead of becoming the new Jim Morrison, Jackie discovered the joys of broadcasting. 'We were kicking about Radio Luxembourg after a gig. "Baby" Bob [Stewart] was doing his programme and he says, "One of you guys have a blatter at this," and me being me I was in like a dog. And I thought, This is great!'

With an idea now of his future Jackie left Barber. 'The last job was at the Nord Sea Jazz Festival. We played after Count Basie and before Duke Ellington. I wanted to stop when it was all there.'

Back in Ireland Jackie became a presenter with Downtown Radio. 'I'm also the Information Co-ordinator and Press & Information producer. Isn't that terrific? Although sometimes I hanker for the carefree days when all you had to do was to be at the gig and make sure you were in tune!'

But, despite his corporate responsibilities, Jackie has never given up music completely, playing first with the Jim Daly Blues Band and then forming Blues Experience with Daly's long-serving guitarist Ronnie Greer, keyboard virtuoso Paul McIntyre – who has worked with Phil Coulter and others – and drummer Colm Fitzpatrick of Rosetta Stone fame.

The band is fronted by Greer who plays the blues with a ferocity and an exhilarating intensity that is truly of world class and who, like virtually all Irish musicians of his vintage, began his career with showbands. 'When I was fifteen, in 1965, I played with The Secrets, then I became involved in cabaret in the late Sixties, playing with Mark Scott & The Marksmen in the Talk of the Town and the Abercorn, backing people like Candy Devine.'

More crucially Greer also began playing in the late Sixties with Ireland's greatest-ever blues musician, the late Jim Daly, a relationship that lasted for 25 years. 'Jim was playing the Golden Jubilee in Cromac Street and was always willing to let young people sit in, which I did, and the rest is history.

'Jim is an out-and-out bluesman, an authentic Chicago-style pianist *à la* Otis Spann and Maceo Merriweather, who was the guy who influenced Otis Spann, and some nights, when he turned it on, his playing brought tears to my eyes. If you had a blindfold test and heard Jim, Otis Spann and Maceo Merriweather, it would be very hard to distinguish who's who. Jim, when he turns it on, can be as good as any of them. And he doesn't compromise – if you move away from that particular style of music, rather than play something he doesn't really feel he is contributing to, Jim will stop playing and fold his arms and wait until the number's over, and then move on to his type of music. He's done that many's a time!'

The Blues Experience:
Jackie Flavelle (left),
Ronnie Greer,
1995

In the mid-Seventies Greer doubled with the Kenny McDowell-led Bronco, resident at the legendary Pound music club. 'When you first hear Kenny it's overwhelming because he's a really great singer. But Bronco was a pressure gig because I replaced Jim Armstrong who had a technique that far outweighed anyone else and you got all these air guitarists there waiting for me to fall flat on my face! But the Pound was an institution. It was good times within bad times in Northern Ireland. It was a place where there never were the problems that permeated other aspects of society. People from all sections of the political divide went, united by the music.

'Bronco was a cover band mainly although we did the odd original number and Kenny was always very fussy about the material he chose. There was an element of him trying to educate the punters, of him trying to introduce someone new – who he thought was outstanding – to the public at large. And there was a coterie of people who went to hear the band who looked for that, but there was the other average Joe Public who would have wanted to have heard "Sweet Home Alabama" or "Sunshine Of Your Love" so I suppose Bronco's strength was ultimately its weakness as well.'

When Bronco split Greer concentrated on his work with Daly. 'By now black artists were coming over more frequently and we backed Memphis Slim, Byther Smith, Lefty Dizz, Fenton Robinson, Cousin Joe, Phil Guy, Eddie Burns, Carey and Lurrie Bell and others. You never have any preparation with them – you just go on and play, but it's not too difficult if you understand the idiom and they were all amicable, though some of them, if they threw you a solo, were taken aback by what came back, so you never got another solo all night! But it was only when these guys started telling me that I was good that I started to believe I was. Lurrie Bell was the best guitar player I've ever played with and he said, "Man, you was smoking!" And I remember Lowell Fulson sighing, "Man, you sure make me feel homesick!" And Sonny Terry said, "Hey, I'm gonna use you on my next album" – but he used Johnny Winter instead! Dr John was the best experience. He brought things out of me I didn't know were there.'

The good doctor's then-infamous drug problems were nonetheless apparent. 'He came into the dressing room and took his cap off and all his bits and pieces were inside the cap. The second night they had to virtually carry him into the gig because he could hardly walk, but he still played great. But the first night we had a nice time with him backstage and he actually started singing the "Dirty Dozens" for me personally and by the time he'd finished all 25 verses, twenty people had gathered and everybody clapped and he was laughing and delighted.

'I found him a very nice guy. Jim and I were out with Van Morrison one night and Van said he found him a strange sort of a guy, into all the voodoo and stuff. Maybe Van has more experience of him than I would have, but my experience of him was that he was really nice.'

A gig with Little Willie Littlefield, with Van Morrison's cousin Sammy Stitt guesting on harmonica, was broadcast. 'A while later Jim rang me and said,

"I'm at Sammy's house with Van and Van wants to see the video," so I took it up. Torry McGahey, who had been in The Freshmen, was our bassist and Torry's been bald since he was about four and hasn't changed over the years, so every gig we ever played someone would always say, "Hey, didn't yer man play with The Freshmen?" or whatever. So we were watching the video and Van suddenly says, "Hey, that wee lad played with The Freshmen!"

'I actually had played with Van once in Lurgan in the Calypso Ballroom after Them before he went off and made his fortune in America. I was playing with the relief band and his own guitar player didn't show up – an English guy called John Cox – and I went on. If I remember correctly the band was booed off the stage after four or five numbers.

'I've been in Van's company several nights and the thing about Van is, for all his fame, he's still an enthusiast at heart. One night I was asking him about various people he had played with and he talked till three o'clock in the morning recounting stories about John Lee Hooker and so on. It was rather nice that someone like that showed that kind of enthusiasm. That's why he gets on well with Jim because he knows Jim's heavily into the music and he can feel comfortable with him.'

With Jim Daly semi-retired during the last years of his life, Greer began working with Blues Experience, accompanying American bluesmen such as John Primer, Big Jack Johnson, Philip Walker and others. 'Philip and me were trading solos one night, matching each other, when he started playing with his teeth and I couldn't match that. So the next night I said, "I hope you won't do that on me again, Philip," and he said he wouldn't. But during the set he did start doing it. I said, "I thought you weren't going to do that!" and he said, "I had to, man, you were sitting there right on my shoulder!"'

Despite his musical success Greer has always refused to turn pro. 'I'm a sales manager in a steel stockholding company and I make a good living. In fact when [English blues guitarist] Dave Peabody saw my BMW once, he jokingly said, "Hey, I thought you were a real bluesman!" And by not going professional I've probably played with more great musicians than if I'd gone to America and joined a blues band, because here, every time someone of note comes over, we play with them.'

Blues Experience have just released their first album, *The Official Bootleg*, on the Good Vibrations label. 'It was recorded live in Magherafelt, on mini-disc. Hi-fi buffs don't like it because it sounds like a real gig. It's a document of a night in Magherafelt and with every live recording you're going to have a few flaws, so I think it's a bit ropey here and there, but it has its moments.'

Postscript: Flavelle is now retired from Downtown Radio and has become a successful, freelance pro musician, playing several nights a week in various jazz, blues and country line-ups. Blues Experience are effectively defunct, apart from the very occasional gig, but Greer now co-leads The Kenny McDowell/Ronnie Greer Band.

SECTION 4
ROCK IN A HARD PLACE

Henry McCullough,
onstage in Warsaw, 2001

HENRY McCULLOUGH
PROLOGUE

When local promoter Nigel Martyn broke the news to me over the phone I was so shocked that I had to sit down.

Nigel's news wasn't that a loved one had died: it was that Henry McCullough was to be presented with a Lifetime Achievement Award from the Ards Guitar Festival – and that the organisers wanted me to present it to him, in front of the Queen's Hall audience.

I could think of no worthier recipient, for through the showband era and the beat-group era and the folk-rock era and the rock era, Henry had been one of the most charismatic and compelling performers in Ireland and beyond. But, in common with most of the human race, I find the thought of making a speech in front of hundreds of people about as appealing as the thought of having my toenails ripped off. So my first thought was to wimp out, but because of my huge admiration for McCullough I found myself agreeing and trying to sound nonchalant.

The deal was that this was to be a surprise for Henry. At the end of his festival gig I was to bound on stage and make my speech and the presentation. The possibilities for a fiasco seemed endless. What if Henry got off stage before I got on? What if – and the more I thought about it, the more inevitable this seemed – the audience all buggered off to the bar as soon as Henry finished and they saw some nonentity shuffling on stage and beginning to mumble into the mike? What if nobody listened to what I had to say and the hubbub of conversation drowned me out?

But making the presentation turned into one of the most satisfying experiences of my life. As I started to speak I saw every face in the audience light up in delight and I got a moving sense of how beloved Henry is by audiences. Every face was beaming with pleasure, everyone was delighted that Henry was getting an award he so richly deserved. Every statement I made about Henry's career was greeted with rapturous applause, every compliment I paid him was cheered.

When I finished speaking and turned to present Henry with the sculptured artwork that was his award he embraced me for a few seconds and then spoke graciously to the audience. And then he left the stage visibly moved and to a tremendous ovation. I joined him in the dressing room and he was clearly thrilled. Touchingly he told me – and has repeated to me since – that what made the award even more special for him was that I had been the one to present it to him.

Trevor Hodgett

And presenting it to him was certainly special for me for I have seen Henry play dozens of times and been thrilled every time by the power and passion of his playing and by his uncompromising commitment to his artistic vision.

On stage in Ards, on 29 October 2001, this, recreated from my notes, is what I had to say:

'Every year the Ards International Guitar Festival presents a Lifetime Achievement Award. Last year, you'll remember, the award was presented to Davy Graham. I've been asked to announce this year's winner which I'm delighted to do because it's hard to imagine a more deserving winner than the man to whom we have just been listening, the great Henry McCullough, for Henry's musical achievements over decades really have been colossal.

'He played in showbands, like The Skyrockets and Gene & The Gents; he played in a beat group, The People. He played psychedelic rock with Eire Apparent, who toured the world with Jimi Hendrix. He pretty much invented folk rock by adding his electric guitar to Sweeney's Men. He became an international rock star with Joe Cocker & The Grease Band and, yes, he really was the only Irishman to play at the Woodstock Festival. He even became a pioneer of the rock musical by working with Andrew Lloyd Webber on the original recording of *Jesus Christ Superstar*. And, of course, with Paul McCartney & Wings he had hit records like "Hi Hi Hi", "C Moon" and "My Love".

'Since the mid-Eighties Henry has been back in Ireland leading his own magnificent bands. Henry is a riveting performer and I think what makes his playing so compelling is the sense that he is a driven man, utterly possessed by the power of his music. He plays blues, he plays country and he plays rock 'n' roll and he plays them all with searing intensity – whatever he's playing, a Henry McCullough performance is permanently at white heat.

'Henry rocked through the Sixties, through the Seventies, through the Eighties, through the Nineties and he's now rocking in the twenty-first century.

'He's a great survivor, he's a great guitarist, he's a great performer and he's a great guy. We're so, so lucky to have him, so on behalf of Ards Guitar Festival, Henry, let me congratulate you and present you with this wonderful trophy. Henry McCullough!'

HENRY McCULLOUGH

The year 2001 hasn't been a bad year for Northern Irish bluesman Henry McCullough, for in recent months he has sold several million records and reached number two in the American album charts. Not, admittedly, with his solo CD, *Belfast To Boston*, admirable though that album is, but with the recent Paul McCartney & Wings compilation *Wingspan* – for of course it was Henry who played lead guitar on Wings classics like 'My Love', 'Live And Let Die' and 'Hi Hi Hi'.

Sales of *Wingspan* were boosted by an acclaimed television documentary shown around the world. 'I watched the documentary with great joy,' declares McCullough, who returned to live in his native Northern Ireland in the mid-Eighties. 'The music was great and it made me realise more than before that I'm part of rock history. I actually sent McCartney a wee note to say I'd enjoyed watching it and it brought back many memories and I got a nice letter back from him to say thanks and he hoped I was well and to keep plucking them silver strings. And he drew a wee caricature of himself, with that little rounded face of his. It was nice to hear from him.'

McCullough, whose career had begun in Irish showbands, joined Wings in 1972. 'I got an invitation through [Wings guitarist] Denny Laine to go for an audition with McCartney. We played for two or three days. He says, "Do you want the gig?" and I says, "Aye."'

Despite the fame, Wings didn't make Henry's fortune. 'I was on £70 a week. Enough to get yourself a motor. There were no session fees but we got a £500 bonus for the *Red Rose Speedway* album and there was the odd perk – like after the album we jetted off in a Lear jet to Morocco for a few weeks.

'McCartney is a perfectionist. You just have to go along with that. Ninety per cent of what we played on each song was the same every night, so it was almost like being back in the showbands. If he had a song he would say, "This particular lick would fit in here," so you would play that lick. But if there was a section where there was a gap, you were allowed to make up what you wanted, as long as it fitted.'

On the recording of 'My Love' McCullough asserted himself, and created one of the greatest solos in all of rock music. 'I thought, At least give me a go at doing something instead of having to play something that you made up last night. So five minutes before the take I said, "Listen, I have to change this solo." So that panicked him! I didn't have a clue what I was going to play. If it hadn't worked out I'd have felt a right fool. But I got it in one take. When I

Trevor Hodgett - Includes material previously published in the *Irish News* (5 September 1998; 22 September 2001), *Blueprint* (September 1996) and *Blues In Britain* (March 2002); plus additional material

listened to the playback I realised it fitted perfectly, so it proved a point to McCartney regarding myself.'

A *Top of the Pops* appearance promoting the record was a less-glorious experience for McCullough. 'I was totally langered,' he admits. 'As we got to the solo I knew I was going to throw up. I only had time to leap off stage and dive behind scenery – still playing the solo as I was being sick. The worst of it was I'd sent my mother a postcard: "Watch *Top of the Pops* on Thursday." McCartney was very tolerant and never said anything. He'd seen everything in his Beatle days so nothing shocked him. I think he just thought I was having an alcoholic burst out and being typically Irish.'

Bizarrely, McCullough played drums on 'C Moon'. 'We were in the studio and I was just sitting around the drums and McCartney was futering about on the piano and the music started moving – and then it was, "OK, let's record this." And so I stayed on the drums. And I was quite surprised recently to see a *Top of the Pops 2* which was all McCartney and on "C Moon" there I was, as confident as you like, battering away on the drums. I knew I'd played drums on the record but I'd forgotten *Top of the Pops* and to see it was really weird.'

However, some of McCartney's music, and the associated videos, disenchanted Henry. 'Wearing a white suit and lying against a tree pretending to sing "Mary Had A Little Lamb" – it's a far cry from John Lee Hooker!'

Wings' first tour was low-key. 'We just got in the back of the Transit, with dogs and kids and the truck behind and just turned up at universities. He would stick his head in and say, "Is it all right if we play here tonight?" and of course that was it. That was the bonding period, in the back of a bloody Transit with no windows, because we all wanted this to work. That would have been the poor man's *Magical Mystery Tour*. We all got on real well. If you don't have a happy working group it doesn't work. McCartney needs that, like everybody does.'

Henry toured England and Europe with Wings, the band, once, succumbing to rock 'n' roll cliché by trashing their dressing room. 'We were playing football in the dressing room and it went from knocking over the odd carton of popcorn or whatever to kicking the ball a bit harder and knocking down something else. It was like mob rule: the more you thrashed it the more someone else would thrash it. But after it was done we looked at the mess and we felt really stupid.'

McCartney, at the time something of a drug-squad magnet, was busted on Wings' European tour. 'The office had sent out a bit of grass, but, as opposed to doing it subtly, they'd just put it in brown paper and taped it up and by the time it got to Sweden there were twigs sticking out.'

McCartney's insistence on having his wife Linda, a non-musician, playing keyboards seriously compromised the band. 'Well, of course it was frustrating. It was brought to his attention and hers. It was for the future of the band that we would have had these discussions because everybody wanted it to work as much as Paul himself. Well and good, let Linda come along but let's bring in a piano player to do the job properly. Let Linda play something else and sing her little harmonies and have a good time . . . but it was not to be. So there was just that little weird side to it. It was established that this is the way it's going to be, boys. And that was that. It was no more brought up and nobody moaned. She wasn't a musician at all but at the end of the day she was able to play something. She was taught the parts by Paul and she never ventured too far from that – she could shuffle maracas, she could play the tambourine. I think she handled it really well.

'And the band was great live. We had a lot of great, rocky numbers. I had a great time as everybody else did. The odd time he would have done "Long Tall Sally" as an encore and he was brilliant at it. We were like a bunch of kids really after the gig and all the rest of it.'

Inevitably, however, the constraints of playing in a band musically controlled by someone else began to grate on McCullough and he walked out in 1973, during rehearsals for the *Band On The Run* album. 'I had a row with McCartney over what to play and where to play it. And it was quite severe: "You'll fucking do this," – like I'm the boss. "We'll see about that, you c——!" And I just packed my guitar, stuck my amp in the car and set sail. And that was my stint in Wings done.

'I didn't call him, and the next day he said, "Where's Henry?" And Denny Laine said, "He's gone." Paul knew it was coming. I think he preferred it that way because at some point he may have had to have given me the sack which he didn't want to do. The fact that I left at that particular time was good for me and it was good for him. I think if it had gone on for another three or four months it wouldn't have worked. It wouldn't have come to blows but it would have been man against man. And that is the situation that we all try to avoid.

'I don't resent anything. He was great to work with. He is a very respectable family man. He liked to come home, sit down, watch Cilla Black and smoke a joint. Who doesn't nowadays? We got on really well and I left of my own accord. Two months later he drove to Victoria where I was staying, wrote me a cheque for £5,000, and says, "Here Henry, thanks very much. I really appreciate it. Nice one." We drank a half-bottle of whiskey, smoked a couple of joints, shook hands and that was that. He's a lovely man. A genuine, hard-working person and a dedicated artist.'

Working with the sainted Macca was the highest-profile gig of McCullough's career but by the time he was hired to join Wings McCullough was already a vastly experienced player, whose career to date represented, in microcosm, something of a history of Sixties popular music: from showbands to a beat group, The People, to psychedelic pop with Eire Apparent, to folk rock with Sweeney's Men, to rock stardom with Joe Cocker & The Grease Band with whom he became the only Irishman to play at the Woodstock Festival and with whom he played on the original recording of the pioneering rock opera *Jesus Christ Superstar*.

McCullough still recalls his apprentice days in showbands with affection, when he played in such bands as The Skyrockets and Gene & The Gents.

'Being allowed to go out and play music was fantastic,' he recalls. 'We did everything from Chuck Berry to Jim Reeves to old-time waltzes to comedy, like Peter Sellers and Sophia Loren's "Goodness Gracious Me" – the punters all loved that. It initiated me into the showbiz end of music, which stood me in good stead later when I got involved with McCartney, because he was a bit showbandy, with us all wearing the same jackets. Only flashier than The Skyrockets!

'Cecil Kettyles, the leader of The Skyrockets, I remember, used to turn out our pockets to see if there were any Dexedrine [pep pills] and confiscate them. And I remember we played a seminary once and me being the only Protestant they had me sit in the van while the priest came out and blessed it!'

In backward, rural Ireland, McCullough's next showband, Gene & The Gents, had a unique selling point – their singer was a black South African. 'He was a novelty. Can you imagine it down in Mayo or somewhere – this guy flying around singing "My Boy Lollipop"!'

With the advent of the British beat boom, Henry began to feel stifled. 'Chrissie Stewart, the bass player in The People, who had moved from Belfast to Blackpool, heard I wasn't too happy in the showbands and gave me a call. That was my chance: to go off and join a beat group! There was great money in showbands but I arrived in Blackpool to find these four boys going out for £7 a night and living in one room.'

The People retreated to Dublin – and took the scene by storm. 'It was great in Dublin – but after we peaked there, there was nowhere else to go but London. Into the van, gear in back, writing in lipstick 'Off to London'. In London we lived in the van, all five of us, including the roadie. Then we got this gig at the Middle Earth with Pink Floyd, with Procol Harum, at the time of "Whiter Shade Of Pale", headlining. Mike Jeffries and Chas Chandler were in the audience and came up and said, "Sign this contract!" We said, "No problem." They sent us to Majorca for three months to write original material and we came back with suntans but only one song – because of too many banana daiquiris.

'We did a package tour with Hendrix, The Move, Amen Corner, Pink Floyd, The Nice and The Outer Limits, who became Yes. It was incredible, but Hendrix was always very distant. You could have a smoke or a drink with him but at no time did I ever feel at ease with him. No one ever did. He wouldn't snub you but you'd be afraid around him. He had this thing about him. You could never go up and say, "How're you doing, Jimi?"'

The band moved to New York, living in the Chelsea Hotel, and Henry began a long-running romance with Janis Joplin. 'I walked into the bar in the hotel and there was yer woman sat with the hair flying and guffawing and we got chatting – and if you watch the movie *Janis* you'll see her shouting, "I'm really in love with this Irishman I just met!" She wanted us to go to the Bahamas. I hadn't been too far from home and I thought, Could this be the end of me? She was like a big sister and I was like a toyboy trailing behind her.

Jimi Hendrix (left), Robert Wyatt of Soft Machine (centre), Henry McCullough (right),1968

She was brilliant – always lovely San Francisco clothes, always the best of dope. She wasn't into heroin then – just Acapulco Gold, which is lethal weed. Then she got into heroin and was more inclined to stay in her room all day.'

Eire Apparent toured the States extensively, with Hendrix and with Eric Burdon & The New Animals. 'Eric Burdon was a psychedelic man. He would slip you this and that when you didn't know about it, then he would switch on this tape recorder and ask you these absurd questions. And then he'd play it back. You can imagine what that was like. He'd write it all down and say, "This is for my new film." He wanted to be the Lone Ranger, I think.'

In Toronto disaster struck when McCullough was busted for marijuana possession. 'They took me to court and let me out on bail and Chandler and Jeffries gave me a one-way ticket to Dublin. I was shell shocked getting the sack but I was the most rebellious in the band and they probably felt if they got me out it might be easier to manipulate the rest.'

Back in Ireland Henry joined seminal electric-folk band Sweeney's Men with Johnny Moynihan, later of Planxty, and Terry Woods, later of The Pogues. 'At that time the folk musicians and the rock 'n' roll musicians had started coming to each other's gigs, and I became friendly with Johnny Moynihan. I joined when Andy Irvine went to Romania. Electric guitar, tin whistle and bouzouki was a strange mixture. It lasted three months. We didn't know how to intertwine the electric guitar and the acoustic instruments. [Famed Irish scene-maker] B.P. Fallon managed to hustle us back together [in 1986] for a radio show but it was a hell of a mess because over the years Johnny and Terry had become enemies. It was live but Johnny would put his accordion down – "I'm going for a piss," – and walk off when Terry started to play. It didn't turn out the way we had hoped.'

Needless to say the band mystified and enraged rural Irish audiences. 'There were rows and ructions about getting paid. In Longford once nobody applauded and there were taunts. Afterwards the promoter paid us half and said, "You're the worst band we've had." When we were leaving a few of the lads were thumping on the bonnet but eventually they let us go.'

Henry joined Sweeney's Men after the band's first album, *Sweeney's Men*, and left before its second album, *The Tracks Of Sweeney*, although two songs which he co-wrote are on the latter. 'I was doing the Cambridge Folk Festival with Sweeney's Men and we went to London for a couple of gigs and I was staying in the Madison Hotel, which was a haunt for people like John Lee Hooker and Freddie King. Joe Cocker was staying there with [keyboard player] Chris Stainton and they were looking for a guitar player for The Grease Band. I was getting a wee bit bored with not having drums or bass, so I went down to audition at the Marquee and that was it.'

'At first we used to split the money five ways, until Joe began to have more success and then the money would go back to the office and we got £50 a week. No royalties or session fees. You did it all because it was all rolling with the flow. You never thought what would happen if it broke up.'

Was it a thrill playing with such a phenomenal singer? 'Once you get

Sweeney's Men,
Cambridge Folk Festival,
1968

involved working with people, regardless of how talented, you become immune to anything like that. It's like mates: "Go out there and sing a bit, Joe."'

The Grease Band were reportedly wild rock 'n' roll outlaws. 'We were fairly wild. Get paid, go to the bar, go home, get sick . . . no it wasn't quite that bad! We did one tour with Gene Pitney and we were wilder than him but nothing serious.'

Cocker cracked America after his phenomenal performance at Woodstock. 'All the performers were staying at the Holiday Inn, about twenty miles from the festival. When I woke up there that morning I had four lines of cocaine. In those days it was three or four grams a week – three to four hundred pounds' worth – just for your personal use. Just to open your eyes, brighten you up and get you going – like having seven cups of coffee in one go with a Liquorice Allsort on the side! Then I headed down to the bar and there was Jerry Garcia and John Sebastian and so on, all flashing peace signs. You would nod and acknowledge each other but any company that was kept was usually in the toilet – taking drugs. At eleven o'clock we got the call to board the helicopter, an old army job, which had landed in the garden. The inside was all decked out with camouflage netting so we felt like we were going into battle. It was exciting but everybody felt tense and there was no conversation.

'Our keyboard player Chris Stainton had taken LSD, and when we were up there he said to the co-pilot he was going to throw up, so the co-pilot opened the sliding door wide enough that Chris could get his head out, without his shoulders, and he was sick over half a million people.'

Not surprisingly Stainton was still feeling queasy after the helicopter landed. 'There was a big marquee backstage and Chris put his arm round one of the poles and slid to the ground. I remember Phil Lesh of The Grateful Dead went over and kissed him on the head. I suppose he must have agreed with him about something.'

Surprisingly McCullough didn't feel nervous playing in front of the largest crowd ever gathered for a rock gig. 'You get more nervous playing in someone's front room,' he insists. 'But to walk out in front of a sea of faces stretching as far as you could see was incredible. The gig was a real peak for us. The first time I ever got to turn up full volume with Joe. When we came to the final number, "With A Little Help From My Friends", the sky just exploded. It was incredible. Chris was playing the best organ ending I ever heard at the end of the song and then the heavens started going berserk and the rain started coming down in torrents. I think that helped make it special. It was the perfect gig, I suppose.

'Afterwards me and [bassist] Alan Spenner missed the helicopter out so they got us a spare, a wee bubble job. It was like a Volkswagen! That was terrifying altogether, because when it lifts up, it leans forward. Back in the Holiday Inn we just had time for a bottle of Scotch and a couple of beers and then off to the next gig. Just another day in the touring schedule really.'

McCullough played on Cocker's first two albums, *With A Little Help From My Friends* (1969) and *Joe Cocker* (1970), but disastrously missed some of the sessions for the latter. 'Janis Joplin turned me on to heroin – she was the first woman that injected me with drugs, in her room in the Chelsea Hotel with the scarves round the lights and joss sticks. We were in bed and she did it to herself. She says, "Have you ever had this?" I says, "No," and I can mind her saying, "Hey boy, you not able to handle this?" So I says, "OK, hit me, hit me." It was like being in a cotton-wool ball. A lovely drug but so fucking dangerous. But I ended up getting hepatitis from that first time that I ever had a needle put in my arm. Oh, it was lethal. Two or three days later my arm went dark purple and I didn't know what was happening. And that ruined a lot of work for me out in LA when we were doing the *Joe Cocker* album. That's when [pianist/guitarist/arranger] Leon Russell came in because I was in bed fucking sick from fever and everything.'

Subsequently Cocker was talked into leaving the band to form Mad Dogs And Englishmen, with Russell. 'The night before Joe left to go back to the States for the Mad Dogs tour we stayed up all night together. He was as nervous going there as we were being left on our own.'

The Cocker-less Grease Band's subsequent tour of Europe with [blues legend] Freddie King was ill-fated. 'We all got blind drunk on the plane and aggro started. Our bassist pushed me and I fell and broke my hand, so I had to just sing on that tour.'

More happily The Grease Band played on the original, ground-breaking *Jesus Christ Superstar* album. 'I loved it. It was so unusual. I could never read the guitar parts so I would go in an hour beforehand and Andrew Lloyd Webber would sit at the piano and show me how it went. He wasn't after session musicians – he was after feel. He knew if he took the time beforehand, it would be worth it.'

By and by The Grease Band fizzled out and McCullough's Wings adventure began. When he walked the plank and left McCartney before the *Band On The Run* sessions, he was soon followed by the band's drummer Denny Seiwell. 'Whenever Denny Seiwell left Wings we got together with [keyboard player] Mick Weaver and [ex-Eire Apparent bassist] Chrissie Stewart and it was a band called Druth. We lived in Chicago for three months and then we went to San Francisco and did the Andy Fairweather Low album *Spider Jiving*. [Atlantic Records' founder] Ahmet Ertegun came down to hear Druth. He mustn't have liked us very much but it was great because he was in a white suit, with a big cigar: "Hey Ahmet, give Aretha me number!"

'Anyway, that all fell through and I met up with Joe again and we decided to put something together. We went up to this ranch in Santa Barbara and in six months we rehearsed one song – "With A Little Help From My Friends". Why? Well, the bass player was into smack, the drummer Jimmy Karstein was into guns, Mick Weaver and his old lady were into each other – I think she might have changed sex at some point – and I was drinking tequila first thing in the morning with a teaspoonful of mescaline. A few psychedelic freaks, a smackhead and the drummer into guns: it makes a fucking great combination!

And Joe was trying to keep his belly in by lying on a bottle of Courvoisier. Everybody was just too out of it.'

A biography of Cocker, *A Little Help From My Friends*, by J.P. Bean, alleges that at this time Henry pulled a gun on Cocker. 'Jesus, I didn't read that,' gasps an appalled McCullough. 'No, no, not at all. Are you serious?'

McCullough later recorded several solo albums, including 1975's *Mind Your Own Business* for George Harrison's Dark Horse label. 'I didn't spend that much time with him, but he seems a nice chap. But when he lost the ["My Sweet Lord" copyright] lawsuit everybody on the label had to go their own way.'

McCullough also worked with Eric Burdon, Carol Grimes, Ronnie Lane, Roy Harper ('He's one of the greatest, I think. A great talent, a great gentleman and a smashing person.') and Frankie Miller, but while touring with Miller a classic McCullough mishap occurred in Sausalito, when he was arrested for a driving offence. 'They let Frankie go but I got a handcuff job. I wasn't worried about the drink-driving so much as about the chunk of dope in my pocket but I managed to manoeuvre myself around and lifted the dope out of my pocket and ate it. They flung me in a cage inside a cage – a real Hannibal Lecter job. I was in my rock 'n' roll clobber with leopard-skin trousers and flung in with these derelicts. Who were they? I don't know; nobody I knew.'

Strangely, Miller told nobody about Henry's plight and he was left to stew for two days until his absence was noticed and he was bailed out. 'Frankie

Henry McCullough, backstage at the Elmwood Hall, Belfast, 1994

wasn't apologetic, no. He's a real wee Scottish gurrier!'

In the mid-Eighties an accident nearly ended Henry's career. 'My hand slipped down a kitchen knife and severed the tendons on three fingers. Thankfully it was the right hand. The fingers were dropping off but they did microsurgery at the Ulster Hospital and put them back together again. It was a difficult time but it's all good for a laugh. It makes you cool your suedes. Everything in life works itself out. If you feel strong enough in yourself, you know you can cope.'

Since that nadir McCullough has worked extensively throughout Ireland and, strangely, has developed a parallel career in Poland. 'A Polish lecturer from Coleraine University had heard me and asked if I'd like to go to Poland with my Irish rock 'n' roll – I think it was some kind of cultural vibe he was pushing on me – and I went and the audiences enjoyed it a lot. They found it novel that someone from Ireland should be able to sing a bit of blues or country. The touring end of it has been fantastic – they treat me extremely well, the musicians that I play with are of the first quality and the audiences enjoy it a lot and are very affectionate towards me.'

Two of McCullough's albums, *Blue Sunset* (1997) and *Belfast To Boston* (2001), have been recorded in Poland. 'For *Blue Sunset* I was asked would I like to go into the studio for a bit of *craic*, so we started recording at two o'clock one day and we were finished by six o'clock!'

A particularly stunning performance is of McCullough's own, harrowing composition 'Locked In And We Can't Get Out'. 'It's about Northern Ireland. Even with Clinton having flitted through and maybe some light at the end of the tunnel, I think for many years the majority of people here will be locked in and can't get out, because of an old situation. But I wouldn't call the song venting any anger – it's just a wee rock 'n' roll song really.'

The stand-out track on *Belfast To Boston* is the title track, performed solo on acoustic guitar, a song that resembles a traditional Irish folk song of emigration except that it includes disorientating lyrics about taking psychedelic drugs with Native Americans. 'That track is what pleases me most about the album. It's based in part on my career but heavily embellished. I mean, can you imagine taking a load of psychedelics with a bunch of Indians! Sure, you'd be scared out of your bloody wits! It's a little story about coming from Ireland, travelling around America, doing a little bit of this and that and coming home again. And then there's the instrumental section which would be the "Homecoming Dance". It's an emigrant song with a little bit of psychedelia in the middle.'

Along with *Wingspan* and *Belfast To Boston* another triumph for McCullough of late has been the presentation to him of a Lifetime Achievement Award – a specially commissioned sculptured artwork – by the Ards Guitar Festival, an award that was previously won by Davy Graham. 'I was absolutely delighted,' declares McCullough. 'It's a very, very nice thing to happen to anyone. And it's a lovely trophy – I have it on the table. It's a lot more personal than getting an oul' bloody gold record to hang on the wall. I was absolutely bowled over. It's probably my most prized possession that I have in the house.'

In 2003 McCullough celebrated his sixtieth birthday. 'I'm happier now than I've ever been,' he asserts. 'That's because I'm more clear-headed and that's down to giving up alcohol. Alcohol was taking over and now I've lost that particular devil. I just stopped, five years ago, and I feel better and it shows in the music. At gigs I was letting myself down badly on occasion and I felt I had to become a professional drunk or a professional musician again. And the greatest love won.' McCullough's 2003 CD, *Unfinished Business*, includes 'Failed Christian', a searing self-composition. 'The first lines state I'm a failed Christian and I don't go to church,' he explains. 'But I'm not a failed Christian in the sense of not believing in God – and that faith helped me get through stopping drinking. I say wee prayers now I never said before – for my mother, for Hank Williams, for Elvis, for Alan Spenner of The Grease Band, for everybody I know that's dead and gone.' McCullough doesn't just pray for Hank Williams – for the album he has also re-recorded his own song, 'I Couldn't Sleep For Thinking Of Hank Williams'. 'Hank lived what he was writing about and the myth of Hank continues to grow. But who'd want to win recognition in history but not see 30? I've now lived twice as long as Hank did and I wouldn't want it to have been any other way.'

Henry McCullough, onstage at
the Warehouse, Belfast, 1995

HENRY McCULLOUGH
THE MENAGERIE, BELFAST

If he had not followed a musical career the great Henry McCullough – ex-Joe Cocker & The Grease Band, ex-Paul McCartney's Wings, the only Irishman to play at Woodstock, etcetera, etcetera – could, on the evidence of this gig, have found equal success as a boxer. When a troublemaker persistently pushed his microphone stand so that the microphone several times rapped him in the mouth, the veteran singer/guitarist launched himself offstage with electrifying speed and unleashed a flurry of combination punches that Barry McGuigan would have been proud of. The barrage of textbook left and right hooks left the yobbo dazed and bewildered and, as he was led out of the building, McCullough strolled nonchalantly back onstage and picked up the song exactly where he had left it, his wide-eyed band quickly joining in.

Before and after his exhibition of the noble art McCullough played with his usual white-hot intensity, performing electrifying versions of his own compositions such as 'Failed Christian' and 'Locked In And Can't Get Out', an anguished, despairing howl of pain and horror at the Troubles. Of the covers, 'House Of The Rising Sun' was sombre and reflective and, boldly set to a new tune, strikingly original.

McCullough's four accompanists were excellent throughout and, interestingly enough, featured bassist Chris Stewart, who in the late Sixties toured the world with McCullough in Eire Apparent, mostly supporting Hendrix, but who has recently, after 30 years, returned to live in Northern Ireland.

Trevor Hodgett : Concert review originally published in *Blueprint* (March 2000)

Eire Apparent, 1969

EIRE APPARENT
SUNRISE

Producer: Jimi Hendrix
Recorded: Record Plant, New York and TTG, Los Angeles
Label: Buddah Records (203021). Reissued on Sequel CD (NEX CD 199) in 1992 but now deleted
Personnel: Ernie Graham (guitar, vocals), Mick Cox (guitar, vocals), Chris Stewart (bass), Davy Lutton (drums), Jimi Hendrix (guitar), Robert Wyatt (background vocals), Noel Redding (background vocals)
Titles: 'Yes I Need Someone' / 'Got To Get Away' / 'The Clown' / 'Mr Guy Fawkes' / 'Someone Is Sure To (Want You)' / 'Rock 'n' Roll Band' / 'Morning Glory' / 'Magic Carpet' / 'Captive In The Sun' / '1026'
Singles extracted: 'Rock 'n' Roll Band' / 'Yes I Need Someone'

Eire Apparent were a Belfast band who in the Sixties had it all – and ended with nothing. They had talent to burn, major management, Jimi Hendrix as their record producer and toured Britain and the world with Pink Floyd, Hendrix and The Animals. And yet they somehow failed to achieve the fame that had seemed inevitable. Ex-members Ernie Graham, Henry McCullough, Chrissie Stewart and Davy Lutton did variously go on to achieve success with Wings, Joe Cocker, T-Rex and others, but the quality of their only album, the Hendrix-produced *Sunrise*, makes the band's obscurity a mystery.

The band began life as Tony & The Telstars, a top-twenty cover band. As they became more musically ambitious the name was changed to The People. The People consisted of Ernie Graham, Chrissie Stewart and Davy Lutton, who survive until the end of our story, plus Eric Wrixon (keyboards), who had played in Them, and Tiger Taylor (guitar). The band, with Michael Niblett temporarily replacing Stewart, recorded on *Ireland's Greatest Sounds: Five Top Groups From Belfast's Maritime Club*, a studio compilation album on which they perform Buddy Holly's 'Well All Right' and The Big Three's 'I'm With You'. 'We were in a state of flux at the time,' comments Graham. 'Members were coming and going and we were on the brink of deciding we had to get out of Belfast.'

The People's escape route was provided by The Wheels, a Belfast R&B band based in Blackpool, who encouraged The People to join them in Lancashire, where Chrissie Stewart soon reclaimed his position as bassist. 'The People were quite a souly wee band – towards the Graham Bond side of things – and the whole northern-soul scene adopted them,' recalls Wrixon.

Graham remembers harder times. 'The Mecca Ballroom scene was

Trevor Hodgett · Album retrospective originally published in *Mojo* (June 1998) and the *Irish News* (19 May 1995), plus additional material crumbling. Clubs were taking off and people didn't want to go to ballrooms.'

The Wheels compounded The People's problems by poaching Wrixon, who made two singles with his new band, before becoming a founder member of Thin Lizzy.

Meanwhile The People replaced him with a guitarist, Henry McCullough, a star with Irish showband Gene & The Gents. 'We spun him a story there was a really good scene in Lancashire,' recalls Graham.

McCullough picks up the story. 'I arrived straight from the showband scene with seventeen mohair suits and found these four boys, with check hipster trousers, all living in one room, going out for £7 a night. There was only one bed, so we took it in turns to sleep, or sometimes we did a Three Stooges job and lay like spoons together.'

Soon tiring of poverty The People relocated to Dublin, where they took off in a major way, with Dave Robinson, later supremo of Stiff Records, fulfilling a semi-official management role before his departure for England. 'Those were the most successful gigs The People ever had,' declares McCullough.

Inevitably the band decided to try their luck in London, but found themselves paying serious dues, as McCullough recalls. 'We lived in the van. The roof had a hole, so we had to park under a bridge. Any time we came across a gig we used to go down to the toilets in Leicester Square to change our gear and have a wash and brush up.'

'We were desperate,' remembers Graham. 'We were starving. Then we bumped into Dave Robinson and he got us a gig supporting Procol Harum in the Middle Earth club. They spent one-and-a-half hours playing songs all the same tempo, then we came on at five in the morning and blew the place apart with real, raw rock 'n' roll. Afterwards seven top managers, including Hendrix' managers Chas Chandler and Mike Jeffries, were outside our dressing room. It was fairy-tale stuff. We said, "If they're good enough for Hendrix, they're good enough for us!"'

The band's memories of Jeffries – later killed in an air crash – are unsentimental. 'A very difficult guy to know,' says Graham.

'A bit of a sly customer,' adds Stewart, 'whereas Chas was very open and brash – told us we were going to be stars.'

Graham recalls Chandler particularly affectionately. 'Chas was a smashing bloke who knew the business backwards. He wasn't a good musician, but he had a good ear for what would be popular.'

McCullough, however, resented Chandler's attempts to mould the band, now renamed Eire Apparent. 'He said, "Henry, you can't stand like that, you've got to stand with your legs apart." I said, "Look, I can't get into this." But I went along with getting green velvet trousers and big furry hats and having my hair permed. It was ignorance on everyone's part.'

The band recall with dissatisfaction their first single, 'Follow Me'/'Here I Go Again', which was produced by Chandler. 'It was a very quick recording,' sighs Graham.

'We weren't keen but Chas was the boss,' Stewart agrees. 'We were an R&B/rock 'n' roll band, but the manager said this was the path we had to take.'

The band was sent out on one of the most extraordinary package tours of the Sixties. 'We did a tour with Jimi Hendrix, The Move, Amen Corner, Pink Floyd and The Nice,' recalls McCullough. 'We got to do ten minutes!'

The band also toured America. Graham explains: 'We went out for a 60-day tour with The Animals, ending on St Patrick's Day in New York. At the end Jeffries decided Hendrix' future was America. He offered us the choice: stay with the company or go back to England and start from scratch with no manager.' The band decided to stay and began a second tour, with Hendrix, Soft Machine and Vanilla Fudge. However, catastrophe struck when McCullough was arrested for marijuana possession in the hotel room he shared with Graham.

McCullough recalls the experience nonchalantly. 'There was a little bit of grass on the dressing table. When I got back these police were there. The usual trip. It wasn't as frightening for me as it was for wee Ernie, because he burst out crying. He was afraid they were going to do *him* for it, but I said, "No, that's mine." I spent the night in the cell, then was let out on $750 bail.'

Graham remembers the incident bitterly. 'Henry had the knack of mixing with shady characters. I'd warned him: don't involve me. But he had people in our shared room, smoking dope, and they attracted the attention of the house detective. I got back and found three policemen there. I was arrested for doing nothing and held overnight, before Henry gave a statement I wasn't involved and I was released. But for the rest of the tour, every time I heard footsteps I imagined people coming to arrest me.'

Pending trial McCullough continued to work with the band, from what was now their home base in New York. 'Chandler and Jeffries said, "We'll get you back to sort it out." When the time came they wouldn't pay the airfare. They said, "It's really bad for the image." They gave me a one-way ticket to Dublin and I was there before Ernie, Davy and Chrissie knew I had gone.'

Stewart recalls the debacle similarly. 'We weren't told till next morning. We all felt bitter. We were young and naive and believed in management, rather than our own judgement.'

Graham's recollection is different. 'Henry wasn't sacked. He couldn't stay in New York because he wouldn't get his visa renewed. We felt, "There's nothing we can do, Henry: *you* have to go back – but we don't want to." I had least regrets. Henry had landed me in the shit and I wasn't particularly forgiving.'

McCullough, who subsequently played with Sweeney's Men, Joe Cocker's Grease Band and Wings, was replaced by English guitarist Mick Cox. 'He was very into Clapton-style blues and he was a very good lyricist, but he wasn't one-tenth the musician Henry was,' asserts Graham. 'Henry was a great live guitarist – he could play things off the top of his head.'

The band began work with Hendrix on *Sunrise*. 'We spent four months making it at the same time Hendrix was making *Electric Ladyland*,' reminisces Graham. 'I was at all the sessions for *Electric Ladyland* – I loved watching Hendrix work and he tolerated me! But Hendrix was a very private person. Nobody could really say they were Jimi's friend. I knew one side of him, but we shared a few girlfriends and I heard some hairy stories about violence.

'Later, on tour in New Mexico, I went back to my room and I heard someone whistling at me – it was Jimi, whose room was opposite. He had the white label of *Electric Ladyland*, so I was the first person to hear it, in his room, with Jimi Hendrix.'

Sunrise, with every track written by band members (mostly Graham or Cox), provides a perfect, utterly disarming snapshot of a mid-Sixties pop group becoming psychedelic. On the one hand the lyrics for, say, 'Got To Get Away' could have been written for Gerry & The Pacemakers; on the other the album is deliriously awash with lashings of phasing, panning, wah wah and every brand of distortion available to the aspiring acid rocker.

'Hendrix played on every track,' enthuses Graham.

'He was a great producer,' adds Stewart. 'We were all young boys and he got something out of us. And he was a lovely guy. He would get his manager to phone me to come over for a jam. I was very fond of him – he was a real nice guy. Very shy.'

One track, the haunting '1026', was in fact produced by Jack Hunt. 'Jimi was busy and it was an impromptu thing with [Jimi Hendrix Experience bassist] Noel Redding, [Soft Machine drummer] Robert Wyatt and ourselves,' remembers Graham. '1026 was the number of the suite Chrissie and I shared in the Chelsea Hotel, from March until September.'

The band decided to leave Jeffries and return to England. 'Chas got Jeffries to buy him out and we got concerned about what we were hearing about Jeffries' business dealings,' explains Graham. 'Also we were told we were worth more to Jeffries as a tax loss than if we were successful. He could keep us living comfortably in the States but he wasn't going to push us. Whereas we thought if we went back to England with an LP . . . When we made that decision the LP was mixed by Hendrix in one night, so it doesn't do justice to the work he did.'

Back in England the band became unhappy with Cox. Graham: 'On tours of America we only had time for five songs. In England we were expected to do one-and-a-half hours. We found Mick lacking when we tried to do *Sunrise* material because so much of the guitar was layered and Mick wasn't up to it on stage.'

Cox, who later released an eponymous solo album, backed by Kokomo, and recorded on several Van Morrison albums, was replaced by ex-People guitarist Tiger Taylor. The new line-up toured Germany and recorded the irresistibly upbeat 'Rock'n'Roll Band', featuring a startling Hendrix solo, which was added to the British release of *Sunrise*. 'Tiger was really unreliable,' muses Stewart. 'One morning we went to his room and he'd done a moonlighter back

Ernie Graham,
mid-Seventies

to Belfast. He was a really good player, a really nice guy, but he always ran away in the middle of the night, when he didn't have to confront anyone. He was shy.'

Taylor later joined Anno Domini, another Northern Irish band based in London, with whom he recorded *On This New Day*. However, just before that album's release he, again, disappeared to return secretly to Belfast, and his career in Anno Domini ended. He later led his own band in Dublin and played with The Freshmen.

Meanwhile the end was nigh for Eire Apparent. Graham explains: 'We were earning fairly good money and the top Polydor A&R man was coming to see us on Tuesday, about a second LP – and I was told on Monday that Chrissie and Davy didn't want to go through with it. I was deeply hurt: I wasn't talked to, I wasn't given a clue. It was very disappointing.'

Stewart recalls a less traumatic demise. 'We just ground to a halt,' he says. 'We didn't achieve the fame that management expected and we just ended up doing clubs.'

Stewart went on to record as a member of Spooky Tooth and Ronnie Lane's

Slim Chance and also toured with Terry Reid, Peter Green and Juicy Lucy. He has also appeared on over 30 albums as a session man. 'I did the Janis Joplin live album, *Farewell Song*, that came out after she died, because [her backing band] Big Brother were so bad, God bless them. The only thing they kept was the guitar. [Drummer] Denny Seiwell and me overdubbed. It was really hard 'cos they were slowing down and speeding up.' From 1975 Stewart worked as Frankie Miller's regular bassist.

Eire Apparent drummer Davy Lutton later recorded two albums, *Riding On The Crest Of A Slump* and *Why Not?*, with the band Ellis, before joining T-Rex, with whom he recorded the 'Teenage Dream', 'Light Of Love', 'Zip Gun Boogie', 'New York City', 'Dreamy Lady', 'London Boys', 'I Love To Boogie' and 'Laser Love' singles and the *Zinc Alloy*, *Zip Gun* and *Futuristic Dragon* albums, before leaving the music business.

Graham later recorded a self-titled solo album, backed by members of Brinsley Schwarz – including Nick Lowe – and Help Yourself. 'I was deeply hurt by how the band had split up and I'd split up with my girlfriend, so the album was fairly introspective. But I was very happy with it. The track 'Sebastian' was an in joke – he was a hash dealer in London who had promised me a couple of pounds of Leb if I wrote a song about him!'

Graham next joined Help Yourself, contributing to the *Strange Affair* album, in 1972, before forming Clancy, who released two excellent albums, *Seriously Speaking . . .* and *Every Day*, for Warners, in 1975. 'When the dollar hit the floor American labels started getting rid of British bands and we were one of the casualties.'

Graham recorded one more single, 'Romeo And The Lonely Girl', written by Thin Lizzy's Phil Lynott, which was released on Stiff in 1978. 'Ian Dury's band The Blockheads did the backing. But 'Sex And Drugs And Rock'n'Roll' came out at the same time and took off. Stiff had to concentrate everybody on that and mine got lost.' After this further disappointment Graham drifted out of the music business.

Thus only two ex-members of Eire Apparent, McCullough and Stewart, are still musically active. But lest that fact depress, let Graham have the final word. 'I wasn't a great musician – I was a frontman – but I think to myself, You haven't had a bad life. I'm quite happy – I've got a family; I live a very comfortable life; I've no pressure on me. And I was very fortunate – I was paid money to do something I'd have paid money to do. I travelled the world; I met some of the greatest musicians; I lived and worked with Hendrix. I've no regrets.'

Postscript: Ernie Graham died after an illness on 27 April 2001; Chrissie Stewart returned to live in Belfast where he became an occasional member of Henry McCullough's band, and survived a brain haemorrhage.

SKID ROW
PROLOGUE

During my earliest days as a full-time writer I was pretty tenacious in seeking multiple opportunities for pre-selling any one interview or concert review – conscientiously, of course, writing things up in different ways and never (well, almost never) selling to publications that were direct rivals. Reviewing a concert for say, a newspaper and a magazine, or an Irish newspaper and a UK newspaper, was a common occurrence. One had to make a living. The *Irish News*, a Northern Ireland daily with pitiful rates of pay but a strong arts commitment (at that time under the leisurely arts editorship of Colin McAlpin), was a fairly regular recipient of 'second-bite-of-the-cherry' pieces where the time and travel aspects of an interview would have been justified primarily by a more substantial commission elsewhere. (That said, I did interview as many local musicians as I could find solely for the *Irish News* during the mid-Nineties, with the expenses incurred being generally no more than a round of scones and cappuccinos and one side of a C90.)

Thus, at some point in 1994, when it was announced that Gary Moore's new supergroup, BBM – with ex-Cream legends Jack Bruce and Ginger Baker supplying the two *B*s (though not to be, as it turned out) – would be performing in Belfast I rang around to see if anyone fancied commissioning an interview. Personally, I'd never been particularly taken with what I knew of Gary's playing or music, but it would be no problem to bone up for any encounter, should one be on the cards. Things were soon looking good. *Guitar Magazine* was ecstatic about the prospect of a Moore interview – at that time the guitarist was apparently turning down a lot of interview requests, particularly those from the world of guitar-buffery. At the same time, in the wake of serious chart action from his two recent blues albums, his profile was at an all-time high.

The fee being offered was very attractive: from memory, £400-and-something, which at that time in my rather wings-and-prayers career was good news indeed. I would, of course, also be spinning out a thousand words for 40-odd quid to the *Irish News*. As it transpired, when my request for an audience was passed through Gary's publicity people the answer was yes. Not because of a guaranteed front cover with the UK-wide *Guitar Magazine* – but *only* because of the prospect of half a page in the *Irish News*. Being a Protestant from east Belfast, and the *Irish News* the paper of choice for the Catholic community, crossing that chasm was, for all Gary's huge international success, still a big deal to him. I was, of course, happy to facilitate this proud moment in cultural relations.

Colin Harper

Skid Row, on tour in Sweden, 1970:
(l–r) Noel Bridgeman, Gary Moore,
Brush Shiels

Alas, BBM never did make it to Belfast. Given such a trio of famously fractious individuals it was probably inevitable that one of them would eventually look at one of the others with the wrong expression and the whole thing would go pear-shaped. My interview was cancelled and, given the pre-emptive purchase of a few cut-price Moore albums from Terri Hooley's Good Vibes, my wallet a little lighter. Still, seven years later all that revision came in useful after all.

After a period away from the limelight and, indeed, the blues, Gary had come back to that particular idiom with an album whose title was in no way designed to lead anyone up the garden path. It was also, I had to admit, blisteringly impressive stuff. Resilient publicist and, by this stage, long-time acquaintance Alan Robinson was particularly keen to get people on board. I got the impression that Gary – not, perhaps, such hot property as he once was – might have threatened to come round and play a four-hour version of 'Parisienne Walkways' at him if meaningful column inches were not forthcoming. In the event, Alan did what looked to me, as a perennial browser (if not buyer) of magazines, a terrific job on the *Back To The Blues* campaign. My modest contribution to the cause was an album review in *Mojo* and (reproduced here) an interview feature for *The Irish Times*.

What struck me about the album was the apparent reconnection with the spirit of Skid Row, Gary's legendary if largely unchronicled Dublin trio from the late Sixties, comprising one Brendan 'Brush' Shiels on bass and Noel Bridgeman on drums. I had become, and remain, fascinated by Skid Row. One of the great pleasures of compiling this book was in the filling in of its gaps. For too long had I failed to address what can only be described as the glaring omission of an encounter, professional or otherwise, with the once and future Skid, Brush Shiels. We finally met in a Transit van outside the cabaret lounge of a delightful pub in a one-street town in Cavan, as the deadline for delivering a finished manuscript loomed. But just being around this most extraordinary of men is enough to see the world, and its pressures, in a different light. As Noel Bridgeman had promised only days before, as he politely declined his own invitation to revisit that era, 'I think you'll find him an interesting fellow . . .' He was right. This man who had never once doubted he had the capability, and the band, to conquer the world, and who had ended up with nothing, had the character and the will power to reinvent himself, for the sake of a living, as a national clown – yet a wise man in fool's clothing. 'It doesn't bother me, Colin,' said Brush – repeatedly, time and again. 'It just doesn't bother me . . .' And it really doesn't.

As for Gary, I never met him. I would have liked to, but a possible opportunity for a face-to-face interview in London didn't work out, so the telephone it had to be. He was immediately appreciative of my already published review in *Mojo* – it's always nice, and never expected, when an artist makes that gesture of acknowledgement to a writer – and amused by my enthusiasm for both Sweeney's Men and Skid Row. Would my fantasy band, he quipped, be

The Bell/Brush Band, mid-Seventies:
Eric Bell (left), Brush Shiels (right)

Sweeney's Row? Well, perhaps not. But by its very distance and opacity that era will forever be a magical place. For Gary, the magical era was just before that: growing up in Belfast. He had only recently, he coyly admitted, brought his son over to visit some relatives in the city. At dead of night the pair of them had sneaked bicycles into the grounds of Ashfield Boys, his Alma Mater, and done wheelies to their hearts' content. For Gary at least, those were the days.

GARY MOORE
ON THE SKIDS

'Wow! Nobody's asked me that one before,' says Gary Moore, self-exiled Irish guitar hero and a man who has quite palpably just made his best record in twenty years. Unashamedly entitled *Back To The Blues* (pithily following a couple of profile-lowering forays into more contemporary sounds) it sounds uncannily like a Marshall-stacked, all-cylinders-firing homage to his time in the late Sixties with Brush Shiels and Noel Bridgeman in Dublin's premier power trio, Skid Row. Minus the drum solos, of course. A passing query on the chances of a Skid Row reunion was, then, my winning entry into Gary's book of interview firsts. With such an incendiary approach – neither as mannered as his previous blues projects nor as slick as his hard-rock albums – had he not noticed himself this spiritual reconnection with the ghost of Skid?

'I've never thought about it like that,' he admits, 'but certainly it's got a lot of energy, mostly because we did it so quickly. If you take a long time over a record you end up making something different from what you intended. This time I stuck to the plan and I was so proud when we finished it: it was exactly the record I'd wanted to make. I went in feeling very free-spirited, it was done quickly, there's no pretences and what you see is what you get. And, yeah, I suppose I did want to show what I could do.'

Asked if he felt his back was against the wall, with the experimental pop albums *Dark Days In Paradise* (1997) and *A Different Beat* (1999) having failed to engage his, or anyone else's, audience in significant numbers, Moore's response is both honest and sanguine: 'Most musicians make the same record every time, and that's fine,' he says, 'but the people I respected when I was growing up – like Jeff Beck – they weren't afraid to try something new. I've always tried to follow that rule myself. I would have got bored if I hadn't. I've made a blues album [this time] because I wanted to make a blues album. The same with the last record, which was an attempt to marry guitar with dance rhythms. With something like that you're really crucified before you start: people who would be into what I do would probably hate those rhythms and the people into dance music would probably hate me!'

One unexpected facet of interviewing Moore is the warmth of his personality. There may be a mid-Atlantic twang in his singing, but his speech is still 'soft Belfast', his tendency to self-deprecating humour surprising (particularly given what is probably now a decades-old reputation for being 'bolshie') and his demeanour friendly and open. Yes, he is doing a telephone interview – hardly an aspect of normal life for most people – but he is not doing so under

Colin Harper · Originally published in *The Irish Times* (23 February 2001)

any guise or façade. Gary Moore, it seems, is a real person in a rarefied business, who just happens to have an extraordinarily rich history.

Born in Belfast in 1952, Moore has gone through life like some musical Zelig with a time machine. He has played in all manner of musical settings – beat groups, country ballads, psychedelic folk music, jazz fusion, Celtic rock – always, of course, coming 'back to the blues'. One track on the new album, 'I Ain't Got You', comes straight from the 1965 Yardbirds repertoire – a repertoire Moore has affectionately and validly plundered before. During the summer of '65, when the North was awash with beat groups, Moore's school band, The Beat Boys, won their heat in a talent competition at Pickie Pool (an outdoor swimming pool) in Bangor, and got their picture in the local paper: 'Yeah, and I also remember doing another one around that time run by Eddie Kennedy at the Club Rado in Belfast,' he says. 'We actually won – the prize was £15 – and he handed us this empty envelope on the stage and said, "Don't worry lads, we'll sort out the cheque later." I'm still waiting! But there was a great scene in Belfast then. I remember seeing The Who at the Top Hat. I had a band called Platform Three by that time and we had to do a gig that very night. I remember finishing the gig and running all the way to where The Who were playing, hearing the sound of "The Kids Are All Right" from way up the street, throwing my three shillings or whatever it was at the guy on the door and pushing my way up to the front. It was a wonderful moment and a great time to be growing up.'

By 1969, aged sixteen, Moore had relocated to Dublin, joining Skid Row – where his recording-career proper began – and hanging out with people like Granny's Intentions, Dr Strangely Strange and progressive folkies Sweeney's Men. Of the latter, the esoteric Johnny Moynihan would periodically guest (on tin whistle, of course) with Skid Row while the more no-nonsense Terry Woods would prove a useful man for a vulnerable prodigy to know: 'Terry was very, very good to me,' says Moore. 'When I was living with Skid Row Brush used to be a bit of a bastard sometimes, but Terry would always give him such a bollocking if he upset me. One time Brush turned tail in fear like I'd never seen before in my life – and actually apologised to me the next day, which was a novel experience! I haven't seen a lot of these people in years but it doesn't mean I don't think about them. I did play with Dr Strangely Strange a couple of years ago – that "difficult third album"! [*Alternative Medicine*, 1997] It was great to see them all. They're very special people and they were very good to me in Dublin in the Sixties. I mean, they were the guys to hang out with then – the coolest people in town, very arty and bohemian. So if you got in with them you were somebody.'

Outside of Dublin Skid Row, unfortunately, were nobodies – though they did once jam with Led Zeppelin. Or did they? 'Er, kind of!' says Moore. 'They felt sorry for us, basically, because we were all skint. Skid Row wasn't just the *name* of that band! We were all staying at the Holiday Inn in Los Angeles, they were playing at the Forum and they used to come and see us every night. They

BBM, 1994: (l–r) Gary Moore, Jack Bruce, Ginger Baker

got pissed one night and John Bonham and Robert Plant got up: John sang and Robert played the drums. So, no, we didn't quite jam with Led Zeppelin!'

It is, as his publicist rightly points out, rare indeed to find such a thorough Sixties veteran still only in his forties. Common perception, however, would probably pigeon-hole Gary as an 'Eighties artist' who came through a period of seemingly joining and leaving Thin Lizzy every other week to a respectable semi-retirement, like Eric Clapton, with a kind of AOR blues formula. The deferential *Still Got The Blues* (1989) and *After Hours* (1990) were and remain the most successful albums of his career, happily coinciding with a market ripe for 'Blues Brothers' stage shows and Levi's-ad retroism. A 1994 album with Jack Bruce and Ginger Baker, as BBM, and the following year's *Blues For Greeney*, were doffs of the cap to old heroes Cream and Peter Green respectively, and also Moore's last UK chart placings – thus far. The BBM tour almost got to Ireland, but not quite. Since then, not a sausage for the concert-going Irish Moore fan: 'You know, every time we get offered dates it just doesn't come off,' he sighs. 'Every time there's a problem – though we've just been offered two shows in Dublin in May . . .'

Mention of potential opportunities like the Galway Arts Festival or the Monaghan Blues Festival spark an immediate interest, and Moore promises to have his management look into it. With an album as blisteringly joyous and refreshing as *Back To The Blues* the time is surely right. As they used to say back in the last century: 'We want Moore!'

BRUSH SHIELS
REMEMBERING SKID ROW

Several subsequent 'name' musicians emerged from pioneering Sixties bands like The Yardbirds and Cream, and yet those acts have managed to find a venerated position in the twenty-first-century world of digital remastering, CD box sets and biographies. Even Taste, at the time of writing, have entered the world of remastered compilation-dom. Wherefore art thou, Skid Row? That their early singles, on Joe Colgan and Donal Lunny's independent Song label, have never made it onto CD – let alone the various B-sides and US-only tracks of their major-label era – seems incomprehensible. Similarly, the basic CD availability of their three albums proper (1970's *Skid*, 1971's *34 Hours* and the unreleased third album – first issued on vinyl, somewhat indecisively, in 1990 as *Skid Row: Gary Moore, Brush Shiels, Noel Bridgeman*) is less than ideal. They're probably all available somewhere in the world, but certainly not in Ireland.

Too often referred to as merely the musical kindergarten of Gary Moore and (very briefly) Phil Lynott, Skid Row made music so idiosyncratic, contrary, eclectic and, at times, inspired, that it should remain, at the very least, a thing of great fascination to the student of the Sixties. That their records were invariably made in little more than a day – a slightly bizarre, if admirably economical, ethos that Brush Shiels maintains to the present – should remain a thing of great instruction to those who insist on pottering about in studios for indefinite periods of time. If nothing else, a record involving Brush Shiels is just that – a 'record' of his work that day, a moment captured.

The basic facts of the Skid Row story are simple enough. Emerging out of the beat-group scene in Dublin, Brush formed Skid Row (initially named My Father's Moustache, before common sense prevailed) in 1967, featuring himself on bass, Phil Lynott on vocals, Bernie Cheevers on guitar and Noel Bridgeman on drums. For a period around this time Brush ran his own club, the Ghetto, as a focal point for happenings with fellow progressive types of the day like Tara Telephone and Dr Strangely Strange. Belfast guitar prodigy Gary Moore replaced Cheevers in 1969, and in the summer the first Skid Row single 'Misdemeanour Dream Felicity'/'New Places, Old Faces' was released on Song. Having trouble with his voice, Phil was soon 'let go' with Brush and Gary now taking the vocals. Lynott then formed Orphanage with Pat Quigley, Joe Staunton and Brian Downey. During the summer of 1969 Terry Woods would briefly be a member.

Another single, 'Saturday Morning Man'/'Mervyn Aldridge', also surfaced on Song that year, with Robbie Brennan briefly replacing Noel Bridgeman on

Colin Harper · Previously unpublished; from an interview conducted at a pub in Butler's Bridge, County Cavan (February 2003)

drums. Bridgeman had momentarily joined fellow Dubliners, Granny's Intentions, who were then in London working on their first and only album, *Honest Injun*, for Decca. Noel recorded three tracks and then returned to Skid Row. Gary Moore then joined, or lent his services, and the album was completed.

From psychedelic-influenced beginnings, the classic Skid Row sound developed as a combination of breezy country ballads, Cream-like heavy blues, angular King Crimson-ish high-volume prog-rock and an overriding fascination in finding a Brubeck/Coltrane-influenced, rock-based fusion entirely their own. Clearly, the challenge of combining pummelling riffs with generally poignant lyrics and folksy melodies in weird time signatures and with blisteringly fast solos was one that all involved enjoyed immensely.

A concert in Dublin with Fleetwood Mac led to a management contract with Mac manager Clifford Davis. By the end of 1969 Skid Row had been signed to CBS, and soon relocated to Britain. The first UK single, the curiously atypical country-flavoured 'Sandie's Gone (Parts 1 & 2)', appeared in April 1970, with first album *Skid* released in October. The first of four studio sessions and two concerts for BBC radio, mostly under the patronage of DJ John Peel, was recorded in July 1970. During that year they made their first visit to the US, performing with many of the other exploding 'British' progressive rock bands of the time, and toured Europe with Canned Heat, playing live on German TV's *Beat Club* along the way. *34 Hours* – a more indulgent, less song-focused set, though still running the stylistic gamut from country swing to free-form jamming in a late-period Hendrix fashion – was recorded early in 1971, its release trailered by the definitive Skid Row single 'Night Of The Warm Witch'/'Mr Deluxe'. A second tour of the US followed, supporting The Grateful Dead, although the financial strain and apparent laissez-faire approach of Davis' management was becoming hard to bear.

An untitled third album, ironically their most cohesive and accessible (albeit revisiting some previously recorded material) was recorded in autumn 1971 just before Moore quit – telling the press that the band were just playing too fast and it was time he found his own thing (which, for all that, turned out to be, frankly, playing fast). Eric Bell was drafted in to fulfil some UK Christmas dates, with future UFO guitarist Paul Chapman coming in as permanent replacement. The band re-recorded exactly the same tracks as the Moore version of the third album, but momentum flagged and neither was released at the time (the Moore version finally surfacing via Castle Communications in 1990). Brush subsequently returned, broke, to Ireland, forming the short-lived Bell/Brush Band with Eric Bell, and periodically reviving the Skid Row name to get work – before discovering the best way to make a living was simply to play songs with three chords, turn on the blarney and act the goat.

At this activity – with a uniquely look-no-safety-net cabaret routine interspersing Elvis, Hank Williams, Thin Lizzy and Paddy Reilly covers with flashes of stunning prog-rock virtuosity if the moment is right – he has somehow risen to the position of national icon. Being persuaded, by future Boyzone/Westlife manager Louis Walsh, to release rollicking versions of Irish ballads 'The Fields Of Athenry' and 'Dirty Old Town' as a twelve-inch single in 1988 sealed his fate. In a sense, the Irish nation has taken to its heart one of its greatest musicians with the unspoken understanding that he keeps his musical abilities to himself.

It would, though, be entirely wrong to suggest that Brush has a sour attitude about all this – in fact, one of his great attributes is his genuineness and friend-liness with punters of all ages and interests. He is a 'people person' to the core. Somehow, embedded in his character, is the ability to be completely Zen about life's ironies. On the one hand he appreciates certain kinds of music and has the ability to play and write astonishingly complex material; on the other he has the ability to make a decent living in the lounge bars and on the talk shows of Ireland doing something that has no aspirations on a musical level whatsoever.

Interviewing musicians for the past decade, I've certainly met a few people with colossal chips on their shoulders, but Brush Shiels is not one of them. There are people whose lives are disproportionately consumed by this or that press cutting from 30 years ago, this or that event that supposedly blighted their career, their unrecognised genius or whatever else. Indeed, one individual I can think of, convinced that his band played the best set of the entire Woodstock Festival yet didn't feature in the movie, has allowed himself to be racked ever since by conspiracy theories on the matter. Had Skid Row played Woodstock, Brush would most likely recall it as just another gig. Then again, maybe his life, and the memory of his band, would have been very different.

Brush – you say you haven't had a rehearsal since 1972, since when you've become significantly more successful.
Since I've stopped playing, you mean! I stopped 'playing' in 1972 and I've been basically making a living ever since. I gave up the ghost in 1973. The real Skid Row was the only Skid Row – Gary Moore, Noel Bridgeman and myself. I only used the name after that 'cos I had to make a living. As soon as I could make a living without using the name I stopped using the name. To make a living I had to stop 'playing'. So from '73–'74 I didn't play at all – I just stood out the front and jumped around. Somebody said to me once, 'Why are you so confident?' And I said, ''Cos I'm a lot better than most people think I am.' So, basically, I'd have enough confidence *not* to play, if you know what I mean. I couldn't see the point of it when I saw people like T-Rex, Slade and so on – these guys were coming in as I was going out. I thought they were awful, I still do – though, Lord have mercy, I hope he [Marc Bolan] is in Heaven.'
Were you ever in a showband?
No, but I was in the next thing along – beat groups, which they used to say were a kindergarten for showbands and they weren't far wrong. Then I was in the first soul band in Dublin, The Uptown Band – I enjoyed that. I was playing rhythm guitar at one point but [somewhere along the line] I was offered a job in a band if I could play bass. I was a footballer before I was a musician; that was kind of a problem in as much as they were gonna pay me to play football

in 1964. I signed for a team in the League of Ireland – Bohemians. Some strange things happened. I heard this album by Oscar Peterson, *Night Train* – still one of my favourite albums, with jazz guys playing the blues – and I heard this bass-guitar solo on there by Ray Brown and I thought, Jesus! So I remember spending about eight months listening to that one album, *Night Train* – somewhere around '66, '67. I stopped playing football altogether then – same way as I stopped playing music later. I can just stop. I stopped playing football when I was nineteen and I never kicked a ball again! I still meet guys today and if they call me Brendan I know they're gonna talk about football – it's very funny! There were a few reasons why they called me 'The Brush' – the long hair and the beard, that was one, and that term 'sweeper' was in in football, so it was all sorts of things like that.

I was working class and I was always more interested in country lyrics than jazz lyrics – I had no interest in why 'The Lady Was A Tramp' – and I reckoned that the working class in general had more interest in country lyrics than they had in Cole Porter or whoever. I remember reading something about Charlie Parker and he was asked what his favourite song was, and he said it was a Hank Williams thing, 'I'm So Lonesome I Could Cry'. It was because of the lyrics, and I know exactly what he was talking about.

So I originally came from a country thing to a jazz thing and [with Skid Row] I ended up playing heavy metal, because I reckoned you could do this Jimi Hendrix thing very easily if you had a good guitar player. So I was looking for a good guitar player. Gary was standing in for someone with The Few, from Belfast, playing a show in Dublin. We were playing down the road in the 72 club, in Middle Abbey Street. We had a very good guitar player, Bernie Cheevers – he was actually 'Electrician of the Year' with Guinness at that time – got a medal and all that! So he was gone, off to be an electrician. But I knew Gary was good as soon as I heard him, doing a lot of stuff off the [John Mayall] *Bluesbreakers* album. I offered him a job that night. He said, 'You'd have to talk to my father.' So I went up to Stormont to see his da, Robert, and he just asked me to look after Gary. So I says, 'No problem.' I reckoned it wouldn't take more than six months to get this band off the ground – I knew exactly the way to do it. Philo was the singer at the time so it was Gary, myself, Noel and Philo – it couldn't fail.

[But] we did a television show – either *Like Now* or *Zoom* – doing 'Strawberry Fields Forever' and Philo was singing badly out of tune. His throat wasn't right, as we found out later, but he was tricking around with some girl and a balloon – which was fair enough, I suppose, because the reason I gave him the job in the band was because of his looks. He was told not to bring his girlfriend along – a lovely girl, Carol. There were no girlfriends allowed at the gig or in the van. The idea was, 'We go to the gig, look at the girls and piss-off the blokes' – and that worked.

Tell me about the early Skid Row recordings.

There was a guy called Tony Boland, who was a friend of Andrew Loog

Oldham, who ran the Immediate label, and he wanted us to do a demo for them. So Tony brought us into Eamonn Andrews' studio [in Dublin] and we did this demo, of 'New Places, Old Faces' and something else . . . I thought the first single we did on Song was 'Mervyn Aldridge', but maybe I'm wrong. The Song label was Joe Colgan and Donal Lunny was his MD, in charge of the music. He was everywhere, Donal! But a local single – ah, it was just something to do that week. It never occurred to me that we weren't heading for America anyway.

So your live show was the main thing?

Yeah, we had a great show – and even without Philo we had a great show. There was a film out at the time, called *The Defined Ones*, with Sidney Poitier and Tony Curtis, and if Philo had stayed in the band we were going to base the live show on that, with this pretend 'falling-out routine' – tearing shirts off, throwing the bass across the stage. We did it once at UCD, and it was a great show. [Manager] Brian Tuite – his band Granny's Intentions were top of the bill on that show and after seeing us he offered to manage us and it seems to me like practically the following week he brought someone to see us, Mike Smith, and he offered us a deal. In the meantime Phil had gone over to Manchester to get his throat done – he had terrible trouble with his tonsils, and his mother had offered to pay to get it sorted out. But he wasn't even on the plane and we were rehearsing without him – and we thought we sounded great. So when he came back I let him go!

Dublin must have been a good scene in those days.

It was happening seven nights a week, plus seven afternoons! There were gigs all over town. There was only one gig in Cork, the 007 club, and aside from that there was only Belfast. But in Dublin there was loads of gigs – the 72 club, the Apartment, the Moulin Rouge, the Scene club . . . it was a great time. We were all immature existentialists – Jack Kerouac's *Dharma Bums* vibe was in the air, that kind of thing. But it never occurred to me that I wouldn't get to America and do exceptionally well.

But first you all moved to England.

We would have based ourselves in England almost right away, maybe six months after Gary came in, but that was a mistake. We'd have been better staying in Ireland. It was somewhere in 1969 anyway. Then Philo arrived with Eric and Brian [as Thin Lizzy] maybe four or five months after us. John Peel put us on right away. He'd seen us playing at the Stadium with Fleetwood Mac – he'd come over with them – and that was when Clifford Davis offered to manage us. There and then. He'd never seen us before. But, again, I took everything for granted. I've a strange attitude: I don't get excited easily but I have a good time all the time! It's like a football match – just go out and do what you have to do, but enjoy yourself.

Our first major single, 'Sandie's Gone', was a country type thing, which got a 'power play' on Radio Luxembourg at the time. The average kind of heavy-rock fan is not able to deal with that – they'd think you've gone soft. It's a strange thing – you could be jumping over the drums and playing the guitar with your teeth and all that but if you slow it down and it's not 'Stairway To Heaven' or something like that then people think there's something seriously wrong with it.

But didn't Cream have a similar dichotomy with whimsical studio recordings and a heavy live show?

Well, the thing was – even when they slowed down they still had a slow blues feel. They were trying to write hit singles, too, like 'Wrapping Paper'. But Jack Bruce and Ginger Baker – they had come out of the Graham Bond thing, which was jazz. Everybody at some stage [in those days] was tricking around with either Charlie Mingus or Charlie Parker, and you got to the blues because it was fashionable, mainly. You wanted to make a living and the record companies were saying, 'If you sounded like *this* we could give you a deal.' I remember people like Manfred Mann, who were basically a jazz group, seemed to get rid of the polo-necks and become a blues band overnight. One minute there was jazz, next there was trad jazz – Ottilie Patterson, Chris Barber, Lonnie Donegan and that sort of thing. They all realised that the blues thing was coming in so one minute Lonnie was doing this, the next he was doing that – and skiffle was as close as you could get to the blues at that time. And out of that skiffle thing came people like The Beatles. The reason sometimes you were the way you were [musically] was that there was a very good chance of getting a good recording deal, getting to America and making a lot of money. Success was more important than the music!

Clifford Davis, your manager, is rather suspiciously listed as producer for all three of the Skid Row albums – did he actually have any musical involvement?

Well, unfortunately he did have something to do with the first one, insofar as he *was* the producer, which is why the sound is so bad. But he did keep telling us that he *wasn't* producing it, that Peter Green would be along later! So we did it in one go, and that was it – starting at maybe ten o'clock in the morning and finished at ten o'clock at night, overdubs and all. Peter Green didn't turn up, so we just started mixing it. The second one took 34 hours – that's why it's called that. I still make records in a day.

And then your first tour of America . . .

The first gig we did was in the Fillmore West with Frank Zappa and Boz Scaggs. Then we toured with Ten Years After, Jethro Tull, The Allman Brothers . . . we came back from America and we were told, 'The next time you go to America you're going to be huge.' And there was a very good chance we would be. Gary came back and said he wanted to do the twin guitar thing [like the Allmans]. That was fair enough, though it didn't really interest me. It never occurred to me to get another guitar player to do the same job. The only mistake I made was really not playing the guitar myself – I should have started practising then.

We toured [Europe] with Canned Heat – but we got no money. I think £15 a week was the most we got, and that was nothing at the time. I don't know

Brush Shiels,
mid-Seventies

if even Clifford Davis was getting paid at the time. The record company wasn't paying for anything. So I would say Clifford wasn't getting too much out of it. He had our music publishing which would basically be illegal now – your manager can't be your music publisher. Gary [later] got out of it because he wasn't 21 when he signed, but anything I wrote was kept – I've never been paid by them, ever. Well, no, they did give me £60 once, for a pram, but that was all I ever got!

Clifford Davis: a good guy or a bad guy?

Ah, he just got caught up in different things. If we'd had a manager who wasn't managing Curved Air and Fleetwood Mac at the same time . . . He didn't travel around with us – he just left us in America to make our own way round. It was badly done: we had nowhere to stay, just sent over on a wing and a prayer, on $5 each a day or something. It was tough going. We didn't have a lot to eat. But we survived. And it never occurred to me that we wouldn't crack it.

'Night Of The Warm Witch', from the second album, sounds like the classic single – yet it didn't chart.

No – well that would have been my problem in as much as the country numbers took away from it – there weren't enough songs [on *34 Hours*] and some of the songs on it were just jamming. If we'd had six songs that were fairly similar it would have worked great, but putting the country things on wasn't such a good idea, for that time, in the long run. Now, it might be – but that 'Night Of The Warm Witch' was good, I liked that.

So the second album was better than the first in your view?

It makes no difference. It was just something you did in a day, you know?

And then it all fell apart.

Where we were going by the end was heading more back to the twelve-bar blues – it had been getting so intricate that nobody knew *what* we were doing. That was the problem, and it was basically my fault. I'm very extreme: I'm either very intricate or I won't play at all.

I remember the day that Clifford Davis and ourselves parted company – he sent three guys down to the Marquee in Wardour Street and they took my guitar and my amp and I had nothing – nothing at all. After all that touring America, nothing. And then I came back to Ireland – no guitar, no money, nothing. Not even a gig. And I was exactly the same as I am now! After touring the world, filling the Stadium, and everyone knowing me, I was on the dole queue. I still had the best leather coat – but then it wouldn't have bothered me if I'd had the worst leather coat. Like, so what? Next week we start again! But I can honestly say that the best days I ever had were with the lads – with Gary and Noel and Philo. I loved playing with them. They were great days. These days it's completely different. You get more philosophical as you get older. I've got two sons, Jude and Matthew, who play with me now and again and a lot of people say, 'That's great,' but I say, 'You must be joking!' But, no, it's not the same as playing with your mates.

If Gary rang and said he wanted to get the band back together – you, him and

Noel – would you do it?
I might do it for one night, but that'd be it. It'd be a great night, but the main problem would be it'll never be as good as it was. At a certain stage we're all only cabaret.

So here we are now, we plug in and we play. We come here to do this because you have to have somewhere to go to, do something and go back from. You would think that the gig would be the most important thing – but we take the gigs for granted. Whether it's full or empty, we get paid anyway. But we never go down badly. Once we play, we can't go down badly – we always get back whatever we give. Anybody can go down as well as I can. But they don't seem to. They put too much pressure on themselves. I don't put *any* pressure on myself. Even when I'm not playing an instrument I'm very confident. I did a show there in Croke Park a few months ago – there were 71,000 people and it was the first time I went on anywhere with backing tracks, no band. But it had no effect on me other than I enjoyed it, ran around Croke Park, had a good time and then I went home and watched television. I'm very hard to intimidate, even when I'm not playing!

No regrets, then?
Watching the Biography Channel, the amount of guys who've got to the end of what they're doing and have had a good time – they're very few and far between. Success – there's an awful lot of problems that seem to come with it. Everyone has problems with their life anyway. You start off by wanting to play to the best of your ability and then you get to a point where you find out what I call the 'Hucklebuck syndrome'. No matter what you're playing, whether you're Duke Ellington or Charlie Parker, the punters always tune in to what I would call the 'Hucklebuck' in your set – which is usually the simplest thing. Like 'Whiskey In The Jar'!

Do you still get enjoyment out of music?
I get enjoyment out of trying to work it out, which is a slightly different thing. It's like trying to do a cryptic crossword. Just lately Jude was interested in a couple of Django Reinhardt things and a couple of Charlie Parker things and a couple of Duke Ellington things. I hadn't heard them for a while so I said, 'Put them on and we'll work them out,' and it reminded me of things and I thought that was nice. But you still see the music sometimes as something that you work out, and you enjoy the working out of it more than anything else.

Are you a contented man?
Well, I reckon if you put me in a room with everybody else you've been talking to you might find I have less hassles!

Postscript: By the end of our evening in Butler's Bridge, I suggested to Brush that he let me look into the possibility of organising a compilation of Skid Row's surviving BBC radio sessions and the early singles – which should be available by the time this book is published. He was also musing on the prospect of a brand new Skid Row album before the year was out. No, really . . .

Eamon Carr, from the sleeve
of *Happy To Meet*, 1972

HORSLIPS
PROLOGUE

When I was at university in the mid-to-late Eighties Horslips occupied a curious place for my generation on the edge of experience – legendary but distant, a world away, the stuff of elder brothers' record collections. Curiously, the musical world of the Seventies seems a whole lot closer and certainly more acceptable today – be it as kitsch or cred – than it did in the Eighties. Album covers like the works of art that sleeved *Happy To Meet, Sorry To Part* and *The Book Of Invasions* solidified the notion that here were people with a vision, people who cared about what they did – daft outfits notwithstanding.

It seemed incredible to me that Horslips, with music as expansive and stirring and, surely, I thought, as epochal in the history of Irish rock, did not exist on television. There were, of course, as one later learned, plenty of TV appearances still in the can here and there, but to a large extent the Eighties was the decade before pop music became a retro media commodity. Early in 1990 something billed as 'Johnny Fean & The Spirit Of Horslips' – Fean being the former guitarist and chief vocalist of the band whose spirit was being invoked – was billed to play the rag ball at Queen's University, Belfast. It was a few months after I'd left the place but I determined to sneak back in for the evening and build a stable door of celluloid posterity just before the horse finally bolted. Hiring some gear and roping in a few pals to assist on sound and cameras I produced and vision-mixed as-it-happened a multi-camera, near-broadcast-quality film of the show. For me, it would be merely the first of several grand-scale follies/visionary enterprises to come.

'Hi, I'm looking for The Spirit Of Horslips,' I'd said – a few hours before show time – to a couple of blokes hanging around the stage door.

'Er, that'd be us,' said one of the blokes, with mild embarrassment and representing, as it transpired, a west-Belfast 'Blues Brothers' type act moonlighting en masse for an Irish college, village hall and social-club tour as, essentially, Johnny Fean's own tribute band. Give the man some credit, he was a good few years ahead of his time there! Also on board the Fean wagon were a trio of wannabe models doing their best on hip-shaking backing vocals, and a Father Ted-ish manager who had probably been hanging in there somewhere in the underbelly of Irish showbiz since the showband era.

Johnny himself was pretty relaxed. 'I'll probably get a few more years out of it yet,' he'd mused. (And he wouldn't be wrong.) The gig was great fun and the film turned out pretty good, too, for a bunch of amateurs. It didn't help, I admit, that Johnny had lost his voice and that the following week's show at

Colin Harper

Horslips from the sleeve of *Happy To Meet*, 1972:
(l–r) Charles O'Connor, Johnny Fean,
Eamon Carr, Barry Devlin, Jim Lockhart

some old ballroom in the backwoods of Leitrim was ten times better – but one has to try.

Ten years on, with their back-catalogue finally rescued from the oblivion of mediocrity that had beset it when an ex-manager had supposedly flogged it on (in the form of nth-generation masters) to a Belfast record distributor in the early Eighties, I met up with Eamon Carr and dutifully recorded the tale of the band he had been 'in denial' about for the past two decades. It's nice to hear a music-biz story with a happy ending, and nice to hear the music on CD without a wall of murk in the way. As to whether or not there will ever *be* a reunion of this venerable institution it was perhaps telling to note that, at the time of writing, Johnny Fean has announced the comeback of . . . yes, The Spirit Of Horslips!

HORSLIPS
IN THE BEGINNING

One of the most innovative and influential bands in Irish rock history, the Horslips legacy had been sullied for nearly twenty years – between their split in 1980 and their long-overdue victory in a Belfast court in 1999 – by poor-quality vinyl, cassette and ultimately CD reissues and compilations. In a nutshell, a former manager of the band had sold inferior-generation album masters to a Belfast record distributor in the wake of the split, and for various reasons too complex to explain here the fight for justice has only recently been resolved. With bitter irony this was a group who had always owned – and exercised complete artistic freedom over – their own recordings from day one, licensing to labels in the UK, US and Europe rather than selling out to the corporate machine. Now that the rights are back with the group (whose case was sustained by financial guarantees, in a spirit of brotherhood, from U2) stunning remasters of their original albums, with upgraded artwork from the group's in-house designer Charles O'Connor, are appearing via Demon Records, with aspirations for a box set of rarities and a retrospective video to come. A full-scale reunion is unlikely but the original five are tentatively recording together again, on odd weekends at Charles O'Connor's place in the north of England, just to see what happens.

'We started as an experimental unit and we wound up as a burned-out experimental unit!' says Eamon Carr, the group's drummer and lyricist. 'One of the first big gigs we did was a festival in Sligo, playing support to Fairport Convention, The Chieftains, Bridget St John and possibly also Tír na nÓg – and we wound up in 1980 sharing stages in America with Blue Oyster Cult, Molly Hatchet and The Outlaws. Quite a strange span. People fix on that glam image we had but it was maybe only two years. In a way we were like Hawkwind – a "people's band".'

There is no denying the Horslips legend within Ireland: their best-known 'Celtic rock' anthems are still covered by bar bands, while increasingly their music is being used in TV advertising and even, in the case of 1973's 'Dearg Doom', as a backing track for the 1998 Irish World Cup squad's single 'Put Them Under Pressure'. Eamon Carr has become a respected cultural commentator with Dublin's *Evening Herald*; bassist Barry Devlin is now a film-maker, with several U2 promo videos on his CV; flautist/keyboard player Jim Lockhart is an eminent and influential radio producer with RTÉ, responsible for RTÉ's *Dave Fanning Show*, Ireland's equivalent to BBC Radio 1's *Evening Session*; Charles O'Connor, multi-instrumentalist, has gone back to graphic design

Colin Harper · Originally published in *Record Collector* (November 2000)

(though there was a low-key solo album, *Angels On The Mantelpiece*, in 1996); while lead guitarist Johnny Fean remains the only member still treading the boards, playing in London pub bands and occasionally fronting his own tribute band, The Spirit Of Horslips.

Having checked out the Caravaggio in Dublin's National Gallery – Carr has a Masters in fine art, after all – we settled down in the gallery's echoing café to retrieve some echoes of how it all began: 'In 1972 myself, Barry and Charles were all working in Arks Advertising agency in Dublin,' says Eamon. 'Charles was a graphic designer from Middlesbrough who'd played in a céilí band at the college of art there and came over to Dublin because of Irish traditional music – he was the most traditionally minded of all of us. I was a copywriter in the agency, as indeed was Barry, and I had a sort of poetry and music group called Tara Telephone, with Peter Fallon [brother of legendary rock publicist B.P. Fallon], Declan Sinnott and Lucian Purcell. Jim Lockhart had come to the poetry readings that I had and would produce his tin whistle and play 'Blue Rondo A La Turk' and 'Take Five' on it and I remember thinking, That's very interesting. He knew his jigs and reels, too. So Charles and Jim could certainly play and Barry and I could play enough. There was a guy called Spud Murphy – a photographer with us in the agency – and he played guitar with us but left before we really started gigging. He went on to work with *Sounds* and photographed John Lennon's *Imagine* sessions.'

During the Sixties and early Seventies Ireland's live-music scene was dominated by showbands – essentially dance bands with brass sections, covering the pop hits of the UK and US and usually fronted by Elvis wannabes – who played host to the early careers of several Irish rock guitarists, including Rory Gallagher, Henry McCullough and Eric Bell. But Dublin also had quietly thriving progressive rock and folk scenes, which produced some now highly collectable records (a great CD compilation is surely waiting to be done) and which provides a backdrop to the emergence of Horslips. Some acts, most notably Skid Row and Dr Strangely Strange, did acquire deals with UK labels but unfortunately John Peel's notion of financing a Tara Telephone album (as Ireland's answer to Principal Edward's Magic Theatre) didn't quite happen. 'I can remember with Tara Telephone asking Joe Dolan, ex-Sweeney's Men, could we come down to his gigs and do some stuff. I also knew Henry McCullough [ex-Sweeney's Men and Eire Apparent, latterly The Grease Band] and in fact I'd written a poem about Henry and recited it on TV, on the *Late Late Show*, around 1969 or 1970. Sweeney's were devastating, just awesome. Prior to that you would have had The Dubliners and there was a thing called the Dublin Blues Appreciation Society, of which I was a member. There was a band called Blues House with Ed Deane on guitar who, I think, wound up in Bees Make Honey later on. Brush Shiels [the driving force behind Skid Row, Ireland's answer to King Crimson] ran something called the Ghetto club, a once-a-week type of thing, and it could have been anything: Terry Woods with an embryonic Woods Band; Dr Strangely Strange; Mellow Candle with Clodagh Simonds –

who also worked at the ad agency with Barry, Charles and myself. Clodagh is still recording and doing amazing stuff – lives down in west Cork. There was also a great a cappella group called The Press Gang and Alec Finn [later in trad legends De Danann] was playing blues with The Cana Band . . .

'You met these lads in the same coffee shops or the same pubs. So there were poetry readings going along with blues sessions and folk sessions and there was also a beat-group scene which Them used to come down from Belfast and play. There were a few venues around Dublin – Stella House, the Five club, the Scene club, the Apartment, the Club A-Go-Go – that people like Them and The Gentry would play. There weren't any bars at these venues, that was the weird thing – but you could get a couple of hundred kids paying money to get in. People like Skid Row would have played these places in the later Sixties. Thin Lizzy were also knocking around. We got a couple of early supports with them, one in the Stadium, very early on – before they went to England. I'd encouraged Philip [Lynott] down to the poetry readings – Phil's line was, "Will there be chicks there?" He was nervous as hell, actually a sensitive lad and a fine poet. But slightly before that Skid Row had already been in the British charts with their first album [*Skid*, a UK number 30 in October 1970], so there were possibilities that things could happen. The showband scene was where the money was – the people I'm talking about weren't making any money. How they existed was always a mystery!

'The first Horslips gig was in a Dublin art gallery, Gallery Langois, and it was an afternoon thing. We performed the set twice as people wandered around the gallery – like a gigantic dress rehearsal, and very useful. We did that again a few weeks later, then ventured out doing odd art schools and colleges. People sat on the ground for those gigs – there were time changes all over the place, definitely not music for dancing to!

'But the momentum began to build and we felt we had to get a single out. Chrysalis and Transatlantic had shown an interest in us but it didn't make sense to go with those people – I think we probably felt it was still evolving. We were being managed by Michael Deeny, an Oxford graduate from Lurgan, Northern Ireland who, with his partner Paul McGuinness [later U2's manager], had started doing promotions. Charles designed posters for him. He ran a festival in the RDS with The Crazy World Of Arthur Brown and Manfred Mann's Earth Band – and we were on the bill and he saw the reaction to us. It took on a life of its own. We were just about holding down our day jobs, gigging quite extensively at that point. The plan was that we were about to stop at any minute, when it made sense.

'Around the time of Tara Telephone I remember thinking that Mike Vernon had set up Blue Horizon – and it just seemed like something you could do. In Tara Telephone we had actually published booklets of poetry. It was very much underground stuff. We knew the lads in The Liverpool Scene, who were a huge influence. We published poetry collections and broadsheets and also a magazine called *Cappella* – we had Ginsberg in it, Séamus Heaney, Pete Sinfield from

Horslips, onstage, mid-Seventies:
Charles O'Connor (left), Johnny Fean

King Crimson, Marc Bolan. In fact, I think we might have rejected one of Marc's! So having done that the idea of putting out a single didn't seem such a big task. There was a pressing plant in Dublin and we'd seen singles with picture sleeves in France.'

Johnny Fean had yet to join the band, but with Declan Sinnott from Tara Telephone on guitar the debut single 'Johnny's Wedding' – a rocked-up trad tune – appeared in a picture sleeve and was a surprise Irish-chart hit. 'Suddenly,' says Eamon, 'we had all this talk of being "Canny Advertising Agents in Pop Success". In fact, people like Bowie and Roxy Music were probably infinitely cannier – but there was a tradition of "art school" about us that a lot of other Dublin bands at that time, with the exception of Dr Strangely Strange, didn't have. The first single created a demand. The second single was a folk song that Barry had learned called "Green Gravel" and we were delighted with this because it was the root of "St James Infirmary Blues", which probably swayed us to record it. It was a minor hit and meant that we started getting gigs in ballrooms – and some were disastrous. We were playing maybe 45-minute spots in the intermission. People would dance like billy-o to the showband, then we'd come on and start mucking around with the "Ace And Deuce Of Pipering" or "Dance To Your Daddy" or something!

'We were perceived as some kind of hippy novelty act, but the cannier promoters realised that there was an audience for the showbands and then *another* audience coming in to look at us, so they'd bring us back on the off-night, like a Wednesday or Thursday. We were then able to buy a PA system and a van, which had previously belonged to Ashton, Gardner & Dyke. At which point we thought, We've done the single, we could probably do the album. But then we thought, No, because the Dublin studios weren't great and we were thinking along the lines of Pink Floyd's first album. Actually, our lights man was a guy called "Ashtar From Mars" who kept stopping the van on the way back from gigs convinced he'd seen flying saucers. I always like to think the Sixties came late to Dublin – like, in the early Seventies!'

Hiring a rambling Georgian House in Tipperary, the group brought over The Rolling Stones' mobile studio – another novel idea for the time – and, with Johnny Fean now on board as guitarist, recorded the seminal first album *Happy To Meet, Sorry To Part* over three weeks. It would prove the first of a sterling run of albums to explore the then uncharted territory between British progressive rock, Irish traditional music and Irish mythology – with a healthy dose of self-deprecating wit and absurd stage wear from the Slade school of fashion. The packaging for that first album was as extraordinary as the music – a die-cut octagonal design with a lavish booklet, which Charles had created. 'The sleeves cost as much as the production of the record,' says Eamon. 'It was basically a homage to his concertina!'

Released in November 1972, the album went ballistic: 'It was frightening. The first pressing was, I think, 35,000 and it sold out in two weeks. The pressure was on to get another pressing out by Christmas. It sold enough to qualify as platinum – except that those terms weren't being used in Ireland at that time. It was being distributed by Release Records, who distributed the showbands – and they were great because showband stuff sold in all sorts of shops up and down the country, so our record got great distribution. And that was it: we were a band, an identity had been formed and by that stage we couldn't get off the train.'

Thirty years later, the train is being shunted back out with the sparkling new polish of digital remastering. Not all the albums may be essential but some are and the rest, at the very least, are splendidly entertaining period pieces. And as for that name – well, you try saying 'Four Horsemen of the Apocalypse' after a few whiskeys . . .

HORSLIPS
THE BOOK OF INVASIONS

Coming to prominence in early Seventies Ireland, with a pioneering and still definitive fusion of rock with Irish trad, Horslips had not only imagination, intelligence and bravado but enough self-belief to back up the vision with their own record label – licensing beyond Ireland to various labels including RCA, Atco and DJM. Well-educated and meeting through several members working at a Dublin ad agency, they brought a keen visual and literary sense to a fusion that was arguably waiting to happen.

By 1972 the creatively stifling Irish showband era was waning, and Horslips' debut coincided with Christy Moore's similarly influential *Prosperous*. Although following two distinct directions, both releases built on foundations laid by Sweeney's Men five years earlier to bring an awareness of long-neglected Irish traditional music to a generation of young people raised on rock, if largely starved of local access to it. Horslips became not only an indigenous answer to the likes of Fairport Convention in Britain, but massively popular on a mainstream level. By the time *The Book Of Invasions* appeared, in the autumn of 1976, they had had a rough taste of international touring but had also already dabbled in Celtic mythology for *The Táin* (1973), a Jethro Tull-ish song cycle commissioned for a Dublin theatre production.

Taking its title from a twelfth-century manuscript which documented/

Colin Harper · Commissioned for *The Mojo Collection* (Jim Irvin (ed.), Mojo Books, 2000)

Horslips, reunited for a memorabilia exhibition in 2004: (l–r) Charles O'Connor, Eamon Carr, Jim Lockhart, Johnny Fean, unknown, Barry Devlin

mythologised the settlement of Ireland, *Invasions* would be their masterpiece. Time to craft the material was bought with the release of a pure trad album (*Drive The Cold Winter Away*), a compilation (*Tracks From The Vaults*) and an extraordinarily successful Irish-only single version of what would be re-recorded as the new album's opening track, 'Daybreak'. *Invasions* itself was virtually an album's worth of potential hit singles with brief conceptual inter-ludes. Indeed, three tracks – 'Trouble With A Capital T', 'The Power And The Glory' and 'Warm Sweet Breath Of Love' – were subsequently released as singles in either the UK or US. On the back of radio play and previous ground-work on the road, the album charted in both the UK top 40 and *Billboard* top 100. Richly impressionistic, by turns wistful and epic, this was an epochal moment for Irish rock. 'Dealing with Irish myths,' says lyricist Eamon Carr, 'was firstly a useful device and secondly helped us, and our audience, to explore our own identity. We started out just mucking around playing gigs in pubs, and somehow we became a "people's band" – in a way that very few bands do.'

Shortly after *Invasions* the group succumbed to the black hole of 'breaking America' and split in 1980. A few years later, U2 – with promo videos directed by Horslips' Barry Devlin – succeeded in that task, while all things Celtic went on to become a huge international industry. In 1999 Horslips finally regained their record rights (illegally acquired, and endlessly repackaged, by a Belfast businessman shortly after the split). Most members now work successfully in the Irish media, but pride is both strong and justified and a reunion is not unlikely.

Rory Gallagher,
onstage in the Seventies

RORY GALLAGHER
PROLOGUE

I never saw Rory Gallagher live. True, I probably had a few opportunities when I was at school and his concerts in Belfast were still fairly regular, though becoming less so. But I never did, and there it is. Much as he was a hero to many in the North, Rory just never really made it into my own peculiar little orbit until it was too late and I, as 'the writer from Belfast', was asked to write obituaries for both *Mojo* and *Record Collector* following his untimely death in July 1995.

I have a recollection of interviewing, together, in an empty Lyric Theatre on the banks of the Lagan, Andy Irvine and Eric Wrixon. I can't imagine what the context of both these men being there at the same time could have been, but there they were, by fortune at the right moment to bury and to praise. I believe we went on to the Rotterdam Warehouse for a drink afterwards, Andy judging this a good enough moment to come off the wagon and raise a glass. Though I had spoken to him on the phone before – around the time of my writing, three years earlier, a Sweeney's Men sleeve-note – this was the first time I had met Andy Irvine and, as I recall it now, I was profoundly impressed by his demeanour and his aura of integrity. I borrowed albums, put calls through to Jan Akkerman in the Netherlands, to Davy Spillane on a mobile somewhere in London and to somebody representing Samuel Eddy, and gave the two pieces my best shot in the time available. It was a first, rapidly drawn glimpse into the world and the character of Rory Gallagher and there was already enough to make me sorry I had never known him.

Three years later, and shortly after my long-in-waiting piece on Anne Briggs had appeared in the magazine, *Mojo* editor Mat Snow rang to ask if I'd be interested in writing a full-scale retrospective on Rory. Mat was a very good editor – his restructuring of my Briggs piece, as it appeared in the magazine, was a masterclass in the art – and a decent fellow besides. It was nice to be asked and, in hindsight, this was probably the point in my writing career where I had accumulated enough self-confidence and experience to take on a full-scale biography. Which was just as well as Bert Jansch, wildly out of character as it was, was about to ask me to do just that. But getting back to that feature on Rory, I didn't need to be asked twice.

Donal Gallagher was about to reveal the first fruits of a systematic remastering of Rory's back-catalogue, via major label BMG (though, in true *Mojo* style, direct referencing of any such products in the text would be quietly removed), and he was the obvious first point of contact. We agreed to meet soon, in Cork. In the meantime, ultra-fan Dino McGartland generously made me welcome at his home in Omagh where I watched videos of the great man, borrowed vintage interview cuttings and got a sense of what Rory was all about to the legions of the faithful. I was drawn particularly to what some may view as the edges of the Gallagher map – the early days, the last days and the consistently expressed interest in folk music. The archetypal Seventies era, of checked shirts and endless tours, seemed less important in understanding the man. Either way, though I would later meet – and come to admire, in his role as Nine Below Zero's bassist and de facto manager – Rory's 'golden era' bass man, Gerry McAvoy, I opted not to interview those who were primarily associated with that era.

Around this time I had allowed myself to become gently arm-twisted into managing The Adventures – Belfast-based Eighties hit-makers on the reunion trail – and it was, of course, only slightly unethical to feature key man Pat Gribben as an interviewee in the Gallagher piece. (In the event, Pat's entirely sincere quote didn't make the final *Mojo* edit. As to The Adventures' reunion, we managed a handful of very well-paid shows in Belfast, a less successful foray into Dublin, a photo session, some local TV, a bunch of positive press cuttings and some promising, if protractedly recorded, new demos before I finally jumped ship pleading, quite rightly, the combination of an utter lack of the necessary ruthlessness to take things any further and, in more specific terms, a looming commitment to write a book on British folk music from the Sixties. There is only so much incongruity one's headspace can accommodate.)

Meeting Donal in Cork was a very pleasurable experience. Rory is a lucky man to have someone of such dedication, tenacity and fundamental decency as the ongoing executor and champion of his recorded legacy. John Wilson and Richard McCracken are lucky men, too, in being co-beneficiaries of Donal's long-fought renegotiation of Taste's royalty situation. And the fans are perhaps luckiest of all, given the quality of the retrospective CD and DVD programme to date, with no doubt many more carefully crafted releases yet to come. (It may be surprising to some – as it was to me – to learn that during the first quarter of the reissue programme Rory was BMG's biggest selling artist after Elvis Presley.)

I've met Donal on several occasions since then, and was delighted to play even a small role in oiling the wheels between himself and Bert Jansch during the painstaking process of readying Rory's acoustic demos – with embellishments from the likes of Bert, Martin Carthy and other musicians – for release as the final Rory album proper, *Wheels Within Wheels* (BMG, 2003). I'm also grateful to Donal for providing a terrific foreword – an affectionate account of Taste's brief residency in Bangor, Northern Ireland, during the late Sixties – to *Seaside Rock* (North Down Borough Council, 2003), a modest, affectionate little booklet I completed shortly before throwing in my lot, for better or worse, with the Belfast Education and Library Board.

There was a time, post-Jansch and pre-library, when I pondered very

Taste, mark 2, 1968:
(l–r) John Wilson,
Richard McCracken,
Rory Gallagher

seriously on the possibility of pursuing a Gallagher biography. Such a project, by the right person, is certainly dear to Donal's heart. In truth, I probably wouldn't have been the right person to do it, but either way the moment passed. By the time 2000 arrived I was effectively burned out from a year's toil on *Dazzling Stranger*, and though I find myself continuing to write books of one sort or another, the idea of dedicating another great swathe of life to the chronicling of someone else's holds no attraction. For better or worse I'm now someone who works in a library, who used to write about music. And still does, when no one's looking . . .

Rory Gallagher, 1976

RORY GALLAGHER
REQUIEM FOR A GUITAR HERO

'He suffered a lot. His health was bad. He had a problem with drink. His relationships with women were all messed up because of his work. And he got a lot of hassle from the authorities and the establishment. But still, he stayed true to what he wanted to do . . .' Speaking to *Hot Press* in 1992, Rory Gallagher was describing his admiration for crime writer Dashiell Hammett. It was painfully obvious to the interviewer, Liam Fay, and perhaps also to Rory, that he was all but dictating his own epitaph. Bloated from a once lean figure due to medication for fighting liver disease, shielding any kind of light from his eyes with dark glasses and yet typically honest in recounting his own increasing 'ragbag of neuroses' – obsessive picture-straightening among them – Gallagher's quiet decency was the same as ever, but otherwise he was a shadow of the man he had been. It seemed that after a life of relentless gigging and quite peerless devotion to his fans he was aware that he was reaching the place where life runs out.

'I've toured too much for my own good,' he said. 'It hasn't left time for very much else, unfortunately. You don't develop any family life and it makes relationships very difficult. There's always a certain percentage missing from your life. As a human being you only have so much to give, not just in terms of your physical body but in how you deal with people.'

Perhaps nobody else in rock 'n' roll had given more generously of his time, his encouragement, his gratitude to both his peers – many of whom he admired and spoke of as a fan himself – and to the legions of fans who loved him. One such, Dino McGartland, who runs a Gallagher fan magazine, crystallises the man's enduring qualities: 'Even if you only sat down with him for fifteen minutes in your life he made you feel special,' he says. 'I only met him once but I hear it from a lot of people.'

Rory Gallagher died, aged 47, from complications following a liver transplant at London's King's College Hospital on 14 June 1995, a Wednesday. Strange to tell for someone so long on the margins of media favour, the worldwide obituary machine went into overdrive, and nowhere more so than in Ireland. Devastatingly sincere tributes flowed into *Hot Press*, the island's premier music publication, not only from fans, broadcasters and journalists but from all shades of Rory's peers in the business. Many had only met him in passing but were clearly as impressed with his soft-spoken, generous character and unquenchable enthusiasm for music as they were by his playing – distinctive and virtuosic as it may have been. Jimmy Page, Paul Rodgers and Slash

Colin Harper · Originally published in *Mojo* (September 1998); plus additional material

lined up with Gary Moore, U2 and The Dubliners. Bono marked him perceptively as 'one of the top ten guitar players of all time but more importantly one of the top ten good guys'; a spokesman for Jeff Beck noted wryly that 'both could have been Rolling Stones, but good sense prevailed'. Even Van Morrison issued a statement. But the truth was, as a columnist for *The Irish Times* noted, under the stark headline 'Lest We Forget', that Rory may have been on many people's minds on the Wednesday, but how many had been thinking about him on the Tuesday?

William Rory Gallagher was born on 2 March 1948 at the Rock Hospital in Ballyshannon, a sleepy little town in Donegal. His father Danny, from Derry, was working on a hydroelectric project in the area. Rory was bought his first guitar at nine, although brother Donal remembers him tuning into American radio in search of blues music when only six. Seeing Elvis Presley on TV was a potent inspiration and other early, enduring musical heroes included Chuck Berry and Lonnie Donegan. When Rory was eight the family had moved to MacCurtain Street in the cosmopolitan centre of Cork city, whence his mother Monica had hailed. Still at school, with a fast-developing ability on his instrument, Rory was determined to play: 'I had tried to get a group together at school, which lasted one night! I was still doing the odd show on my own – talent shows and charity shows, Pioneer [a total-abstinence association] rallies. So when I saw an ad in a paper – "Showband needs guitar player" – I said, "Well, I'll give it a bash." These fellas were doing two or three gigs a week and I could plug into an AC30 – the amplifier I had at home was a 4-watt Selmer! I handled the rock 'n' roll department basically. The two years I had with them was fun – at the age of sixteen I was playing the showband gigs in England in Lent [a six-week period wherein Irish dance halls would close] – which gave me the chance on nights off to go down to the Marquee and see The Yardbirds or Spencer Davis.'

The rewards also stretched to the £100 cost of his famous Stratocaster. The showband era has its own mythology in Ireland today, but more as a lifestyle experience than a musical movement with any great legacy. At its peak, there were said to be around 600 matching-suited acts shuttling up and down the island, packing them in on a vast circuit of rural ballrooms (fourteen of which were owned by future Irish prime minister Albert Reynolds) with gruelling five-hour shows encompassing UK chart covers, comedy, Elvis and Jim Reeves. Genuine beat groups were quite literally the poor relation. In joining The Fontana [Showband], later updating its name to The Impact, Rory was simply one of many creative souls obliged to learn their craft in a mohair suit. But he was always agitating for change: 'We were the first to break the showband dress code, wearing more Beatle-y clothes. The name change, too – Fontana was too showbandy . . . We had a chance of a single in England – in fact, we did a TV show in Dublin with a song I wrote, "You Fool Me All The Time" [an acetate of which still exists], and I thought we could break in England. But the others weren't convinced, so eventually I just gave up the ghost.'

With an outstanding commitment for a gig in Hamburg, Rory and The Impact's rhythm section agreed to fulfil it. The promoter had insisted upon a four-piece at the very least; Rory sent him a picture of his new trio with a tone-deaf acquaintance posing by a Vox Continental: 'We went over there in a van, didn't even have a key for the ignition,' he recalled – 'Just a screwdriver. No locks on the door either – we had to tie ropes around it!'

The trio played seven sets a night, fifteen minutes off in the hour, for three weeks. True to form, Hamburg was a steep learning curve but it was already long past its heyday: 'I could still see people hanging around the Star club – like Lee Curtis & The All Stars – completely dressed in black leather. Lots of Liverpool hangover bands. Still a strong atmosphere. The Top Ten club was still going. We auditioned for it and failed – too loud!'

The trio fizzled out on their return to Cork but when a local showband, The Axles, dissolved the following year – 1966 – leaving their bassist Eric Kitteringham and drummer Norman D'Amery free, the idea was resurrected. They called themselves Taste.

Pat Egan, a columnist for Ireland's *New Spotlight* magazine, remembers the buzz the newly unleashed guitarist created, at least in Dublin. It was well before Thin Lizzy with Eric Bell or Skid Row with Gary Moore, but Gallagher didn't have the market quite all to himself: 'At that time it was Henry McCullough and The People,' says Egan. 'Henry would have been the opposition at that stage – *the* other guitar player.'

'That would be true all right,' says McCullough. 'But I was probably in showbands longer than Rory – I think he was the first of all of us to get out of it. Even when I was in The People we were still playing covers of Wilson Pickett. Rory had already got himself on the first rung of the rock 'n' roll ladder and I think anybody who was involved in music at that time couldn't help but admire the man. I mean, there wasn't anybody in that period of Irish music for younger folk to revere – apart from the likes of Dickie Rock or Brendan Bowyer – and Rory was the first to get out there and do it properly. He became a hero to a whole load of people who didn't know anything about the blues.'

'The First Irish Rock Star' was a title Rory would later endure, and one which Phil Lynott – actively chasing the rock-star myth – would doubtless envy. But while the beat-group scene in Dublin had the thrill of a real 'underground', with up to a dozen clubs spanning the mid-Sixties, the market elsewhere in Ireland was patchy. Beat music in Ireland was a city phenomenon. In the south, Galway, Cork, Limerick and Dublin had venues prepared to put on the groups and, as an alternative to the ballrooms, there was something of a tennis-club circuit elsewhere. The early Taste did play occasional gigs in the ballrooms, compromising to the frankly bizarre union rules about band sizes by simply bringing in extra people to stand at the back and play tambourines. But for all the adulation in Dublin, Taste mark 1 were musically a far cry from their peers – still touring Ireland, even at the height of the beat craze, for a fiver a night. Any showband could offer a musician 70 to a hundred pounds a week. If Taste were getting used to being outsiders, they found themselves among friends in Belfast.

Attracted by the British mainland success of Van Morrison's Them – who had been signed by Decca's Dick Rowe (known forever as the man who turned down The Beatles) very largely on the back of a frenzied live performance in the city – Taste arrived in Belfast during the early part of 1967. It was the tail end of a vibrant R&B scene, centred on the Maritime Hotel. For a while Rory actually lived at the Seamen's Mission next door and often hoped that Van, in a lean period post-Them, would come back and play at the venue he had all but made: 'I only actually saw him once then – in a boutique!' Rory recalled. 'When I got up there I was expecting everyone to be carrying rosettes for him. But he'd come back and found it difficult to get work there. It was only in the Seventies that they realised who they had.'

The city was awash with bands playing the rawest blues in Ireland, with venues to support them. In Rory's era a band could play three nights a week in Belfast with other gigs around the province. Roger Armstrong, now MD at Ace Records, booked the band many times for Queen's University and it was fitting that their last-ever gig – filmed by BBC Northern Ireland and now, predictably, long-since erased – took place there, on 24 October 1970. What little that survives on record of Belfast's beat scene from the initial 1964–66 era was collected together on *Belfast Beat, Maritime Blues* (Ace, 1997) although BBC Radio Ulster had already celebrated the scene with a documentary produced by Owen McFadden and presented by John Kelly in 1990, to which Rory contributed: 'It was one of the happiest times of my life, really,' Rory recalled, of his Belfast days. 'It's always very exciting when a band is on the edge of breaking but aside from that, you know, the friends, the atmosphere. And also the good atmosphere between most of the bands – and a good little bit of competition as well. We weren't too fussed about how big we were, how much money we were making, that kind of stuff . . . Anywhere that was anti-showband we would play!'

By the time Taste arrived in Belfast the Maritime's original promoters, the 'Three Js', had been ousted by a professional ballroom dancer called Eddie Kennedy. By July Taste were causing such a sensation at the club that Kennedy, in a repetition of the moves which had led to Them's record deal three years earlier, rang the only guy in Belfast with any real music-business contacts in London: record wholesaler Mervyn Solomon. Solomon by this stage had his own studio and label, Major Minor, and had already tasted success with local boy David McWilliams' 'The Days Of Pearly Spencer'. Taste's first single, coupling 'Born On The Wrong Side Of Time' with 'Blister On The Moon', made its debut on Solomon's label in late '68. But the very day after Kennedy had invited him to the Maritime, before anybody had signed contracts, Solomon had them down at his studio.

Clearly intended as demos, the tracks recorded that day, with Rory doubling extensively on harmonica, reveal a British-style rhythm-and-blues sound much more akin to the Beck-era Yardbirds than to Cream, albeit nodding towards the progressive sounds of the mark-2 Taste. Without hiding the fact that the great majority of the session had been carelessly wiped, Solomon and Kennedy released the seven surviving tracks, briefly, as *In The Beginning* in 1974 before Donal Gallagher (Rory's brother, latter-day manager and ongoing keeper of the flame) had it withdrawn, beginning a lengthy and frustrating process of litigation that would drag on almost to the end of Rory's life.

Kennedy, as manager, took his new charges to England in May '68. The first gig was supporting Captain Beefheart in Nottingham. But somewhere between their first and second sessions for John Peel's *Top Gear*, in August and October, Taste's line-up changed. Hindsight has shown that Kennedy's plan was divide and conquer, taking the money for himself: 'We were told there was a deal on the table but Polydor weren't happy with Norman and Eric,' John Wilson recalls. 'I now don't believe that for one minute. It was a Tuesday, back in Belfast. Eddie Kennedy said, "The band's gonna be splitting after a gig tomorrow night at Romano's – do you and Charlie want the gig?" We said, "Yeah, of course." Eric had a motorbike and after the show he and Norman got on the motorbike and drove to Cork. It was very sad, but there was no hard feelings. The next night we were in Scotland doing a gig and that's the way it went on. Playing live was what the band was all about. During that whole period we never rehearsed. It was just magical. I've never experienced that dynamic again, and I don't believe Rory did either.'

Richard 'Charlie' McCracken, on bass, and drummer John Wilson were both northerners. From showband Derek & The Sounds, they had become Cheese, in thinly veiled imitation of Cream. Cheese were already themselves carving a niche in London, but any desire to fill what was now the gap left by Cream's own disbandment – and Taste actually supported at Cream's Albert Hall swansong later that year – would be adequately rewarded by the accolades heaped upon this powerhouse new trio, and mirrored in a similarly brief, mercurial career.

Taste released two albums: the pile-driving *Taste* (1969) and the more elaborate *On The Boards* (1970), which, in featuring Rory improvising memorably on sax, betrayed the guitarist's fascination with Eric Dolphy and Ornette Coleman. Two posthumous concert documents, *Live At Montreux* and *Live At The Isle Of Wight*, Rory always regarded as illegal. Recorded fast, on eight-track – giving an explosive sound that Gallagher still admired years later – the material on *Taste* had been in the set for months. Their only single (not a medium Gallagher ever cared for), 'Born On The Wrong Side Of Time', recalled Cream. Other tracks doffed a cap at Hendrix and tellingly also at folk-baroque pioneer Davy Graham, whose earlier arrangement of Leadbelly's 'Leaving Blues' was easily adapted for the power trio. Gallagher would often tell interviewers that his favourite guitarists were Davy Graham, Bert Jansch and Martin Carthy, and during his solo years would periodically indicate a desire to play as an acoustic artist, envying their band-less, responsibility-free lifestyles.

By the time *On The Boards* was recorded, Taste were huge all over Europe and had toured America as guests of Blind Faith. At one show, in Los Angeles, the members of Led Zeppelin turned up. Taste were featuring a riff-heavy version of Willie Dixon's 'I Need Love' in their act at the time; within a few months they would have reason to drop it.

Following a fraught performance at the Isle of Wight in August 1970 Taste embarked on what was only revealed in the last week as their final tour, of Britain and Ireland. There had been problems in the band for months – a situation described in the press, when the story finally broke, as 'ludicrous' and 'absurd'. As late as the 26 September issue of *NME*, Rory was talking matter-of-factly about the next album as if it was really imminent. All the numbers were already written, he claimed. He still spoke with overriding enthusiasm: 'There's no point going on stage and playing unless you play as well as you can. If you're a musician you should enjoy playing.'

Taste had never had secrets from the press. They'd pioneered the process of taking reporters on the road with them, but one of their old friends, Roy Hollingsworth of *Melody Maker*, was astonished at the farcical situation he encountered at Newry Town Hall: 'I found Rory in the changing room and he succeeded in talking about everything except the split. You can't help liking the guy because he's so nice. It wasn't a case of him making no comment. He just smiled at questions. If the fact be known, he will not discuss it because he does not like putting people down. He just talks about music . . . Throughout the whole of the evening not a word was passed between Rory and the others. The atmosphere was, to say the least, unnatural.'

Taste were victims of their own rapid success and inexperience. Eddie Kennedy had steered them from a fiver to £2,000 a night in two years. He and his avarice were understandably upset at the split: 'Gallagher could have been a dollar millionaire by next year,' he told Hollingsworth. Well, somebody might have been. Wilson and McCracken formed a new band, Stud, recording three albums with no great success. Kennedy was still in charge, history repeating itself, until Wilson realised the awful truth: 'I just couldn't believe he could do something like that,' he says. 'We couldn't even afford to take legal action.'

Years later, Gallagher could and did. And years later Wilson regrets the sordid end of a band that he believes could have gone on to greater heights musically and commercially. Nevertheless, 'Rory did have a strange personality,' he says, looking back. 'People would see the band onstage and imagine Rory was some sort of real wild guy. But he wasn't like that. For the two hours we gigged he was Rory; for the other 22 hours of the day he was some other bloke. Didn't have a lot of close friends. Did his own thing. Didn't really mix with other people bar saying hello and shaking hands. In fact, during our whole period together there was never any association with women. It sounds stupid, but he was just a really nice guy and very, very shy.'

Every cloud has a silver lining, and even the death-throes of Taste, at their final concert, gave musical life that would flourish years after the event. Pat

Rory Gallagher, 1976

Gribben, guitarist/songwriter with late-Eighties chart act The Adventures, remembers it vividly: 'It was the first gig I'd ever been to and it was amazing. I couldn't sleep that night at all. The next day when I went to school I'd made my decision: this was it, school didn't matter any more. There was no way school was going to help me buy a Stratocaster! I can still hear to this day, in all the guitar players around Belfast my age, the Rory Gallagher-isms. Everybody wanted to play like him.'

Gallagher would continue to play regularly and spectacularly in Belfast throughout the troubled Seventies, when virtually all other international rock artists of any note declined to take the risk, and his consequent influence in the province speaks for itself. It was no surprise that Ulster Television was the first to assemble a Gallagher documentary tribute, within three weeks of his death, and no surprise that his official website is run from Belfast or that tribute concerts take place annually in the city. Gallagher may have been 'The First Irish Rock Star' but he was a Belfast phenomenon.

Most people's recollection of Rory Gallagher today is of a lean, frenetic figure storm-trooping around festival and city hall stages all through the Seventies with a permanent checked shirt and archetypal battered Strat, flanked on one side by Gerry McAvoy, splay-legged, head-banging and writing the text book for the pummelling school of bass guitar. Rory's live shows were high-energy affairs. 'It would start with the encore – that's what it was like,' says Dino McGartland. 'We'd go home shattered.' Any number of *Old Grey Whistle Test* specials, or his record number of *Rockpalast* broadcasts on German TV, bear this out.

Dave Pegg, from Fairport Convention and later Jethro Tull, shared many's a festival stage and after-show pint with Rory and remembers the first time he saw him perform: 'It was the early Seventies, at Birmingham Town Hall. Our roadie Robin Gee was working with Rory at the time. I was sitting with Robin as it came up to the last number and he said, "Watch what they do after this one," and sure enough the audience got up on its feet and went absolutely bananas. He knew exactly how to manage a crowd.'

'A lot of groups get annoyed with audiences that are too rowdy, but I think I know where the line is,' Rory told *Beat Instrumental*, just prior to his debut solo tour in 1971. 'You don't see the old greats on the blues scene preaching about sitting still.' Blistering, sweaty, rowdy blues-rock became increasingly Rory's calling card as the Seventies wore on into the Eighties, in parallel with the influx of lowest-common-denominator admirers washed in with the 'New Wave of British Heavy Metal'. But Gallagher's own musical palette was always much wider than that, and nowhere more evident than on his first solo album.

Recorded in February 1971, with new players Gerry McAvoy and Wilgar Campbell, from Belfast band Deep Joy, and with the incomparable Vincent Crane from Atomic Rooster guesting on piano, *Rory Gallagher* is a beautiful, subtle album of virtually end-to-end highlights. It stands alongside Jethro Tull's *Aqualung* and with *Led Zeppelin III* as one of that year's defining moments from the riff-based, acoustic-friendly end of progressive rock. Not quite as macho as Zeppelin, nor as wilfully quirky as Tull, Gallagher had created his own sound, drawing from modern jazz chordings and octave soloing, urban and delta blues, straight-ahead rock and Celtic folk. On slide and acoustic work there was an affinity with Jimmy Page, but with altogether more lightness of touch. His use of the guitar's volume controls, feedback and sublime tone was more akin to Paul Kossoff but it was the sound that Rory made his own.

'It had a nice atmosphere,' Rory recalled, years later – 'Not as hard or rocky as some of the Taste stuff, nor the later recordings either. A tight little sound – all live vocals and live lead guitar. Recorded very quietly with one little Fender amp and a twelve-inch speaker.'

The new trio pursued a gruelling touring schedule, which eventually caused Campbell to leave. They cut two more albums, *Deuce*, released in December '71, and the similarly splendid *Live In Europe*. The latter, with two posthumous Taste concert sets to compete with, was a definitive snapshot of what made Gallagher great on stage: a breathless Celtic 'gumbo' of folk, blues and rock. *Deuce* was an attempt to capture that live energy in a studio and, as the glorious remix prepared for the 1997 CD reissue testifies, it more than succeeded. Gallagher's songwriting – something he always worked hard at, however formulaic the sound of later albums – continuing on from the debut, was richly flowing, and the earlier comparisons, with an added dash of Doc Watson flat-picking and Townshend-ish sweeps on unresolved chords, held true. Perhaps surprisingly, Smiths' guitarist Johnny Marr has acknowledged that playing along with this album as a kid was a particular inspiration with regard to his own musical development.

When Campbell opted out, Rory drafted in McAvoy's London flatmate, the improbably named Rod De'Ath, together with Belfast-born pianist, Lou Martin. The showband promoters would have been proud: now Rory had a proper band. Two so-so albums, *Blueprint* and *Tattoo*, were recorded during 1973, and while the late-Nineties remastering process brings them a little more to life, their highlights are already heard to much better effect on the next live set, *Irish Tour*.

This 1972–73 period was, nevertheless, Rory's time of peak public and critical acclaim. Everybody wanted him to work with them. He did sessions for Chris Barber, Muddy Waters, Jerry Lee Lewis and turned down serious invitations to join The Rolling Stones and Deep Purple. Recording with 'The Killer' was quite an eye-opener: 'There was a strange sense of violence and madness around when Jerry Lee was in the room,' he once mused. 'Whenever anyone annoyed him he'd immediately pull up his left trouser leg and go for his sock as if he had a gun in it. There was always a borderline of danger about him which I think is necessary for real rock 'n' roll.'

He recalled Waters' *London Sessions* with more fondness: 'It was a real honour,' he said, twenty years later. 'The whole thing has stuck in my memory like a video. I can plug it in at any time and replay it in my head. Muddy taught me an awful lot during those sessions and I came out a much better player than I went in . . . After the recordings I drove him back to the hotel a few times. I've kept the car ever since as a sort of shrine . . . It's falling apart at the seams now but I can still see Muddy in the front seat, smoking his cigars. I only wish I'd had a super-8 camera to capture all that stuff. I know one of the guys from Chicago took some shots and I'd love to get them for my grandchildren, if I ever have grandchildren. It's a beautiful memory for me.'

Rory ousted Eric Clapton as Best Guitarist in *Melody Maker*'s 1972 poll – a big deal at the time. The following year the title was won by another non-Brit, Jan Akkerman from Dutch band Focus – an act that Rory admired. But then he admired so many musicians – Ornette Coleman, Waylon Jennings, Bob Dylan, any number of up-and-coming and now mostly long-forgotten bands. He just loved music. Indeed, when Taste broke up he had turned a negative into a positive in an interview with Pat Egan in *New Spotlight*: 'I don't believe in public squabbling between members of bands,' he'd said. 'That saga that's going on between John Lennon and Paul McCartney is the greatest ever waste of space. Just think of all the young bands who could benefit from the columns taken up with their nonsense.'

One of Rory's last recordings was for an album called *Strangers On The Run* by Irish bluesman Samuel Eddy. It also featured Jan Akkerman. They were both, in those England–America-centred days of the early Seventies, outsiders who won: 'You may have a point there,' says Akkerman. 'If there's anything chauvinistic it's the British trying to protect their marketplace like nobody else. I think we had that in common. I never had the pleasure to meet him but I knew his style of playing and I admired it. He was the king of the white blues players as far as I'm concerned.'

The new four-piece band cut its teeth on an unprecedented four-month tour of America in 1972. Gallagher had been living in London for a period, but when he came 'home' in the Seventies he wanted that to be the dependable sanity of Cork: 'If you hang around London you get wrapped up in the most absurd situations that you never intended to be in,' he told *Sounds*. 'You get talking to someone and the next thing you're agreeing to write some pop opera, or you say, "Yeah, I'll come and play on Mantovani's next session." Things like that are totally out of context.'

Irish Tour, the album and its accompanying film by Tony Palmer, represented exactly Rory Gallagher's context. A beautifully shot document of time and place – a valedictory tour of Ireland in 1973 – it opened in the UK the following year and toured America alongside Gallagher's own dates there to sensational response. Young girls with lank hair reach out their arms to the stage, someone in a suit roves among the young men motioning them vainly to sit down and a backdrop of waves crashing onto the rugged coast bleeds into 'Walk On Hot Coals' – a crescendo of live noise and the face of an ecstatic 25-year-old with sharp sidies and a wrecked guitar.

Rambling around the faded streets of Cork and its rural fringes, Rory described his simple lifestyle and ambitions: 'I don't regard myself as a top-twenty musician at all,' he says, in the gentle brogue that typified his offstage manner. 'I just want to continue playing, I just want to be able to walk into a shop and buy a bar of chocolate if I want to or go into a bar and have a pint without being besieged all the time . . . I don't want to get into the Rolls Royce and the mansion and the cloak-and-dagger sort of living.' Slightly edited and sonically remixed, the film was reissued for DVD in the late-Nineties. It is both sad and ironic that the cloak-and-dagger lifestyle Rory so casually denounced would become his own way of life towards the end.

Tour after tour, album after album flowed on relentlessly. Rory had a razor-sharp memory, and even in later interviews, troubled by self-doubt and barely concealing his fear of the future, would revel in talking about the many great gigs he had been a part of and the people he had met. Wonderful stories abound, like the time his faithful roadie and bodyguard Tom O'Driscoll dealt so ruthlessly with a stage invasion he actually threw his employer off-stage with the mêlée, or the time brother Donal turned an unrecognised Bob Dylan away from the dressing-room door. Another tale recalls the time Rory, guarded by Tom, was trying to soothe Jerry Lee's furrowed brow in an LA dressing room after John Lennon had walked into The Killer's auditorium and stolen all the attention. Rory's gentle ways were having the desired effect until Lennon appeared and O'Driscoll dropped to the floor begging for the autograph of the 'king of rock 'n' roll'. Lewis went bananas – and went for his sock. 'Lennon could see all this,' said Rory, 'so he quickly signed Tom's piece of paper and then went across the room to Jerry Lee. He did exactly what Tom had done to him. He went down on his knees, kissed Jerry Lee's hand and said, "I've been waiting twenty years to get the autograph of the *real* king of rock 'n' roll." Jerry Lee was delighted. He signed the scrap of paper, they started talking then and everything was fine. It was a wonderful moment.'

The touring continued throughout the Eighties but the young man who had started the Seventies with the world at his feet was becoming a marginal figure in popular music. It was partly of his own making. 'I think he had the amount of success that he really wanted, then rode the rest of it out,' Henry McCullough once told me, and that view has a ring of truth. The attempt to crack America, over the course of 25 tours up to 1990, never quite got there. His mistrust of the music business after Taste had coloured his judgement of new opportunities, while protracted litigation, ending in 1992, against Eddie Kennedy and his heirs was both psychologically depressing and a drain on resources. 'I don't like to think about it because it upsets me,' he said, even subsequently. 'The whole thing has made me very wary of music-business people. I don't give a damn about the money – it's people who let you down that bothers me most. I don't think I'd have stuck with it for so long if it wasn't for Donal. He's a superb character, a gift from God.'

Donal had set up an independent label for Rory – Capo – retaining ownership while licensing to Demon Records. Rory's only albums after 1982

– *Defender* (1987) and *Fresh Evidence* (1990), both darkly tinged but supremely powerful works – were products of this arrangement. Because of careful world-wide licensing they were also, commercially, his most successful releases. Indeed, it is fair to say that the parameters of '*Guinness Book*' chart statistics fail to reflect the sheer scale of Gallagher's consistent popularity – not only as a live attraction but as a national and international recording artist.

Donal spent rigorous time and money in slowly reclaiming ownership of Rory's back-catalogue, and in dealing with the business affairs, touring arrangements and personal foibles of an increasingly whimsical individual. An interview with *Q*, in 1990, revealed a man apparently obsessed with superstitions, astrology and unattainable perfectionism in the studio. *Fresh Evidence* had taken years, one scrapping, two remixes and three attempts at mastering before Rory was satisfied. The writer, David Sinclair, did his best to put a positive gloss on things but Rory's talk was simply racked with self-doubt. There was a blues revival going on all around him, with Bonnie Raitt, John Lee Hooker and Gary Moore shifting units by the truckload, but Gallagher was somehow failing to catch the bandwagon. An unsatisfactory self-compiled set, *Edged In Blue*, a couple of years later, was a belated attempt to do so. Sinclair enquired, hopefully, if Gallagher intended going on forever like the old blues greats: 'That was my ambition,' he replied, 'but over these last four or five years I've wondered if I can keep it going. I'll go for about 60. That would be a fair time to retire.'

It was less the interview but the photograph that appeared with it that concerned so many fans and friends. Gallagher had been out of the limelight for ages and consequently his deterioration – bloated and unwell, with bad skin and watery eyes – seemed instant. Gallagher brushed it off as simply lack of sleep and fresh air after so much time in the studio. One old friend, Martin Carthy, recognised the truth: 'I remember thinking, Jesus Christ, he's put on a lot of weight, and then seeing the pockmarks on his face and thinking, Why on earth is he taking steroids? It's a very distinctive blemish. I know, I've had family members who've had to take them and it's very depressing – one of the things they prescribe to build up your resistance.'

Donal candidly confirms that Rory had developed a drink problem during the Eighties, but is adamant that this was not the major cause of the damage to his health. Donal would 'bet my last penny Rory never even smoked a joint in his life' but he was nevertheless seeing private medical practitioners on a twice-weekly basis, concerning fatigue, insomnia, fear of flying and all manner of other phobias. Unfortunately, beyond the freedoms of the Internet – where Donal believes the truth may yet come out – the full story cannot be told for legal reasons. Suffice to say that I found his views considered and compelling.

'He was on a lot of prescription drugs by different doctors,' says Mark Feltham, a member of Rory's band from 1984 to the end and as close to him as anyone, 'and I think they were confusing his mind, to be honest. Rory had an anxiety problem and always had from a young age. He was extremely sensitive and I think quite often that sensitivity leads to drink, to calm the nerves.'

The one notorious show that has sadly coloured many people's views on Rory – dominating, quite inappropriately, at least one prominent obituary – took place at London's Town & Country on 29 October 1992. A single brandy reacted tragically with his medication and Rory simply fell apart onstage. It would be his final London gig. 'People accused him of being drunk,' says Dave Pegg, 'and I got upset about that. He wasn't that sort of person. He wouldn't do it to himself let alone an audience that had paid to see him. He was one of the few people you meet in the music business where the punter is the prime concern. He may have appeared to be drunk but he was seriously ill.'

It had been the debut of Rory's new band. The long-serving Gerry McAvoy had left in 1992 and taken with him drummer Brendan O'Neill – both having joined re-formed pub-rockers Nine Below Zero and consequently finding the logistics of their double roles impossible. A new band was assembled, with David Leavey on bass, Richard Newman on drums, and with Jim Leverton (primarily a bassist) and John Cooke alternating on keyboards. Mark Feltham remained, on harmonica, and still believes this one to have been Rory's best band. Rory himself was dressing in black now, eschewing the image that had become his trademark: 'It's a psychological thing,' he said, mournfully. 'The denim jacket and check shirt have become like a stigmata to me.'

The new band played a series of mostly festival dates in America and Europe, ending on a tour of Holland in February 1995, where Rory's illness became really serious. But he was still the old Rory: 'We were doing the Paradiso in Amsterdam,' says Feltham, 'and I can remember him walking over the other side of the road, against all the traffic, just to give some money to a busker. He was always for the underdog.'

The last Irish show was in August 1992, on Dublin's College Green. Recorded on DAT, Donal still holds it as one of his brother's finest hours. It had been heralded with an interview in *The Irish Times*, with Rory fighting to scotch rumours about his alcohol intake that were reaching his family back in Cork: 'The idea that you can't play the blues unless you're an alcoholic is nonsense,' he said, pounding the table, 'and potentially a lethal notion to be selling to young musicians . . . Sure I drink, but not to excess. And the key reason is the absolute fear of the darkness taking over. [But] you have to step over a certain line, not necessarily to connect with evil, but to take yourself as close to the brink as you can to give the music that essential edge. It's a dangerous balance.'

A last feature that same year in *Hot Press* could barely paper over the cracks. Rory was becoming maudlin and increasingly homesick. In London he bought Irish papers, listened to Irish radio on long wave, kept up with Irish music releases. 'I'd love to go back and live there if I could get myself together,' he said. 'It could be good for me. I have one or two friends in Ireland and I'd like to get up to Donegal as well and get the old mind sorted out. It's probably what I really need right now.'

Rory Gallagher,
mid-Seventies

'I only met him once,' says Andy Irvine, one among many Irish folk players whom Rory admired. 'I remember it was at the Irish Centre in London, where he was staying, about fifteen years ago. He was just sitting there, and I had to look at him about three times and think, That's not Rory Gallagher, is it? There was absolutely no kind of 'I am Rory Gallagher' vibe out of him. I think he came over and got talking to me, and I was incredibly flattered that he knew who I was and knew my music. We talked about the bouzouki and things like that. He was an "ordinary bloke" – there's no reason why people who are big stars like that shouldn't be ordinary people, but very often they're not. I just thought he was a really nice guy and when I heard he'd died I just couldn't believe it – I didn't even know he was ill.'

The abiding impression of Rory in his final years is of a lonely, shy man who had simply lost confidence in what he did. He had a house in Earl's Court but never lived there. Instead, he lived – alone, albeit close to Donal's house – at the nearby Conrad Hotel, using an assumed name. His phone number was religiously guarded. His own material had long reflected a fascination with the 'hard-boiled' spy stories of Dashiell Hammett and Raymond Chandler, and now it was encroaching on real life. For some reason he never did get back to live among friends in Ireland, but made generous appearances on albums by any number of Irish artists: The Dubliners, Phil Coulter, Samuel Eddy and Davy Spillane among them. 'He was kind enough to play on my album *Out Of The Air*,' says Spillane. 'We slotted together perfectly, played very easily and casually together – it was no problem. I didn't know him that well personally but he was a very generous, personable man and I greatly enjoyed his company. He was very good to me.'

But for all this ongoing openness as a guest player on other people's records, Rory was turning down numerous offers of gigs, even cancelling tours at the last minute, and seemed to have few close friends. One occasional foray into company would be to see folk gigs at the nearby Troubadour club. He was friendly with the organiser Nick Flynn, and it was a nice, no-hassle environment to see the live music he loved, particularly Martin Carthy. Rory had introduced himself to Martin in the early Seventies: 'I didn't see him again for years after,' says Martin, 'but there was like a bond always there. He was a great help to me at one point – encouraging – because everybody goes through down phases. But he was always Mr Positive. "Look on the bright side," he'd say. "Things are never as bad as they seem." It was lovely of him to do it, and it was nice that I was able to do the same for him later on.'

Martin met Rory in person perhaps only half a dozen times. One time, the last time, he came to the Troubadour to see Martin playing with his daughter Eliza and was fascinated by what a feeling it must be to have a child to make music with. Sometime later, in 1994, Martin was on tour in Scotland and got a message from Nick Flynn that Rory was in a bad way: 'He was due to do this tour of Switzerland. It was the first time he'd been on the road in ages. He was living in that damn hotel, on his own. I'd basically go and get a £10 phone card and just tell him what he'd told me, basically: "You're a musician, make music – it's what you're good at."'

After a career in hard rock and blues, the music Rory wanted to record at the very end of his life was something akin to the gentler sounds he was enjoying so much at the Troubadour. Donal has uncovered demos with scribbled notes relating to bringing in Martin or Bert Jansch on certain tracks. (*Wheels Within Wheels*, an acoustic album with posthumous contributions from Carthy, Jansch and other players from Rory's 'wish list', was painstakingly compiled and produced by Donal and released in March 2003.) Rory had got as far as sending demos to Jansch, hoping to arrange a still more extraordinary collaboration: 'He actually wanted to work with Anne Briggs,' says Jansch, referring to the legendary English traditional singer who had disappeared from music twenty years before. 'So he contacted Anne and sent a tape up, but she thought he was a pop star and rejected it out of hand. I tried to get her involved after that but she just wouldn't have it. I then suggested Maggie Boyle, and myself and Maggie actually worked on a couple of numbers. He wanted to do stuff like "She Moved Through The Fair" – close to Davy Graham's version – and he had a few Clannad songs in mind. Maggie lived in Yorkshire and came down to London especially to meet Rory and record the stuff that we'd arranged but he didn't show up. He just drew a blank, couldn't remember having arranged it. I grew disheartened at that point. Having to go through Nick or his brother, it was such a palaver to get through to him it was just off-putting.'

Terri Hooley, godfather of Irish punk, had braved the 'palaver' of cancelled meetings a short while earlier, finally getting access to Rory in his hotel room for what was certainly his last TV interview. Appropriately, it was for an Ulster Television series documenting the history of rock in Northern Ireland. Hooley recalls Rory warming to the subject at once, and he spoke fondly of his days in Belfast and with Taste. The happiest days of his life. He name-checked Davy Graham, Carthy and Jansch, described the relationship of Irish music to the blues and played a splendid 'Celtic' arrangement of Elvis Presley's 'That's Alright Mama'. Right back to Elvis, where it had all begun.

In the centre of Cork city, pedestrianised and bustling with activity, there is a pleasant little square called Rory Gallagher Place. Off to one side is a stone-and-copper sculpture in memory of the city's twentieth-century hero; just around the corner is the art college where he took night classes in painting, fitting it in around the showband. On the corner of MacCurtain Street, where he lived, there's a bar called Gallagher's. It's fleetingly but significantly referred to in Roddy Doyle's *The Commitments*. It was a story based very much on Gallagher's own; Doyle had even wanted him in the movie, in the part given to Joey 'The Lips' Fagan – the trumpet philosopher who had toured the world and played with the greats, but whom no one now remembered or believed. Cork City Library has now opened its Rory Gallagher wing; a few miles up the road in Midleton a popular gig venue, the Meeting Place, has walls strewn with memorabilia and Gallagher's name on the door. Even in Paris a street has been named after him – Rue de Rory Gallagher. Remember, this was a man who toured like there was no tomorrow. He was massive in France, and he had many friends there. A federation of music promoters has its offices in the street; they simply had to have Rory Gallagher's name on their stationery. In Ireland, *Hot Press* has instituted a discretionary Rory Gallagher award for musicianship in its televised annual awards. Around Europe there are any number of tribute nights. Is there any other musician, bar Elvis, so tangibly honoured?

He had been unwell for years, but there were still numerous unfulfilled projects in the air when Rory Gallagher died. A Taste reunion, for a peace concert in Belfast, had already been agreed; a recording date with Bob Dylan had been arranged, with Dylan wanting to record Gallagher's 'Could Have Had Religion' with the main-man on guitar. Dylan was Gallagher's songwriting hero – the last books he read were Dylan biographies, given to him at the hospital by Mark Feltham – and it would have overwhelmed him to find, as Donal did subsequently, that Dylan already owned all of Rory's albums.

Of BMG's enhanced reissues, *Deuce, Photo Finish* and *Fresh Evidence* are particularly recommended to newcomers. The series was completed with further releases in September 1999, followed by a double-album of BBC recordings. Fender have recently created a Rory Gallagher guitar, using his own Strat as their template. Visually, projects involving Taste at the Isle of Wight and various *Whistle Test* and *Rockpalast* broadcasts are likely. Film of Taste at the Woburn Festival 1968 has recently come to light, along with showband-era and Taste mark 1 audio recordings. A box set is likely in the longer term. It is true that Rory always put live performance before recording, but he certainly never regarded the latter as throwaway. In the fullness of time, his rightful place as a significant rock songwriter and studio artist will be confirmed. His place as a paragon of decency already is: 'His sort of character just doesn't exist in the music business,' says Mark Feltham. 'In fact, it doesn't exist in *any* industry. He was just a wonderful human being.'

'He was a nice guy 30 years ago and he didn't change,' says Eric Wrixon, a fellow traveller from those heady days back in Belfast and Dublin. 'He's a loss as a human being and that's more important than anything to do with his music.'

'He was a person of his time,' says Andy Irvine, 'and it was a very exciting time for everybody who was part of it.'

One interviewer, sometime after Taste had split, expected Rory to be disparaging about his old band and their music. His answer was one that would encapsulate his whole career: 'If I said that everything I did two years ago was crap I'd be a con man,' he said. 'Whether you saw me two, six or ten years ago I was doing my best.' And, on the night, almost every night, that was all that mattered.

SECTION 5
FOLK IN THE SEVENTIES

GAY & TERRY WOODS
PROLOGUE

Having conscientiously avoided doing so for several years, on the basis of his somewhat exaggerated reputation for belligerence, it was delightful to finally meet Terry Woods, in Dublin, in the early spring of 2001. The impetus on that occasion was the looming opportunity of taking sometime at the Tyrone Guthrie Centre in Annamakerrig to work on a history of Sweeney's Men, as explained above. For the same purpose, and also for a short feature in *Record Collector* (in which she delighted in letting her colleagues in Steeleye Span find out that, once again, she had had enough of them), I had already met up with Gay Woods and was to meet also, in Galway, with former Sweeney's manager Des Kelly. The game was afoot.

Separated for over twenty years by that stage, it would be nice to say that Gay and Terry had succumbed to the rose-tinted spectacles of nostalgia for their musical and marital partnership of yore. As I say, it would be nice. Still, under exteriors of such caustic invective that even Victor Meldrew and Sybil Fawlty might retreat wounded from the bile-filled battlefield, I do believe that Gay and Terry conceal a certain lingering affection for each other, at least musically – though nostalgia, in itself, occupies but a broom-cupboard in the rambling mansions of their psyches. Before 'The Osbournes', there was 'The Woodses'.

Terry had long laid down his instruments for a career in rock-band management when we first met, and was, with that particular hat on, able and willing to give advice to some young rock stars-in-waiting of my acquaintance. He has, however, since then revived the name of The Woods Band and has taken to the stage once again. I'm afraid to say (certainly to the current Mrs Terry Woods, whose regard for the music business is far too sensible by half) that I may be if not entirely responsible then certainly an unwitting catalyst in her husband's retaking of this perilous path. During 2001 I was involved in an ultimately only partially realised recording project with British R&B legend Duffy Power. Cutting a very long story short, Duffy wanted to record his first album in aeons and I – through sheer fandom, a little spare money and a lot of potentially useful contacts among musicians – became his co-producer. In particular, Duffy wanted to record with an unknown Belfast singer, my friend Janet Holmes, whom he had heard on a compilation and excitedly lauded as a world-class talent whose voice would blend wonderfully with his own. He was absolutely right – on both counts.

With the project not long under way, I had a hunch that Terry's instrumental skills could bring something special to one or two of the songs that

Duffy had in mind. I also had a hunch that Terry's own Sweeney's Men/Woods Band classic 'Dreams' had lain forgotten for too long. Terry heard Duffy's demos and was, in his own words, 'very turned on' – digging out guitars and citterns from wherever they were and making himself available, in principle, to record. By this stage Nick Drake's string arranger Robert Kirby was also on board. Things were looking good. Unfortunately, having transformed three guitar/vocal tracks into smouldering jazz/folk epics, the logistical difficulties of embellishing multi-tracks from London, in Belfast, to the singer's vision without the singer present became too overwhelming. Agreeing to call it quits in June 2001, Duffy continued working on his album in London while I decided to do two things: pull together an album of vintage Duffy Power BBC recordings, as a gesture of goodwill, and begin work on a Janet Holmes solo album. If Duffy believed her a major talent, that was good enough for me.

The BBC album became a fascinating project, with some incredible recordings emerging from attics, cupboards – everywhere, in fact, but the vaults of the BBC itself. It was released, to the delight of both Duffy and myself, as *Sky Blues* (Hux Records) early in 2002. So what of the Janet Holmes project? Well, that's a story in itself. The album was completed over the course of a year and remains, at the time of writing, unreleased. But whether it ever sees the light of day or not, it is a work that all involved are very proud of. Suffice it to say, for the moment, that this time 'Dreams' *did* make it onto the set list and, in the middle of winter at a rustic studio in County Wicklow, under the expert supervision of Altan engineer Alastair McMillan, both Gay and Terry Woods generously turned up to record their parts. It would, of course, be lunacy to imagine that they did so on the same day.

THE WOODS BAND

Gay Corcoran (born in Dublin, September 1948) and Terry Woods (born in Dublin, December 1947) grew up as neighbours, began performing music together on a makeshift stage at Dublin's Neptune Rowing Club in 1963 and were married in May 1968. That same month Henry McCullough, arguably the hottest electric guitarist in Ireland at that time, joined Sweeney's Men alongside founder member Johnny Moynihan and the previous year's recruit, Terry Woods. For the next three months, frustrated not by imagination but only by the limitations of available PA systems and the narrow perspectives of their established 'ballad group' audience, this most legendary line-up of Sweeney's Men attempted to fuse rock music with Irish and American traditional material and original songwriting loosely in that vein. They were almost certainly the first ensemble in the British Isles to seriously pursue such a goal and, despite a frosty reception from a part of the audience at the 1968

Colin Harper · Originally published, in substantially edited form, as a sleeve-note to a reissue of *The Woods Band* (Edsel Records, 2001)

The Woods Band from their eponymous album sleeve, 1971

Cambridge Folk Festival, it is now generally acknowledged that in terms of both direct influence and historical priority this is where British folk-rock began.

McCullough, an ex-member of Hendrix protégés Eire Apparent and a future member of both Joe Cocker's Grease Band and Paul McCartney's Wings, may have been the most public face of the Sweeney's Men prototype fusion but, perhaps surprisingly, one of its key protagonists was singer, songwriter, twelve-string guitarist and banjo player Terry Woods. Far from being the arch hillbilly one might have assumed from his contributions to the eponymous *Sweeney's Men* LP debut, Woods was thoroughly open to influences from all quarters. The folk-rock experiment with Sweeney's Men was ultimately stillborn, but once that group had finally called it a day, fizzling out as a somewhat acrimonious duo of Woods and Moynihan in November 1969, he was free to pursue a very clear concept of how the union could be achieved. He would do this, in partnership with Gay, not only in the bitterly divided first line-up of Steeleye Span – whose first album, *Hark! The Village Wait*, remains a classic of the British folk-rock era – but with an unrecorded version of Irish psychedelicists Dr Strangely Strange, a brief and intriguing liaison with members of King Crimson and ultimately with his own group, The Woods Band: that rare combination of a first-generation folk-rock group which is not only now legendary but was actually recorded. The album, the sole surviving evidence of that group, is not only a crucial, if previously obscure, piece of the jigsaw in the story of the British folk revival but a record which reveals still the greatness of Gay Woods' voice and the indefatigable vision of Terry Woods as a musical pioneer.

Brought up in the ruthless and now discredited environment of an education with the Christian Brothers, Terry's youthful rebellion took the form of an obsession with American music. Initially attracted to the widely available music of people like The Everly Brothers, Woods sourced his way backwards from these pop harmonies – in a time when such knowledge was deeply arcane in Ireland – to the pre-war, pre-bluegrass sounds of hillbilly 'brother duets' and most seminally The Carter Family. An early owner of a twelve-string guitar – an instrument only really known through Leadbelly recordings and unusual in the British Isles at that time – Woods would visit and play with the nearby Corcoran brothers, Terry and Austin, who shared his interests. Their younger sister, Gay, was similarly inclined: 'I suppose we were all mini-bohemians,' she says. 'When the girls at school were looking at The Beatles I was listening to Mike Seeger!'

With a handful of initially makeshift venues like the Coffee Kitchen, O'Donoghue's pub and the Neptune Rowing Club, and a handful of people like Johnny Moynihan, Andy Irvine and Gay and Terry, 1963 was effectively the beginning of Ireland's folk underground. Debuting that year as a duo, Gay and Terry were apparently the very first act to play at what was to become the epicentre of the scene, the Neptune Rowing Club: 'I was so shy at the time,' says Gay, 'I just didn't know what I was doing but I did it because one of my brothers and Terry Woods were doing it.'

Gay subsequently left school at sixteen and started working as a typist, but Terry had other ideas: 'We went to France in the summer of 1966,' she recalls. 'We played a bit in youth hostels there and it got into Terry's mind that we could make a living at music. A lot of people were doing it at the time, just taking to the road. We were privileged in that Terry actually got in touch with an agent and lined up a few gigs – in Scotland. How my mother let me go I don't know! It was a great scene, around Glasgow, and there were lots of parties with people like Billy Connolly. But I was so young – it just got too much for me. When we came back to Ireland we split up, personally and musically, and that's how he was able to join Sweeney's Men.'

Sweeney's Men – featuring Andy Irvine, Johnny Moynihan and Joe Dolan – had already enjoyed two hit singles in Ireland, on the Pye label, and Terry replaced the somewhat erratic Dolan in June 1967. Dolan had left for Israel with some notion of joining in what became known as the Six Day War. Common jocularity suggests he arrived on the seventh day. Gay and Terry, however, soon resumed their relationship and were married in May 1968 – by which time the *Sweeney's Men* album had been recorded, for Transatlantic (though not issued till August), with Andy then deciding to go off adventuring towards the Balkans. His replacement, debuting at a concert in Dublin's Liberty Hall as Andy literally bowed out, was Henry McCullough: 'It was the most exciting thing ever,' says Gay, 'Henry walking on, with his long hair, his fringed jacket and his red guitar. I was at Cambridge as well, when they were booed off for going electric . . .'

Still working as a secretary, Gay travelled with Sweeney's Men on weekends, though like Moynihan's then partner Anne Briggs, who also travelled periodically with the group, she never sang or recorded with them. In retrospect Moynihan, at least, concedes this as a tragedy. Gay's own recollection is more practical: 'They never asked me!' Henry left in August 1968, after an invitation to join Joe Cocker's Grease Band, while Johnny and Terry continued on as an increasingly fractious duo, working mostly in England and recording a second album, with Gay remaining in Dublin: 'Terry and Johnny are both eccentrics but they are two opposites,' she says, 'and it was impossible for them to co-operate. But I remember getting phone calls from Terry [around September 1969] saying that he'd met this guy from Fairport Convention who was interested in doing something with them.'

The individual in question was bass player Ashley Hutchings, who was essentially on the verge of leaving Fairport Convention – a successful west-coast-American-influenced English rock group – with a view to either joining Sweeney's Men or forming a new group based around himself and one or more of the members of Sweeney's Men. Former Sweeney Andy Irvine, who had just returned to London from his lengthy sojourn in Eastern Europe, was also a part of the equation. There are various recollections of the precise nature of

Gay and Terry Woods, onstage in Rotterdam, 1973

Steeleye Span, 1970

these plans and, particularly, as to whether any actual rehearsals took place involving Hutchings, Woods, Moynihan and Irvine: Irvine recalls one; Woods is more doubtful. 'It started as an idea between Ashley and myself,' says Terry. 'We used to play football together behind the Prince of Wales in Highgate on a Sunday afternoon. This was after the Fairport car crash [an incident that had killed one member and hospitalised others in the group earlier that year]. Ashley was unhappy with the direction that they were going in and Sweeney's Men was coming to its natural conclusion. It wasn't going to go any further, but I wanted to continue to play. Our ideas were very similar: in essence, for a band from Ireland and England that would have a similar feel to The Byrds and we would use music from this side to create what The Byrds were doing in America. When it seemed a natural thing for me to do I said to Ashley, "Look, my wife is a really, really good singer . . ." Gay was in Ireland, she came over to England [around December 1969], we played a few things together and he said, "Yeah, she is!" The idea was then to try and recruit Johnny and Andy. But Johnny and myself had reached an end. It seemed that Johnny didn't want to work with me and, frankly, I wasn't too pushed about working with Johnny.'

It transpired that if Johnny was not to be involved, Andy's interest in the project was also diminished. Both men would return to Ireland and spend the next couple of years pottering about with low-key gigs and odd recordings (Johnny on Anne Briggs' Topic LP *Anne Briggs*, Andy on Christy Moore's 1971 Leader/Tara LP *Prosperous*, both of them on Dr Strangely Strange's 1971 Island LP *Heavy Petting*) before Andy's co-founding of the hugely successful progressive Irish folk group Planxty, in 1972. As it transpired, Johnny would join the same group the following year.

'We let the thing go with Johnny and Andy,' says Terry. 'We then tried Bob and Carole Pegg, we tried the Dransfields and eventually it came down to Tim Hart and Maddy Prior and, of all those people, that seemed an interesting line-up.' Gay, however – at that time the least assertive of all involved – feels that herself, Terry and Ashley should have been content to work as a trio. It wasn't to be. Tim and Maddy agreed to join, with certain provisos: 'There was always a "but" with Tim,' says Terry, 'and the proviso was that they had x amount of gigs themselves and they wanted to continue to do those gigs while we were rehearsing. We were naive enough to say yes. In retrospect we should have copped that Tim is very much a manipulator and he was never going to do anything that didn't create a winning situation for him and/or Maddy – I don't know whether she was as strong a part of that as he was.'

With Gay and Terry initially sleeping on floors, waiting for Tim and Maddy to commit to the project, things were not on an even footing: 'I should just have gone home immediately,' says Gay, 'and I'm sorry I didn't because from then on I was treated like a serf by everybody and it was horrible. Eventually, this nice couple downstairs from Tim and Maddy's flat in London offered their bungalow in Wiltshire to us to rehearse. But the bitterness started immediately – lines being drawn, metaphorically at least, as to where everyone's food began and ended and so on. And to this day that kind of spirit has not left that band.'

'Their attitude to Gay and myself was very bad,' agrees Terry. 'We were rather naive. Unfortunately Ashley wasn't well enough to take a stronger stance. He spent a lot of time in his room. He and I would go for walks, play a bit of football round the back – but he had all the legal stuff coming in to do with the crash, and he was suffering mentally because of that.'

The group recorded a BBC radio session in March 1970 with things holding miraculously together long enough for an album, *Hark! The Village Wait*, to be recorded shortly after. 'I'd signed on to an agency to start temping,' says Gay, the sole bread-winner for herself and Terry at that time, 'and I remember getting a phone call one day saying, "You can give up the job, we have a deal." The album came together very quickly – I think it was the urgency of Woods and Hutchings.' The deal itself, with RCA, had only been secured through the influence of its eventual producer Sandy Roberton, a loose connection of Hutchings', after representations to various labels by Terry and Ashley had been turned down.

'I think we must have recorded the album in April,' says Terry, 'and it was during the recording that it became impossible to work with Tim and Maddy. It got beyond music. They were exceptionally nasty – he was particularly nasty. We had an agreement that if any one or two of the five left the band that the name Steeleye Span would cease. But after the falling out in the studio Gay and myself went up to my sister, who lived in Nottingham, and I think a week later we heard that Martin Carthy had joined the band. It was more than galling but, worse than that, there were threats, legal threats, issued to us – and we ended up signing stuff that we should never have signed. It was such a nasty way for such a great thing to end – for Gay and myself at least.'

Sometime during the summer of 1970 Gay and Terry regrouped by joining their old friends, and fellow Dubliners, Dr Strangely Strange – a whimsical group based around Tim Goulding, Tim Booth and Ivan Pawle and often referred to as Ireland's answer to The Incredible String Band. Goulding had recently married and left the group, with a tour of Norway, Sweden, Belgium,

Holland and parts of Germany booked. 'I had to play keyboards at one gig – four notes,' says Gay. 'That was fun. It was a pity it all fell apart but it was falling apart anyway when we joined. It seems to be a pattern in my life. Don't ask Gay Woods to join your band . . .'

'It turned out to be the last real tour they were doing,' says Terry. 'Goulding was very much part of the whole Strangely Strange experience. So I didn't think anything was going to happen for them afterwards and also it was very obvious that it wasn't a vehicle for Gay and myself long term because, personality-wise, we weren't quite like them. But it was enjoyable and we had a fun time – staying in the Reeperbahn in Hamburg was certainly an eye-opener for Gay and myself!'

Terry and Gay returned to England and recorded a radio session for BBC's *Top Gear* as a duo in November 1970 – a session, sadly now erased, which neither can remember a single thing about. Tracks performed were: 'I Feel Concerned', 'A Nobleman's Fair Daughter', 'January Snows' and 'Van Dieman's Land'. Only 'January Snows' would make it to the eventual Woods Band album. There would, however, be one more curious interlude: 'When we came back from the Strangelies tour,' says Terry, 'we ended up living in London, just off the Cromwell Road, with Ian MacDonald of King Crimson, and him and Mike Giles [also in King Crimson] did some playing with us. We were thinking about putting some mad thing together! It was really interesting – *really* interesting. I can't remember if we ever recorded anything. There might be a radio programme somewhere but that would be the height of it. But that was wonderful, I enjoyed that.'

Mike Giles did manage to record with Gay and Terry, on their 1975 album *Backwoods*, but back in 1970–71 Terry had re-focused on what kind of band he wanted and who he wanted in it. The pair returned briefly to Ireland to do some recruiting. Two of those required were guitar hero Ed Deane, formerly with popular Irish beat group Granny's Intentions, and drummer Pat Nash. 'The other man I desperately wanted in the band was Paddy Keenan,' says Terry. 'I met with Paddy and talked about it but he was very young and I think his father held him back from going.' Paddy would later make his reputation internationally as the particularly fiery uilleann piper with The Bothy Band, whose 1975–78 recordings remain a benchmark in the contemporary presentation of Irish traditional music. Had Woods succeeded in recruiting Keenan for The Woods Band, the history of Irish music, and their own standing within it, might well be significantly different. As it was, Planxty, debuting in 1972, were to be hailed as the benchmark marriage of pipes and songs in a progressive-folk setting.

'We rented an old house near an RAF base in Bensen, outside Wallingford,' says Terry, 'where we rehearsed the band before we recorded in Morgan Studios. That would have been in spring 1971. We knew what we wanted to do. We had the material – it was just a matter of rehearsing it. We had been playing some of the songs with the Strangelies and one ['Dreams'] I had recorded with Sweeney's and I wanted to try it again with the band. Because when it was done with Sweeney's it was after we'd tried to go electric with Henry McCullough. At that point of time we had problems convincing the record company to put money into us.'

The second and final Sweeney's Men album, *The Tracks Of Sweeney* (issued in December 1969, by which time the group was defunct), does indeed have an air of incompleteness about it – sparse arrangements of material that could have been recorded more dynamically, had there been a bigger budget available. As it was, though, a few tracks, including the early version of Terry's composition 'Dreams', do stand up as powerful performances. Perhaps ironically, the band version, though fuller in sound, was looser in arrangement – an attractive looseness, certainly redolent of the funky ensemble playing of The Band, which pervades the whole album. In terms of Irish folk or folk-rock music, which began flourishing in various styles and directions with the three-pointed emergence of Planxty, Clannad and Horslips in 1972, the sound of *The Woods Band* is a curio – more obviously a natural successor to *Hark! The Village Wait* and closer, perhaps, to the English folk-rock ethic in general.

While Terry had clearly had problems convincing record labels to back his ideas in early 1970, by 1971 folk-rock was momentarily hot property in Britain, perceived as the next big thing, with major labels like CBS and EMI becoming involved. Terry had several interested parties courting his new band and opted, unfortunately as it transpired, to go with a completely new label, the Greenwich Gramophone Company – a subsidiary of Decca funded by Les Reed and managed by yet another King Crimson acolyte, Tony Reeves: 'Tony was a friend of ours who really liked what we were doing,' says Terry. The label was to launch with three bands: The Woods Band alongside a new group featuring former Thunderclap Newman guitarist Jimmy McCulloch and another new group, Greenslade, featuring former Colosseum organist Dave Greenslade. 'Tony had very definitive ideas and it seemed a good bet,' says Terry, 'to go with a company that was starting. Unfortunately, it didn't work out for Tony, and/or Les Reed, and the three bands suffered.' *The Woods Band* catalogue number was GSLP 1004, indicating at least four (stereo) releases, though what those were is a mystery for others to investigate – certainly, there was to be no Greenslade album on the label. Tony Reeves, though, did make a guest appearance on *The Woods Band*, playing bass – as he would on the eventual Greenslade debut for Warners – while Gay's brother Austin, on bass and acoustic guitar, and organist/pianist John Ryan also made cameos. The album was issued, presumably in the latter half of 1971, in a luxuriantly rich-purple gatefold sleeve embossed with a gold Celtic brooch design and featuring inside moody photographs of the four key players.

Only a limited amount of live work was done in Ireland, though Michael Deeny, future manager of Horslips, did promote a few concerts for the band, including one at Dublin Stadium. During the winter of 1971 there was a joint tour of the UK with Greenslade and the Jimmy McCulloch group, followed by a Woods Band tour on the Continent, which Terry recalls as being fun: 'But the record company hit the doldrums about that time. We needed the record company behind us if we were to go forward and suddenly there was no record company. The ass went out of it, really.' Terry consequently became the group's manager by default, trying vainly to keep his musicians afloat financially and 'being driven round the twist! Eventually I said, "Look, there's got to be a better way of living," and that's when we decided to pack it in, in that way, and come back to live in Ireland. It was disappointing. *The Woods Band* album wasn't financially successful but we got a lot of good reviews. That was one of the strange things about Gay and myself – we got a lot of good reviews. But you can't really live on reviews, you can't eat them! I'd always wanted to be part of something successful, on the one hand, but on the other hand I never wanted to sell my soul for success. I was a bit of an oddball in that way. There were other things that I liked doing.'

Strangely enough, Gay and Terry ended up renting a cottage in rural County Meath from, of all people, Johnny Moynihan. With Johnny and Terry by now not on speaking terms (and still not), it was left to Gay to negotiate the rent. She doubts it was ever paid. Eventually reinventing themselves as a duo and becoming effectively Ireland's answer to Richard & Linda Thompson, four further albums were recorded between 1975–78: *Backwoods* (1975), *The Time Is Right* (1976), *Renowned* (1976) and *Tender Hooks* (1978). There were also two singles released. *Tender Hooks*, reissued on Cooking Vinyl in 2000, is the only album of the series available on CD, although a short BBC *In Concert* set from the period was released on Windsong in 1995.

'Coming back to Ireland wasn't exactly a retreat from the music business,' says Terry – 'It was a retreat from the bullshit of the music business at that time. We both felt we were being beaten from pillar to post. We wanted some life and we wanted to play. We happened to be a married couple and we had a life as well as our music – and for quite a long time we actually managed to combine the two. One thing that we should have done but never did, and we threatened to do it, and talked about it – we should have gone to America. Because I think our music would have had a greater degree of, if not success, acceptance there.'

Gay's perspective is rather different: 'I was always just wanting to be a girl at home growing vegetables, potting onions and things like that, and having babies. But I was always being torn away from that to go off touring so it was quite a neurotic time for me. I think Terry was chasing some sort of fame. He just wanted to play – he should have just joined a band and left me at home! We probably wouldn't have been happy then either. But, God, looking back, we got around.'

The Woods Band was reissued on vinyl, on the Mooncrest imprint Rockborough, in 1977, boasting an alternative cover design – a mid-Seventies shot of Gay and Terry outside Moynihan's cottage – and a rearranged running order. The original album currently commands £70 on the collectors' market,

Steeleye Span with Maddy Prior (second left) and Gay Woods (fourth left)

with even the reissue valued at £15. The existence of a European bootleg CD of the album, dubbed from disc, only illustrates the level of demand for what has become an enduring cult classic.

Gay and Terry split as both couple and performing duo in 1980. Both subsequently embraced radical new directions musically. Gay immediately formed a theatrical new-wave group, Auto Da Fe, independently issuing an album and several singles within Ireland between 1980–86. Almost incredibly, she was persuaded to rejoin Steeleye Span in 1994, replacing Maddy Prior and recording three studio albums with the group before leaving acrimoniously, once again, at the end of 2000 for exactly the same reasons as before. Terry, meanwhile, after a spell of honest toil as a factory worker, rejuvenated his profile by joining punk-folk band The Pogues in 1986. Leaving ten years later, having flirted with the brink by way of that group's notoriously excessive lifestyle, he subsequently relinquished both alcohol and performing, spending several years operating as a uniquely experienced manager of young rock bands in the Dublin area. Reconstituting a new group of young players under The Woods Band moniker during 2001, he has since re-entered the fray as a working musician.

While Gay, tantalisingly, has mused upon the prospect of a Woods Band reunion involving herself, Terry sees no likelihood of it ever happening. Some things, he believes, are best left in the past – but celebrated for what they were and are. Asked how he views *The Woods Band* album now, he parries with non-committal brilliance: 'Through a dark haze! Though there's one thing I would like to say: I've always thought Gay's voice was incredibly special. It gave me enormous pleasure listening to Gay sing. And she never got her due.'

AUTO DA FE

Regarded by vocalist and visionary member Gay Woods as 'a progressive rock band for the Eighties', Auto Da Fe's lyrical stance and career ethos were certainly a step removed from the mainstream of their era, yet their musical clothing of artificial drum beats and synthesiser washes identify them inextricably with the early Eighties pop world of Howard Jones, Human League, Ultravox and suchlike. Similarly, a proliferation of singles over albums – albeit singles released largely only in Ireland – would have suggested chart action to have been a prime concern. In fact, the whole thing was driven at least partly as a reaction to Gay's increasingly 'bad experience' with the music industry of the Seventies, during which time she was one half of a marital and professional musical partnership as Gay & Terry Woods.

Aside from being in a career situation she wasn't entirely at one with, Gay was also burdened with the act's creative responsibilities: 'We had these publishing contracts with Chappell Music and I'd be writing and playing the dulcimer trying to fulfil our obligations! He would go off to the pub and I'd stay at home writing. With hindsight, I think that Terry should have kept writing more but he thought I was better. I think I may have written some nice songs in those days, but a lot of them were awful.'

Suffering a miscarriage in 1979 was the final straw: 'I lost a lot of weight and all of a sudden had this metamorphosis. A stillbirth the previous year had been a kind of catharsis anyway and it just changed my whole psychic equilibrium. So after the miscarriage I made a decision – I made a decision! – that this was it, no more babies. I just wanted to go back to work as a typist, but I wasn't let [by Terry]. He said, "Let's form another band." He had met a group of jazzers called Metropolis and somehow I heard a tape of them and thought, That's the musicians I would love to play with. So we had a few sessions with them, and that's how I met Trevor Knight, the keyboard player – and that was the end of Terry Woods!' Believing her intensely combined career and marriage to Terry to have been too much, too young, Gay feels, with typically mischievous perspective, that 'my whole relationship with Terry Woods was definitely unconscious. The moment I became conscious I left him!'

In 1980 Gay and Trevor formed Auto Da Fe, initially basing themselves in Holland (where The Woods Band had previously toured) and using Dutch musicians: Theo Wanders, Wout Pennings and Carel van Rijn. After this initial foray, Gay and Trevor soon relocated and regrouped in Ireland, with the first of a series of line-ups – Ireland was where their career would almost entirely

Colin Harper · Originally published as a sleeve-note to the BBC *In Concert* compilation, *Songs For Echo* (Hux Records, 2001)

be based. Live shows and a fresh, anarchic approach to songwriting were to be the focus of the new group, with recording deals less to the fore. 'It was my idea about this band,' says Gay, 'that it should be just live – to play, get paid and go home and not to get involved in some of the record deals I'd had in the folk-rock era. So what we did was mostly stay in Ireland. In fact, we only did two or three gigs in England.'

That handful of English dates – including the Marquee, the Reading Festival and two BBC radio concerts – had been organised by a UK manager recommended to the band by Thin Lizzy supremo Phil Lynott. Although Gay looks back on this brief attempt to crack the UK as 'the beginning of the end' for Auto Da Fe and its original ideals, it is at least fortuitous that they had the opportunity to be recorded by the BBC for, although the group did indeed make studio recordings (a string of mostly Irish-only singles and an album via two small labels, Stoic and Spartan) Gay herself propounds the commonly held view that Auto Da Fe were primarily a concert experience. The presence of Lynott himself on one of the BBC concerts is explained not only by his long-standing friendship with both Terry and Gay Woods, dating back to Dublin's compact music scene of the late-Sixties, but by his own musical preoccupations during the early Eighties.

'I think Phillip was looking for other things to do besides be who he was with Thin Lizzy,' says Gay, 'so he started doing some solo work and solo gigs. He wanted Trevor Knight in his band. I think that's how we linked up again.' Impressed with the songwriting, Lynott produced Auto Da Fe's first three singles, 'November November', 'Bad Experience' and 'Man Of Mine' (the latter in collaboration with Midge Ure, also working on Phil's solo recordings of the period), and gave the group a leg-up with the support slot to an Irish solo tour he was doing. All of which was helpful, but the group was able to survive on being, for Ireland at least, the right act at the right time. All the singles received strong TV and radio airplay, and consequently Auto Da Fe's well-attended concerts made profits. The plan was working.

The fourth single, a cover of Gene Pitney's Sixties hit 'Something's Gotten Hold Of My Heart', was actually released in the UK (curiously credited as a Gay Woods solo release), prior to Marc Almond's chart-topping version, but made no headway there. Following the summer-y, radio-friendly 'All Is Yellow', the release of the frankly baffling 'Credo Credo' in 1984 may have been a bridge too far. Having that year released the mini-LP compilation, *Five Singles & A Smoked Cod* (a Dublin dialect pun concerning chipped potatoes), the following year's album proper, *Tatitum*, reprised most of its contents adding only four new tracks. It effectively brought together all of the group's six single A-sides to date plus their next, a bizarre choice of cover indeed: Perry Como's 'Magic Moments'.

Giving her penchant for absurdity one last flourish, a final single, 'Bring Me A Bouquet' – referred to by Gay, of course, as 'Bring Me A Bucket' – sneaked out in 1988, although the group's real swansong may perhaps better be remembered as their three-song appearance the previous year at Ireland's epic-scaled unemployment-awareness concert, Self-Aid. For completists, one Auto Da Fe performance appeared on the album of the event.

Gay once again withdrew to County Meath, this time to raise her daughter by Trevor (although they have since separated). But in 1994 she received an unexpected phone call. Would she consider rejoining Steeleye Span? This time around Gay remained long enough to record three studio albums – *Time* (1995), *Horkstow Grange* (1998) and *Bedlam Born* (2000) – along with a concert video and a live album, entitled *The Journey*, of an all-the-line-ups reunion concert. Eventually, however, acrimony over business and personality issues reappeared and early in 2001 Gay announced that she had left the band for good. She nevertheless stands by her work with Steeleye, being particularly proud of the last track she recorded with them, 'I See His Blood Upon The Rose', for *Bedlam Born*. That track, fused with modern dance rhythms, is how she articulates her vision for any future solo album.

As for Auto Da Fe: 'I'd love to do that again! But nobody wants it except me. I've no idea who we sounded like. I don't think I had any reference points from other singers or musicians – I don't think so – because I had suppressed so much of me for so long I just started to write like there was no tomorrow. It just bubbled up.' With none of their studio material available on CD, and the group itself having been sidelined, even within Ireland, as a vague memory or a distant, parochial event of no consequence by pundits and public alike, the release of the BBC concert recordings (as *Songs For Echo*, Hux Records, 2001) is welcome indeed. If nothing else, it demonstrates Gay Woods' extraordinary capacity for reinvention – a reminder of some value in the light of her intention to deliver, post-Steeleye, one last album and the first truly solo work of her career before bowing out. But then she could just be having us on.

Postscript: Terry Woods unveiled his new Woods Band with the album *Music From The Four Corners Of Hell* in February 2003. Gay is currently taking a degree in psychology at the University of Essex (commuting there and back, from County Meath, on a weekly basis).

MELLOW CANDLE
PROLOGUE

Once the notion of this book was up and running, no longer, I deemed, could that unopened box labelled 'Mellow Candle' be ignored. Few writers, it may be conjectured, have such a box (and I *am* speaking metaphorically here – I believe it unlikely that anyone in the world, with the possible exception of former Candle Alison O'Donnell, *actually* has a box with such labelling on it). Many writers, however, will have something else in its place – an aspiration to tackle, at some indeterminate point in their careers, this or that subject which has always intrigued them. Personally, I couldn't contemplate authoring any kind of book on Irish music without first meeting somebody from Mellow Candle, whose exquisite, strange and long-buried music cried out for the posthumous oxygen of celebration. Luckily, somebody at *Mojo* agreed.

Lois Wilson, a fellow Candle fan, needed no further prompting to say yes to a piece for the magazine's July 2002 issue. Consequently, I took a pleasant day off from the library and went down to Dublin to pretend to be a music writer again, waxing lyrical with Alison O'Donnell, carrier of the Candle's flame and one of the group's two singer-songwriters. I should say, though, that as a flag-waver on the subject of Mellow Candle, I was no pioneer. My friend John O'Regan – a remarkably prolific writer and broadcaster based in Limerick – has been quietly championing the Candle's cause for years and continues to give valuable support to Alison's present-day musical ventures. Credit where it's due!

Having written the piece – and consequently having, to my great satisfaction, something Mellow for inclusion in this book – I was surprised and delighted to receive an e-mail from Sarah McQuaid, a fine American singer and music journo based in Dublin, whose company I had most recently enjoyed on the second of those week-long creative sojourns in Annamakerrig referred to earlier. (Indeed, Sarah, liking the Annamakerrig vibe so much – and I can only envy this – extended her own stay to several months and subsequently joined the centre's fund-raising committee.) Sarah had pointed out that *Mojo* piece – and, in particular, its description of chief singer-songwriter Clodagh Simonds as a 'reclusive genius' – to one of her drinking buddies . . . yes, you've guessed it, the perfectly unreclusive (so long as you're not wittering on all night about Mellow Candle) Clodagh Simonds.

The Simonds/Harper connection was thus made and, several amusing e-mails and a couple of months later, we met – over peanuts and whiskey at the same Dublin Hotel where I had previously met with her old friend Alison – and re-lit the Candle for an hour. Clodagh had differed from Alison in her

Colin Harper

Mellow Candle, mark 2, 1971: (l–r) Clodagh Simonds, Alison O'Donnell, David Williams, Ted Carroll (manager), Pat Morris

recollections on one or two matters – as surely any two people would from such a distance – and reckoned that, given the looming prospect of this book, perhaps it might now be an apposite time to change the record and finally say yes to a Candle interview, and to give the world some idea of exactly what she's been *doing* for the past 30 years.

And there would be more surprises to come. Shortly after the publication of the piece, and after years of Alison hoping that long-lost Candle man Frank Boylan might see something in print and make contact, he turned up. Sadly, it was entirely coincidental and nothing at all to do with anyone's retrospective journalism. And in which far-flung corner of the globe had the fellow been hiding? Dublin. Alison went along to one of his gigs: 'It was great to see him playing again,' she said, 'although it felt quite weird, too.' Given that something which might end up being viewed as – although it is by no means claimed as such by me – a 'definitive' history of the band was in the offing, various work-in-progress drafts were passed not only to Clodagh and Alison but also, through Alison, to Frank Boylan, Dave Williams and former manager Ted Carroll. The end result is a very broadly agreed telling of the tale.

Clodagh and Alison have followed very different paths since the days of Mellow Candle. Both now back in Dublin, after various years in America, South Africa, London and wherever else, they remain tremendously talented and determined musicians in their own divergent fields. More importantly, for all the long-buried pain of their dream-group's dissolution they have each acquired an admirable resolve to leave the loose threads of acrimony flutter-ing impotently in the past. Collaborating on the expanded piece below has perhaps tested that resolve but it has not been found wanting. I wish a Mellow Candle album for every reader, and I wish Clodagh and Alison every success with their current work.

MELLOW CANDLE

Swaddling Songs (Deram, 1972), the sole album from the mysterious Mellow Candle, has both the virtue and the stigma of being Britain's rarest major-label release of the folk-rock era – *circa* £500 for a mint-condition original. Is it any good? No, it's brilliant. Dynamic arrangements, exquisite harmonies, lyrically intoxicating and mischievously mysterious, the voices, songs and vision of the writers within Mellow Candle are, like a wardrobe into Narnia or the sleep-induced faerie of *A Midsummer Night's Dream*, the gateway to another world. Often compared, erroneously, to Renaissance – with whom there is only the superficial comparison of piano-led arrangements – Mellow Candle occupy a unique place in the prog pantheon, an Irish group with almost no Irish reference points and bearing more relation to Jethro Tull as fronted by Siouxsie Sioux and Judy Dyble with Vincent Crane on the keys. It's crazy but it's true.

The tale begins at Dublin's Holy Child Convent school in 1963 with three pre-teen girls – Clodagh Simonds, Alison Bools (later O'Donnell) and Maria White – singing Helen Shapiro covers and subsequently Simon & Garfunkel material alongside Clodagh's earliest compositions, and enjoying a virtual block-booking on the music room at lunchtime. As much as the similarity of line-up suggests it, the trio were determinedly uninfluenced by the contemporaneous showband-interval-act success of another Irish schoolgirl trio, Maxi, Dick & Twink: 'At first we were The Gatecrashers and then, from when we were about twelve years old, we were Mellow Candle,' recalls Alison, over coffee and scones in a suitably elegant Dublin tea room. 'I've actually got an acetate and other material from that period of us singing when we were ten or eleven, which I've been offered quite a bit of money for. But I'd never part with it. I saw something recently on a website asking whether we would have been so creative had we not been "repressed" in a school run by nuns, but it wasn't like that at all because those nuns gave us free rein. They encouraged us and when we were sixteen they said, "Leave school, because you'll only want to do this – do it now."'

But even before that, as fifteen-year-olds in the summer of '68, the nascent Mellow Candle had released a UK single, bankrolled by hip actor David Hemmings and Yardbirds manager Simon Napier Bell. How? 'We sent tapes to everybody,' says Alison. 'We even sent one to RTÉ and they told us to bog off! I remember us getting on a bus and thinking, Well, it's their bloody loss! We were very young, about thirteen, and God knows what we looked like, dressed in kimonos and whatever. But Clodagh was very single-minded about

Colin Harper · Includes material published in *Mojo* (July 2002); plus additional material

it.' One tape, sent to Radio Luxembourg DJ Colin Nichol, scouting for Hemmings' production company, Hemdale, hit the jackpot. The girls went to London: 'The three of us were completely overawed with how swinging it was. We were allowed to buy some clothes on Carnaby Street and we thought this was the bees-knees. Colin Nichol was looking after us, walking in front of us through Soho saying, "Come on girls, keep up, stay behind me," – very strict – with all these people leering out of doorways! So we went to meet David Hemmings and Clodagh's eldest sister, who was a model at the time and had this mews house and we were just absolutely bowled over. And then we went in to record with this 22-piece orchestra and The Breakaways – Cliff Richard's backing group, backing us! This was just heaven! It was a great song – great for its time, very dramatic. "Feeling High" it was called, with the other side called "Tea With The Sun". People said, "How old are these girls? What are they taking?" But it was a one-off thing – I guess they probably thought, quite rightly, that we weren't ready to do anything with them.'

The single, released on Napier Bell's own label, SNB, failed to set the hit parade alight, though a copy today, unavailable as the recording is in any reissued form, would certainly light up the eyes of any self-respecting Candle fan. So back to Dublin and the drawing board it was, via a year-long sabbatical: 'The only things we were interested in,' says Alison, 'was being in the school musical, the school choir – anything to do with music. So my mother said to me, "Tell you what, what you should do is a secretarial course – I'll never ask you to do anything else but it's something for you to fall back on." She made me do it and I'm bloody glad she did! I did it for a year – bunked off half the year and forged various absence notes, but I passed. Clodagh's mother made her go to Italy to learn Italian for six months and I think more or less the same thing happened: she just drifted back into music. This takes us up to 1970 – when the boys came in.'

Pat Morris, a huge Jethro Tull fan, came in on bass and David Williams on guitar. During her loosely defined year out, Alison had performed with Dave in a covers band, Blue Tint. By the time the new Mellow Candle came together, Dave was trying his best to finish a degree in philosophy and psychology at Trinity College: 'He wasn't paying much attention to that but he got through it – passed with a 2:2,' says Alison. 'Could have done a lot better but we were all obsessed – music was what we wanted to do.' Maria White had drifted away and there was as yet no drummer. Not that this mattered, as attested by the stunningly complete-sounding demos from this period, on the posthumously released *The Virgin Prophet* (Kissing Spell, 1994): 'We practised six hours a day – and socialised afterwards. People were now coming over to look at us because they'd heard about us. We had some very good helpers then – people like Pat Egan at *New Spotlight* – who were behind us all the way. Maybe all they could do was write about us every week, but they did and we got noticed.'

The first gig was supporting The Chieftains at Dublin's Liberty Hall; the

Mellow Candle, mark 1, mid-Sixties: (l–r) Alison O'Donnell, Clodagh Simonds, Maria White

second a John Peel-compered festival in Wexford including esoteric English underground act Principal Edwards' Magic Theatre – an act whose sound, heard from a distance of 30-odd years, bears striking if coincidental similarities to that of Mellow Candle: 'When we saw them we were fascinated,' says Alison, 'especially because they were so theatrical. That was something we hadn't seen before and we thought they were wonderful. But we had a whole repertoire before we ever saw or heard them. That whole festival was very interesting. There were some very, very good acts – Principal Edwards', Continuum and Fairport [Convention] of course, who we were jealous of because they had it in their contract that they had to have a crate of beer at the back of the stage or something. How can we get a contract like that? we were thinking. Not that I ever drank beer in those days!'

Ted Carroll, then managing Thin Lizzy among others and latter-day head of reissue specialists Ace Records, became their manager. The following year, 1971, would prove more fruitful, with a number of Irish festivals springing to life, but in 1970 there still weren't many gigging opportunities in Ireland, even in Dublin, for anyone outside the showband formula. 'We went for a gig once and got it,' says Alison, 'and the next thing we heard was that Horslips had got it instead 'cos their manager undercut us by five quid or something – and I remember for a long time thinking, Bloody Horslips! How could they do that?! But of course it wasn't them, it was the manager.'

In Dublin, on the folk side of the fence, one of the best gigs of the time was the Mug's Gig, at Slattery's on Capel Street: 'That's where we met Donal Lunny and Andy Irvine [the club's organisers],' says Alison, 'and started going to trad sessions and jam sessions with them – and that's where the trad thing started for me. It came from them. Neither Dave nor I had really "Irish" backgrounds – my mother's English, my father's Irish. So we weren't brought up with traditional music and there really wasn't [in our writing] a slant in that direction, yet later I assumed it, in a way that I couldn't understand. I have a grandfather and two great-uncles, military men, who were all conductors and composers and they came originally from Galway – all from an Irish-speaking, music-playing family. I only found this out when I was 21, way past the Mellow Candle situation. So there was obviously something there that beckoned me.

'But Andy was exotic because he [had] travelled a lot and his songs about his time in the Balkans were a very strong presence. You'd hear it through everything he played – his experience and what he had lived through. It came out all the time. But Andy was very reserved in those days. Donal Lunny was a bit more forthright. They used to hang out together a lot and we'd run into them at sessions – and they liked what we were doing. They'd come to see us, and so did Luke Kelly – he used to hide behind a pillar but you'd see him there, watching the whole show. And Thin Lizzy liked us – Phil asked Clodagh [guesting on piano] to do *Shades Of A Blue Orphanage* [Decca, 1972] because he liked the band.' Jamming one week with Andy Irvine and the next with Skid

Row, Mellow Candle were the clergy of their own broad Church: 'In fact, the very day that Dave and I got married, in January 1972, we played that night with Thin Lizzy [at the Royal Dublin Stadium] – and that was a great gig.'

Eamon Carr, at that time leading a double, if eminently sensible, life as daytime employee of an ad agency and free-time observer and partaker (with the newly formed Horslips) of the Dublin underground music scene recalls wondering, of art-school-ish musos and Mellow Candle in particular, 'how on earth these people made a living.' One might still wonder.

'Clodagh was living at home for a long time as her mother was fairly well-off,' says Alison. 'Frank was just "the hippy" – I don't know where he got anything from but whatever he needed in life just seemed to materialise. Dave used to sometimes go off and work on the oil rigs or the roads for a few weeks. But it was very much a hand-to-mouth existence, unless we managed to scavenge off our parents. I remember Clodagh and I once went to sign on the dole – 1970, the only time I've ever done it – 'cos we didn't have any money. We had to sign on for six weeks or something and in the last week, as we got to the counter, somebody came and said, "Excuse me, can you come to the manager's office?" So we went in there and on his desk, open, he had an article from *New Spotlight* magazine. "What is the meaning of this?" he said. "You're obviously earning some money," – although we were actually barely getting by! – "If I ever see you in here again I'll call the police!" So that was the end of that! We scarpered from that place with our tails between our legs.'

Penury or otherwise, the various demos revealed on *The Virgin Prophet* demonstrate that not only the songs but the devilishly involved arrangements which would ultimately make the group's sole album proper so revered were already in place. So could the Candle replicate on stage what became the record? 'Yes, because we were so well rehearsed,' says Alison, emphatically. 'But we were a bit precious onstage. Ted Carroll used to say to me, "Alison, you look like a fishwife with your hands on your hips." Nowadays, of course, I bounce around all over the place but in those days I was Miss Cool. But that wasn't put on – we were just so focused on the music.'

Having visited London to record demos for the label, with a session drummer (Caravan's Richard Coughlan), Mellow Candle signed to Decca's progressive imprint, Deram, in April 1971. Perceiving it a necessity following the Deram demos, the group recruited Willy Murray as drummer – a Glaswegian then living in Highgate. Another change occurred at this stage when Pat Morris, a carpenter by trade and not entirely at one with the group's hippy lifestyle, opted out, with fellow Dubliner Frank Boylan, from another Ted Carroll managed outfit, The Creatures, stepping into his shoes. The new line-up in place, Mellow Candle left Ireland and relocated to London's Belsize Park, briefly occupying rooms in a boarding house with Gay and Terry Woods.

With occasional trips back to Ireland for events like the RDS' Headland Festival, the Dublin Arts Lab's open-air gig at Blackrock Park and the Ballyvaughan Festival in County Clare, there were also UK support gigs with

Lindisfarne and Steeleye Span, interspersed with periods of extreme poverty: 'I can remember once that we had to ring up Lindisfarne's roadie,' says Alison, 'and say, "Look, can you lend us some money 'cos we have nothing to eat?" He said, "I'm not going to lend you any money," but he came round and brought tons of food and gave it to us. That's the way we lived for a lot of the time, we really did.'

With Decca's 'house guy' David Hitchcock on production, *Swaddling Songs* was eventually recorded at the end of the year, in December 1971: 'I do remember we had to record it in a very short space of time,' says Alison. 'It was all done very fast. But having said that, the circumstances were very conducive: dimmed lighting, plenty of dope probably. And the only track we had trouble with was "Heaven Heath" because it has a harpsichord on it – and Clodagh had never played one. It's got a delayed action and in those days you couldn't shift it around half a second with an edit button. There were 23 takes. We ended up playing it live, with her playing slightly ahead of everyone else. There was not much overdubbing generally, though I do contribute three voices to "Vile Excesses". I'm very proud of the album but it could have been better.'

Mellow Candle, mark 2, 1971:
(l–r) Clodagh Simonds, Alison O'Donnell,
Pat Morris, David Williams

Because we were tired when we did the vocals at the end there's a couple of places where the intonation's a bit off. But it's simply because we were absolutely exhausted – recording from ten o'clock in the morning 'til three in the morning. You just can't sing for that long.'

Imperfect perhaps, but only to the most demanding ears. To the layman the finished product remains a masterpiece, individual songs or arrangements redolent perhaps of this or that artist of the time but the whole resembling nothing before or since. Even comparisons involving individual components of the album are almost certainly coincidental – for example, a certain similarity in aura between Alison's 'Messenger Birds' and quintessential English folk-rock goddess and former Fairport Convention vocalist Sandy Denny's *The North Star Grassman And The Ravens* album of 1971: 'I hadn't heard that then,' says Alison. 'I wrote that song when I was sixteen or seventeen. Clodagh also liked Sandy – and Willy [later] played with offshoots of Fairport and knew that whole set very well. They mixed with them all at one stage, whereas I didn't.' Willy would indeed go on to work with both Sandy Denny and Richard & Linda Thompson in their post-Fairport careers, but whilst the Fairport circle may not have been a particularly strong influence on Clodagh's approach to writing, The Incredible String Band were another matter entirely – particularly the enigmatic Robin Williamson: 'He was very much one of her idols,' says Alison; 'A bit of a god to us all in those days.'

If nothing else, the tantalisingly unreachable opacity of Clodagh's lyrical concerns bear the hallmark of the mischievous and mystical Williamson, though Alison maintains there was always a real-world truth beneath the wordy abstractions: 'She was very into – well, we both were in those days – mystical, spiritual things. Clodagh's writing from her imagination and experience in a way where the premise is true but everything else is invented around it. She's never too obvious. There are kernels of truth, but she has imagined a lot.'

Housed in an arcane if not entirely unsuitable Heath Robinson-style sleeve design – a strange decision given the presence of two obviously photogenic women in the group – the album was released in April 1972. To quote a Simonds lyric, it, and the accompanying single release of album tracks 'Dan The Wing'/'Silver Song', 'sank like a stone'. The *NME* murmured 'tax loss'. Either way, Deram put no support behind it or the group. 'We were never able to actually do anything with it [touring-wise],' says Alison. 'The record company just didn't follow through, didn't do anything for us. That's the truth of it.'

Perhaps inevitably, band and label parted company. Perhaps unwisely, if indeed there was any choice in the matter, the band also left the safe hands of Ted Carroll's management. Although Ted was the frontman in the management of both Mellow Candle and Thin Lizzy – who were beginning to break through in the UK at this time – he was in fact in partnership with Brian Tuite (who ran a sound-hire business) and another individual, a 'sleeping partner' back in Dublin. Between them they were effectively subsidising these career-building gambles. It was around this time that Ted set up his now legendary second-hand and rare-records business, initially as a market stall (referenced affectionately in Thin Lizzy's classic 1973 single 'The Rocker'), primarily to keep *himself* above water.

With Mellow Candle, Ted thought that by bringing in Willy Murray they would have access to a wider range of useful contacts, but these didn't materialise. Ted had tried very hard to get work for Mellow Candle but getting people interested in a non-club band, as they clearly were, was extremely difficult. Thin Lizzy on the other hand were a three-piece who could play the clubs and keep themselves going, for quite a lengthy period as it transpired, until they finally became a cash-generating concert act. This was a game plan not open to Mellow Candle who were, in a musical sense, already a fully formed concert act but without the profile to justify a leap to that level. From time to time even Thin Lizzy, more so than Mellow Candle, returned to Ireland for live work at a higher level which would, aside from morale-boosting, subsidise further groundwork in the UK until eventually they were in the right place at the right time with their break-through 1973 hit single 'Whiskey In The Jar'.

Even at the time, and certainly in retrospect, both Ted and Brian believed that the band should have stayed longer in Ireland – even six months longer – building up finance, support and experience. But, eager to find that yellow brick road, the members of Mellow Candle had persisted in requesting to go to the UK. For better or worse, the management relented.

Losing the contract with Deram and having difficulty in finding a booking agent for England, morale in the band began to sink. At the same time internal frictions were appearing amongst the band members, all of whom, with the exception of Frank, fell under the spell of Scientology. For some, the spell lasted longer than others and for Frank the resulting tension in the air was too much. He left. Morale went from bad to worse.

Pete Harmon, the individual who stepped into Ted's management shoes – and who had come in, as far as anyone can recall, either via Willy or the new bassist, ex-Spyrogyra man Steve Borrill – ended up having a nervous breakdown and somehow blowing money set aside for a Dutch tour. Things could hardly get any worse. By then even the name had changed to Grace Before Space and, with Clodagh's writing moving in a more complex direction and with Willy and Steve – both of whom shared a strong background in progressive rock – bonding well and becoming, in effect, a kind of musical axis of their own, the band which had once been so focused now became prey to those dreaded 'musical differences'. It fell to Clodagh to bring things to a head: 'I was probably the biggest space cadet in the band,' she says, 'and at nineteen my experience at handling such delicate situations diplomatically was pretty limited. But, in a way, I was the one who had to handle it, because I was the problem. The material I was writing at that time was pretty challenging, and also very different to what had gone before. That was something I had no control over – it isn't something you can just switch off and pretend isn't happening. I just started writing in a different style and it wasn't everybody's cup of tea. The various internal tensions were becoming unworkable. I think we were all pretty much at rock bottom at the time, what with one thing and another – no manager, no money, no gigs, no label. It was certainly a bit of a mess. The only workable solution I could see was for Dave and Alison to go one way as a self-contained, easily expandable unit and for me, Willy and Steve to go the other way. It meant that we'd have to find another guitarist and another singer but all in all I felt it was the only thing that would keep everybody happy. I was wrong. I was such a hippy, and the acrimony and bitterness that followed came as a huge shock to me. I remember saying to Willy a few days after the split, "Let's forget the whole thing – I never want to be in a band again," and we just let Steve drift away. It was a very sad parting, and not without bitterness, but at the time it seemed completely inevitable.'

Things in Mellow Candle were indeed far from mellow, and there wasn't too much grace filling the space either: 'We also had a debt which we had to pay back,' says Alison, 'which a friend of Dave's family had taken out. [When the split became inevitable] I had to go with David 'cos I was married to him! But Clodagh and I had been making music together since we were ten, forged together, and that was a very difficult wrench.'

Mellow Candle/Grace Before Space finally called it quits in 1973. Dave and Alison moved to South Africa where they embraced Irish traditional music with a new band, Flibbertigibbet, recording the 1978 album *Whistling Jigs To The Moon* and working on local television and radio. Alison subsequently became active in the unofficial anti-apartheid movement, touring in a musical, working in a series of satirical-theatre revues and helping to run a club in Johannesburg as a platform for free expression. During the mid-Eighties she wrote and performed with Earthlings, a contemporary jazz group, before relocating to London where she spent sometime in public-sector administration. At the same time she was active in making available on CD and promoting some of her earlier recordings, including the Flibbertigibbet album and previously unreleased Mellow Candle demos. In 1997 she moved to Brussels for a period, working with jazz and folk musicians and, once again, in musical theatre – appearing as principal boy in pantomime and coaching principals for several subsequent seasons.

Alison now leads a double life – geographically, between Ireland (where she returned to live in 2001) and Belgium and, musically, between fronting the virtuoso Belgian-based Irish trad group Éishtlinn and, until recently, being a member of an even more unlikely act, Oeda: 'Four women singing in French, Flemish and English – all original songs – and three instruments: fiddle, guitar and double bass. Oeda was a Flemish princess – who couldn't sing. She was tone deaf, but very beautiful!' Currently a member of Dublin's Goilin singers' club, Alison remains an extremely proactive player in the city's traditional music scene.

Dave and Alison separated in the early Eighties and he currently works as a sound engineer and music producer with the South African Broadcasting

Mellow Candle,
mark 3, 1972: (l–r)
Clodagh Simonds,
Frank Boylan,
David Williams,
Alison O'Donnell,
Willy Murray

Corporation in Cape Town. 'We're still good friends,' says Alison. 'He's a terrible correspondent but I do often e-mail him.' Dave continues to be involved in music-making, playing mostly fiddle these days and gigging with an Irish band called Shanty. He is also involved in regular releases of MP3 collaborations, with a political edge – including one, 'Sherriff Bush And Deputy Blair' credited to the Nukular Stompers, which caused a tremendous stir in both the MP3 scene and the international media when it became available during the build-up to the 2003 war in Iraq. Despite the interest, Dave and his colleagues were disinclined to release the track commercially.

Of the other members of Mellow Candle, Frank Boylan worked with Gary Moore and various UK rock bands during the later Seventies and then disappeared. 'Every time something's in print,' says Alison, 'we always hope he'll see it and say, "Ah, that's where they are!" and pop up. But he never does.'

Clodagh's career since the demise of Mellow Candle has been somewhat shadowy to the casual observer but she is, at the time of writing, back to being a full-time participant in the world of music although, even during odd periods of work in administration – including a period in London as one of Virgin-supremo Richard Branson's personal assistants – she never, in a spiritual sense, really left it. Guest appearances on the Mike Oldfield albums *Hergest Ridge* (1974) and *Ommadawn* (1975) gave her the courage to pursue a place within music – a very new concept in the mid-Seventies – where composition, multi-tracking and the studio as an instrument could replace the (still relatively standard) imperative of live performance.

'I felt very bruised and hurt from the whole experience of being in a band,' she says. 'It left me with enormous questions about how to be true to your muse, how to be true to your passion, and yet never upset anybody. I still don't know if that's possible.'

Working with Willy on some demos, produced by Tom Newman, and then taking them to America in 1976 there was a chance of a fresh start. The pair had ostensibly gone for a three-week holiday, but Clodagh ended up staying for ten years and Willy for twenty. Frustrated, despite label interest, by being unable to persuade anyone to take them on with the proviso – daring if ahead of its time – that there would be no touring in band format, both worked briefly for Virgin Records. In 1977 Clodagh composed the music for a theatrical adaptation of Max Ernst's *Une Semaine de Bonte* and, the following year, for *The American Mysteries* – both written and directed by Matthew Maguire, and presented at New York's leading off-Broadway theatre, La Mama ETC.

Following *The American Mysteries* she spent the best part of a year in West Virginia, again writing music for theatre productions. Returning to New York in late 1979 she briefly studied Persian music and, a little later, composition and theory. And then, of all things, she found herself once more the member of a band: 'Willy and I formed this band called The Same,' she says, 'performing all original material, varying in line-up from gig to gig – anything from a basic team of four to a line-up of eight or nine, with back-up singers, additional percussionists and so on. That's one of the reasons we called ourselves The Same – we never were!'

Never viewed by Clodagh as anything more than a fun thing, the band nevertheless featured several future musicians of note, among them Stan Adler (Lydia Lunch's bass player), Steve Bray (Madonna's drummer) and Carter Burwell, who went on to score film music for many of the Coen brothers' films, amongst others. Spanning 1981–82, and with the cachet of residencies at CBGBs and the Mudd club, Clodagh and Willy decided to opt out before it became a fully fledged touring and recording outfit, with all the requisite problems and obligations that entails.

Between 1982 and 1986 Willy worked extensively as a fashion photographer in New York, LA and Dallas (also, much to his delight, reaching the dizzy heights of *Playboy* Recruitment Officer). During the same period Clodagh took various day jobs in New York, but kept her musical interests alive with an informal choral group and the continued study of music from other cultures. She returned to London in 1986, studying orchestration for a while with John Bonnar – a member of Dead Can Dance and an associate of Brian Eno, whom Clodagh and Willy had befriended in London before their New York days. While Clodagh performed with Bonnar during this period – at a showcase evening at the Queen Elizabeth Hall for artists on Eno's label, Opel – and recorded more demos with Tom Newman, the years spanning 1986–92 were to be fallow in terms of her musical goals.

'I wrote very little,' she says – 'Partly because I didn't own a piano, partly because I was completely exhausted most of the time. I was working full time [once again for Virgin], which I hated though I had no choice. It was very draining. I'd just go home of an evening and watch TV, open a bottle of wine . . .'

A sustained yearning for music eventually compelled her to resign from the day job and retreat to west Cork, where she lived for the next six years 'poor but a lot happier!' Whilst there she worked with an a cappella group and began a project (yet to be completed) setting ninth and tenth-century Irish poetry to music. Once again, in this volume, the Zelig-like figure of Donal Lunny appears, in this instance helping an old friend with the demo-recording first steps of this unusual project: 'He's amazing,' says Clodagh. 'He's one of those rare people who puts friendship ahead of business. He's such a source of encouragement, always full of compliments and positive remarks.

'But around that time, when I was so broke I couldn't afford a bottle of gas, I put an ad in *Record Collector* [hoping to sell an original copy of *Swaddling Songs*] and one of the responses I got was from a Japanese guy, a Mr Fujisaki. It transpired that he ran a little record label and asked if I had any material to do an album. And of course I had tons of material. Tom Newman was up for it and came over with some equipment for a few days and we did a very, very simple six-track mini-album. Strangely, it got very, very elaborately packaged [as *Six Elementary Songs*] with a beautiful sleeve. The whole thing is pretty rough but I suppose it's of interest to collectors.'

In 2000 she recorded a version of Syd Barrett's 'Golden Hair' with multi-media artist Russell Mills, which featured on his album *Pearl & Umbra* (on Bella Union). Currently based in Dublin, she is now devoting all her time and energy to recording a collaborative album with Mills and his associates Tom Smyth and Mike Fearon, collectively known as Undark. During the early months of 2003 she also completed her first film score, for Dublin director Graham Cantwell's *A Machine That Works*, a short film set in New York.

As for Willy, he returned to Dublin in the Nineties and died in 1998 of pancreatic problems. 'He and Clodagh were great mates, and she was there at the end,' says Alison. 'He was only 47 or so. Thing is, when we first met him in London he was a real health nut. He introduced us to Earl Grey tea, which we thought was very grand! Perhaps his lifestyle became less healthy after he went to New York.'

Suggesting some comparison to Susan in the final Narnia story Clodagh, in Alison's view, now 'looks on Mellow Candle as something that's all very nice, but it's way back when and she doesn't want to have much to do with it. I often have to call her and say, "Look, I'm doing this or that interview, do you want to join me?" – "Nope, you go ahead." It's gone, in her mind. She's not sentimental about people or things in her past, whereas I am!'

Yet, for all that, Clodagh's view on the Mellow Candle adventure isn't entirely unforgiving: 'I'm not ashamed of Mellow Candle or of the album,' she says, 'but I suppose most people find what they did when they were eighteen a bit embarrassing. The album was quirky and unique all right but we had a great producer in David Hitchcock, who I sometimes feel doesn't get enough credit. To be honest, in retrospect I don't think we were destined to be major-league players. The album was unique, yes, but we weren't particularly brilliant live. We were more concerned with the music than with being entertainers, which was all very noble. But at a time when all around us the beginnings of glam-rock and theatricality were starting to blossom, it just might have been a fatal error of judgement! We were probably in the same league musically as, say, Trees – we were never in the league of Steeleye or Fairport or Pentangle because we didn't have a virtuoso. I think our strength was in the songs rather than the performances. I was never a particularly good singer or much of a keyboard player, and I'm not really a performer by nature – more of a writer. Personally, I'd be quite happy in a box under the stage! Dave and Frank were both very respectable players, but I think probably Alison and Willy were the strongest performers. It's a personality thing.'

For those who had long admired the group's one album (reissued on CD in the UK on See For Miles in 1993, and currently available on import from Japan) the emergence in 1994 of another album's worth of material – albeit chiefly, if not entirely, studio and home-recorded demos of material that would end up on *Swaddling Songs* – was a rare delight. We must be thankful that former manager Ted Carroll bore no grudges and that, at the time, Clodagh, Dave and Alison needed the money: 'Ted provided half the material [for *The*

Virgin Prophet],' says Alison. 'He helped me significantly with that. He made it available, didn't charge any money, did it as a labour of love, got his company to put it together in decent sound. Clodagh hadn't much money at the time and we got a little bit of money for doing that, just a little bit. But since then she hasn't been too happy about the reprints of any of these things. But it's out there in the public domain now. [When the band split] we had three new songs in the pipeline, one of which I can still hear in my head to this day. It was about Dún Laoghaire and had di-diddlies in it, like "Boulders On My Grave". But we never did it. So it's all "out" now, unless anybody has a secret live recording.'

Eighties neo-hippies All About Eve once covered 'Silver Song' and Steven Malkmus, frontman of Nineties alt-rock-band Pavement, did 'The Poet And The Witch', but are there any other Candle covers out there? 'I'm not sure,' says Alison. 'Maybe there are in Japan – because that's where we get our royalties. We keep getting played on the radio out there but it's so inscrutable: "What's the station, who's playing it!?" But I've never performed any of those songs again myself. It's a sacred thing. And yet the stuff I did with Flibbertigibbet I still do to this day. I don't know that I'd like to hear myself sing it now – I wouldn't be able to sing that high on "Messenger Birds". I was eighteen then and my voice is lower now. However, technically, I'm a much better singer now but I couldn't sing it in the original key.'

And yet, in the final analysis, to have once been a part of a magical, unique piece of work must be a source of great pride: 'Yes, it is,' says Alison. 'And I think it's stood the test of time. I do look forward, I do new projects and they're all different but I am, still, the keeper of that flame. I did once worry that the rarity aspect would overshadow how much it's a stand-alone piece of work. As you yourself wrote, and I wrote a song about this, "It's dated but still lovely." I was very struck by that phrase and I think that's right.'

'It baffles me,' says Clodagh, reflecting on the undiminishing cult of the Candle. 'But I suppose there is still a thread from then to what I'm doing now. I've always been interested in voice, in what you can do with harmony, and while I'd like to think I've grown up a bit lyrically there is a lyrical thread that runs through my work. But Mellow Candle does all seem a very, very long time ago.'

KEVIN BURKE, ARLO GUTHRIE & PADDY KEENAN PROLOGUE

'Glad to know an eight-track changed your life,' said Kevin Burke, by e-mail. 'Not many people can say that!' And I've no doubt that he's right. Strangely, by the time this book came around I realised that the only member of the legendary Bothy Band I had never met at one point or another in the course of writing about Irish music for a decade or thereabouts was, in fact, the only one who had altered the course of my life: Kevin Burke.

Much of my interest in music, and in music of a time before that of my own era of growing up in the late Seventies and Eighties, can be traced to the innocuous gift (or off-loading) from an uncle of an outmoded eight-track cartridge machine (the short-lived precursor to the cassette player) at some point in the late Seventies. Coming with several cartridges of mostly early Seventies American country and singer-songwriter music, this opened up a strange and distant and insatiably appealing world for me. It was, after all, still a time before the print and broadcast media had discovered a vast, mineable seam in bygone musics of the rock era. This stuff wasn't easily found! To 'discover', in this way, an album like Arlo Guthrie's *Last Of The Brooklyn Cowboys* – seemingly self-contained, in a richly drawn world of its own – was a wonderful thing. (I eventually wore out the cartridge and, amazingly for a Belfast record store in the early Eighties, found and purchased a rather expensive vinyl import as a replacement. Now Kevin tells me that, to cap it all, somewhere out there exists a deeply obscure quadraphonic vinyl version. I will, of course, now have to seek the blighter out.)

What most intrigued and inspired me on *Last Of The Brooklyn Cowboys* were the opening strains, fading up through the sound of crashing waves, of Kevin Burke, unaccompanied, playing the Donegal fiddle tune 'Farrell O'Gara'. It probably didn't occur to me then that having Artist A play a tune on Artist B's album with no involvement from Artist B whatsoever is a rather odd thing. It just seemed right – as Arlo would eventually explain to me. It was also, almost certainly, my introduction to Irish traditional music and it always tickles me, like the possessor of a magic ring, that earnest discographers of Irish trad (usually non-Irish people) never seem aware of this very first, exquisite recording by the great Kevin Burke – who within months had joined Paddy Keenan, Micheál Ó Domhnaill, Tríona Ní Dhomhnaill and Donal Lunny in The Bothy Band, godfathers of every Irish trad band to come.

While The Bothy Band never played any part in my life, I do have a kind of semi-detached regard for them – from repeat showings of TV performances

Arlo Guthrie,
Roscrea Heritage
Centre, 1988

they recorded for BBC Northern Ireland in the Seventies and suchlike. Sometime in the early Nineties I was asked to annotate the CD release of a couple of the band's BBC Radio 1 *In Concert* recordings. I was happy to give it a go and extremely fortunate to have the help of Altan's Frankie Kennedy in trying to identify the various un-introduced jigs and reels! It was only after the CD appeared that one became aware that the ownership of Bothy Band copyrights had become a rather prickly issue – as the great Paddy Keenan was more than happy to discuss when we met at Dublin's Harcourt Hotel a few years later.

As for Arlo, I first encountered him at the Galway Arts Festival in July 1996 – a show that I reviewed for the *Independent*. During the course of writing this book I became aware that Tom Stapleton – who kindly supplied the photo to prove it – had brought Arlo to Ireland for a gig at Roscrea in 1988. But back in 1996 it seemed like this was Arlo's first-ever tour of Ireland, though a holiday long before had inspired his greatest album. 'Jeez, I thought that guy was dead,' had been the opening remarks that night in Galway. We fell about laughing. It was the start of a wonderful evening, yet one that was to be eclipsed two years later at Belfast's Elmwood Hall.

Like Roy Harper, in various ways, Arlo is a complex man, gliding through the long, gentle twilight of his career with an enviable cottage industry under his wing, his son on board as musical accompanist and somehow maintaining an equilibrium between a wacky, blissed-out public persona and personal, often musically expressed, concerns of a profound nature. I interviewed Arlo in a hotel breakfast lounge the morning after the Belfast show. Perhaps to him it was another town, another interview but for me it was tapping, at last, the source of an ancient magic.

KEVIN BURKE & ARLO GUTHRIE
LAST OF THE BROOKLYN COWBOYS

'We were going for a "feel" here,' says Arlo, side-stepping any suggestion of a concept album. 'It wasn't specific to an era exactly but I think the cover says it, too: we were going for "that", going for a mythical place somewhere that included all these things on the record. By 1973 we were beginning to see the end of the folk boom and the beginning of disco. I think we began to realise that we weren't looking for radio play and, frankly, dealing with even the records we'd made up to that point we weren't getting any either! So we just concentrated on making records that we loved listening to.'

And 25 years on, this wellspring of tender loving care, some great players and an obviously luxurious budget has proved its worth. 'Virtually unknown, even in the States,' as Arlo admits, and with a strangely beautiful cover-shot silhouette of Arlo and wife Jacqui this was artistically the most compelling outworking on one single disc of all his crazy, eclectic influences – here and there flashes of hillbilly hoe-downs, old-time gospel reverence, ragtime frivolity, sensual Hispanic horns and the delicate binding spells of mystical thought and hazy nostalgia. Nostalgia, at least in part, for Ireland: 'We went there, five or six of us just goofing off, in 1972 and ended up going just wherever the road went,' he says, 'until we found ourselves in Milltown Malbay, in Wilson's pub. There was a young kid there who took out a fiddle and started playing with us. That day there was 50 people in the pub; we came back the next day and the whole town was just full of people. The third day you couldn't get near the place. I mean, people came by busloads just 'cos they'd heard some music was going on somewhere and the whole town just erupted into this spontaneous celebration, which we found overwhelming – just fabulous. When we couldn't play from hurting, this kid showed us round – and he never stopped fiddling. I said, "Hey Kevin, if you're ever in the States come look me up," figuring, "He's never getting out of County Clare, never mind Ireland." Two weeks later the phone rings, "Arlo, it's me, Kevin – I'm in New York. How do I get to your house?"' Thus, two years before the monumental first Bothy Band record – and little known to trad chroniclers even today – Kevin Burke made his scintillating, evocative debut, playing Donegal reels against the ocean, on an Arlo Guthrie record: 'He'd be fiddlin' away on these cliffs,' says Arlo, 'with the wind and the surf, and we loved that so much that we put the sound of it in there – that was just for us, we didn't care any more! We just wanted to make records for ourselves, and that was such a nice time we put that "time" in there and hoped that in some way it would draw people into that "place."'

Colin Harper · Album retrospective originally published in *Mojo* (March 1999)

The sense of place is richly drawn, with each song glimpsing an episode of some unattainable dream world based on a mythic Old America – end of the Wild West, turn of the century. The songs were the fabric, but some of the most sensational embroidery, for sheer atmosphere alone, was on a definitive reading of Dylan's 'Gates Of Eden', courtesy of one Ry Cooder whose own artistic star was still awaiting its ascendancy: 'I guess he probably made his reputation playing with us as much as anyone else,' says Arlo. 'He was part of a crew that lasted a long time at Warner Brothers. Ry and myself and Randy Newman were the folks that Lenny Waronker liked working with. Lenny went on to become the president of Warner Brothers and he stayed there a long time until just recently. So it was the cream of the crop that we got to play with and that was through his personal interest.'

Arlo credits engineer Don Landy and arrangers Nick De Caro and George Bohannon with much of the sound on the record, but it was clearly a team effort: 'By this time we had the foundation of a great team of people making the records. The backing singers particularly – they were also on "City Of New Orleans" [a fluke US hit the year before] and they were really just the best, the tops. I'd been working with some of these guys on the previous couple of records; the production team, too. Lenny Waronker was in the driver's seat and my friend John Pilla was working his way into becoming a professional producer. It wasn't until three years later, with *Amigo*, that I think we really nailed a *great* record. We'd ironed out all the bugs by then. But, of course, for some people it's the bugs that give the character. But this record was the beginning of that and we were all very pleased with it and, I think also, disappointed that our era was fading 'cos we were just getting ready to make some good records.'

Material-wise, there was one Dylan, two Woodys, two 'trad. arr.' Kevin Burkes, four magnificent Arlo originals and a trio of bizarre oldies. 'Troubled Mind' had been a Forties hit for Woody's cousin Jack Guthrie, while 'Miss The Mississippi' was an obscure old Jimmie Rodgers tune and 'Lovesick Blues' a Hank Williams-era yodelling exercise: 'We also went a little bit out on a limb and did a piano rag I'd written and put some horns to it. This guy George Bohannon arranged it and, actually, we're doing that one this year as part of a whole show with a big symphony orchestra – undoubtedly it'll become the next record!'

Few of the songs, sadly, remained long in the live repertoire, though '"Gates Of Eden" I've been doing for years,' he says. 'It's a little busy on the record but it was busy with such great players I couldn't bear to take 'em out.' And now it's all there on glorious remastered digital. Any good? 'Er, I don't know,' he says. 'I haven't heard it.'

PADDY KEENAN
KING OF THE PIPERS

'I do have a bit of a reputation, I know,' says the well-spoken, slightly weather-beaten but raffishly positive and gently ebullient gentleman sitting opposite me, drinking coffee, at the bar of a Dublin hotel. It's a statement that few who are remotely in touch with Irish music could deny, but had they been sitting here chatting to this thoroughly likeable fellow in the flesh, or had they been standing in awe at his packed-out, stone-cold-sober and 100-per-cent blistering performance in the same venue the night before, they would have had to reconsider the evidence. But reputations, of the serious boozing, unreliable, outrageous-behaviour variety are hard to stop once they start, as Paddy Keenan, 'king of the pipers', knows all too well.

'And the more you're known, of course, the bigger the reputation grows,' he goes on. 'If something happens it might be minor but by the time it gets back to you it's huge! Here's an example: I was over in Los Angeles with Dolly Parton, Emmylou Harris and Linda Ronstadt and when I came back, maybe six months later, this guy came up to me in the street and said, "Hey, Paddy, is it true that when you were over with Dolly that you ran up and felt her boobs to see if they were real?"'

He seems genuinely embarrassed at even the thought of it. 'And another one was when this guy came to me and said, "Hey, didn't we have a great time in Lisdoonvarna?" And I said, "Well, I wasn't there." "Aw, you were – sure we were drinking together." "Damn it, I wasn't there!" I said. And you know something, if my wife hadn't been with me in France at the time she'd have believed him 'cos this guy was so convinced. And the worst part of it was, when this guy was finished and I was blue in the face saying I wasn't there, he walked away saying, "Ah well, you must have had a better time than I did if you can't remember it." I mean, what can you do? You've just got to walk away from it.'

Paddy Keenan, gypsy-blooded former member of The Bothy Band – the most revered Irish trad act of the Seventies – has been trying to walk away from it for sometime, to the point of leaving music altogether for a number of years in the Eighties and trying to get a quiet, family lifestyle together selling antiques in the wilds of west Cork. It's not the first time that this soft-spoken, shambolically glowing individual that all other pipers look to for inspiration, imagination and near-reckless emotion has tried to get away from piping either. And just like the first time he's found that it can't be done.

'It happened in the late Sixties,' he says. 'I fell in love with the blues for three years and tried to pawn my pipes but I just couldn't get rid of them! I

Colin Harper · Originally published in *Folk Roots* (June 1997)

was playing more guitar at the time, and harmonica and singing – I was making a living busking. Anyway, about two years later a friend of mine wrote to Paul McCartney. She was mad to get me back on the pipes for some reason and it was at the time that The Beatles were making their last records and were all looking for new instruments, new religion, new whatever. So she wrote and said, "I've got this friend who plays a very unusual instrument and he's the top guy at it," and so on – and she did actually get a reply from him! I was supposed to go and meet him, but I was hippying around London, having a great time and I just didn't want to play the pipes – I swear to God I was kind of embarrassed about them! But after three years I did take them out, took them into St James' Park and tuned them up and there was a crowd of people around me throwing money in the box and I thought, "God, what have I been missing?" So I came back to Ireland and got together with Triona and Micheál, and then Tony McMahon and Paddy Glackin, and that was the beginning of The Bothy Band.'

Which we'll come to presently. But what was he up to before he tripped off to London? 'I'd been playing with my family,' he says – 'My father and brothers and myself plus members of The Fureys. We were called The Pavees. Finbar [Furey] lived with us for something like six years up to about 1968 and my dad was tutoring both of us at the time. Finbar and Eddie then went off and became a duo, while George and Eddie formed a band called The Buskers and then they all joined up later as The Fureys. But for years we played together, and actually did some taping. The instrumentation was pipes, banjo, fiddle, mandolin, guitar and vocals.'

All of which was pretty innovative for the time: 'Well, yeah, it was. Finbar and Eddie were doing it, but The McPeakes were probably the first act to popularise the use of pipes in that kind of set up. Anyway, we did some professional recordings for an American company but they were never released – they're still there waiting for my OK, so you never know. There's stuff there from '66 to '72 and I would like to get it out, hopefully by the end of the year.'

Keenan seems like a man who's come to terms with his past, both good and bad. The good stuff's the music, the bad stuff's the business side of it all and the riotous lifestyle that blinded him to the rip-offs at the time. All that, he assures me, is very much in the past tense – both alcohol and the chances of rip-offs happening again. He has a brand new album, *Na Keen Affair*, out on his own label, Hot Conya, with a lawyer negotiating licensing and distribution deals for him. And he has, with the very occasional relapse (if rumour is true, which as we now know isn't always the case), gone teetotal. So does this positive-thinking Nineties vibe mean we can expect future unearthings from The Bothy Band, too?

'Well, as long as they ask me about it!' he says, with a degree of mirth. 'The last time something like that happened [The Bothy Band's Radio 1 *In Concert* album, issued on Strange Fruit in 1995] somebody came up to me in the street and said, "Hey, have you heard the new Bothy Band album?" – and he gave

Paddy Keenan,
mid-Nineties

me a copy of it. I enjoyed some of it, I found myself very much out of tune on some of it – but it captured the energy, all right. It was so nice, when Tommy Peoples was there, to play with him because you could play as you wished. I didn't have to think about him, he didn't have to think about me, because we blended so well. And I don't think you'd ever find a bunch of musicians of the same quality getting together without some kind of competition.'

So how did it all start? 'I left home at about seventeen and my father was very strict about music – especially the fact that I was a piper and he wanted to mould me as the piper of the future. I suppose I loved the pipes in the beginning, then rebelled and ran away. So I wasn't in touch with Irish music for a while.

'In 1969 or 1970 Tony McMahon asked me if I'd like to join a band called 1691, with Peter Browne, Matt Molloy, Tommy Peoples – most of the people who ended up in The Bothy Band, actually! I remember touring with Micheál Ó Domhnaill and Mick Hanly around that time – they were playing in Brittany and I'd decided to hang around with them for a month. And I suppose that's where I got to know Micheál and then The Bothy Band later came out of that. I think that was 1972, but I'm getting a bit lost here . . . Anyway, I'd come back to Ireland and I was playing a bit with the family again and then I recorded a solo album in 1974. Actually, I'd recorded an album a year or two before that with a skiffle band who were busking around Grafton Street. They called themselves The Blacksmiths, because we couldn't think of a better name in the studio . . .'

Another lost gem? 'No, I think it's a load of crap! But we were just having fun, you know. The guy who had us do it was a freelance producer. We'd signed a contract for one album and he went on and sold it to EMI. I released a solo album of piping on Gael Linn in 1974 that got great reviews and then of course EMI brought out *The Blacksmiths Featuring Paddy Keenan*, which was terrible. But I was having a load of fun drinking, playing, having a great life and in fact that's really the way it continued with The Bothy Band. We were having such a great time we didn't think enough about money.'

Indeed. Money. It's hard to avoid the topic when you're talking about The Bothy Band. It's a tragedy of the music business that so many innovators and great entertainers of the past – whose works continue to sell consistently around the world on CD – have been, legally or otherwise, deprived of their rightful rewards. Does it feel, now, like a bitter irony that everyone and their dog name-checks The Bothy Band as an influence while nobody involved ever made any money out of it?

'Well, there was money made all right,' says Keenan, without sounding especially bitter. 'Someone was making it. Actually, we'd started the record company [Mulligan] ourselves but then certain shares went to a certain person and suddenly the money was going elsewhere. But I wouldn't hold my breath for the rest of my life, waiting for some rewards to come from it. I still do have a share in the company, but royalty-wise I haven't seen a statement let alone a royalty since 1975 from that whole Bothy Band period. I don't want to go into all that stuff, but the point is it did leave a sour taste about the record business and I felt sorry not just for myself but for the other musicians who'd put so much work into it, trying to build a company to facilitate other musicians who wouldn't have got a chance.

'Anyway, since The Bothy Band split I played a lot on my own – solo stuff, occasionally with another musician if we could afford it. I did some tours of Europe and then a short stint around 1982 with a group called Last Night's Fun, with Johnny Moynihan, Tommy Peoples, Eddie Stack and myself. We spent a month or two in the States and then I came back to Ireland and decided to get away from the music altogether. I took a couple of courses – one in general engineering, one in furniture restoration – and got into antiques. I bought a place in Clonakilty, west Cork and opened a shop. The reason for that was to get away from the whole club scene – the booze, the hangovers, all that sort of stuff and also so I would have some other business to fall back on, so I could pick and choose what gigs I wanted to play. Because some of the bread-and-butter gigs were becoming a bit strenuous. The other thing, also, being that after a number of years with The Bothy Band and various other bands and various situations with record companies and bad management, financially it just wasn't that great.'

But for someone like Keenan, you just can't leave the music for long. A combination of domestic circumstances and itchy feet saw to that: 'Around 1989, '90, I went over to Germany and did a tour with Oisín,' he says, 'and then I travelled around Europe for a bit and went back down to west Cork and lived for a year on my own, to get away from everything. I was married to Michelle, a French girl, for a while but we were separated by then. That was why the shop had come about – it's difficult to settle down as a married man when you're travelling all the time and it's in your blood. In 1991 I went to the States, did a short tour and it went so well, with venues asking me back, that I stayed six months. I decided I'd move to the States and live there for a while, and put together a small group and hopefully do something original. But I'd always had in mind, even with The Bothy Band – and I was always shouting at them to do it – to try writing our own stuff. It never really happened, although we tried it once in Paris for the live album [*After Hours*, 1978]. A lot of that was scrapped, though it's on a shelf somewhere.

'About a year after the band split up Donal [Lunny] and Christy [Moore] came to me and Donal said, "Paddy, you've always been looking for something new – well, we've got it." And that was the beginning of Moving Hearts. So I spent a month with them at the Baggot Inn listening more than playing but I decided no, I couldn't go ahead with another three or four years of my life doing the same thing – I'd had such a bad time, financially, with The Bothy Band. But I did recommend Davy Spillane, who was down the country playing in pubs, so it was a great break for him and he's done very well out of it.'

And does Keenan, as one might suspect, relate more to a piper like Spillane than, say, the more austere, elegiac playing of Liam O'Flynn? 'Well, no actually

Kevin Burke,
New England, 1972

– I respect all pipers from beginners to advanced players. I like to see mood. I'm a mood player – I use music to express my mood because I'm not a very good speaker. My presentation on stage isn't great. But back then I was feeling a little stale, a little limited with the Irish music but then I thought, Well, I don't want to be bastardising Irish music – if you'll pardon the expression – if I'm going to do something new then I'd like it to be original. This was my intention back then with The Bothy Band – and Moving Hearts was a great idea.'

Which raises the question, Has the new solo album fulfilled that desire? 'No,' he says, with quite remarkable candour. 'It had great ideas but there was meant to be more in the way of original compositions there. Then nobody's ever happy with what they do, are they? But no, the next album will be *the* album – the one that I'll be happy with and that hopefully everybody else will be. Right now what I aim to do is put together a small band, make records and go out live.'

And what about those people who desire nothing but the pure sound of Paddy Keenan, king of the pipers, unhindered by the sounds and rhythmic constraints of other instruments? 'Well, I will eventually record a full solo album on all the different sets of pipes – just pipes – but if I go on stage now and bleed my heart to people like that they wouldn't notice – they want excitement. But within that excitement during the concert I will bring people down and you can do it in that context.'

Sounds remarkably similar to the doctrine of Martin Hayes, unquestionably (on fiddle) Ireland's most innovative, entrancing performer of moment. Is there a chance they could ever work together? 'Oh yeah, I love Martin Hayes,' says Paddy. 'With Martin it's not technical – although he can be technical – it's mood playing, and his mood will move you. Very, very much so. He's a moody person, too, and I think it takes that to create good music. If you're going round with a permanent smile on your face it's going to be superficial, so therefore your music's going to be superficial. I reckon that if we did do something together it would be worth listening to.'

So where, after a recording break of some fourteen years, does he plan to go from here and is there anything else the public needs to know about the renaissance of the legend? 'All they need to know is I hope I can make it in the next three years 'cos that's about all I've got left in me, I think! But I'm determined to do it on my own. I've been very diplomatic in letting record-company people have a listen to the new record if they want, but I'm not interested in selling this album to anybody. I want to hold on to it and to protect myself from here on. And I would like, at some point, to give chances to people who aren't yet out there 'cos there's a lot of great music around, and the other thing is I'd like to see musicians get what's rightfully theirs.'

Including The Bothy Band, perchance? Like, say, a reunion? 'Well, there have been offers,' he admits, with a twinkle in the old eye, 'and very lucrative ones, too. But a lot of the reason for The Bothy Band being recognised as one of the great bands is because it's finished! But I know that a lot of them in the band would love to reunite, do an American tour with contracts up-front of course . . . So you never know! If someone comes and offers us a huge amount of money we might just do it!'

But then again, if the Paddy Keenan I saw playing in Dublin the night before our chat can turn in an album that captures that amount of adrenalin and marry it to wholly original material, who would care for the past anyway? *Na Keen Affair* confirms to the faithful that Keenan is still the man; the next one, if it lives up to his own expectations, should confirm it to everyone else.

ARLO GUTHRIE
ELMWOOD HALL, BELFAST

Somewhat akin to the very concept and, one imagines, coiffeur of Tom Bombadil creeping into and out of the narrative in Tolkien's *Lord of the Rings* with little concession to any sense of time and place, and little effect on the plot, Arlo Guthrie is rock 'n' roll's Anomaly with a capital *A*. He knows it, he thrives on it, he plays it to the gallery and right there and then it's 100 per cent what the gallery want. This particular gallery was in the place in which the Ulster Orchestra rehearses, and it was packed full of expectant nostalgists of every age.

But to bracket Arlo Guthrie – Woodstock veteran, son of Woody, flag-waver for the rose-tinted ghost of free love and wry chronicler of a Thanksgiving Day littering incident 30-odd years ago – as a nostalgia act is way short of the mark. As you'd expect from a man with a snowy shock of hair, a harmonica harness round his neck and a tendency to say 'man' rather more than one could reasonably get away with in contemporary life, Arlo is reliving the Sixties on a professional basis. But he's living the Nineties, too. Somewhere in the second half of the show, when laughing heartily at every quip is beginning to hurt, we see little glimpses of the real man. Introducing a powerful new song, 'Wake Up Dead' – an almost uplifting reflection on the processes of terminal illness – we learn that back home 'when I'm not up here pretending to be someone' he visits hospices and runs a charity for the dying.

For those who perhaps only knew the hits – the dope anthem 'Coming Into Los Angeles', the celebratory 'City Of New Orleans', the quite unique 'Alice's Restaurant', all of which were delivered with gusto – it may have been surprising that someone so inextricably linked with an era that's long gone has a razor-sharp take on modern life. But if Arlo ever stood for anything it was the idea that 'folk music' meant songs by people, for people, about people; songs, he mused with irony but real affection, that might just change the world. His good heart is still burning and like a master of his calling, like the jester in *Twelfth Night*, he knows that the way to influence is not to moralise but to entertain, and every now and then to point out some piece of grief amongst the merriment. He spoke with genuine sincerity about playing in Belfast ('Believe me, it's hard for me to find a place I haven't played before . . .') and how he and his dad wore out a record long, long ago by a group of traditional singers from the city (The McPeakes) and how, maybe, some of that spirit had made its way into his own songs. God knows, Belfast in these modern times could certainly learn something from the well of humanity it glimpsed, if only in passing, from this fine old cowboy on his travels.

Colin Harper · Concert review originally published in the *Independent* (2 April 1998)

CLANNAD
PROLOGUE

The setting-up of interviews with celebrities is usually a mundane business, involving the passing of requests through publicists or managers and hearing back a few days later. The only possible intrigue in the process might be trying to find out who that middle-person would be and, more to the point, what their phone number is. Only occasionally, and almost certainly during the pursuit of some personal goal, would one resort to intrepid activities in order to nail that scoop. Rarely, these days – and sadly, in my view – will any kind of print or broadcast interview with a 'celebrity' occur without there being an active promotional campaign behind them. I imagine TV researchers on regional talk shows, in particular, spend most of their time sitting around waiting for spuriously topical PR bumf relating to this or that minor celebrity to arrive on their desks. And I imagine, when first I met Máire Brennan, in the early Nineties, that she must have had something to promote at the time because she was, indeed, appearing a few miles down the road from me on a regional talk show.

Having a hunch that Máire might have something to say on the topic of Pentangle influence – surely, I reasoned, a subject of some interest to the readers of my latest hare-brained scheme, *Rosemary Lane*, a Pentangle fan magazine – I raced down to Broadcasting House, in the centre of Belfast, and blagged my way in to the after-show do. I got the impression that this was something people didn't do very often. Still, we arranged to meet at her home in Dublin shortly after that, and the interview was very interesting – exploring not only the correctly guessed influence of The Pentangle on the early Clannad sound but moving on to Máire's recent conversion to an evangelical faith. Alas, having typed up the Pentangle section myself I paid someone else to type up the rest only to find that, being in the process of moving house at the time, the tape and the transcript wound up at the wrong address, disappearing with someone else's junk mail before the faux pas was discovered. Leaving aside exclusively Christian journals, Máire's testimony in print would have to wait for her autobiography.

A few years later, in 1996, it was her band's turn to be the subject of some spuriously topical PR. About to embark on a long tour, after a period of inactivity, someone had decided it was some kind of anniversary (an issue that clearly, from the text below, bemused the actual membership of the band) and the boys were made available for interviews. I arranged to meet them in the lobby of Dublin's Shelbourne Hotel, moving on to the tea room of that august

Colin Harper

Clannad, 1979: (back row, l–r) Ciarán Brennan,
Noel Duggan, Pádraig Duggan, Pól Brennan;
(front row, l–r) Máire Brennan, Áine Brennan (Enya)

establishment for what would prove the first of many happy interviews over cream scones and coffee in the years to come. Never underestimate the ice-breaking potential of a cream scone. Acquiring CD copies of Clannad's various recordings for Gael Linn and Tara without any bother, the problem became the rare and vinyl-only first album for Philips. Locating, by phone, a Dublin-based second-hand dealer who had one going spare, it transpired that the easiest way to make the transaction was at the very door of the Shelbourne. This was to give a new, and ever-so-slightly absurd, spin to the phrase, 'I've just bought your first album . . .' which would, indeed, open my encounter with the trio of folk legends waiting patiently on a sofa within.

The interview had been commissioned by Mark Paytress, features editor at *Record Collector*, although the editor, Peter Doggett – incidentally, one of the finest and most informed, if largely unsung, writers on music I have had the pleasure to know – had reservations. Irish folk was not then, and is not now, a core genre for that magazine. But there was, nevertheless, a great story behind Clannad's eventual pop success in the Eighties and Nineties and Peter was ultimately happy with the end result, and gracious enough to say so. Being *Record Collector*, the piece required an accurate discography to append it. Alas, being Clannad – 'a shower' in the unattributable words of one former associate – these were, in fact, the last people one should have gone to for accurate information. All three of the boys – Ciarán, Pádraig and Noel – were fairly convinced, after a period of pondering the matter, that there may well have been that joy of record collecting, a non-album B-side, sometime in the Seventies. Could they remember what it was called? Of course not. Or the A-side, perhaps? Nope.

Still, a few years on and somebody has obviously cracked the mystery as the track in question – a Gaelic title I must be forgiven for not, myself, now recalling – appeared as a bonus on a European first-time-on-CD issue of that elusive (and, if I remember correctly, somewhat pricey) first album. As to that live album the boys predicted, well, we're still waiting.

CLANNAD
THE FAMILY WAY

Very few bands have been in the business for 25 years and yet remained largely anonymous as individuals. Nor have many continued to increase their record sales while contributing significantly to the saving of an ancient tradition and, at the same time, creating a sound that is wholly unique and immediately identifiable as their own. But that's the stunning achievement of Clannad, the Irish band whose gentle, traditionally informed sound is now a familiar part of today's cultural landscape – far more so than their lone top-five hit, 1982's 'Theme From Harry's Game', might suggest.

Clannad is an abbreviation of '*an clann as Dore*', an Irish phrase loosely translated as 'a family from the district of Dore' – or, to be precise, Gweedore in north-west Donegal. It's one of the most windswept and isolated areas of Ireland, but a dot on the map that has proven remarkably rich in international music success. Clannad vocalist Máire Brennan is rightly proud: 'You look around here,' she told me recently, amidst those very hills, 'and there is a strong kind of vibe with us – Altan, Enya and even the likes of Daniel O'Donnell. This is just a tiny bit of Donegal and to have international acclaim focusing on such a tiny place is extraordinary.'

Máire, on that occasion, just happened to be at home visiting her parents and took the opportunity to pop into the only hotel for miles around to say hi to traditional protégés Altan, who were celebrating their signing to a major label (Virgin) with numerous bemused record-industry types from London and a bandwagon of TV and radio people. An occasion like that or, indeed, the international success of a band like Altan wouldn't have happened were it not for the pioneering contribution of Clannad in the Seventies. They gave native Donegal songs in Irish a contemporary but still reverent treatment when it was commercially unacceptable to do so; touring as hard as anyone around Europe; and using one-off label deals to their advantage until major success came along (via 'Harry's Game' in 1982) – giving them a rare bargaining power for financial security and artistic freedom.

Anniversaries, though, have always been a bit vague. RCA are telling anyone who'll listen that it's the twenty-fifth; the band aren't so sure: 'It's very hard to define when you start from,' says Noel Duggan, guitarist and founder member. 'Máire wasn't with us for the first year in 1970, then we made our first album in '73 and went professional in '76 – so it's not 25 whatever way you look at it!'

Ciarán Brennan, bassist and writer of Clannad's most commercial material, has a more stoic perspective: 'To me, our starting point was 1976. But it doesn't

Colin Harper · Originally published in *Record Collector* (June 1996)

matter to us any more – it's just nice to know that we're still selling, still charting. It's a satisfying thought.'

Clannad were founded in 1970, albeit as a part-time act, by brothers Noel and Pádraig Duggan and their nephew Ciarán Brennan – one of a large family of siblings whose father Leo ran (and still runs) a pub in Gweedore and fronted a showband. The musical background was an inspiration: 'With my father having the showband,' says Máire, 'that meant he'd have lots of sheet music coming into the house in the Fifties and Sixties. It was quite different to the average rural Gaelic household – with music and musicians and guitars everywhere. But, like everybody else, once you'd got a radio, in your teens you tuned into the forbidden Radio Caroline and Radio Luxembourg!'

Máire was drafted into her brother's trio as a harpist before anyone discovered she could sing, while another brother, Pól, drifted in shortly after on flute, guitar and vocals and provided the band with a 'pop idol' frontman. The early Seventies were a time when the traditional music of Ireland was being rediscovered and reinvigorated by the younger generation, with crossover bands like Planxty and Horslips doing for traditional Irish music something akin to what Fairport Convention, Steeleye Span and The Pentangle had done for English music a couple of years earlier. Along with The Rolling Stones, Joni Mitchell and The Beach Boys, whose songs were regularly covered at early Clannad performances in the family pub, such artists were a key influence: 'We kind of related to Pentangle,' says Máire, 'because of the acoustic side of things, with guitars and double bass. We were very much a group like that. I used to listen to Jacqui McShee and sing her songs sounding like her. In fact, there was one Pentangle album we used to do all the songs off. Not all at once, maybe, but a couple a night!'

'It was mostly the Danny Thompson sound for me,' says Ciarán. 'Somebody played me Pentangle when we formed the band and I was amazed – it was so nicely percussive with the double bass and I loved the jazz influence from Terry Cox on the drums. It was very encouraging to see that something like that was happening in England, so we kind of said, "Well, there might be room for us all."'

Taking a Pentangle-influenced sound and traditional material they'd collected themselves from singers in their own area, the group performed at the 1970 Letterkenny Folk Festival and won a competition to record an album with Philips. But it wasn't exactly a case of wheeling into a studio the following week: 'It didn't actually happen till we did an appearance at the National Song Contest in Dublin in 1972,' recalls Ciarán. 'The record company didn't think there was a market for people singing in Gaelic. They thought we were a novelty act, with a harp and the harmonies and all that. I don't think they wanted to honour it until we were plastered all over the town with this song contest.'

Even back in Donegal, the native language – which is currently enjoying a wide acceptance culturally and musically – was frowned upon at that time: 'When we did cover versions it was great,' says Máire. 'But when we'd do a

Gaelic song they wouldn't clap. Strangers would clap, but it was seen as a poor-man's language, really. It was in the poorer areas that Gaelic was spoken, so by speaking Gaelic it was as if you were letting yourself down. But the music intrigued us, and the more we got into it the more beautiful the melodies became and the more interesting the stories behind them. Then someone down the road would say, "Hey, I've got a version of this song," and it would gradually build up. But the record company didn't want all these Gaelic songs, which is why it took us three years to do two days in the studio!'

Currently out of print, as it has been for many years, the *Clannad* debut album is a wonderful period piece, featuring seashore sound effects, an occasional jazz drummer, Tim Rose's then ubiquitous 'Morning Dew' and a self-penned Gaelic rock 'n' roll number from Noel amongst the traditional fare. By the time of their next album, Clannad's sound had matured into something less derivative, but if you've ever wondered what a Gaelic Pentangle would have sounded like, then this is the one to find. Later Seventies pressings came in a laminated sleeve, but an early Eighties reissue, handled by Tara on behalf of Philips, had to be cut from an ad hoc master created from a mint vinyl copy when the original metal plates and master tape were found to be lost.

Although most of their essential recordings from the period are now on CD, barring the debut and live albums, the original Clannad discography from the Seventies is something of a meandering path, as Ciarán explains: 'Philips had an option for a second album but a certain date had elapsed and my father, who was representing us, said, "Sorry, we're going somewhere else." After the fiasco of the first one, which had such a small royalty – about two-and-a-half pence – we decided to do one-offs. Whoever came up with the lolly, we recorded for them.'

The second and third Clannad albums, *Clannad 2* (1974) and *Dulaman* (1976), were recorded for Ireland's state-funded traditional label Gael Linn and both came in gatefold packaging. They define the band's sound of the period: acoustic guitar/flute/harp-based traditional music from Donegal, sung mostly in Irish, with occasional hints of what would later become the group's trademark sound. The layered harmonies and 'Enya-esque' staccato strings on 'Arise And Dress Yourself' from the '76 recording is an obvious example, while the fuzzed electric-guitar solo on 'Dheanainn Súgradh' from *Clannad 2* (provided by future Bothy Band guitarist Micheál Ó Domhnaill) anticipated their subsequent dabblings in mainstream rock. The latter was paired with 'Eleanor Plunkett' for an Irish-only single.

The mid-Seventies found the group building a substantial following in Europe, which prompted their decision to go professional in 1976. *Clannad In Concert* was recorded on inexpensive two-track over several shows during the group's Swiss tour in 1978 and is a fine record of their live act with two tracks in particular standing out – the blistering ten-minute finale of 'Níl Sé Ina Lá' from the first album, and Máire's interpretation of W.B. Yeats' 'Down By The Sally Gardens'.

A further set of recordings, clearly also from this era – possibly a stray set of masters from the same tour – later appeared as *Ring Of Gold* on the Celtic Music label in 1986. Although the label is long established, the group regard the release as a bootleg. Another bootleg concert set from the period, recorded at the Ballisodare Festival in Ireland, has since appeared on CD in Italy, while a heavily imported various-artists set entitled *Festival Of Irish Folk* was released on the back of some similarly titled mid-Seventies German tours organised by legendary folk entrepreneur (and Krautrock icon) Conny Plank. This included studio material from the band's second and third albums. The bona fide *In Concert* was notable for appearing on Ogham, the band's brief experiment at running their own label.

Their next release, *Crann Úll* (1981), was recorded at Plank's studios in Cologne and while initial pressings appeared on Ogham the set was fairly quickly licensed to Philips. It has subsequently appeared on CD on the Dublin-based Tara label, for whom the band recorded their next album, 1982's *Fuaim*. If *Crann Úll* is generally seen as unexceptional, *Fuaim* was a revelation. By now a six-piece, featuring their classically trained sister Enya (Áine) Brennan on keyboards and vocals, Clannad had produced a work that, with hindsight, marks something of a watershed. It was to be the last (and best produced) of their independent releases, and introduced greater musical experimentation, with the addition of Enya on Fender Rhodes, guest sax/clarinet contributions and a jazzier, still pastoral sound that was moving somewhere close to Jethro Tull territory. Indeed, keyboard player Peter-John Vettesse, who was at that point updating the Tull sound on the latter's *Broadsword* album, would prove a key contributor to Clannad's controversial *Sirius* experiment five years later.

After eighteen months or so Enya left the group to pursue a phenomenally successful solo career, taking with her Clannad's long-time manager Nicky Ryan. Meanwhile, the group signed to David Cavanagh Management and the modern Clannad era – of big productions, self-written material and ever-expanding line-ups – was ushered in with the timeless and massively successful 'Theme To Harry's Game'. The tune was commissioned by Yorkshire Television and released as a single on the company's own label later in 1982. Ciarán explains: 'We were asked along to Windmill [Lane] Studios in Dublin one morning to watch this three-part series called *Harry's Game*, based on a book by Gerald Seymour. They were thinking of using "Mhórag 'S Na Horo Gheallaidh", a Scottish Gaelic song on *Fuaim*, but we said, "Look, this doesn't make sense – this thriller about Northern Ireland with Scottish Gaelic music." I suggested we'd write something new, which we did in about six hours.

'On the trip down, I'd been reading this book of verse that my grandfather had had and it had, in Gaelic, the words, "All things must pass, the moon and the stars will go out," and so on. So I took some jolly nonsense words, like "fal-la-la-fol-de-rol", and slowed them right down to something moody. There was this Prophet 5 [voice sampler] in the studio and it all fell into place.'

'Harry's Game' not only got the Irish language into the UK charts for the first time, but had major labels baying at the door: 'Now we were on *Top of the Pops* singing Gaelic like we'd always wanted to, and there was no record company that was going to say, "Don't be doing that,"' says Noel.

The group signed to RCA, who promised them the greatest artistic freedom, and Richard Dodd, the producer commissioned by Yorkshire TV to work on 'Harry's Game', was kept on for their first RCA album, *Magical Ring* (1983). Recorded with the luxury of 24-track equipment and three weeks to get it right, it was a massive step forward in terms of sound and material. Although traditional material was still a part of their repertoire, Clannad were now a part of the commercial marketplace, with a particular skill in soundtrack work which was to prove handy. Ciarán: 'The next album, *Legend* [1984], gave us a bit of breathing space for a second album proper after *Magical Ring*. We'd heard there was this *Robin of Sherwood* TV show happening in England, so we got the manager to phone up about it. He was told, "Oh, we were trying to get in contact with *you*!"

After *Legend* came 1985's *Macalla* (meaning 'echo'), which took the band's sound and mystique a stage further. A sinister, nocturnal cover photo ably reflected the increasingly windswept anthems that the group, and Ciarán in particular, were producing. The album was crammed with latter-day Clannad classics, like 'Closer To Your Heart', 'Almost Seems Too Late To Turn' and Máire's duet with U2's Bono, 'In A Lifetime'.

'RCA asked Máire to do a duet,' says Ciarán. 'We don't like demands like that, but she just happened to meet Bono in a pub round the corner from the studio and invited him in. Three days later it was done. On the first day he was kind of mumbling odd Gaelic things and kept asking us, "What's the title of this bloody thing?" I was listening to Tony Williams' Lifetime at the time so I said, "In A Lifetime". We all sat around and contributed lyrics. Simple as that.'

The track, with suitably windswept video in tow, was another hit in the UK but did nothing in America, increasingly a challenge to the group. However, the next album, *Sirius* (1985), featuring session heavyweights Robbie Blunt, Russ Kunkel and Bruce Homsby, was a concerted attempt to crack it: 'We'd always wanted an American producer and a shot at the American market, and *Sirius* was a very calculated try,' admits Ciarán. 'But it went horribly wrong, because the public didn't want it.' *Sirius*, named after the Greenpeace ship, wasn't without its moments, but it took the carefully evolved Clannad sound of harmonies, jazzy inflections and traditional influences too close to bombastic AOR, as uilleann pipes battled it out with stadium-rock drums.

The next clutch of albums – *The Collection* (1988), *Atlantic Realm* (1989), *The Angel & The Soldier Boy* (1989) and *Pastpresent* (1989) – were, as if retiring hurt, two more soundtracks and two compilations. *The Collection*, on K-Tel, anthologised their entire career while *Pastpresent* focused on their Eighties work and featured two otherwise unavailable tracks.

In 1989, Pól Brennan left to pursue various projects, including opening a studio and involving himself with the nascent Womad festival. But the group bounced back with 1990's *Anam*. '*Sirius* was an interesting album,' says Ciarán, 'but it took too long, over a year. We'd been relying on all these different producers – Richard Dodd on *Magical Ring*, the Moody Blues' Tony Clarke on *Legend*, Steve Nye, who'd worked with Japan, on *Macalla*, and Russ Kunkel on *Sirius* – so by the time the Nineties came I felt I had to take control, reacquaint ourselves with our acoustic sound. We recorded *Anam* at my house in Rathfarnam. I had a 16-track studio set up from doing *The Angel & The Soldier Boy* animation soundtrack for the BBC, so we recorded *Anam* on the same gear and told RCA in America to forget about it. We were only selling about 80,000 records in America, which is a drop in the ocean. It wasn't worth touring America, for us or them. They'd released 'In A Lifetime' twice and still couldn't get Bono and Máire into the top 200. They just didn't know what to do with us in the States.'

At least, not until a friend of the band happened to be on a skiing holiday with a top man from Atlantic Records. He played him *Anam* and the band was soon signed to a US deal with Atlantic. Around the same time Volkswagen were using 'Harry's Game' in a US TV ad and the music was creating more public interest than the car. The song was added to US pressings of *Anam* and the band have gone from strength to strength in that territory ever since.

Banba (1993) continued the gentle, airy pop/rock formula of *Anam* with Ciarán writing virtually all the songs and producing. As far as the public were concerned, though, the focus of Clannad was Máire Brennan: 'I just like to be in the background,' says Ciarán. 'There are a lot of people who hunger for fame but, with the other three of us, that's gone a long time ago.'

Máire has since further enhanced her profile with two solo albums, featuring her three younger sisters, two of whom – Deirdre and Brídín – now tour as backing vocalists with Clannad: 'I feel busier now than I was five years ago,' says Máire. 'It's amazing – you'd think it would settle down, but there's a huge interest in it, and music is such a lovely thing to do. When I was growing up nobody was singing Gaelic songs, not like now, so I'd like to think there is a future for it. When we started singing Gaelic songs we were told that we'd need to change our outlook on life, but we didn't change it for many, many years. When we did, it was only because it was time to move on.'

The new album, *Lore* (1996) which – anniversaries notwithstanding – breaks a long lay-off designed to avoid burn-out. The album continues the formula honed to perfection with *Anam* and *Banba*, and initial CD copies include a bonus disc of six previous hits. So what next? 'I don't know,' says Ciarán. 'We could very easily do a Springsteen and go back to being acoustic. We thought this one was going to turn out that way, but it developed into something that would have been difficult for just the four of us to do on stage. There are ten people in the current touring band. This world tour will take about a year and we'll be recording all the shows digitally. With such long breaks between tours we may as well start recording everything, so that we'll have something in the bag, at least!'

MÁIRE BRENNAN
THE OTHER SIDE OF THE RAINBOW

Colin Harper · Book review originally published in *Folk Roots* (April 2001)

These days the name Clannad is probably more associated with a kind of obscenely budgeted, pseudo-Celtic blandness than any great musical integrity. Yet let us not forget that here was a group whose first five albums were recorded almost entirely in Irish (commercial madness at the time) and who, on the evidence of this simply but attractively written memoir, survived the Seventies through luck and determination alone. As Máire notes, with typical lack of pretension, there would have been many parents who would have harangued their penurious, pipe-dreaming children into getting 'proper jobs' long before the freak UK hit with 'Harry's Game' in 1982 finally turned things around for them – and by that stage there had already been four of the Brennan offspring through the Clannad ranks, with others yet to follow.

Máire Brennan,
mid-Eighties

Máire grew up the eldest of nine in the remote county of Donegal during the elsewhere-swinging Sixties, with Catholicism and family being key touchstones. Those factors blended with the sounds of the day to create, by stealth, the family group that debuted on record in 1973 as Clannad. Individually and collectively the members had made several Irish TV and festival appearances before this, and the parallel story of Máire's convent schooldays and her incongruously hippy-ish group's evolution offer a fascinating glimpse into a now strangely remote era. Eventual group success exacerbated long-brewing personal turmoil for Máire, as the lifestyle consumed her sense of self-worth – a sense that had remained adrift since a secret abortion in 1970 and a subsequently failed marriage. Máire makes it clear that her brothers Ciarán and Pól were always the creative heart of the group, with herself merely the frontperson. Thus, while Clannad form the backbone to this story, the flesh is in Brennan's personal journey from Catholic guilt and lifestyle excesses to her current redemption. In that sense, it compares well to Frankie Armstrong's memoir, *As Far as the Eye Can Sing* (also written, as is Brennan's, with a discreet co-writer), in that Armstrong's career in music is effectively a thread through a life dedicated to women's issues and social justice.

The Clannad story may now be over – in my own view they ran out of steam creatively a long time ago – but Máire's current fulfilment as an individual has impacted on her professional life, with recent work, after initial misgivings, now aimed at the contemporary Christian market. Much as I share Brennan's spiritual views, I've never been one to proselytise or excuse the pap that makes up the bulk of Christian music and literature. Initial flickings-through on this book were not promising, but after a little perseverance – essentially, through a melodramatic first chapter that one suspects to be a narrative contrivance of the co-writer, Angela Little – I found its simplicity of style revealing a truly compelling story, honestly told and refreshingly free from any hard-sell agenda. On that basis, I would recommend it. Me, I was still turning the pages at two in the morning.

Shaun Davey (left),
Liam O'Flynn (centre),
Rita Connolly, *c.* 1990

SECTION 6
THE HIGH
KINGS OF TARA

THE HIGH KINGS OF TARA
PROLOGUE

As Maurice Lennon suggests, in one of the pieces below, there are people in the music world, particularly in the folk-music world, who get the wrong idea about John Cook, inscrutable MD of Tara Records. On the one hand he's a very generous and witty fellow; on the other – in matters of business – he's made of steel; a man who does business in black and white, with no grey areas and certainly no room for nods, winks, favours and sentimentality. When Topic Records in the UK released their potted history of the British folk revival, *The Acoustic Folk Box*, in 2002, reviewers composed thinly veiled and wildly disproportionate pokes at the bogeyman who, as the compiler had no doubt made them aware, wouldn't allow the use of a certain Christy Moore track. Christy, we were told, had shrugged his shoulders and said it was fine by him, but . . .

Who was this dastardly individual? How dare he scupper the definitive aspirations of such a monumental project? It was, of course, that mild-mannered, dobro-playing accountant and well-known connoisseur of cappuccino, John Cook. Meeting with John in the early spring of 2003 – in a coffee shop, of course – for our first decent chinwag in a while, I made him aware of this new-found infamy. It was certainly good for a laugh. The truth was that John has found, invariably, that the only way to do business and to cover one's back in the business world – which the nebulous concept of 'the folk world' is, and has to be, a part of – is through watertight contracts. All contracts pass through John's lawyers, and let it suffice that he doesn't use the firm of Cutts, Korner & Cheapskate. For John to do a deal involving the potential return of a royalty percentage on one track from an 80-track compilation hardly requires a genius to point out that not only would the lawyer's fee not be covered, but there may well be a danger of not quite recovering the cost of a cappuccino. And that, in the world of John Cook, is a serious business indeed.

If every other label in the folk world runs on wings and prayers, that's their concern. The fact that Cook has kept his operation afloat for 30 years, with a gentle but consistent stream of quality product throughout, should say enough about his judgement as a businessman, while the fact that many of these recordings are high-budget and often musically ambitious – hence risky – affairs speaks volumes about his commitment to music. There are few indeed, in the business of music, who walk that tightrope so well.

My introduction to the Cook empire was inadvertently through a friend, Joan Meneilly, who loaned me an nth generation cassette copy of the exquisite Shaun Davey/Rita Connolly album *Granuaile* sometime around 1990. This was

Colin Harper

striking, extraordinary music and quite unlike anything I'd heard before. Joan, a trained singer and Ph.D.-level ethnomusicologist, found her own escape from the drudgery of low-paid, temporary work – as I did, at the same time, through being able to string a few sentences together – by setting herself up as a piano teacher. The keys to freedom, indeed. Somehow, and I don't recall the circumstances, this battered cassette was to become a way in to not only a whole seam of music but an unlikely provider of direction to my eventual career as a writer.

It was 1994 when I finally decided there really was very little to lose in jumping off the low-paid, no-prospects bandwagon to nowhere that I'd been on since graduating in 1989. I bought a house and resigned from the particularly miserable occupation I was in at the time. My old school friend, and fellow veteran of the Queen's University history department, Mark Simpson – currently a national current-affairs personality with the BBC – was then serving his time as a reporter for the *Belfast Telegraph*. As I recall, he seemed rather alarmed that anyone in their right mind would give up permanent employ for the unknown waters of freelance journalism, let alone freelance music journalism. Let alone freelance weirdo-folky-never-heard-of-it journalism. This was, I believe, a path entirely unknown to career advisers.

Unwittingly, though, Mark gave me not one but two great leads to follow: he recommended approaching Tom Collins, genial editor of Belfast daily, the *Irish News*, whose interest in the arts, he said, was well known. Whether it was my bad hearing or Mark's slip of the tongue, I ended up making my pitch not to the Belfast-based *Irish News* but to the Dublin-based *Irish Times* – to be told of my faux pas, and with very good humour, by arts editor Paddy Woodworth. I can't remember the mechanics of it but, somehow, from that point on, I became a regular contributor to both papers.

My first piece for the *Irish News*, published in March 1994, was an interview with Rita Connolly whose first solo album proper had just been launched in Dublin with a press reception, hosted by her new manager, the legendary Pat Egan – a key figure in the late Sixties/early Seventies Irish rock scene. In a sense, then, my first assignment was quite literally a free lunch.

My first major piece for *The Irish Times*, by happy coincidence, was an interview with Rita's partner, the maverick architect of *Granuaile*, Shaun Davey. It was to prove the first in a long line of pieces on Shaun and his circle – not only Rita Connolly, of course, but legendary uilleann piper Liam O'Flynn and folk-rock stalwarts Stockton's Wing. All these artists would be united, during an almost feverish mid-Nineties period of releases from the label, by the patronage of John Cook and by the production skills of Shaun Davey.

Events involving Shaun and his own work would prove to be rare though periodic. I was lucky enough to preview and review, almost without exception, all of the Irish concert premieres and revivals of his work from 1994 onwards. The one exception was the lack of a proper print review for the monumental, and to date unrepeated, *Gulliver*. I did manage a few lines in a subsequent *Irish News* piece on Shaun and a somewhat diplomatic review on Radio Ulster the following day – which Shaun, I recall, heard and found most amusing. In essence, I found it a dense, though powerful work, largely unburdened with the motifs and immediacy of Shaun's 'trademark' pieces, though featuring odd moments of magic on first-hearing, particularly the massed-choir treatments of Psalms 65, 69 and 88. As the maestro had told me, 'Some of the most beautiful verses in the English language are connected in some way to liturgy and prayer.' He wasn't wrong.

I met Liam, in a professional capacity, only the once, although his keyboard player and regular touring partner Rod McVey lived a couple of miles down the road from me, and worked with me on a couple of local recording projects during that period. Regarding Stockton's Wing, my main point of contact was their new-found singer and songwriter Eamon McElholm, who was fresh out of university and living in Omagh during that time in the mid-Nineties when I was actively looking for unsigned Northern Irish artists to promote in the *Irish News*. Most of the people covered in that series fall outside the remit of this book, but Eamon was able to adapt his writing – from what may be called the Paul Brady tradition of mature pop music, in which he was and remains a master – to fit perfectly the trad-based, harmony-laden, pop-folk sound of Stockton's Wing.

Some of the best mainstream songwriting I've ever heard remains languishing on unreleased Eamon McElholm demo tapes. Eamon was a key factor in the group's brief renaissance, their gunfighter at the last-chance saloon, and it seems to me a huge waste of talent that, since the demise of Stockton's Wing with the protracted illness of the man who really *was* their visionary and engine room, fiddler Maurice Lennon, Eamon has made do with the path of a jobbing trad guitar accompanist. Perhaps his time will yet come. In any event, the writing of this book provided a perfect opportunity to meet again with Maurice Lennon to find out just what did go wrong with the Wing, and about his own tremendous return from oblivion with concept album, stage show and multi-media plans built around the legend of Brian Boru – bankrolled, of course, by the only man in Ireland upon whom such a mercurial talent could depend: John Cook.

Given that I was travelling down from Belfast for that first encounter with Shaun Davey, John Cook had offered quality hotel accommodation if I wished. I declined on principle (yes, I had them!), but it was a generous offer and, as Shaun told me that very day, entirely typical of the man. Sometimes I've disagreed with John's approach to things, or expressed gentle frustration at what might sometimes appear to be a sacrificing of imagination for over-caution (long indeed have John's ears been deaf to the undeniably fabulous idea of a Shaun Davey 'best of' . . .). But John does what he does, and he does it well. Andy Irvine, an increasingly fervent believer in the concept of the artist owning and marketing their own work – cutting out the middlemen – once told me that, as far as he was concerned, 'all record-company people are bastards,' only to find himself immediately adding the caveat, 'Well . . . maybe with the exception of John Cook.' He is indeed an exceptional fellow!

JOHN COOK
A TARA STRENGTH

'I suppose you could say I've achieved what I set out to achieve,' says John Cook, munching on a cheesecake, quaffing cappuccino and trying, in between, to summarise the tale of Tara in a Dublin city diner. 'Quite simply, there are some high-quality albums which will stand the test of time, and that's already proved itself. I like to push musical boundaries, and I like to think we've produced material of cultural merit, as well as great musical merit. I don't think there's an easy option – if we knew what the punters wanted we'd all be at it – *that's* the easy option! But in the long term, a quality product will always last the course and that's what we've done: we've created our own niche, and it's all about quality.'

Which is just as well, because nobody could accuse Tara of quantity. The label has released precisely no new albums in the last year, although there's plenty happening on the back-catalogue front and a new Liam O'Flynn album, together with a Maurice Lennon/Paul Roche duo album, will be recorded this side of Christmas. But who, pray tell, is John Cook? Known in the record industry as the inscrutable, dobro-playing accountant with a ready line in dry wit, nerves of steel and a penchant for cappuccino, Cook has single-handedly built up the label from its origins as a modest offshoot of a Dublin record shop 25 years ago to an iron-clad outlet for quietly ground-breaking music based on the Irish tradition, and has become a benchmark to rivals in standards of packaging, production and recording ever since. As for Cook himself, his artists see him, with a mixture of deference and affection, as 'the enigma': 'I think John's a great man,' says Maurice Lennon, fiddle maestro in Stockton's Wing. 'He's stuck his neck out for people and he's the leader in the field in terms of *real* folk music in Ireland. It's very rare to find characters like John Cook, in the record business or otherwise! It takes a while but when you get to know his way of operating then the communication lines are opened up. Some people tend to misrepresent him but if they're given the opportunity they'll find he's actually quite easy to work with. He's been very helpful to our agents abroad, for instance, and that's been very important. They could ring him up and ask for, say, 100 promotional copies of an album and it would never be a problem – we've heard this from a number of agents, that he's one of the most helpful people in the business in that regard.'

A modest individual of soft-spoken, indeterminate accent, Cook has chiselled out enduring marketability for his artists with a knife-edge balance of vision, prudence and acumen. Not a man given to reckless enthusiasm or

Colin Harper · Originally published in the *Irish Voice* (late 1996) and *Folk Roots* (December 1997)

rash expenditure, he does occasionally confound expectations with the odd flight of fancy – like recently signing a Limerick-based pop band called Treehouse Diner because he liked them and only afterwards worrying about how one markets such an item. But upon such pragmatism has Tara's roster of world-class acts been built.

Born in Scotland, educated in England and Ireland and skipping an offer to study economics at Trinity College, Dublin, Cook went into the hotel business as an internal auditor in the mid-Sixties. After that and a period of international travel, he combined his passions for music and accountancy and opened a record shop in Rathfarnam, Dublin in 1969. Over a period of three years Cook built up the business to peak level before selling it to a chain of stores which had just changed its name to Golden Discs, formerly known as Tara Records. And here the tale begins: 'Tara had existed at the retail end,' says Cook, 'but not as a label. It was set up in the early Sixties by Jack Fitzgerald. He had one store on Tara Street in Dublin, specialising in American imports. It's a bookie's office now. I knew Jack all those years I was in the hotel business, for no other reason than I was a particularly good customer, and after I sold him the store I started doing odd bits of admin work for him. And around that time, 1971, there was one import – from England this time – that was doing exceptionally good business . . .'

That album was *Prosperous* by a young Irish singer called Christy Moore, at that stage a lowly cult figure, travelling around the British folk clubs. A previous album released in England had sunk without trace, but this one, recorded by Bill Leader – who had already recorded legions of latter-day greats in their musical infancy, for Topic, Transatlantic and his Leader/Trailer labels – was where the great 1970s shift in Irish music began. The four individuals who went on to form Planxty – Andy Irvine, Donal Lunny, Liam O'Flynn and Moore himself – were on that album and, to satiate demand from his customers, Jack Fitzgerald bought the rights to the record and re-released it himself the following year on a label of convenience entitled Tara.

'There was quite a gap between that album coming out and anything further being released,' says Cook. 'When Planxty came together they did three albums with Polygram – one of the major labels operating in Ireland at the time – and then the band broke up. That would have been the mid-Seventies, and it was about that time that we were thinking of developing the Tara label and started putting aside capital to finance recordings.' Several other independent labels were cropping up in Ireland at this time, most of which were vehicles built around one major act – Claddagh with The Chieftains, Mulligan with The Bothy Band, Oats with Horslips – and this would, initially, be the direction Tara would take.

'Planxty had started this whole strain of Irish music that was coming more into the centre,' says Cook. 'So when the band decided to get back together in 1978 they put themselves up for a record deal and we started bidding against the major labels. I decided that if we were going to start a label in earnest the best way to do it, even if it's costly, is to get a big album and a recognised artist. It goes a long way to getting your label known.'

Quality, big-budget product followed at a steady rate thereafter, with two albums from Planxty (*After The Break* and *The Woman I Loved So Well*); two Christy Moore solo projects (*Live In Dublin* and *The Iron Behind The Velvet*); a couple of albums from Irish-language band, Clannad (*Crann Úll* and *Fuaim*); and the first three albums from a promising new act called Stockton's Wing. All four acts are now of course legendary names in Irish music, hugely respected by the current generation of trad stars and, with the exception of Planxty (gracefully retired as a unit), all still going strong. Indeed, it has been a trademark of Cook's modest empire that acts have left his label to bigger and better things – and several have also returned: 'It's not particularly by design,' he says, 'but a lot of the acts we've recorded have either gone to or come back from major record companies. We can never aspire to be a major company but we seem to operate in a little niche just below that level. We go for the family atmosphere, keep it as an Irish-owned-and-managed production company, producing high-quality albums with long shelf life, retaining the rights to them and marketing them over a period of years. Marrying artistic interests with commercial interests is a tricky business, and sometimes that produces differences of opinion, but I have good relations with most of the people I've dealt with over the years. Bands will leave the label and bands will come back to the label – Stockton's Wing being a prime example . . .'

'We were enticed away by Polygram and a few other companies,' recalls

Maurice Lennon, 'and went off and did our own thing for a number of years until the early Nineties and then when we went looking around for someone to back us, at a time when we really *needed* an album out, nobody wanted to know. But John Cook was there for us. So he's stood by Stockton's Wing through thick and thin really, and I think he's got his money back – otherwise he wouldn't have done it!'

Cook, with one of those cavalier gut-feeling instincts that sets him apart from the simple, passionless accountants of the mainstream record industry, re-signed the Wing when everyone else thought they were burned out, and steered them through a difficult period of low morale, limbering up with 1992's low-key *The Crooked Rose* and allowing them to recreate a luxuriant full-band sound on 1995's exquisitely crafted re-birth, *Letting Go*. Featuring new frontman/songwriter Eamon McElholm, it's arguably the best album of their career. The story illustrates a rare sense of vision that seems at odds with Cook's prudent, cautious image: 'Well, I'm cautious to a degree,' he says. 'I mean, I've always liked the notion of pushing music in new directions, such as orchestral albums – which can be costly and gets you into a higher-risk area. But with regard to a band situation, if you can increase the number of people on tour and make it feasible either by the venues that you fill or by under-writing it, I'll do it. The best presentation possible – on stage or on record – is what it's all about for me. We ran Davy Spillane's band out of our office for three or four years, so I've an accurate idea of the extent you can push a live touring situation with a band.'

Spillane, bringing traditional Irish pipes into a jazz-fusion setting and more recently the esoteric and potentially lucrative new-age/film-soundtrack area, built up his reputation with Tara before moving on amicably to a major deal – in his case with Sony. Clannad set the trend in 1981, after four albums with various labels during the Seventies and then two with Tara, using the bigger budgets available courtesy of Cook's 'maximise quality' philosophy to begin experimenting with the studio techniques that led to the breakthrough UK hit single, 'Theme To Harry's Game', and subsequent international success. That success was soon mirrored by erstwhile Clannad member Enya, whose sole recordings with the band, on 1981's *Fuaim*, were bankrolled by Cook. In the Clannad case, Cook's involvement in their leap to the bigger league, via a bidding war that left RCA the winners, meant he was in a position to reap his own modest recompense – in effect, the Irish rights to several subsequent Clannad albums on RCA and, of course, the rights to continue marketing and licensing his label's own Clannad product around the world.

Tara has never embraced the 'Celtic bandwagon' themselves, but are quite happy to license material for compilations to other labels that do. It's the way a successful business works. With this in mind, the fact that Clannad, Stockton's Wing, Davy Spillane or any other great act may move on is less of a concern to Tara than it would be for others: 'It would be our policy, I suppose,' says Cook, 'that any album we'd record would have to be a "stand-alone" album – an album that could sell and be marketed on its own merits because so often artists go on to do something else, the band breaks up or whatever. Moving Hearts' album *The Storm* would be a very good example of that. Moving Hearts achieved probably the most successful fusion of Irish music with jazz and rock. They did three albums with Warners in the early Eighties before coming to me and recording that one instrumental album which has proven to be one of the back-catalogue's biggest sellers – and the band have only come together for maybe half a dozen gigs since it was recorded.'

Marketing product from bands that break up or go into semi-retirement is child's play to Cook. The real test is marketing a kind of music that has no precedent, costs a fortune to record and costs another fortune to perform live on a stage. And, of course, Cook has done that, too. Years before the phenomenal worldwide success of Bill Whelan's *Riverdance* – with its combination of traditionally inspired music in an orchestral setting – Cook had been releasing albums of exactly that by the first and greatest of the genre's composers, Shaun Davey. He also went on to release a pre-*Riverdance* symphony by Bill Whelan, *The Seville Suite*. But he didn't go into it lightly: 'Back in the late Seventies Shaun and Bill basically had the Irish advertising market cornered – they did an enormous amount of jingles for radio and TV, which is how both of them acquired much of their first experiences of orchestration. At that time Shaun was approached by the national broadcaster, RTÉ, to write a piece for the RTÉ Symphony Orchestra based on Tim Severin's recreation of the voyage of St Brendan from Ireland to America, and that's how *The Brendan Voyage* came about. It was duly performed and then the question of recording it came up. Looking back at the catalogue, it was the one album I agonised over more than anything else. It was such a departure from anything that had been recorded up to that point, in putting Irish pipes together with an orchestra and a rhythm section, plus one had very high costs involved in recording it. I agonised for many days over that, but of course I don't regret it. It's still a great album.'

Indeed, seventeen years on a remastered, repackaged version has just been released on the American market along with four other titles, including Andy Irvine/Davy Spillane's ahead-of-its-time *East Wind* (1992) album, as part of a 'Roots of *Riverdance*' marketing initiative. Back then, though, Davey was a fine-art Masters graduate who had only previously released one obscure yet charming singer-songwriter album on the short-lived York label in 1972, involving members of The Strawbs, after which he almost formed a band with Donal Lunny (at the time in between Planxtys), worked with a band called Midnight Well and disappeared into advertising. The release of *The Brendan Voyage*, however, launched him as a contemporary orchestral composer of international standard and led to further commissions for work in a similar vein, several of which – *The Pilgrim*, *Granuaile* and *The Relief Of Derry Symphony* – have been released on Tara. Although Shaun has more recently allowed soundtrack commissions (for the BBC TV series, *Ballykissangel*, and the film, *Twelfth Night*) to be released on other labels, he remains essentially loyal to Tara and to Cook in particular: 'He's the main-man, really,' says Shaun. 'I don't wish to record with anybody else and I hope he finds it possible to continue to record the odd thing that I write. He's very committed to his artists. I mean, some artists go on to other labels – for example Davy Spillane, who I know John likes and respects enormously still. I, on the other hand, have never looked for another record company. Every few years I'll go back to John with a project and he will or will not, as he sees fit, go with it. We might have the odd musical disagreement in those situations, but I suppose I'll always go with his judgement.'

Most of Shaun's works feature the truly exceptional vocalist Rita Connolly and the universally recognised master of Irish piping, Liam O'Flynn – both of whom have also recorded solo albums for Tara under Davey's supervision as producer: 'Shaun is a superb producer,' says Cook. 'Certainly, the last Liam O'Flynn album he produced, *The Given Note* (1996), would be one of the best-produced albums in the catalogue. But of course everything else has improved as well – studio techniques, recording facilities, the advent of CD . . . It all helps towards a better end product, and the better quality the product the more able it is to last the course. In fact, it's interesting to note that with *The Brendan Voyage* its tenth year of release was its second-highest year of sales, so that's a good example of a consistently selling album. It doesn't date.'

Cook's policy of 'less is more', putting quality before quantity and aiming for only two or three recordings per year, has paid off. Almost none of the Tara catalogue has been deleted. In fact, as digital technology has become available in recent years, much of the Tara catalogue has been remastered or even (in the case of Shaun Davey's *magnum opus*, *The Pilgrim*) re-recorded for CD. It all adds to the notion that the sign of Tara on the spine of a CD is a guarantor of music in a class of its own, unencumbered by trends and bandwagons in Irish or popular music generally and, furthermore, of a quality in sound, musi-cianship and presentation that scales an enviable height.

Nevertheless, quality doesn't automatically equal huge global sales and some markets, particularly America, have remained effectively out of reach for a relatively small label in Dublin. But the enigmatic Mr Cook has, of course, a few ideas on that front: 'We've licensed tracks from some of our artists to other labels there,' he says, with an accountant's zeal. 'It's a good marketing exercise. For instance, there's a track from one of Liam O'Flynn's albums on Windham Hill's *A Celtic Christmas* album which did very well, and we licensed a Clannad album to Atlantic a couple of years ago. We also get a lot of requests for the use of instrumental tracks in film and television. Sometimes the money is negligible, but it all contributes to the cause!'

It certainly does, and even if the great American public refuses to buy the newly revamped *Brendan Voyage* in epic numbers, at least it's there for the cognoscenti – and few of those would deny that the estimable John Cook deserves to be quaffing cappuccinos and cheesecake for sometime to come on the back of what has already become a quietly exceptional life-work.

SHAUN DAVEY
DAVEY & MORRIS

Shaun Davey, the renowned self-taught composer for orchestra and uilleann pipes, first came to prominence with *The Brendan Voyage*, released on Tara in 1982. Before that, he'd been dividing his time between music for advertising and dabbling in production, both of which he's continued to do when time allows. But like all pioneers and visionaries, the man who invented the ethnic/orchestral genre has a dark secret, known only to a handful of genre collectors. And it lies in the sinister, singer-songwriterly depths of the early Seventies. Valued at £100, titled *Davey & Morris* and straddling the folk/progressive crossover, this long-forgotten album heralds a grimace from the composer. 'I find *my* role in the thing very disturbing,' he says. 'It beats me – *I* certainly wouldn't pay £100 for it!'

Davey is significantly prouder of his second major work, 1983's *The Pilgrim* – a vast, ambitious work for over 200 performers (soloists, choirs and orchestras from the seven Celtic nations of Europe) based entirely on medieval religious texts in such commonplace rock 'n' roll languages as Irish, Welsh and Cornish, and commissioned by a French festival at a cost of £100,000.

Subsequent work has included the song-cycle for group and orchestra, *Granuaile* (still perhaps his most immediate and accessible work), *The Relief Of Derry Symphony*, numerous scores for theatre and television and, most recently, a marvellously rewritten and re-recorded version of *The Pilgrim* available on CD for the first time. Most of his work also features Ireland's finest singer, Rita Connolly, and ex-Planxty piper Liam O'Flynn. Davey may be frowned upon as a populist by the classical establishment, but his musical achievements remain those of a visionary and a taker-of-risks.

That said, not many in his immediate circle have been allowed to see or hear the skeleton in the closet. This early Seventies oddity has been attracting three figures in progressive folk-rock circles for sometime and, despite Shaun's misgivings, it's actually very pleasant and extremely interesting in the light of his subsequent fame in other fields.

Recorded by Shaun Davey and James Morris in 1973, and released on York Records – a joint subsidiary of both Decca and Yorkshire Television – the album (York FYK 417, with an insert included) sits well with other lost gems from that era. The personnel connections are interesting, too: Planxty man, founder of the Mulligan label and general folk-rock legend Donal Lunny on various stringed instruments and bodhrán; Patrick Halling, who led the strings on Jethro Tull's *Minstrel In The Gallery* (1975), on violin; Strawbs members

Colin Harper · Album retrospective originally published in *Record Collector* (October 1994)

Dave Lambert and Richard Hudson on guitar and drums, with fellow Strawb
Tony Hooper producing. Davey sang on most of the tracks (something he
rarely does today), played keyboards, guitars, harmonica and made his first
orchestral arrangements – very effectively, but in a manner he now finds embar-
rassingly egotistical.

James Morris' claim to fame is that he subsequently founded the now iconic
Windmill Lane Studios in Dublin, where the likes of U2 have recorded. On the
album James sang and played bass.

The music itself has a progressive, early Lindisfarne feel to it but with addi-
tional tricks involving time signatures and oblique lyrics that probably owe
more to Genesis. The most obscure track, 'Ishkamir', is both lyrically and
melodically akin to The Incredible String Band with a string section, while 'Blue
Smoke', based on a slightly sinister piano figure and building in sound, is remi-
niscent of Andy Roberts *circa Homegrown* (1971). Davey, of course, denies it
all: 'Andy Roberts? No, I've never heard of him – and I certainly never listened
to Lindisfarne. Let me see, it was somewhere between The Beatles and Bob
Dylan. John Mayall and Eric Clapton, in their early days, were heroes of mine,
and some of the black blues artists – but lots of people were drawing on the
same influences at the time.'

Davey and Morris had been members of a college band back in Dublin
called Blues Assembly, and when both came to London, for different reasons

– Davey to study for a Masters in fine art at the Courtauld Institute, Morris to train as a film editor – the songwriting partnership continued. 'We were semi-serious about it,' says Davey. 'It was a question of walking the pavements and knocking the doors of record and publishing companies. We got a publishing deal first, and they tried to develop what we did, which involved doing small gigs in folk clubs in Gravesend and places like that. The Strawbs connection was brought about by the record company that finally agreed to let us loose in a studio. At that time, The Strawbs were winding down as a performing group, and Tony Hooper was working as a house producer for York Records. He was very good to us – I've never forgotten that. He encouraged my ideas about orchestration. I suggested that on one or two tracks I'd like to try and write parts for brass – and I meant one or two trumpets, but he said, "No! Use five trumpets! Use five trombones!"' Also on the album was the 'Hi Heel Sneakers'-ish 'Grape Street' – almost the only recorded evidence of the maestro playing lead guitar. 'Well, I did do a very good Status Quo impression for a jeans commercial after that, but that was the end of it,' he says.

So did the album sell? 'No, certainly not enough to impress anyone. And I think the money ran out before a proper single could be produced.' Success as a recording artist wasn't on the cards for some years. Neither of the partners had time to do much performing, and Davey even recalls falling asleep at his lectures during the recording period. 'We both had other things that we had to do, so there was a natural diminishing of our responsibilities. We returned to Dublin. James came back as a fully fledged film editor. That same year I formed a band called Bugle with Donal Lunny. We only did four gigs, in Dublin, and some demos. It was a very experimental band. Donal took a year out of Planxty to pursue these things, but there was only one way for me to go at that stage – I was very keen to cross boundaries and arrange meeting points between certain instruments and traditions, and that had to be thought out on the page.'

One of the fruits of that intensive and ultimately successful direction is the man's current release, the revamped recording of *The Pilgrim*. Should the people who'd pay £100 for *Davey & Morris* also buy this less wallet-emptying item? 'Well, yes, I hope they would, because I subscribe to the belief that we spend our lives trying to do a very small amount of things in our work, and we keep coming back to improve on them. But I think on the album I made with James I can see little seeds of things I did better later on.'

SHAUN DAVEY
OF WINGS & PRAYERS

'I don't believe in God,' says Shaun Davey, matter-of-factly. The fact is offered obliquely, in the context of explaining his background, but it will probably come as a surprise to many of those familiar with the man's music. Hearing Rita Connolly and a host of angels singing '*Christ within me . . .*' as the glorious epilogue to Davey's new recording of *The Pilgrim* – a work that is founded almost entirely on texts of faith from the Middle Ages – it seems extraordinary that this could be the product of an unbeliever. His passion, however, is not for the soul in its afterlife, but for squeezing out a sense of culture in this one.

'It's nice to have had the opportunity, in my lifetime, to record so many things, and to help steer them through with the people they were written for. There's no reason to be concerned with what happens after that.'

Things have changed for the maverick individual who wrote *The Brendan Voyage* fifteen years ago. However he may be regarded in serious music circles the world over (and it's not always seriously), his respectability as a composer for theatre is well established – with scores currently running in two RSC productions at the Barbican – while in terms of the ethnic/orchestral epics which tend to reach the record stores, he's ploughed a lonely furrow for long enough to convince anyone who cares that he's not some joker with a bunch of 1970s concept albums and some half-baked ideas. 'As I recall, very few of the concept albums were actually *about* anything,' he says, with more earnestness than the subject deserves, before wandering off on the subjects of albums like *Sgt. Pepper's Lonely Hearts Club Band* and Rick Wakeman's *The Six Wives Of Henry The Eighth*.

And just what is *The Pilgrim* about? 'Wings and prayers,' he says, sounding wilfully obscure and enjoying every minute of it. But he is conscious of the fact that, in rewriting and re-recording his most ambitious and least-performed *magnus opus* for the digital medium, he has all but rescued from oblivion a work of exceptional qualities – not least in its balm to the savaged soul. 'Well, you see, I believe that Christianity has been a very good force, a very good thing,' he says. 'I believe very much in equality, but the fact is that I am unable to accept the concept of God.' And just how does he arrive at something so spiritually moving from a position of such stoic detachment? 'Oh, well, that's easy,' he says, 'because the most moving music you'll ever hear is music that is not sentimental. You know, some things are better left unsaid – in a way, you don't always want to lay your soul bare. Well, so it is with music. Things need

Colin Harper · Originally published in *The Irish Times* (12 August 1994)

Rita Connolly,
Shaun Davey
rehearsing
Granuaile,
mid-Eighties

to be done in a more oblique way.'

The content may indeed be oblique, but there is nothing fey about the sheer scale of *The Pilgrim*. It premiered at Lorient in 1983 and everything about that very production reeks of a doomsday scenario narrowly averted: a 200-plus cast who saw the score only days beforehand; a barrier of languages; a stage that needed to be rebuilt with its back to the wind; a cost of £100,000 to stage.

The original album, salvaged from the event, was little more than a document to folly. His next work, *Granuaile*, was a pub session by comparison and it, plus *The Brendan Voyage*, were the ones that saw regular performances in subsequent years.

The Pilgrim remained almost entirely unrepeated and unrepeatable until New Year's Eve 1990, when an opportunity to reassemble everyone for a concert in Glasgow presented itself. An intense bout of rewriting and the foresight of Tara main-man John Cook has resulted, at last, in a truly worthy presentation of this most dense and least narrative of Davey's creations.

It is, if not his most immediate work, then certainly the most definitive single document of the man's vision, though he denies this himself. And it's all there bar the kitchen sink: 'Well, the kitchen sink is not there,' he says, with the conviction of a man who may actually have considered it at some stage, 'but it is, I think, *nearly* right – it's as close as it was possible to get. There's about ten per cent of it, fifteen per cent maybe, which in my view needs to be completely re-thought, rewritten and re-recorded.' And will he ever do that? 'Probably not.'

Interviewing Davey is a demanding business. He will stand his ground alone, over years, on the staved pages of his craft, but he will never – willingly – say more than he needs to. The interview, as a whole, is conducted as a process of statement and denial in pursuit of elaboration, and well beyond the drudgery of mere questioning. He is weary from a heavy period of working on his next, and probably final, large-scale creation [the choral epic *Gulliver*, which was unnameable for contractual reasons at the time of this feature's original publication] followed by six weeks in the studio producing an album for his partner, Rita Connolly.

The interview becomes a cat-and-mouse situation, but he begins to enjoy the challenge. Devil's advocacy is one way to the truth, but the master Davey plays Christ in the wilderness. How would he react to charges of gimmickry? 'Well, it's a question of degree.' What is his place in the contemporary classical fraternity? 'I don't think I have a place in the contemporary classical fraternity.' *Granuaile* is a moving experience . . . 'Is it?' What is it that you're trying to do? He laughs. 'I don't ask those questions of myself anymore!' Stalemate. Has he really created an entirely new genre of music? 'Sometimes,' he says, 'I think that there are things that I would write that nobody else would. I think that between Rita's singing and my writing for her, we have invented a partic-ular kind of song which wasn't there before. But I'm not going to make any claims about what I have written. I know that it was waiting there to be done and, anyway, if I make claims somebody's going to say, "Yes, but Seán Ó Riada did it before you."'

The 'Ó Riada gambit' is one sure way of prickling the composer's cool exterior, but he has to think about a recent comparison (in terms of genius, integrity and a pioneering vision) to Jimi Hendrix. How did he feel about that? 'I didn't understand it.'

Much less does he appear to understand, or want to consider, the prospect of his own impending portrait on the walls of history – even the suggestion that he has, already, an accredited place in Irish music. 'I don't, you know, I don't . . . I reject this notion. I don't have an accredited place anywhere! Listen, I can walk round my home town of Bray and *nobody* knows who I am!'

But given the legendary status afforded to his heroes and predecessors (Ennis, Ó Riada, and others), does not the very weight of history hang heavy upon his shoulders? 'No! I don't particularly go around comparing myself to these people because I can't even begin to do that. I don't wish to – it doesn't help me to do that. So I don't have the pressure of thinking, Oh Christ, I've got to be as good as Jimi Hendrix – right?'

There may be a stolid exterior but Shaun Davey – for all his solitary stature and the cultural intensity of his vision – is not a man entirely bereft of humour. In terms of dryness, that humour would give the Gobi desert a run for its money, but surely no man is an island? 'Well, OK, there *are* times I feel, God, Beethoven was so *good* – how can I even be in the music business? How can I look myself in the eye and still try to write music when I can see how good they were? That is a kind of pressure, but it's a fact of life. You have to get on with it.'

And yet the pressure of working in solitary fashion for months on end, on colossal projects like *The Pilgrim*, must be immense: 'There is no hiding place,' he says, 'when you are standing in front of an orchestra and they're playing your piece. It is not a time for excuses. It either works or it doesn't. If it doesn't work, it will 99 per cent of the time be your fault, and that's not very pleasant. You have to accept that that is going to happen from time to time. If you don't put up with it then you stop doing it and, to be honest, I'm not sure that I want to put up with that risk for the rest of my life . . . It's a very tiring process. You can be looking for some sort of satisfaction from a personal progress that isn't always there and there may be – in fact, I'm sure there are – restrictions on my ability to develop as a composer for an orchestra. I've had sufficient motives to brave the storms so far, as it were, and I'm not sure if it's going to be worth the pressure any more.'

He is well aware that his reputation can survive for some considerable time on auto pilot – on the back of repeat performances of existing works. 'One looks at things from year to year,' he muses, 'and, first and foremost, one has to make a living with what one's got.'

And he knows he is now in a position to make choices and changes to his lifestyle. He rejects the notion of a 'greatest hits' album as 'unattractive', but admits to an irritation that his compositions for theatre remain, as yet, largely unrecorded: 'I feel frustrated that people who like *The Brendan Voyage* can't get to hear these things.' He has the very definite air of a man who wants to tie up loose ends and do something else – of a man who has, perhaps, reached a crossroads. So aside from the unnameable work, is this new version of *The Pilgrim* the end of an era – is it the last of the great works? 'I will not become involved in a work that is so difficult to stage, in a hurry, in the future.' So it is? 'Well, yeah, OK. It is.'

LIAM O'FLYNN
LIVING LEGEND

Liam O'Flynn has arrived, a few minutes late, for our rendezvous at the characterful HQ of his record company, Tara, run – amidst a heady froth of invoices, artwork proofs, back issues of *Billboard* and boxes of product – by enigmatic supremo John Cook. Situated in modest anonymity at the end of a narrow, cobbled lane just off the busy Dublin shopping precinct of Grafton Street, the offices of Tara themselves are a geographical metaphor for the current, irrevocable status of O'Flynn – an unassuming individual, largely unconcerned with the hustle and bustle of the mainstream record industry, yet only a stone's throw removed from it and quietly successful nonetheless. Added to which, in the same way that Grafton Street – immortalised time and again through art and literature – is not just any old street, O'Flynn is not just any old musician: he is a part of history.

Every generation throws up but a handful of truly great exponents of the Irish tradition's most esoteric instrument, the uilleann pipes. In the early years of the century Patsy Touhey, an emigrant to America, was the man to be reckoned with; during the Thirties and Forties Johnny Doran, based in Ireland and the last in a tradition of travelling pipers, was the name to silence his peers; while the Fifties and Sixties were the virtually exclusive territory of Leo Rowsome, Willie Clancy and Séamus Ennis – all three maintaining the instrument through a lean period in its survival and all three close enough to the modern era to remain widely revered names to this day. While others have since taken the instrument some way into jazz and rock territories, O'Flynn remains the sole direct link to his three greatest predecessors – maintaining the integrity of the music whilst taking care to present it in consistently fresh, quietly ground-breaking contexts and playing with passion, grace and, on occasion, abandon.

As we meet, however, the great man is more concerned with abandoning his car in the 'strictly no parking' environs of the Tara HQ. Somehow, one expects uilleann-pipe gods to be mystical, otherworldly figures possessed of alchemical secrets and hidden truths, but O'Flynn is an unprepossessingly soft-spoken individual of very ordinary appearance, with very ordinary concerns – like trying to avoid parking tickets. One of Cook's employees whisks the vehicle in question surreptitiously round a corner to somebody's warehouse and, mundane worries addressed, the three of us troop off down the lane to one of Cook's favoured emporiums for liberal quantities of cappuccino and cheesecake.

Colin Harper · Originally published in the *Irish Voice* (late 1996)

Liam O'Flynn,
mid-Nineties

So, Liam, this business about being a legend – 'last of the greats' and all that – must be a hell of a burden? 'Oh, it's great fun!' he says, instantly deflating one's preconceptions and causing a mouthful of cappuccino to move throat-wards a tad sooner than planned. 'You can't let it get to you. Actually, when you talk about burdens of responsibility it reminds me of Willie Clancy being interviewed by some foreign TV outfit in Milltown Malbay. "So, Mr Clancy," they said, "where did you get your piping from?" And he told them his mother was a plumber!'

O'Flynn may not be an alchemist but his sense of humour is certainly a well-kept secret. His press cuttings are strewn with phrases like 'a very private person', 'inscrutable', 'gentle', 'impassive', 'never flash' and so on, and his recent recordings are rich, exquisitely crafted works of art. But to assume that Liam O'Flynn is one of those so-called 'legends' who drift around the record industry years after their moments of glory, to increasingly diminishing interest, or conversely to assume that he is someone whose reputation is founded on his 'worthiness' rather than any more universal quality would be to assume wrongly. He's the real thing. His current, undisputed position as Ireland's greatest living piper and one of its greatest musicians period has been won through an ongoing career of touring and recording with some of the tradition's most influential names of the last 25 years, most notably Planxty and Shaun Davey, plus work on recordings by the likes of Kate Bush, Enya, Mark Knopfler and The Everly Brothers, and soundtrack work on films including *The Field* and *A River Runs Through It*. When he makes a new recording of his own, Liam O'Flynn doesn't trade on his reputation, he adds to it.

The Given Note is the title of Liam's latest offering and its reception in Ireland and Britain has been sensational, with awestruck reviews from folk and rock publications alike. Liam's just about to tour the US, in support of the album, for the first time ever under his own name, with a band featuring Rod McVey on keyboards and guitarist Arty McGlynn – both phenomenal talents in their own right. It's a sunny day in Dublin, the cappuccinos have just arrived at the table, John Cook is footing the bill, and it's a perfect opportunity to acquaint oneself not only with Liam O'Flynn but with that weirdest of instruments, the uilleann pipes. So, Liam, what's the story?

'Well, the uilleann pipes developed out of the Irish equivalent of the Scottish war pipes,' he says, and it's clearly not the first time he's had to answer the question. 'Dates aren't really known,' he continues, with easy authority, 'except that around 1700 a bellows was added and the Irish pipes began to take on their own identity and grow in popularity. You think of legendary harpists like O'Carolan and people like him having these patrons and, when the harping tradition died out around the early eighteenth century, I think it's fair to say that the pipes followed on as the court instrument of Ireland. A lot of the aristocracy took to playing them and it did become a fashion to have, in certain large Irish houses, a resident piper to entertain and all that.

'The biggest breakthrough into developing what we now know as the uilleann pipes was the sort of reed which is in the chanter, because you get a second octave with it by over-blowing. That was a really huge technical break-through and I think even now the uilleann pipes are the only pipes to have that facility. Even since then keys have been added so you can get a chromatic scale, although, I must admit, it isn't that easily accessible.'

And if Liam O'Flynn finds it tricky, you can bet your bottom dollar the development of the instrument has come to the end of its road. Which is no bad thing, for of all the various pipe variations around Europe – Northumbrian pipes in England, war pipes and Border pipes in Scotland, Galician pipes in Spain, the binou in France – the uilleann pipes are the most notoriously complex. Is that not so, Liam?

'It would seem to be!' he says, with impish glee. 'There are three parts to the pipes – the chanter which produces the tune, the drones which are sounding all the time and the regulators – and you've seven reeds altogether. Sometimes, in, say, a slow air, you might decide to use only one drone but almost always it's all three. The regulators are the keys you operate with your wrist for harmonies and chords – they're like closed-off chanters.'

Plus, amidst all that devilish dexterity, having to operate a bellows in tandem with your right elbow – no mean feat. And a curious looking beast, too: 'Yes,' says Liam, 'imagine during the eighteenth century, when it was still largely unknown to people, some fellow arriving along with this extraordinary contraption with its own built-in accompaniment. It's bound to have created some impression. Added to which, a piper's arrival in an area was a big deal in those days – not just because they were entertainers but because they were news-gatherers.'

He may be the inheritor of a grand and rarefied tradition but, of course, nowadays, no one would expect Liam O'Flynn to turn up and read a bulletin of current affairs before his show. If they did, they'd be disappointed. But he has, in a sense, consistently managed to make the news himself by simply being there at the cutting edge of traditional music's progress through the modern era. His very first recording, in 1971, was on a Christy Moore album called *Prosperous*. It was an album which launched not only his own career but the international reputation of Christy Moore, the instantly popular and seminal folk group Planxty – which featured Moore, O'Flynn and the other *Prosperous* musicians, Donal Lunny and Andy Irvine – and the Tara record label itself. It was a record that influenced a generation, and was one of the first to set the pipes alongside vocals, guitars and the like. Clancy, Rowsome and Ennis may have kept the instrument alive in the preceding years but when the history books are written it will turn out to be Liam O'Flynn who reintroduced it to the masses: 'Yeah, they reckon there's more young people playing pipes now than ever really,' he says, moving onto a second cappuccino. 'There's been a huge growth in interest in the instrument, especially considering that 40 or 50 years ago it nearly died out. A handful of musicians kept the thing going. What's really fantastic now is when people come up to you and say, "You were the first person who introduced me to the sound of the pipes." That's a wonderful compliment. And, I have to say, it happens quite a lot.'

While the other members of Planxty discovered traditional music through latter-day curiosity, O'Flynn had enjoyed a more leisurely route: 'I was born into it,' he says, 'through my parents' interest – County Clare on my mother's side, County Kerry on my father's side. My father played the fiddle and he had a very good friend who was a piper and they often played together for fun. So from my earliest memory of the instrument I thought, That's the instrument I want to play. My father knew Leo Rowsome very well, so Leo made me my first practise set and it went on from there. I still play a set of Leo Rowsome pipes.'

Liam's interest in the music took him to sessions around Kildare and into Dublin, but it was in a little village called Prosperous that the idea for, first, a collaborative album based around Christy Moore and, subsequently, a group called Planxty came about: 'Christy was working on the folk-club circuit in England,' says Liam, 'and contacted myself, Donal Lunny and Andy Irvine to work on an album that he wanted to make in Ireland. And because it worked really well, for whatever reason, everyone involved was really anxious to carry it on, so we formed the band. Christy and Donal are from Newbridge in County Kildare, which is about eight miles from where I'm from originally. Growing up we didn't have any contact at all, but there was a little pocket of musical activity centred around this village called Prosperous nearby, and in later years a gang of us used to meet there every Wednesday evening – sometimes Christy would be there, sometimes Donal – so that's how we all knew each other.

'Right from day one Planxty had its own particular sound. It wouldn't have been the first folk band with pipes – you had The McPeakes and The Fureys using pipes and guitars and so on – but in Planxty we were quite sure what we wanted to do from the start. The really powerful, unique thing in the band was the way in which we approached accompaniment – accompanying songs and tunes. It sounds simple when you listen to it but it was really quite complex, with these lines from Donal and Andy weaving together, and it's still something that isn't easily imitated.'

Planxty recorded three albums in their original lifespan between 1972 and 1975 – Planxty (1972), The Well Below The Valley (1973) and Cold Blow And The Rainy Night (1974) – followed by a four-year sojourn before coming back, on Tara, with After The Break (1978) and The Woman I Loved So Well (1980), and finally Words And Music (WEA, 1982), after which its members moved on amicably to other musical avenues of adventure. Not the least adventurous of these avenues was that which presented itself to the band's least obviously adventurous member, Liam O'Flynn. Shaun Davey, at that time a composer of music for radio and TV advertising jingles, had been an admirer of Planxty and had also been involved in songwriting and production work on the Irish folk scene. By the time Planxty finally went their separate ways, he had cooked up an idea to write, by combination of commission and labour of love, The Brendan Voyage

– a ground-breaking descriptive work for orchestra and pipes based on a recent recreation of St Brendan's legendary sea crossing to America. It was a high-risk venture, but it would turn out to be the start of an ongoing, challenging and immensely fruitful relationship for both of them that has continued on through further recorded works like *Granuaile* (1985) and *The Pilgrim* (1984; 1992): 'It's an amazing coincidence,' says Liam, 'in that Planxty disbanded and I immediately found myself going in a new musical direction with Shaun's orchestral work. I had a basic knowledge of theory before working with Shaun but I would never be comfortable having to perform music and reading it at the same time. Coming from the tradition, you learn music by heart so I would only be comfortable with these pieces once I'd committed them to memory and had a bloody good idea what the orchestra were up to as well!'

The new fusion of orchestra and pipes, and the worldwide opportunities that have opened up for Liam to take the piece to international festivals – including stints with the Montreal Symphony Orchestra in 1984 and 1985 – have almost recreated the sense of awe with which rural Irish folk would have greeted a travelling piper in the last century: 'Every new territory I go into with the piece,' says Liam, 'people are amazed by this new "creature", as it were.

Planxty, early Seventies:
(l–r) Donal Lunny, Andy Irvine,
Liam O'Flynn, Christy Moore

But the whole concept of *The Brendan Voyage* was wonderful, with the pipes telling the story of this little boat and the orchestra telling the story of what the little boat encountered. It was a ground-breaking piece, for sure, and it seems to me, as time passes, that the impact it made is an ongoing thing. But right from the start Shaun was very much in love with the sound of the pipes, and when he first approached me with the idea of writing a piece of music for them based on the Brendan voyage we sat down and discussed the instrument, its strengths and the difficulties that a composer would come up against.

'During the whole process of the writing of *The Brendan Voyage* Shaun learned very well indeed, as he says himself, the "inner workings of the instrument" – what was possible and what wasn't. Actually, one of the biggest difficulties I found with the piece wasn't a musical thing, it was finding oneself within a totally different performing environment. The formality of the concert hall, an absolutely quiet audience out there in front of you – that puts some pressure on a traditional musician. So far I've managed to get away with it!'

Admirably so. And is the piece still its composer's key work? 'Well, it was written for me and the uilleann pipes,' says Liam, unsuccessfully containing a chuckle – 'Of course it is!' Davey's most recent works have moved away from the pipes, although the earlier works are still performed on demand. But the Davey/O'Flynn collaboration is still going strong. Liam has recorded two superb solo albums for Tara recently – *Out To An Other Side* (1993) and *The Given Note* (1995) – and both have featured substantial contributions in terms of material, arrangement and production from Shaun Davey.

'There's a lot of Shaun Davey on *Out To An Other Side*,' says Liam, 'because of the arrangements, because we used a little core of orchestral players there. "The Fox Chase", for instance, is the only full-length descriptive piece that's now extant in the piping tradition and I remember about two years before we went into the studio saying to Shaun that I felt it would lend itself really well to the kind of orchestral arrangement that he could give it. The other traditional pieces on that album came largely from my own repertoire and they were complemented by other Shaun Davey pieces on there, so it's a broadly based album. The slower tunes on that album pointed me in the direction of the next one, so when I came to record *The Given Note* I had very clear ideas about how I wanted it to sound.'

The Given Note has indeed marked a significant progression for Liam within the same broad area of sound. The album features a small core of musicians – Rod McVey, Arty McGlynn and additional guitarist/bassist Steve Cooney – plus guest vocalists Andy Irvine and Paul Brady, contributing a song each, and two sets of tunes with members of Galician piping group, Milladoiro. Once again, with Shaun Davey producing, the sound is luxuriant and the arrangements second to none: 'Sometimes it comes together in the studio,' says Liam, on the process of arranging, 'or sometimes we'd meet up in advance, or send the tunes to the musicians and let them become familiar with them and then we'd fire ideas around in the studio from that. For example, Paul Brady's guest spot on the album with "The Rocks Of Bawn" – I wanted Brady on it because I just love his style of singing and knew it would suit the kind of album I was after and, also, although we'd played together in a version of Planxty, we'd never recorded together before. So we all arrived in the studio, sat down and the thing literally happened – and you can sense that, I think, in the recording. "O'Farrell's Farewell To Limerick" which opens the album was another one that pretty much happened on the spur of the moment. We hadn't actually planned on recording it but it got mentioned in the studio. I had flat pipes with me at the time and started playing around with the tune because I figured it would be really nice on flat pipes, plus Steve's open-tuned bass gives it a lovely, original sound.'

Flat pipes? Just when one had got a handle on the instrument along comes another complication: 'Well, the pipes I mostly play are concert-pitch pipes,' says Liam. 'The keys you can play in there are D, G, A minor and E minor but the bottom note is D above middle C. There are other sorts of pipes that come under the heading "flat pipes" – they're flat, or below concert pitch, and they can be in almost any key. In fact, in the last century pipe makers were almost exclusively making low-pitch pipes and they have a different sound – more mellow, quiet, sweet-toned instruments. Séamus Ennis recorded with those sort of pipes. The concert-pitch pipes are more strident and were developed in America by the Taylor brothers, who came from Drogheda originally. There was a need in America, I think, for a louder instrument because of the size of the concert halls.'

Which Liam, with the benefit of modern amplification, will be comfortably filling very soon, regardless of the nature, variety, tonality and size of his instrument. If it's got a bellows, a bunch of keys and a rack of fine cylinders protruding from it at disparate angles, chances are Liam O'Flynn can make it sound like a chorus of sirens on a windswept isle. He's a living legend, he's nothing left to prove, and with *The Given Note* he's just made the ultimate record of his career. So how on earth is he going to follow it? 'Well,' he says, draining an umpteenth cappuccino (while the boss of his record company double-checks the bill), 'John Cook seems to be reasonably happy with it, so we're going to make another one that he's also reasonably happy with!'

Postscript: *The Piper's Call*, the follow-up to *The Given Note*, was released in 1997.

STOCKTON'S WING

Their career has had its ups and downs of late, including the departure of long-time frontman Mike Hanrahan, but the new album from Irish traditional legends Stockton's Wing, entitled *Letting Go*, is very possibly their best work to date and testifies to the strength of character and ideas within their ranks. A great deal of credit for this new lease of life must go to the instantly likeable new 'Wing commander', Eamon McElholm. McElholm is an award-winning twenty-something from an outlying area of Omagh, County Tyrone, which is, itself, an outlying area of everywhere else in Northern Ireland. A hotbed of traditional music, Eamon? 'Well, I wouldn't say it's 100 per cent healthy, but it's healthy-ish, and there's a few people living about here might surprise you – people like Arty McGlynn, the fiddle player out of Dervish, the fiddle player out of Four Men & A Dog . . . So there's a few of us about!' Sounds pretty healthy to me.

So first the important stuff: that name. What on earth *is* a Stockton's Wing, Eamon? 'Apparently it's a beach in New Jersey,' he says, with mildly anti-climactic mystery-solving satisfaction. 'I think it's mentioned on the first Bruce Springsteen album. But I always thought it was a bird or something. I remember the first month I was with the band we were away somewhere and some foreign journalist asked me what a Stockton was. I'd no idea, I had to go and ask the boys.'

That first month was just two years ago – a blink in the eye of the band's seventeen-year history – but the Eamon McElholm story starts somewhere in between. Let's take 1990, for instance: 'Well, I was finishing grammar school in Omagh and Fuji were promoting a *Rock School* competition, open to school bands across the UK. I wanted to enter the competition but I couldn't get a band together from the school so I did it solo. I was the only solo artist in it, which was a bit daunting.'

And, of course, he won it. And then the bright lights beckoned: 'It worked out very well actually, because, in fact, the day after I finished my A levels I flew off to appear on Sky TV. I found myself doing a lot of TV work then – mostly children's television stuff with Anthea Turner, Michaela Strachan, Timmy Mallett, people like that – and that led to a lot of radio work as well. I met a lot of people in London and was offered a few small record deals, but nothing I decided to go for. People were wanting to turn me into a pop singer and I wasn't really into it at that stage. I was influenced by stuff like Bruce Hornsby, Jackson Browne and Van Morrison but I was always very much involved in the traditional scene as well.'

Colin Harper · Originally published in the *Irish News* (17 April 1996) and *Folk Roots* (July 1996)

McElholm wisely invested his time in a Salford University degree course in popular music and recording, the patron of which was Beatles producer George Martin and, once again, there was something to win with the name Eamon McElholm written all over it: 'George had established a John Lennon Songwriter's Award in association with the Performing Rights Society which was open to music students around Britain, and I was lucky enough to win it that year.'

That year being 1991. So what happened next – the Eurovision Song Contest? 'Well, I was doing a lot of work as a solo performer but, because I was doing this degree course at the time, I couldn't take it too seriously – couldn't be slipping off *every* week! But I was involved with a traditional act called Upstairs In A Tent for a while, with people like Eoghan O'Brien from Déanta and Stephen Hayden, brother of Cathal from Four Men & A Dog. I played on and off with the Tent for about eighteen months, although there were a couple of tours of Scandinavia I couldn't do because of exams and so on. There was record-company interest in the band but I didn't feel the line-up was stable enough to record an album and I didn't think there was enough money on the table to do it properly, so I finished with them in January '94, finished my degree in June '94 and joined Stockton's Wing four days later!'

The man has clearly had a ridiculous amount of good fortune. Singer-songwriter Mike Hanrahan had just left the band to pursue a solo career, with which he's currently very happy, and Eamon was recommended to the remaining members by Ron Walsh, a mutual friend at a music agency: 'Ron gave me a call and I met the boys over in Dublin about a week later, played a few tunes together, sang a few songs . . .' Hindsight is all very well – with a killer album hitting the shelves eighteen months later and the band's credibility back on an upward curve – but McElholm didn't land on a gravy train at the time. He had to rewrite the recipe for the gravy: 'I was certainly aware their career had faltered a bit,' he admits, 'but they were very determined to re-establish themselves. I think it was all down to financial matters. At one stage there were ten or eleven people involved, with two trucks on the road constantly, doing massive gigs all over America with Frank Sinatra and Michael Jackson. It was just a financial strain, really. The new deal with Tara Records was already on the cards when I joined. I don't know if my joining actually sealed it, but I know that Tara were very happy with the songs.'

The label's belief in the band was based on little more than Tara supremo John Cook's instinct, given the disappointing sales of *The Crooked Rose* album in 1992. Around that time the band had honed itself down to an acoustic four-piece, but it was clearly time for a completely fresh approach or nothing at all. There followed a period so bereft of Wing activity that, as founder member Maurice Lennon puts it, the band had virtually died. But the decision to disappear for a while turned out to be the saving of the band. Once McElholm was firmly on board, the Wing rehearsed solidly for six months, with the odd gig now and then, and crafted the raw material for their most awesome recording yet.

The resulting album, *Letting Go*, was brilliantly produced by *Brendan Voyage* composer Shaun Davey who fine-tuned the Wing's already complex arrangements into something the band themselves regard as being the closest they've come to the sound they originally set out to achieve. It features six of McElholm's most memorable songs alongside five highly impressive and mostly original instrumental pieces, in classic Wing style. The new music is currently being featured in a thoroughly recharged live act involving a six-piece electric version of the line-up: Maurice Lennon on fiddle/vocals, Paul Roche on flute/vocals, Davy McNevin on banjo/mandolin, McElholm on vocals and guitar, plus a rhythm section. With McElholm's magic touch the new album has, of course, already won an award, this time from the *Irish World* newspaper. The band are working towards another album sooner rather than later, and McElholm isn't ruling out the possibility of a solo album. He can no doubt find, after all, a bit of space on that increasingly crowded mantelpiece for a Brit Award, an Ivor Novello and the odd gold disc. In the meantime, the Wing are flying higher than ever and will be doing so around Britain two or three times before the year is out.

STOCKTON'S WING
EMPIRE MUSIC HALL, BELFAST

Three years ago, Stockton's Wing – a respected but, through an ongoing dalliance with drum kits, not universally revered name on the Irish traditional scene – were hanging on for dear life. Although the professional lifespan of trad acts is closer to that of jazz (where age improves) than rock (where people sell lots of records today and disappear tomorrow), consumer boundaries are blurring and the marketplace will no longer tolerate complacency.

Stockton's Wing (their name plucked from a lyric on a Bruce Springsteen album) had reached that point. That they have managed to turn their critical and commercial fortunes around through sheer hard work and the finest record of a seventeen-year career with the recent *Letting Go* is testament to both exceptional grit and enduring quality. The new energy, evidenced by a thrilling, occasionally incendiary performance at the Belfast Empire, is also to do with changes in personnel. Paul Roche, on flute/whistles, and Maurice Lennon, on fiddle, are all that remain from the original line-up, but they were, and are, the group's key players.

In 1993 Mike Hanrahan, writer and singer of the group's best-known Irish hit single, 'Walk Away', did just that. Other bands would have pulled down the curtain on a respectable career – one that had seen guest spots at Irish concerts by Michael Jackson and Frank Sinatra – but Lennon's unbelievable enthusiasm kept the spirit alive long enough to find a replacement in twenty-something former UK *Rock School* winner, Eamon McElholm. The reinvigoration that he brought has become a sight to behold.

A couple of the Hanrahan songs, obvious crowd-pleasers, were played at the Empire along with a fair smattering of tunes from the group's instrumental back-pages – many of them sets of 'genuine' trad tunes appended with fiery originals in similar style – but the core of the show is McElholm's own songs, from the current album and, presumably, from the next.

A distant cousin of Paul Brady, McElholm's style is similar but fresher and more contemporary in feel. The juxtaposition of rock and folk – with a sheen of class that is missing from most folk-rock acts, as such – has been the Wing's trademark for years. Wonderful, substantial songs like 'Home', 'Anybody Out There' and 'Letting Go' fit perfectly with instrumental work-outs, from the riotous 'Skidoo' (a favourite encore based on the riff from Queen's 'Another One Bites The Dust') to the elegiac and as yet unrecorded Lennon original, 'If Ever You Were Mine'.

The chemistry and contrast between the three frontmen is exceptional:

Colin Harper · Concert review originally published in the *Independent* (3 September 1996)

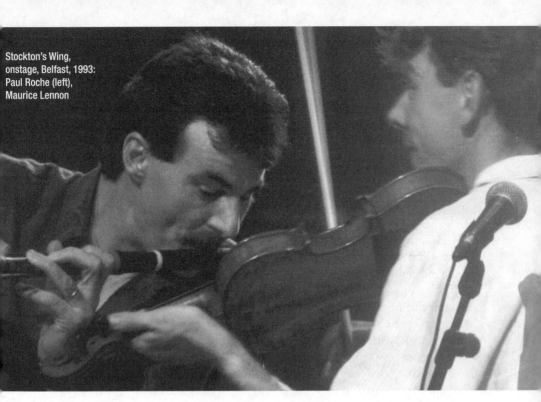

Stockton's Wing, onstage, Belfast, 1993: Paul Roche (left), Maurice Lennon

Roche, a six-foot-six Christy-Moore-meets-Jethro-Tull character, cheerleading with wry banter and wild gestures; Lennon, a mad professor, his mischievous grin and machine-gun eye-contact pushing everyone else to dizzier heights; McElholm, the clad-in-black rock star with sensitive songs and blistering acoustic-guitar technique. With rhythm section in tow, it was an exhilarating, explosive combination.

MAURICE LENNON
RETURN OF THE KING

There was a period in the mid-Nineties, around the release of their fabulous album *Letting Go*, where I seemed to be spending a lot of time with Stockton's Wing – indeed, it was a tremendous joy to me, as a punter, to be able to see the band many times over the course of an eight or ten-week residency at Belfast's Empire Music Hall during the summer of 1996. It was also a telling insight into how much the available energy and inspiration of one member, Maurice Lennon, on a given day could raise the performance from perfunctory – which, with a band that good, was always going to be perfectly acceptable to most people in the audience – to sensational.

Looking back during the work on this book it suddenly struck that I didn't first encounter Stockton's Wing during that period as I'd always thought – I had, in fact, first seen them towards the end of their period with Mike Hanrahan, at a show somewhere in Derry with Óige. I can also recall asking Óige's fiddler, Ruairí Ó Catháin, whether the bloke at the front with the guitar was the main-man. 'No,' said Ruairí, pointing at Maurice Lennon. 'That's the main-man!' While I came to know Stockton's Wing a few years after that primarily through their new singer and songwriter, Eamon McElholm, I soon came to realise that onstage Maurice Lennon was indeed the man with the gear-lever. If Maurice was on form, you could bet your bottom dollar that you were going to see the best gig in Ireland that night.

And offstage, when Maurice was on form, you could be sure the *craic* would be pretty close to ninety. I recall, particularly, the band, myself and a few camp followers gathering for an after-show drink at the band's hotel on Botanic Avenue – a hotel which seemed to have employed, as night porter, somebody whose attitude to residents was straight out of the Basil Fawlty book of social graces. For a prolonged period, it seemed – and this could be a somewhat caricatured memory – this man and Maurice were pursuing each other round the hotel, *circa* two in the morning, with the porter making snide remarks about the quality of customers these days and the likelihood of anyone receiving drinks, and Maurice politely yet doggedly requiring not only a round of drinks but some sort of apology. After a while Maurice, still without drinks, rejoined us in the lounge and, when the approaching footsteps of his adversary could be heard, said, 'Watch this . . .' and proceeded to regale the company with an ostentatiously loud anecdote about the time he met Frank Sinatra – as if Frank was his best pal and, for all the night porter knew, may be popping in for a nightcap himself at any minute. Remarkably, the level of service improved significantly after that.

Colin Harper · Previously unpublished, from an interview in Dundalk (February 2003)

And then – suddenly, it seemed – things went silent on the Stockton's front. A very radio-friendly non-album single, written by Eamon, had been recorded by the group although John Cook, having sounded out the likelihood of various Dublin DJs giving it airtime, opted not to release it. A certain amount of wind went out of the sails at that point. But there were also differences of opinion within the group on how best to move things forward. Maurice took ill and after a while odd bookings as Stockton's Wing were being undertaken without him. In the short term this seemed understandable although even now, during the period of working on this book (late 2002, early 2003), there continue to be periodic festival appearances by some version of 'Stockton's Wing' – based around Paul Roche, Eamon McElholm and Davy McNevin plus whoever else is available that week as fiddler and rhythm section. Fair enough, musicians have to eat – but this lingering, ad hoc afterlife for such a dedicated and distinctive group seems, at best, unlikely to further their reputation.

It was, however, a thrill to hear from Eamon McElholm, just as the finishing touches were being put on this volume, with news of his own plans and recent activities. Towards the end of 2002 Eamon filled an eleventh-hour breach as guitarist in highly regarded traditional group Solas, consequently enjoying a US tour and gladly accepting further work with the group as and when it's been offered. Also during 2002 – in between that work with Solas, duo work with fiddler Desi Donnelly (which has been his bread-and-butter work in recent years) and odd resurrections of the Wing – he finally completed a bona fide solo album, the release of which, this year (2003), he plans to make a priority. As Maurice says, his name may yet be in lights. And as with the name of Maurice Lennon himself, it certainly deserves no less.

Maurice, tell me about the end of your involvement with Stockton's Wing – it seems as if the group resurrected itself with the Letting Go *album in 1995 and then imploded a year or so later.*
Letting Go was a seriously good album, and it still *is* a seriously good album. Stockton's Wing is made up of a group of people and after twenty-odd years . . . We did well to hang in there for as long as we did, really. But Stockton's Wing was my life, it was everything for me. Unfortunately I became ill and spent about four months in hospital. Really, my commitment to the band had taken so much out of me that I had to pull out. I was in too deep. An unbelievably difficult thing to do. I didn't want to do it and yet I realised that it was the best thing that I could do for myself and for all those around me.
Was there a 'last gig' as such?
No, because the illness came upon me really very rapidly so I didn't have time to think about it. I didn't know where I was – other people had to look after me. That's how sick I became. But a lot of that was from pressure, really, because the illness hasn't recurred since then.
And now, several years on, you've come back with a really ambitious project – a concept album about Brian Boru.

I love a challenge – and this whole album was a massive challenge! I approached [guitarist] Anto Drennan with a view to doing the album together but he couldn't give me the commitment that I wanted. I had planned, maybe, that we would write it together. But he says, 'Look, you just go away and write it, bring it back to me and I'll play it.' So I went away and wrote all the music. He's just so busy all the time but he's a really good guy. We're kindred spirits, really. Initially, once the studio work began, myself and Greg Boland [ex-Scullion] were working on it together. I took Greg on as a producer but it was heading in a direction I didn't want it to go. It was almost a Moving Hearts direction – odd rhythms, odd this, that and the other. I wanted it straight down the line. I didn't want there to be any confusion in people's minds about this music. So I got Donal Lunny in to 'root' it – I needed to root it, badly. I could have done that in a certain way myself but I think it's always better, with a big project like this, to take someone from the outside who doesn't have any preset ideas or agendas. I was bold enough to approach Donal and ask if there was any chance he could think back to some of his production techniques with Planxty. I asked him, about a month before we started work on it, to think back to that work, to approach this music in a different light [from his current approach to production]. Actually, I snookered him accidentally – I was going down to record with John Prine in Galway, for a Sharon Shannon album, and I was giving Donal a lift. So I said, 'Have a listen to this for me, will you – tell me what you think of it.' He listened to it and said, 'Put it on again there . . .' It was five already recorded tracks, pretty much finished. So I asked Donal would he like to become involved.

How did Greg feel about relinquishing control?

Ultimately, the decision to change producer was not my call. The record company were very worried about the slowness of the progress and that's what brought about the change in production. Donal's a very safe pair of hands. He's clever and he's very, very subtle. OK, it took a while to come together but when it came together I thought it was well worth it and it will stand up for a long time to come.

So – neither jazz-folk like Moving Hearts nor folk-rock like Horslips.

No! Really, the only link that I would see – though I really liked some of the early Horslips material – would be the electric guitar. And, yes, I suppose they did do a version of 'Brian Boru's March'. Essentially, it's a suite of music for electric guitar and violin whereby the electric guitar, to me, represents the spirit of the land – Ireland – and the violin represents the spirit of Brian Boru, Ireland's king. There are battles between the two instruments at different points. It's like a musical conversation between Anthony Drennan and myself, accompanied by another fifteen of the best musicians I could possibly find.

The sleeve-notes are very extensive and myself and [author] Morgan Llywelyn worked very hard on them. And I'm very proud to say that when she heard the thing first it brought tears to her eyes – because she could sense the spirit of Brian Boru in it. What I did was give everybody in the studio a sheet of paper with the sleeve-notes in relation to each track and I'd have them read it. It was like painting a picture, and me saying 'This is the way we're going to paint it.' There's a track called 'Stone Of Destiny', a reel, and we were going to play it maybe three or four times and it was only going to be three minutes long. Now, on the third time through Donal looks at me and I look at him and he looks at Anto and Anto's looking at somebody else and we're all jamming away, having a great time – and the track ends up at six minutes! Just a groove, answering each other with notes and that's the type of album it is – a musical conversation piece.

'Kincora', your own spoken-word epilogue to the album, is very powerful.

Thank you. It gave me an idea for an album, down the road, of choosing pieces of poetry, reciting the poems and writing the music behind them. That's something I'd like to do. As it is, the live show for *Brian Boru* features narration between each piece of music, depicting the scenes. Strictly speaking, it's a shortened version of the sleeve-notes.

There's a very lyrical side to your playing – though not so prominent on this album, which is more triumphant in feeling. I particularly recall one of your unrecorded tunes at the end of the Stockton's Wing era, 'If Ever You Were Mine'.

That's still doing the rounds. Cherish The Ladies have recorded it. And it was also recorded by Natalie McMaster and the Nova Scotia Symphony Orchestra – and I've never recorded it myself! It's an awesome version – a 50-piece orchestra. Not even John Cook's budgets would stretch to that!

John tells me the album took much longer to record than planned.

Because of the people. There was a little bit of going in the wrong direction at first but getting Anto, Donal and Noel Eccles was a huge difficulty. Anto was working with The Corrs, Noel Eccles was away with *Riverdance*, Donal was doing his own thing with Coolfin at the time . . . Trying to get them all in the one place at the same time was difficult! Donal was working on Christy Moore's album the same time he was working on mine, and his involvement in Sinéad O'Connor's album followed very quickly after that.'

Have you ever been tempted to get involved in Riverdance?

If I was 22 and able to wear a mini-skirt I'd probably have every chance of becoming involved! What I am doing at the moment, though, is acting as musical director for a show in Dublin called *Ragus*, running eleven weeks at the Olympia this summer. We did it last summer for nine weeks and sold out most nights. The story is based around the Aran Islands and its people. The fellow who wrote it is Fergal Ó Murchú – an awesome traditional singer. He came to me a couple of years back. The show was to run at Vicar Street and they needed radical work on musical arrangements. So I produced the album of the show for them and remained as musical adviser. It's lovely to be in Dublin for the summer. I'm toing and froing right now between the Midwest, Chicago, and Dublin.

Presumably you have a view to building something in the US with the Brian Boru *show?*

Indeed. I put on a performance of *Brian Boru* at the Irish-American Heritage Centre in Chicago [in early 2003] – a Sunday-afternoon concert and we had 300 people at it, so there is an interest there. It was a benefit concert for the Heritage Centre library so financially it wasn't a great gain for me but it was an effective way to get the material across to people.

Are you having to take on more mundane work as a musician while developing opportunities for the Brian Boru *show?*

Oh, absolutely. I do that every day of the week. I spent two years with [Galway singer and flautist] Seán Keane recently, which was a fantastic experience. It was a very good discipline. First of all, it's Seán's name on the door [rather than mine] . . . And when it was whittled down to a three-piece the room for error was gone. When it was a big band [of six people] that was an even bigger challenge and I loved that. My role was to stay out of his way and yet enhance what he was doing. But when it became a three-piece – Pete O'Hanlon on guitar, Seán and myself – that was very sweet. It was an unusual line-up but it worked very well. You won't find a better voice in Ireland. He's an awesome singer. I was still working with Seán when we recorded the *Brian Boru* album, so it worked out very well. He asked me to record on his last album but I couldn't do it because I was going away. Working with Seán gave me a great advantage in terms of being able to back the songs for the stage production [*Ragus*] – doing nice, intricate-sounding but very simple arrangements.

What is your ideal for the Brian Boru *project?*

My ideal is to see this put on stage in New York – though it doesn't necessarily have to be me playing it. I need to stick with this and see it through for another couple of years at least.

Almost like a Shaun Davey project then. Of course, it took Shaun a while to establish The Brendan Voyage.

Yes, it didn't happen overnight. It took *The Brendan Voyage* five or six years before it really took off worldwide. It took off in Ireland very fast because it was so unusual, with the pipes and orchestra. I still consider it one of Shaun's best works.

Has Shaun Davey influenced you in any way?

No, I'd have to say not – though his compliments on my viola playing were really fantastic! We remain good friends, of course. Working with Shaun though, funnily enough, was helpful to me because Shaun Davey likes to create a picture – so I'll have to correct myself in that, yes, he influenced me in that regard because I also wanted to paint a picture with the *Brian Boru* album. When you're in the studio with Shaun Davey and you close your eyes you've got to see the picture – that's the way he works. And that's the way I approached this with Donal.

Your playing and sound on Brian Boru *strikes me as more in the Tommy Peoples style than say the sweeter Kevin Burke/Martin Hayes style.*

It's extraordinary you should mention that because I've discovered recently that for me less is actually best. I used to think before that more was best. But unfortunately flash is also cash.

Yet surely the popularity of Martin Hayes & Dennis Cahill disproves that?

But Martin is an extraordinary fiddle player – his musicianship is just extraordinary. Actually, when I put on the *Brian Boru* show in Chicago it was with a five-piece band which included Dennis Cahill. He had the music on the nail, had it down – and he was a great help to me when we performed it there.

It would be understandable for someone in your position, having to rebuild an international career, to be envious of Martin's position.

Sure. I mean, I would love to be where he is – absolutely, no question. But I'm not jealous at all. What I have is a God-given gift to play music and I can use that or abuse it. And I want to use it. I feel that, to a degree, over the years, that maybe I abused the music in Stockton's Wing. Some of it was good but some of it wasn't.

Looking at Stockton's Wing's early publicity photos it looks like you were trying to be a pop group.

Absolutely, we were. That was our mistake and that was our downfall. Some people would say that was our success, but it was our downfall. I heard Mike Hanrahan on a talk show recently saying that if it wasn't for songs like 'Beautiful Affair' and 'Walk Away' Stockton's Wing wouldn't have been as big as they were – and I couldn't disagree more. I really believe that Stockton's Wing became what they were because primarily we were awesome traditional musicians who had just won All-Ireland titles and everybody wanted to know about us. The fact that the songs were successful was a massive bonus, but I believe we would have reached that level anyway.

I understand the Stockton's Wing touring operation in the States during your period of early success was a strain on resources.

It was a loss-making effort. There was another way of doing it, of course, but we made the really bad mistake of thinking that bigger is always better. Whereas with *Brian Boru* I really feel that I can perform this album with two people or with twenty. Because it's the spirit of the music, essentially, that I'm trying to get across. I could sit down with somebody like Dennis Cahill and do it like that, on my own – OK, I'd love to have everyone else around me but if I had to, that's what I'd do. I did one of the tracks on a television programme recently with Eamon McElholm and it sounded huge. So I'm very open-minded about it and I can choose musicians in the countries that I go to, if they're good enough and if they're available.'

Would you agree with me that Eamon is still an unfulfilled talent?

Absolutely. I'd love to work with Eamon again. I really think he should take the bull by the horns. But it can be very difficult for a singer-songwriter. Give him a bit of time. His name will be up in lights yet.

There was talk of a duo album with [Stockton's Wing flautist] Paul Roche around the Letting Go *period – did that fall by the wayside?*

It did. That won't happen. But I'd love to do just a traditional album – just do it and fire it out there. Also, there's a distinctive sound to the *Brian Boru* album,

Maurice Lennon,
1995

and it would be lovely to put a band together to do another album with that
'sound'. But I also feel that I want people to hear my music on a solo basis also.
So there's a lot of contrasting possibilities and a lot of people giving me ideas.
*As a touring Irish musician is it better or worse now than it was in the late
Seventies and Eighties?*
Better *and* worse! Better in the sense that you've more venues now – lovely
little theatres dotted all over the country – and yet you have a radio policy that
is really deplorable in my opinion. The problem is that radio stations [in
Ireland] are supposed to play a certain percentage of Irish music, but it's the
same people all the time. In fairness, U2 are an Irish band – but they're going
to be playing U2 anyway, because they're also a world band. It feels like people
are missing out. I mean, I'm not the biggest ballad lover in the world but there
is absolutely nothing at all for ballad singers today. Luke Kelly was an awesome
singer and, I don't care what anybody says, Ronnie Drew is an awesome singer
– and there's no airplay for the likes of those people.
Are you hoping to take Brian Boru *to folk festivals or have you more presti-
gious concert venues in mind?*
I would love to do the folk festivals because I want to bring the music to the
people – and that's what I do best. Put me on a stage, put a fiddle in my hand

and I'm not the same person as you're speaking to now! A different human being!
You take wings?
I do actually, and I can fly off to strange places . . .
This reminds me of what people have said about Rory Gallagher: energised onstage, but shy, lacking confidence and prone to phobias offstage – like two different people.
I can relate to that one million per cent. I knew Rory and had many conversations with him at the Irish Centre in London, which he used to frequent. We would never have gotten that deep into things but I could certainly relate to him. And yes, I am that 'other person' for 22 hours of the day. But when I go onstage I have my little angels which I call upon.
Rory once said that he had to connect with some kind of darkness to give a true performance of rock 'n' roll – would you say the same of your approach to traditional music?
Oh God, yeah. I have been on that edge. I have stood in front of people and played and thought that my whole world was just going to fall apart absolutely – and yet none of those people would have known that. They would have just thought the gig was unbelievable. So you do go that far, you go right out to the edge and it's a very frightening place to be. You're holding a bow in your hand and you just don't know if you're going to drop it. Sometimes you can actually go that far. But I've a very strong faith and I've seven angels, mentioned in this album, and I call on them to come with me on the stage any time I perform, and they will inevitably be there when I need them.
You must get a lot of people asking you if Stockton's Wing will ever get back together?
It happens all the time. I just say, 'I don't know – I've nothing to do with it, I left it five years ago and I just don't know!' And that's the truth. It's lovely to be recognised as part of Stockton's Wing because the band had such a great relationship with people generally, and had a really good name in that regard. And I'd like to see that 'name' continue in some way. Time will tell.

Postscript: Shortly after this interview took place Maurice was made an offer to reunite the original line-up of Stockton's Wing for a one-off summer festival at Lisdoonvarna. A year later, in May 2004, another one-off reunion was scheduled for Dublin's Vicar Street.

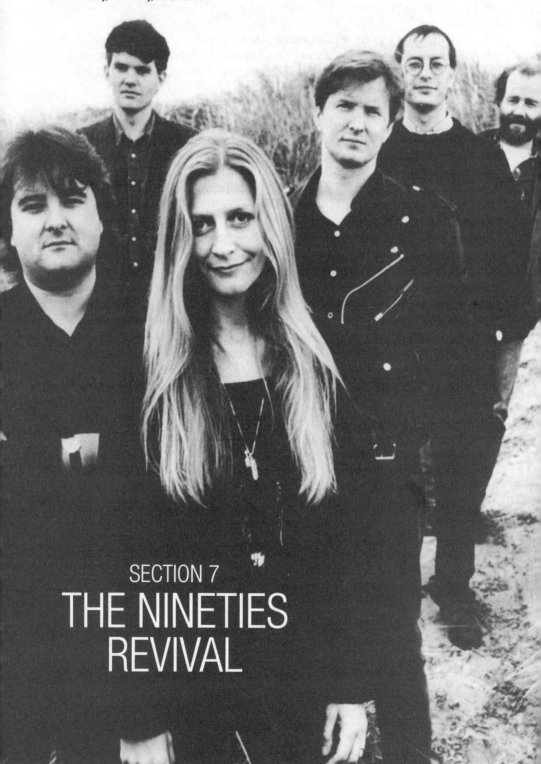

Altan, *c.* 1990: (l–r) Ciarán Tourish,
Paul O'Shaughnessy, Mairéad Ní Mhaonaigh,
Frankie Kennedy, Mark Kelly, Ciarán Curran

SECTION 7
THE NINETIES REVIVAL

ALTAN
PROLOGUE

I would never describe myself as an expert on Irish traditional music (and all that that implies – its history, its jargon, its etiquette and all the rest of it). All I am is knowledgeable (through time and effort) and appreciative (usually through instinct, sometimes effort) of a certain handful of artists who happen to be Irish traditional musicians. I could say the same thing in relation to progressive rock, jazz, fusion, blues, the English folk-baroque guitar school or any number of other little boxes of classification that, however invidious, are an essential tool in the world of music journalism and, if we're honest, in the way most of us think about and relate to music. There are people I know, for example, who would instinctively view anything that sounded 'diddly-dee' as being on exactly the same low level as everything else that sounded 'diddly-dee'. Maybe Altan had to deal with that kind of prejudice in their long haul towards mainstream acceptance. I'd be surprised if they didn't. But there would have been no better man than the late Frankie Kennedy to have done it. Frankie was a gentleman and a scholar, in the best sense of the words, and by great good fortune Altan's breakthrough into popular consciousness coincided with my own first steps as a professional music writer.

Having graduated in 1989, the next four to five years were a dismal catalogue of temporary contract admin jobs broken up with spells of unemployment. But it was also during that period – particularly during 1990 and 1991, before the joys of graduated freedom had devolved into the realisation that hope is, by and large, only there to be confounded – that I was putting in time on a planned biography of English jazz/folk ensemble Pentangle and enthusiastically travelling around the summer folk festivals at Ballyshannon, Glencolmcille, Galway and so forth. I had a certain amount of yearning (ultimately not enough when pitted against that mortal enemy of such whimsy, common sense) to be a performing musician and was keen to meet others in the trade.

Performances by Arcady, Déanta and finally Altan – who I first encountered, during that period, not in the west of Ireland but on a double bill with John Martyn at Belfast's Ulster Hall – made a great impact. I became friendly with Mary Dillon, the incredibly gifted singer with County Derry-based traditional group Déanta, and her husband Paul McLaughlin. It was largely through their friendship, and a vaguely involved association with Paul's own musical project, Óige, that I really got a feeling for how the Irish trad world operated.

By 1993, having filtered out whatever knowledge I had by then acquired

Colin Harper

on The Pentangle and their circle into various CD sleeve-notes, I had somehow become a reviewer for the cred new UK music monthly, *Q*. Within a few years the magazine had become a publication I just didn't want to be associated with, but for a while it was a terrific calling card and a good discipline in terms of learning the critical craft. John Aizlewood was reviews editor at that time and my having brazenly cold-called to tell him he needed *me* to write huge features on people like Bert Jansch spookily coincided with *him* feeling the need for someone to write a couple of CD reviews a month on folk music.

I was in. I was also in a terrible day job at the time – terrible in that it was the kind of day job which also involved night shifts, no prospects and miserable pay. *Q* reviews were often written at two in the morning until the thought, Why on earth am I doing this? gave way to the resolve that, having already one foot in a pretty impressive door, one could probably kick in enough others to actually make a living as a writer. I escaped in March 1994. Whatever the cash-flow headaches of the next seven years, I never doubted that I had made the right decision.

Most remarkably of all, that old line about editors needing me to write stuff about Bert Jansch kept delivering the goods – my first commissioned work for both *Mojo* (December 1993) and *The Irish Times* (March 1994) was, indeed, on Bert Jansch. Some people have been flattering enough to suggest that Bert owes much of his current standing to me – frankly, it's the other way round! Whatever the odds against it may have been, my entire writing career was, and remains, entirely founded on a bit of brass-necked bravado and a certain degree of expertise on a self-effacing singer-songwriter who had, at that particular juncture, been wildly off the radar of fashion for years.

Those first breaks gave me enough time and space to acquire, very quickly, some kind of expertise on other people and other music. When John Aizlewood asked me if I knew anything about folk music in general – well, I wasn't going to say no, was I? Looking back now over the work I did for various magazines and newspapers in those first few no-safety-net months of 1994 – when the great experiment of seeing whether the pen was indeed mightier than the mortgage began – it's clear that, Bert Jansch aside, Altan was my subject of choice. I was happily in a position to make their great album *Island Angel* one of *Q*'s 'albums of the year', and while I would review and interview the band several times over the next few years, at no time was my enthusiasm more intense than during what were to be the final few months leading up to the tragic death, in September 1994, of their founder, Frankie Kennedy.

I've enjoyed seeing Altan periodically since then, and *Blackwater*, their first recording after *Island Angel* and containing Mairéad's own beautiful tribute, 'A Tune For Frankie', was a wonderful way to move forward. But something about Altan in those days before the 'Virgin era' was truly inspirational. Maybe my own heightened adrenalin – to make this mad notion of writing about folk music for a living actually work – enhanced the experience. Then again, what we were all seeing then was still Frankie's own mad scheme – of giving up

Altan, onstage at the Olympia, Dublin, 1994:
Frankie Kennedy in the foreground

teaching to make a living at Irish traditional music when its first golden era, in the Seventies, seemed long gone and unrepeatable. There was surely some serious adrenalin flowing up there on the stage as well. Either way, who could have denied or begrudged the groundswell of goodwill, support and fervour that was becoming increasingly obvious around Altan in those days. It was their time and the time was right, and Frankie's band was the best of its kind. It was icing on the cake that as a human being he was also one of the best.

ALTAN
OLYMPIA THEATRE, DUBLIN

It's always difficult to convey in words the essence and appeal of music from the Irish tradition, but more so to share even a glimpse of what it was to have been there, midnight at the Olympia on Saturday 12 February 1994.

Altan play a music that has always been there and always will be, and it belongs to everyone on the island. This night was like a homecoming – a celebration of all that, and of Altan themselves. From small beginnings to sales, awards and accolades the world over with not one hint of hype or contrivance has not been an overnight thing. It's already a cliché to say it, but just like Clannad ten years ago Altan deserve every bit of their hard-won success, and that feeling was all but tangible in the electricity and warmth buzzing around the auditorium. Every box, tier and stall in the place was full to capacity, with more besides. Steve Cooney and Séamus Begley – the most fearsome act to follow in the whole country – opened the show at the crack of midnight with the universal language of jigs, reels and polkas played at impossible speeds, with Cooney's battered guitar firing murderous triplets and shifts in time at every turn.

When Altan appear the whole place is enraptured. There's Galway guitarist Mark Kelly, pacing stage-right with mad-librarian earnesty; Ciarán Curran on bouzouki, stage-left and statuesque; Dermot Byrne on accordion, Ciarán Tourish on fiddle – both hitting furious, sweatless velocity with the poise of Clint Eastwood; and Mairéad Ní Mhaonaigh, from Donegal, singer/second-fiddler, hair flying, laughing and joking (in English) between the timeless Irish-language love songs and spurring everyone on with an infectious energy. When flautist and founder member, from Belfast, Frankie Kennedy walks on in the middle of the fifth number – visibly weak from the awful effects of chemotherapy – the spontaneous ovation is deafening. We all want him to get better, we all want Altan to be massive – we want them to be *us* to the rest of the world. North and South, we were proud to be Irish, ecstatic just to be there and desperate to share it. They came back time and time again, and it just got further and further beyond the pen of even Joyce himself.

Colin Harper · Concert review originally published in *Mojo* (May 1994)

ALTAN
THE FRANKIE KENNEDY ERA

Back in 1970 a group of musicians from Donegal called Clannad won a prize in a talent contest: to make a record. They had to wait two years to collect, while the poor record company tried (unsuccessfully) to talk them out of singing the whole thing in Irish. Sure enough, it bombed, but a few years on and they were singing away in their mother tongue on *Top of the Pops*. Every generation, said Paul Simon, throws a hero up the pop charts. In Ireland, every generation throws up a focal point for the maintenance of its musical heritage, and sometimes they get to be the heroes in the pop charts, too. During the mid-Seventies Planxty, De Danann and The Bothy Band were the names to be reckoned with in Irish traditional music; twenty years later, in 1993, with *Island Angel* winning industry awards and storming the critics' polls on both sides of the Atlantic – and going on to rack up unheard-of sales of 50,000 within its first year – it was clear that Altan were their generation's saviours and heroes.

Formed around Belfast-born flautist Frankie Kennedy and singer and fiddler Mairéad Ní Mhaonaigh – Mairéad, like the members of Clannad, from the Irish-speaking Gweedore area of Donegal – the origins of Altan go a great deal further back than their first album proper, 1989's *Horse With A Heart*. Frankie and Mairéad, who were partners in life as well as music, had met aged fifteen and had attended teacher-training college together in Dublin during the late Seventies. Their first appearance on record was guesting on an eponymous album by one Albert Fry, recorded for Gael Linn in 1979. In 1981 the pair graduated and were married, teaching Irish for a living and playing the Dublin traditional-session scene with their part-time group Ragairne. Their first record, *Ceol Aduaigh* (meaning 'northern music'), appeared on Gael Linn in 1983, credited to 'Frankie Kennedy & Mairéad Ní Mhaonaigh' and was notable in featuring as a guest player future million-seller Enya – at that time recently departed from her siblings in Clannad.

The Altan story began in earnest in the wake of Frankie and Mairéad's second, again jointly credited, album entitled *Altan*, named after Loch Altan – both a lake in Donegal and a self-composed tune on the album. The tune, tentatively nestling amongst the purely traditional material, gave but a hint of the instrumental compositions nudging the trad style gently onward that would become highlights of future recordings. The individuals who would complete Altan the group coalesced on this album and during the live work that followed it: Donegal-man Ciarán Tourish on fiddle; Ciarán Curran from neighbouring Fermanagh on bouzouki; and Galway guitarist and wry humorist Mark Kelly

Colin Harper · Originally published in the *Irish News* (2 December 1994); expanded as a sleeve-note to the Altan compilation, *Once Again* (Snapper, 2000)

Altán by Mount Errigal,
County Donegal, 1994:
(l–r) Ciarán Curran, Ciarán Tourish,
Mairéad Ní Mhaonaigh,
Frankie Kennedy, Mark Kelly,
Dermot Byrne

(who to this day, of truly international status, maintains a day job in the insurance business – touring commitments being shared with veteran Derry guitarist Daithí Sproule).

Altan had been released on US label Green Linnet, which over the next few years would develop, alongside the career of Altan, from a kitchen-table labour of love to a flourishing global entity. Frankie and Mairéad took what was initially a career break from teaching and toured the US with their new band in support of the album. It was around this period that Paul O'Shaughnessy, who had played on the *Altan* album but remained committed to a day job, was gradually replaced in the touring unit by Ciarán Tourish, although for a period Mairéad, Ciarán and Paul made up a rare three-fiddle front line in the group. The two or three-fiddle approach to the line-up – where in the Seventies either fiddle and pipes, fiddle and bouzouki or pipes and bouzouki had been the norm – was one of two factors which made the Altan sound unique. The other factor was the music itself, the rough-edged, windswept and near-Scottish sound of the Donegal instrumental tradition which had been, up to then, under-exposed in contemporary repertoires and recordings. The fact that Mairéad sang nearly all the song selections (which remained exclusively traditional up to the end of their association with Green Linnet in 1995) in Irish was also a trademark. Although there were precedents, these were still the days before *Riverdance* and the global phenomenon of all things Celtic, and it was commercially a brave stance.

But the group was now regularly on the road in both Europe and America, with an identifiable sound, and over the next four albums – *Horse With A Heart* (1989), *The Red Crow* (1990), *Harvest Storm* (1992) and their arguably still unsurpassed *Island Angel* (1993) – Altan delivered a continually refining, subtly progressive body of work that ultimately saw them crossing over, without any obvious compromise to the integrity of the music they had based their career on, into the mainstream of the entertainment world. While the previous albums had done increasingly well in terms of sales and critical coverage, *Island Angel* – recorded at Dublin's Windmill Lane Studios – saw their compositional and arranging skills, together with a capturing of their onstage energy, combine with 'the moment' for both themselves and for Irish music generally to begin a genuinely mainstream renaissance which is only now showing the signs of ebbing back a little – as every fashion in entertainment periodically must. *Island Angel* stayed on *Billboard*'s US world-music chart for eight months and the group and/or the album were acclaimed in a wide array of end-of-year critics' polls during 1993 and 1994, ranging from *Q* magazine to *The Irish Times*. During the same period, further recognition was acquired through the group's guesting on several tracks for Dolly Parton's back-to-basics album, *Heartsongs*.

The seemingly now inexorable progress onwards and upwards was nevertheless tinged with mixed emotions for the group as its founder, player-manager and visionary Frankie Kennedy had been diagnosed with cancer in 1992. Frankie battled with the disease throughout the breakthrough years, memorably appearing on stage – clearly at an advanced stage of illness, but to justly thunderous ovations – for the encores at triumphal homecoming concerts in Belfast and Dublin during the winter of 1993–94. Kennedy died, aged 38, on 19 September 1994 and was buried in Donegal. Within weeks, his band had begun a tour of England. The decision to go ahead, with the dates in hand and with the band as an ongoing unit, was down to Mairéad Ní Mhaonaigh – effectively the public face of the group and its driving force on stage. Dermot Byrne, who had guested as accordionist on *Island Angel*, was retained as a full member and several years later married Mairéad.

Green Linnet released the first of many compilations, *Altan: The First Ten Years*, in 1995 but even before Frankie's death both group and label had discussed the future and each side accepted the time was right for the group to move on. In October 1995 a deal was signed with Virgin that has thus far resulted in three albums – *Blackwater* (1996), *Runaway Sunday* (1997) and *Another Sky* (2000) – that have seen the group expanding their musical palette and exploring new avenues artistically through added instrumentation, songs in English, original songwriting and so forth. Green Linnet have meanwhile continued to repackage and license the material from the first five albums. Such is the nature of the music business.

Altan worked hard and became, by stealth and dedication, the darlings of the rock 'n' roll media and an inspiration to a new generation of potential traditional musicians. Indeed, every December Gweedore hosts the 'Frankie Kennedy Winter School' – a combination of tutorials, sessions and concerts attended by students from around the world and given by professional musicians of the highest calibre in respect to Kennedy's achievements. Fiddler Ciarán Tourish knows exactly why Altan have become, from such a purely traditional standpoint, a name to be found as readily in *Q* or the *NME* as the *New York* or *Irish Times*: 'It was 100 per cent Frankie,' he once told me, without a moment's hesitation. 'Frankie knew from the beginning what the band should be doing, where it should be going, and fortunately he set the band on a track so that all we have to do is keep it rolling in the same direction. None of us have any intention of letting go the grip. We'll keep going – we've got to keep going, because this is a thing that Frankie set up. I think it would be an insult for us to cut it short, after all the work he put in.'

The handful of times I met them together, during the halcyon days of the *Island Angel* era, Frankie and Mairéad showed themselves to have a warmth and courtesy often rare in the music industry. Working within a shamelessly egocentric business, Frankie Kennedy never expected or touted for press features, but he would always say, 'Thank you,' when something did appear. He respected the way the industry works, but he had a sense of decency and a soul that much of it lacks. He had a sense of humour, too. On one occasion I had referred, in print, to his band's 'rock 'n' roll charisma'. Alas, the picture agency had supplied the magazine in question with a singularly uncharismatic photograph of a different act entirely. The editor was incensed; Frankie Kennedy was in stitches. Another piece featured a sub-heading erroneously referring to Frankie Gavin (from Seventies folk heroes De Danann) – the trad equivalent of calling Jimi Hendrix 'Jimmy Page'. He probably enjoyed that one, too. The last mistake wasn't funny at all. I had written an interview up for an Irish newspaper. Frankie Kennedy, it declared, had beaten cancer. The day after our interview he had been given the all-clear. By the time it was published [in the *Irish News*, 9 July 1994], the illness had recurred.

Sometime later Frankie Kennedy called me from his home near Dublin to say that he'd seen the article. He'd loved it. He'd been in hospital and it had cheered him up no end, he said. A few weeks later he rang me for the last time. Everybody else was off on tour, but as the man who had steered the band this far he was keeping his hand in as much as he could.

'We all looked at it, attitude-wise, the same way that Frankie did himself,' said Ciarán Tourish. 'Frankie fought. It was the most admirable thing that I've ever seen in my life. When we were away, if Frankie wasn't undergoing treatment he was always working away, always doing something. If he wasn't physically there with us, he was still in a managerial role right the way through. Other times, if he wouldn't have been there for a full gig he'd have been there to come on at the end. It helped his morale. Frankie was never a man to sit down and do nothing.'

Hopefully one day some of Altan's incendiary radio concerts from the early Nineties will see the light of day, but in the meantime the contents of his commercially issued recordings with Altan will provide a sense of how Kennedy's vision grew and prospered in a period when nobody in their right mind would have put money on the viability of Donegal music as a way of life at the restless end of the twentieth century.

MARTIN HAYES
THE MASTER OF SILENCE

I first encountered Martin Hayes on a bright sunny evening at a church in Galway – it was in July 1995. It may have been the first time his sombre, soaring tones had graced the gothic interior of a place of worship but it wouldn't be the last. This was a time when I was living alone, getting by on writing and relying on a certain solace in the recordings of Estonian minimalist Arvo Pärt. It sounds pretentious, I know, but the early part of my professional writing career was quite a fragile period and with cheques invariably slow to arrive a little time spent in Pärt's tranquillity really did go a long way. I heard in Martin a musician of the same spirit, and was subsequently intrigued to find that he, too, was a Pärt devotee, and that he, too, had seen his own hard times.

I had already, shortly before that trip to Galway, been entranced by Martin's new album, *Under The Moon*, and had willingly championed it in *Q*. My conclusion there, that 'sparsely accompanied fiddle music has rarely sounded so complete and so essential', duly found its way into the steamrollering international litany of awe-struck press quotage in the man's promotional material. All over the world, that year and into the next, the world's media were discovering Hayes as one the most astonishing Irish traditional musicians of the modern era.

The compiler of such tributes, and Martin's agent/manager for Irish and European work, was and remains my friend Amy Garvey – a strident, energetic, well-regarded and, in those days, oft-encountered personality on the booming Irish trad scene. As a relatively young, relatively inexperienced and regularly cash-strapped writer at the turn of the Nineties Amy showed much kindness to me and, in equal part sharing as professionally proselytising, had introduced me – and many, many others – to Altan. At that stage Amy was Irish publicist – on a contractually part-time, vocationally full-time basis – for the North American record label Green Linnet. To a great extent the wave of publicity and packed houses that characterised Altan's rise during the period leading up to their final Green Linnet album, *Island Angel* (1993), and through to their triumphal signing to the UK 'major' Virgin in 1995 can be traced back to Amy. By 1995 her energies were focused on Martin Hayes, not only as a Green Linnet artist to whom she had an obligation like any other but as an undiscovered, personally unassuming artist of world class upon whom she was prepared to stake her reputation. And she was right.

During that Galway trip I interviewed this wry, cheery, immediately likeable

Colin Harper

fellow and his delightfully sardonic American accompanist Dennis Cahill. Already they had encountered controversy from the trad establishment. Dennis had met some po-faced people from the Comhaltas organisation a few days earlier who had, absurdly, questioned the traditional validity of his chords: 'Fine, pick a date and I'll not play anything from after that date,' had been his checkmating reply. Brilliant. The resulting feature, a basic 'Who are you? How did you meet?' type piece, appeared in the *Irish News* and in *Folk Roots*. It was the start of a long and deeply rewarding association, as fellow professionals on either side of a fence and also as friends.

Four weeks later I caught the pair again at the Stray Leaf folk club, Mullaghbawn, in the wilds of County Armagh – one of Ireland's few folk clubs along the English lines and its hardest-to-find venue of any kind (at that stage a barn behind a pub in a place where road signs are a luxury). In looking through the file and bringing together here most of my published work on Martin and Dennis I realise that I've seen them in concert on at least twenty occasions, probably more – and each one has been magical.

Early on I described Martin in print as the 'Master of Silence' and during the course of a slightly mad recording project of my own in late '95/early '96 I wrote a piece of music of that name as a doff of the cap – the gall, the presumption, indeed! Martin thrilled me by agreeing to record violin parts for the piece if I could make it down to a studio in Ennis, County Clare, on the only free day of his next Irish tour, in May 1996. Needless to say, I was there. Years later Martin added fiddle, in Seattle, to another Harper & Co. recording, from Belfast, of the Bert Jansch song 'People On The Highway', destined for a Jansch tribute album of that name which was released on Market Square in September 2000.

I have, indeed, been privileged to have been in the right place at the right time to witness and to help chronicle the rise of one of Ireland's greatest musicians of all time, and honoured, like Eire Apparent were with Hendrix in their own time, to have made music with such a sonic magician.

INTRODUCING
MARTIN HAYES & DENNIS CAHILL

'I'm trying to reach something which I don't think has been done in Irish music,' says Martin Hayes, sipping tea at a seaside hotel in Galway. 'A communication back and forth, between fiddle and guitar, allowing the guitar, with its whole rhythmic and harmonic potential, to become more fully integrated into it. Up till recently I've been trying to push the fiddle thing, using different accompanists, but now it's reached the point of a bona-fide partnership. I couldn't replace Dennis now with any other guitarist.'

Hayes, fiddler from Clare via Chicago, is arguably the greatest new talent in Irish music for years, while the extraordinary intuitive and technical abilities of Dennis Cahill, his accompanist, represent both the icing on the cake and the key to his future innovations. I say 'arguably' but I have yet to hear anyone argue against it.

The pair have been touring Ireland over the summer in support of Hayes' new album (his second, for Green Linnet) entitled *Under The Moon*, and finish off tonight with a late-night show at the Playhouse, Derry. For anyone remotely interested not only in traditional music but simply in music where the playing is vibrant, inspired and brilliantly performed, Martin Hayes and Dennis Cahill are an act worth travelling a distance to see. Their performance in the echoing ambience of St Nicholas' Church in Galway during July's Galway Arts Festival was breathtaking. Last week's performance in the packed but mesmerised Stray Leaf folk club in Mullaghbawn – unquestionably Ireland's hardest-to-find venue – was better still, if only for the intimacy of the occasion and the closeness between each listener and the infinite nuances of the music. For be in no doubt, Martin Hayes plays traditional music, but you've never heard the like of it before.

Hayes and Cahill met up in Chicago in the mid-Eighties, after living across the road from each other for years: 'We kept meeting in pubs,' says Martin, 'and then one night we decided to swap addresses, to get together and play some music – and I'm going, "Hold on, you're almost living in my front yard!"' Dennis is a native of Chicago and a consummate professional musician – rock, jazz and now Irish traditional music. Martin, although growing up in Clare in a family steeped in the stuff, simply drifted to America, with no real intention of entering the music business: 'I didn't really intend to pursue it as a career at all, though I always hoped I could have some kind of work that would allow me enormous amounts of free time to pursue the music in a leisurely fashion, with no constraints whatsoever! I figured business was the key and even studied

Colin Harper · Originally published in the *Irish News* (8 September 1995) and *Folk Roots* (November 1995)

it at college. I figured you had to make money to support music. But when all my business dealings eventually failed, and I had no means of making money, music became the means of making money – and I became a professional musician by accident.'

After a while playing 'stage-Irish' material at weddings, functions and Irish-American pubs, Hayes became dissatisfied and hooked up with Cahill to form an electric band called Midnight Court: 'A kind of Moving Hearts on steroids – very rocked-out, high-energy, high-speed, unapologetic Irish music, if you could call it Irish music by that stage. It was Irish tunes but it felt more like a Mahavishnu Orchestra type fusion of Irish and jazz and rock.'

Under pressure to change its repertoire to something a tad more main-stream, the band eventually folded, in 1991, after which an exhausted Hayes received an offer to make his first solo album: 'At that stage I needed to play quite easygoing. I had rebelled enough and didn't feel I had any more points to prove. But the whole experience of playing in Midnight Court opened up my ears and allowed me to be more objective. So although you can't hear the influences directly, the effect of having done it impacted the way I did traditional music.'

That first album, *Martin Hayes*, was well received, which the man himself found pleasantly surprising. His decision to play gently, with absolutely no gimmickry and no striving for commercial appeal, had proved exactly the kind of approach that people wanted. Dennis Cahill, also worn out from the Midnight Court experience, had gone his own way for a while and, although now integral to Martin's live performances, doesn't appear on either of his two solo albums to date.

Both albums, nevertheless, showcase Hayes' extraordinary tone, restraint and sense of dynamics – virtues shared and enhanced by Cahill at the live shows. Influenced by Stephane Grappelli as much as any traditional player, Hayes steered clear of the old 78 rpm recordings – which had influenced the likes of Frankie Gavin – and instead went straight back to the older players living in Clare who were themselves inheritors of an unsullied tradition: 'I couldn't find a definite, physical style but there was certainly an aura and an expressiveness about their music that fascinated me, and it's that that I'm interested in evolving and developing – that intangible feeling, that sense of mood and soul that's in the music. And if their intonation or tone or technique wasn't great, let's bring in those things, but not get consumed in them. It would take Dennis and I five gigs to play the amount of notes some people play in one, but the end result is the expression of soul and spirit. We're not doing anything new, we're just "allowing" the music.'

Martin Hayes,
1993

MARTIN HAYES
OLYMPIA THEATRE, DUBLIN

There's a sense, among Irish musicians, that Martin Hayes has come out of nowhere to stay out on his own. There's also a sense, among the people who write about Irish music, that there are no more adjectives, epithets or cross-generic comparisons left to be used about him. Comparisons in print to the likes of Miles Davis and Jimi Hendrix cause Hayes to step back in quite genuine humility and usually to mumble some self-deprecating witticism in that unmistakably soft-spoken east Clare accent. If he is indeed on that level of genius, he'll be the first in history to combine it with being an ordinary bloke.

Bearing more outward resemblance to Noel Redding than to Jimi Hendrix – mad haircut and scholarly spectacles – Hayes was born into a Clare family with deep traditional-music roots. Moving to Chicago in the 1980s with a series of business ideas that didn't work, Hayes found himself playing music for a living, going through a Celtic-rock and jazz-fusion phase before realising that, no, just like the business ideas, the public don't want this either. In 1993, exhausted, he made *Martin Hayes*, a low-key album of reflective traditional tunes. The public responded. A second one, *Under The Moon*, released last year, kick-started a critical-acclaim/cult-following bandwagon that continues apace.

The albums, however, give only a glimpse of Hayes' performance magic. The onstage chemistry between the fiddler and his accompanist, Dennis Cahill (not on the records yet), is truly exceptional. Cahill, from Chicago, is a journeyman guitarist, totally new to Irish music and unencumbered by notions of 'how it's done'. The names of the tunes are almost irrelevant, for between them they so utterly deconstruct the material that it becomes a vast, spacious soundscape aching with the sores and celebrations of centuries, soaring with the slow-burning dynamics of modern classicists like Pärt and Górecki. Seemingly every arts writer and musician in town was there – the entirety of Altan, kings of the trad castle, included – sitting in pin-drop silence at the feet of the master. The creaking of his chair could, without exaggeration, be heard at the back of the 1,200-seater auditorium.

There's a notion that J.S. Bach was a conduit for the music of God – stirring the soul, rewriting the rules, taking the listener by way of austerity and solemnity to previously unreachable heights. What occurs when Martin Hayes and Dennis Cahill lock in together on a stage is, for this writer at least, on that same transcendental level – way beyond the traditional vehicle and onto a different plane of experience. It would seem that the Master of Silence has finally found a business idea that works.

Colin Harper · Concert review originally published in the *Independent* (20 July 1996)

EMMYLOU HARRIS, HAYES & CAHILL
NATIONAL CONCERT HALL, GLASGOW

In pairing up the Master of Silence and the Queen of Doom as a fitting end to this year's Celtic Connections Festival, someone was taking a risk. But it was, however incongruous, an inspired one. Put it like this: if Hendrix had lived to play country he'd want to be in the Emmylou Harris band; if Bach had lived to rewrite the rulebook of Irish traditional music, he'd have Martin Hayes to contend with. It's as simple as that.

Beautifully accompanied by Chicago-born guitarist Dennis Cahill, Hayes struck a mischievous and engaging image on the stage. Swaying like a puppet with Marc Bolan haircut and John Lennon spectacles, his stripped-to-the-bone take on an oft-caricatured and over-familiar corner of the world's music defied superlatives. The effect, ethereal and expansive, was reminiscent of The Pentangle taking their low-volume fusions into The Albert Hall – and mainstream acceptance – in the late Sixties. While Hayes' music commanded attention, Emmylou Harris needed only her very presence on the stage. A slight, statuesque figure, she has found the path to a graceful yet still vital maturity in rock 'n' roll that so many others, in cabaret, therapy or self-parody, can only dream about. Still championing her last album, *Wrecking Ball*, the shadowy desolation of the vast, bare-black stage itself – with a little village of musicians, drums and monitors huddled together at its centre – seemed to mirror that album's desperate emotions.

Given the album's thumbs-down reception by country music buffs it was notable that, in a live context with this band, the new material seemed in no way discontinuous from the old. Harris' abiding gift was to make each song, each lyric speak clearly and resonantly amid such a cauldron of sound. It's why she's still around.

Colin Harper · Concert review originally published in the *Independent* (28 February 1997)

Martin Hayes (left), Dennis Cahill,
Glencolmcille, County Donegal, July 1997

ON THE ROAD WITH
MARTIN HAYES & DENNIS CAHILL

Dennis Cahill is having a bit of a bad day. No, make that a week. 'I think this is the first time I've convinced Debbie that touring isn't one long vacation,' he growls, in distinctive Chicago drawl. 'I mean, you've all the aggravation with airports and none of the relaxation when you get there. I tell you, if I ever make a million I'm gonna give $50,000 to Debbie and Amy and send 'em off on tour – see how they deal with it . . .'

The phrase 'blistering barnacles' comes to mind, and it's hard to suppress amusement. Dennis is Captain Haddock to Martin Hayes' Tintin, cavorting around the world having adventures, meeting faintly ridiculous people on a regular basis and coping with episodic nonsense in notably different ways: Cahill huffs and puffs; Hayes deals with everything on a more conciliatory, cerebral level. Examples litter their conversation like a valve to the pressures of endlessly crafting, on the road, a music of awesome fragility. Here we all are, 'on the road' in Dunlewy, Donegal, on Tuesday 14 July and Debbie – a one-time Cahill 'love interest' from back home, it transpires – has turned up out of the blue for that night's concert and subsequent wind-down at the local pub. Martin, the east Clare fiddle maestro who currently lives (or, at least, picks up his mail) in Seattle and his partner Helen have gone back to the B&B. Amy Garvey, their gregarious agent-cum-European manager, up from Dublin, has run into some friends across the bar. Manus Lunny, a curiously reflective member of Scots folk-rockers Capercaillie, who lives nearby, has joined us. Folk music, in the British Isles, is a small world. We find mutually informative small talk easily enough. 'The feeling I get from the music business,' says Manus, staring into space, 'is like the feeling you get when you lean backwards in a chair and know you've leant too far. *All* the time.'

'Boy, I haven't had this much fun for two weeks,' says Dennis. The pub is admittedly short on atmosphere. We drink up and leave.

The business of touring can be fun, and sometimes it can't. 'Purgatory' is the word musicians use, for those moments of down-time when confidence ebbs away and they wonder what it's all about: 'You go very high with the musical experience,' says Martin, the next day. 'I'm sure it's no different from drink or drugs, and sometimes it's a big let-down without it. I definitely have times of feeling that what I do is absolutely useless and meaningless and the fact of the matter is, I have to do a concert tonight. And there'd be me starting to think that I'm a fraud.' And yet nothing could be further from the truth.

The Donegal sojourn – three intimate shows and a couple of radio interviews

Colin Harper · Originally published in the *Independent* (25 July 1997)

over two days – has been designed by Amy as a rest-cure in the middle of a longer tour to promote their first joint album, *The Lonesome Touch*. They've been touring two years solidly now and in it the word-of-mouth expectations have been realised. The previous week was 'Willie Week' – the annual eight-day traddies' pilgrimage of workshops, sessions and all-night revelries in Milltown Malbay, held in memory of piper Willie Clancy. If you're anyone in trad, it's the place where everybody knows your name – and when your name is Martin Hayes, the 'Master of Silence', increasingly on a par with Jehovah, that can be a bother. 'There's this guy making a documentary on me,' says Martin, unnerved at the recollection, 'and every time I walked out of a door, there he was. I'm telling you, more than once I felt like diving into the street and making a run for it.'

They may be 'fried' (Hayes and his longing for solitude; Cahill and his complicated love life) by the time they get to Donegal, but in a way it is the very pressures of life that fuel the fragile magic they create with, barring inspiration, only three devices: guitar, fiddle and the instrument of silence itself. But however much one strives for solemnity and soul, one has to deal with the mundane and the frivolous. And at this, the first gig was a triumph. Tuesday: a lunchtime recital at the visitor centre of Glenveagh Castle – Martin Hayes, the lord of the trance, in amongst the wall charts and the stuffed otters, with an audience roughly equal in terms of musical diehards and tourists with small children. There'll be a lot of small children on this trip – they like Martin: he's funny, he's gentle and for all the biblical fervour of his international press notices (to the extent where his record company have apparently started asking journalists *not* to use Messianic metaphors) he has a mischievous grin. Kind of Robin Williams with a Marc Bolan haircut – the upshot of which means, regrettably, getting mistaken for Kenny G at airports.

Perhaps inevitably, in its context, this show never attains full-blown nirvana, but the effect is still stunning. 'I've had a request,' says Martin, 'from a bunch of five-year-olds [grin widens, ripples of mirth all round] for a slow air . . .' Of course, this is a relative term – everything Martin plays is slow, or carries well the illusion of entropy as an art form. No fiddler and no guitarist in Irish music play fewer notes than Martin and Dennis, and absolutely no one – past or present – comes remotely close to the sheer spiritual sensation they can, when the moment is right, create. That evening, at the main concert of the day in Dunlewy, the 'mystical thing' happens. For perhaps 25 minutes in the middle of the show – where the music has built continuously, in soaring, soul-penetrating tenacity – one feels entranced. At that same point, Martin tells me later, he felt it, too. It is not something he can conjure up at will, but neither is it an accident: 'There's a kind of soulful experience that's better than prayer or meditation,' he suggests – 'That's more genuine – a space you can work yourself into musically. So you want to reach that space. I'd spent a number of years playing in quiet corners for myself, like I'm pouring music into myself. Somehow in my mid-twenties the experience flipped about and I found that the only time I was getting this same experience now was when I was reaching out to someone else – like the giving is the receiving.'

The crowd – packed, like all three Donegal shows, to the rafters – is explosive in appreciation as each set of tunes ends. Almost anything Martin says in between, in his soft-spoken, near-apologetic tones, will get a laugh simply because it punctures the tension, resolves the silence. If his music is a key to the soul, silence is the torch to find it: 'I remember reading in the back of one of [minimalist composer] Arvo Pärt's recordings where he said that music was the space that silence had chosen to abandon. I liked that. I think that silent moment is the moment in which the audience subjectively create for themselves, in which they're actively participating. You make people aware of the silence. It's a challenge every time.'

Just as Pärt, the Estonian ascetic, has created his own 'tintinabulli' style of composition from deconstructing renaissance music, so Hayes has effectively created a stripped-down, purer form of Irish music – one that reaches back, he believes, to a time before the ancient airs and marches were grafted onto the imported structures of jigs and reels. He's pragmatic about it, and he's loath to be held aloft as a champion of anyone's cultural agenda. His music, traditional Irish 'by accident of birth I suppose', is simply a vehicle in the search for enlightenment. Even an *Irish Times*' reviewer who could not, in a surfeit of received wisdom on 'the tradition', comprehend quite what he was trying to do, compared Hayes, albeit within a truly impenetrable metaphor, to Jesus. But however much these kind of comparisons may skirt absurdity – and long has the Hayes camp revelled in the anticipation of a 'Mother Teresa' review – neither are they wrong in their premise. That said, Martin Hayes, Zen-like master of his art, is not about to kick ass with today's equivalents of the Romans or the Pharisees or anybody else. 'But it is like a missionary thing,' he admits, of his calling.

'What,' I suggest, 'like The Blues Brothers – you're on a mission from God?'

'Yeah, that's it!' he grins, ambiguously. 'I've actually played in that theatre, with my dad's band – the one in the last scene . . .' His dad's band, The Tulla Céilí Band, is, at 50 this year, the most venerable in Ireland. But seriously Martin . . .

'Look at it like this,' he says – 'The evangelists today speak to more people than Jesus ever did and they'll have a minimal effect by comparison. Like, I was reading this interview with someone who was saying, "I'll always be known as the bass player from Kajagoogoo . . ."! Now, that sounds kind of *strange* to me. You could be popular for twelve months on a mega level and touch millions of people a little bit – or you could touch a few thousand people a lot. That's more valuable to me.'

Playing 100-seaters and *really* communicating to those people, and paying his way through life, is all Martin wants. Both he and Dennis have been through the rock 'n' roll mill before and now they've found where it's at: soul music. Without trying, without the push and shove of global hype, Martin Hayes has been compared to J.S. Bach, Jimi Hendrix, Miles Davis and God. He draws influence from spiritually driven minimalists like Pärt and fusion pioneers like The Mahavishnu Orchestra; he is erudite, humble and constantly re-evaluating himself, his music and his goals like no one else in the industry. He is a once-in-a-lifetime – and he's also very funny. 'The muse,' he notes, wisely, 'has no interest in press cuttings.'

The next day, at a radio interview for the local Irish-language station (he barely speaks a word of the stuff and can't understand why broadcasters consistently refuse to believe this) the presenter, in between phone-ins on the subject of 'Batman *agus* Robin', chirpily enquires what they do for a living. 'Hey, it's all we can do,' says Dennis, with a facial expression that says he's heard this kind of ill-informed rot a million times before.

They play a tune. It's staggering, and entirely new . . . sort of. 'Something I heard my dad play when I was six, I think. It just came to me,' says Martin, in the linguistic safety of the car park.

On the way out, the presenter turns to myself and Helen – the one scribbling observations, the other taking photos. 'So, are you all here on holiday?' she says. Again. Did anybody ever put this to Jimi Hendrix, or Miles Davis, or Bach? Over her shoulder, Martin chuckles silently, which seems entirely appropriate.

'No,' I say, firmly and clearly, and in English. 'Martin is one of the world's leading traditional musicians in the commercial arena, Dennis is his accompanist and I'm writing about them for a national newspaper. We're all in pursuit of wealth.'

We go to lunch, we come back for a link-up with a national show and Martin falls about in further silent revelry when it becomes clear, on air, that Dennis' dark past in cabaret is out ('I sang some songs and made sarcastic remarks. Hey, I made a living . . .'). Behind the screen Amy fields calls on her mobile from people who've heard about a 'secret gig', that night, in Dublin. It's so secret that nobody has told Martin or Dennis. Instead, and without secrecy, they're off to Glencolmcille, birthplace of St Columba – the edge of everywhere, the beginning of nowhere.

That night there are no lights, no amplification and the show is unbelievable. We repair, all of us this time, to the best of three pubs in the village. We discuss the processes of music, the state of our souls and what he's going to play on BBC2's *Later With Jools* (an appearance is imminent). Perhaps, feels Martin, he has done all he needs to do – touched a few people, said what he had to say. He doesn't need to be a star, '. . . but everybody wants to be loved, to be acknowledged for what they do'. He is unquestionably the best in the world at what he does, and he makes a living at it. He's a lucky man.

An hour later we discover that, like all pubs in the world, there is a chip van outside – yes, even here. We consume the food on the way back to this night's guesthouse and even Dennis is back on form. 'You know,' he says, 'I've only met two guys from Northern Ireland who don't have a problem. And you're one of 'em.' Thanks. I think.

HAYES & CAHILL
CORNMILL HERITAGE CENTRE, COALISLAND

Over the past three years Hayes and Cahill have taken their remarkable, breathtakingly subtle artistry to some sizeable venues. Indeed, next year the plan is to limit their activities, in Ireland at least, to full-scale concert halls. There can be little doubt now that they have the profile to do it but, as Martin once put it himself, 'the muse has no interest in press cuttings'. Invariably, in my experience, what they do – a contemplative and spiritually charged take on traditional melodies – is enhanced by the intimacy of the space they fill. Tonight, in the plush, woody ambience of this provincial heritage centre with a capacity of perhaps 150, that view was proven once again.

Touring Ireland for the first time in a year, it was thrilling to hear almost an album's worth of new material, and to hear the development particularly of Cahill's guitar technique. Influenced no doubt by a beautiful new instrument, he played even less notes than usual – typically accompanying the laments and slow jigs with intermittent cascades among diminished and unresolved chords, creating a shimmering, harp-like effect. A Blasket Islands air associated with fairy lore was the apogee of the duo's further-developed experimentation with jazz voicings and deconstructed melody/harmony playing. Periodically wailing over the seas in mythic grief, pulling dissonances and chord drones from his fiddle against the tension of Cahill's filigrees, Hayes used the tune to launch an extraordinary 30-minute medley climaxing in something akin to Vivaldi. A live album is promised; another 'album of the year' can be safely predicted.

Colin Harper · Concert review originally published in *The Irish Times* (4 August 1998)

Martin Hayes (left), Dennis Cahill, Glasgow Royal Concert Hall, 1997

MARTIN HAYES & DENNIS CAHILL
ST ANNE'S CATHEDRAL, BELFAST

The first time Martin Hayes and Dennis Cahill played in Belfast, in 1995, it was in the cabaret lounge of a small pub. Though both live in the States, it was also the public debut of their partnership: the most innovative act in Irish music that the decade would see. Comparisons have since been made with Hendrix, Bach, Miles Davis and seemingly everyone else of influence and stature bar Mother Teresa – indeed, his own publicist has taken to actively dissuading commentators tempted to make that final leap into Messianic realms – but Hayes himself remains an affable fellow with his feet very firmly on the ground.

It was amusing, then, for the fellow to be returning to Belfast, not only to a cathedral, of all places, but to surroundings where a ten-second echo dictated the pace. It was, if anything, more magical than ever. The recent high point of a Hayes performance has been the increasingly epic 'long medley' – an ever-evolving, trance-like set of tunes that has been known to reach 50 minutes in length. Whether models of Stonehenge and dancing dwarfs were ever manoeuvred onstage during the playing thereof remains something for the imagination. The pair's current CD, *Live In Seattle*, contains a definitive 30-minute version – opening with the dark, evocative polyphony of a fairy lament from the Blasket Islands, peaking with the delicate frenzy of 'Rakish Paddy', climaxing with a joyous skip through Pachelbel's 'Canon' – and it was this arrangement that closed the show tonight, to typically rapturous applause.

For long-term fans, though, it was 'The Golden Castle' – a new and equally stunning, if more poised, medley – which held most fascination and pronounced the evening's tone with its eerie serenity. Here, Cahill truly confirmed his own uniqueness as an accompanist. Never one for the manic strumming of his peers, he has deconstructed his role so ruthlessly that only the pulse remains, only the faintest rumour of a fragile arpeggio.

Eschewing the riotous lifestyle maintained by most of the people professionally involved in Irish traditional music and taking a large element of his inspiration from the redemptive music of modern 'faith minimalist' composers such as Arvo Pärt and from the technical rigours of Seventies jazz-fusion, Martin Hayes (with Cahill now an integral part) has created a form of music that was simply not there before. And now, at the end of the twentieth century, he stands like a Samson-esque figure single-handedly grappling with Irish music's twin pillars of impish fire and fathomless grief – whose foundations are as deep as the tradition itself – with the implausible intention of fusing the two facets together into one glorious whole. He has already succeeded in doing so.

Colin Harper · Concert review originally published in the *Independent* (3 December 1999)

TAMALIN
PROLOGUE

'One could put money on them' was my concluding remark in a Tamalin concert review, published in *The Irish Times* in November 1996. I had, in the same piece, trumpeted the imminent release of the group's long-awaited debut album 'in a matter of weeks'. It wasn't the first time I had made such a claim in print, and it wouldn't be the last! Whatever their qualities – and on a musical level they were (and may yet be) world class – Tamalin were as delightfully 'through-other' as any bunch of would-be world-beaters could be.

As a would-be commentator with Belfast daily, the *Irish News*, I had set myself the task of chronicling every local band I could find, of whatever musical persuasion, for a weekly series called 'The Class of '95'. Given that many of these aspiring, generally talented and almost invariably professionally doomed people were very organised and business-savvy, it was a shoulder-shrugging joy, in a way, to see that Tamalin, perhaps the most talented of all, always gave the impression of being unable to catch a bus let alone the star-studded elevator to success.

Perhaps I exaggerate, but then again – immortalised in print in a June 1995 piece for the *Irish News* where, yet again, I was promising the world the imminent arrival of something that was still a couple of years away – I have the evidence of Group Captain Tina McSherry herself: 'Yes, none of us is very business orientated,' she admitted. 'It means you get ripped-off all the time. We'll have to get a manager once we sort out the record deal . . .'

By that stage the long-awaited, Donal Lunny-mixed, nine-track album – which had been owned by the group, albeit financed by licensing arrangements with various overseas labels – was in the process of being sold (lock, stock and with four additional tracks in its barrel) to UK label Grapevine. With operations in London and Dublin, and associations with any number of quality artists, a decent stab at the fame game seemed assured. But this was Tamalin – and the bus was leaving the station. Heading in the opposite direction.

During that period of waiting for the mythical Tamalin album I had the great fortune of having Tina contribute – in an archetypically Tamalin-ish way – to my own mad recording project, sometime in 1996. I recall with amazement (and relief) her turning up (late) to the studio, a full band of other hugely talented friends all ready and waiting, favours being owed by the minute, only for Tina to mention that she hadn't got around to listening to the demo of whatever it was I wanted her to sing. Panicking, the clock ticking, I busked it to her once on a guitar out on the studio's stairway . . . and she took it to heaven. From one listen, and in one live take with the band, her transformation on its melody and delivery were akin to the difference between The Beatles' version of 'With A Little Help From My Friends' and Joe Cocker's. I remain, to this day, astounded at the woman's innate musicality.

One of the great pleasures of working on this book has been the opportunity to catch up with a few people. Truth is, after the Tamalin album finally appeared I somehow lost touch with them all – though John, incredibly prolific as he now is on the international trad scene, I managed to see on stages, behind stages and write about from afar on the odd occasion thereafter. So whatever *did* happen to Tamalin? And will their time yet come?

Paul McSherry's phone number was the first that yielded itself to discovery and, in his recollection, Tina and John were the first problems – in a manner of speaking. After a successful tour of Australia and New Zealand in May 1997, with Ronnie Drew, Donal Lunny's new band Coolfin and others, John was put on a retainer – effectively 'on call' – to work with Coolfin, which he would end up doing for three years. There would be live work in Japan and elsewhere and the unit's first album would be released in September 1998. That same year Tina, already with two children from a previous marriage, became pregnant. As an additional complication Paul, married to Déanta fiddler and music tutor Kate O'Brien, had in September 1997 (shortly after the Tamalin album had slipped out) accepted a teaching post in Magherafelt.

Still, all was not lost. Déanta, for example, had already enjoyed several worthwhile years as a viable part-time band – including three albums for US label Green Linnet and manageable bursts of live work – with most of its members holding down simultaneous day jobs as dentists, teachers and pharmacists. It didn't help, however, that Tamalin's laudable realisation that a manager was needed led them towards the unfortunate choice of an individual who was used only to dealing with angsty guitar bands and who had no empathy with either traditional music or the opportunities within which it can flourish. Tamalin were never likely to get anywhere with this man.

The final straw was Daniel O'Donnell (again, in a manner of speaking). Daniel's label, Ritz, buoyed by his quite remarkable success, bought the Grapevine label and all hope of a second album for Tamalin disappeared. The fickleness of record buyers is well-known, but one barometer of the fickleness of record *labels* is that barely six years after hearing from the band about the unbelievably extravagant photo budget for their album cover, a phone call to Grapevine's London office, to request a photo for this book, yielded the aural equivalent of a blank expression. The band were unheard of and nobody knew anything about any photos. Truly, Daniel had turned their minds to blancmange . . .

In 2001 Paul and John toured as a quartet with Donal O'Connor (fiddle) and Michael McGoldrick (pipes). Paul, however, couldn't commit to further work due to the day job and the excellent Tony Byrne came in as his replacement. An album, *At First Light*, appeared, credited to John McSherry and Michael McGoldrick, and a second is planned. Of the others, Joanne is musically dormant and, of all things, working at a Job Centre in west Belfast; Tina currently has five children and lives in leafy Castlewellan; and Kevin 'Dod' Dorris is reputedly earning a living as a pub-session player in Galway. But things are stirring. Paul, John and Tina – all contacted during the writing of this book – each expressed a yearning to, as The Blues Brothers would have it, 'get the band back together'. There's unfinished business and huge talent languishing. Might it be too much to suggest they're 'on a mission from Dod'? Let's hope so.

Tamalin, 1989:
(l–r) Paul, Tina, John, Jo, Dod

TAMALIN
KEEPING IT IN THE FAMILY

The idea of mixing traditional music and rock music isn't a new one. In fact, it's so old that it's had plenty of time to be done badly many times over, and now a four-fifths family group from west Belfast are doing it all over again – and doing it with more subtlety, integrity and imagination than anyone else has managed for years. Of course, like any bunch of folkies, getting them to analyse the thing in any kind of depth is a waste of time. They don't care – they're musicians, they just do it.

Led by the sultry and silken-voiced Tina McSherry and featuring Paul McSherry on guitar, John McSherry on uilleann pipes and Joanne McSherry on fiddle, with Kevin 'Dod' Dorris on bouzouki, the ensemble have just finished recording an album that should instantly establish their name within the international music industry and their sound as perhaps the most exciting and refreshing to come out of the Irish tradition for years. They incorporate elements of Balkan and Breton music in this unique concoction, elements of musicianship on the highest level; they herald, as influences, Led Zeppelin and The Bothy Band in equal measure; they're a little shambolic but a lot enthusiastic – musicians to the hilt. They are, in short, Tamalin. And no one seems to remember how it all began.

'Well, you see, we were all playing on the traditional scene for years,' says Tina, 'as a family. The first big festival we did was Ballyshannon in 1986, as The McSherrys. But it was never a serious thing. We just did it in the summer when we weren't at school or university, and then Paul and I graduated with degrees and couldn't get any jobs so we decided, "Right – we're going to do this?" I think we've started to really take it seriously within the last year although, as I say, we've all been playing together without any direction for ages. Doing this CD has given us something to aim for.'

And judging from the results, which should be widely available within a matter of weeks, they've really hit the bullseye. Although like many of their contemporaries on the Belfast music scene their labours are essentially of a self-financed nature, Tamalin have been lucky enough to have had the professional help and encouragement of two musicians well versed in the practicalities of the business and in achieving work of an international quality.

Former Bothy Band hero Donal Lunny oversaw the as-yet untitled album's final mix, while the whole project has been effectively steered through by Dave Early, percussionist to the stars, as Tina explains: 'We're very easygoing,' she says, 'but Dave gets things happening – a mover and a shaker. We're not very

Colin Harper · Originally published in the *Irish News* (3 February 1995)

pushy. We only really push ourselves. But Dave's really into our music – he heard us a few years back and said he was very interested in experimenting with rhythms in Irish music, which he'd never really done before. So we organised some of the recording costs and Dave organised the rest. We've been lucky there, although it's coming out of our pockets at the end of the day. We'll own it ourselves but we're licensing it to various record companies in different territories and they're giving us advance royalties to pay for the recording.'

Those territories include Ireland, Scotland and various parts of Europe where the band have, in typically vague fashion, already toured: 'Our whole lives are about music,' says John. 'So everywhere we go we bring our instruments and meet people – and end up getting invited back to play.'

Still only in his early twenties, John has already been an Oireachtas champion on his instrument (at eighteen, the youngest ever), beating the legendary Peter Browne in the process. But it could have been Tina: 'Yes, I used to play the pipes,' she says. 'We were given a set by a friend, Noel Fitzpatrick. He couldn't actually play them himself but he was really encouraging to us. I started playing them before John – and then he stole them on me! He used to lock himself in his bedroom and practice. Come six o'clock every Saturday night, without exception, you couldn't get into his room. All you'd hear was pipes – till one in the morning.'

John's own version of the story concurs in every respect save one: it wasn't just Saturday night, it was every night. Clearly, in this case, the practise has made as near to perfect as makes no difference. Tina though – now flautist as well as vocalist – wasn't the only sibling to manage a false start: 'Joanne actually started on the trumpet at school,' she says, much to Joanne's embarrassment. 'She wanted to play the fiddle but they didn't have enough to go round, so she had to progress onto it. It was amazing really – she was asthmatic, so why they gave her a trumpet I've no idea . . .'

Ask them if they come from a musical family and they'll laugh at you (of course they do – they're all musicians, aren't they?). 'Parents, you mean?' says Tina. 'I suppose so. My dad plays classical piano, but he's really into traditional music and that's what got us into it. In fact, the first concert we ever saw was Planxty at the Ulster Hall – the last concert Planxty ever did. It was 1980 or '81 and the place was absolutely jam-packed. My mother brought the four of us along. It was fantastic.'

A seminal experience then? 'Well, I can't remember it,' says John. So, perhaps not.

That said, the whole group are steeped in traditional music and in the Belfast sessions scene and yet, as urban-dwelling radio listeners, are instinctively attuned to the possibility of a crossover audience in contemporary music: 'We don't really want to be part of any scene,' says Tina. 'We're just what we are and we play the music we like. Yes, we're coming from a traditional background, but we're not confined to that. We're going in our own direction: we are Tamalin.'

TAMALIN

'People always ask me, "Aren't you in a band?"' says Joanne McSherry, youngest and quietest member of Tamalin. 'And sometimes I wonder . . .' With her brothers John on uilleann pipes, Paul on guitar and sister Tina on flute and vocals (plus Kevin Dorris on bouzouki), Joanne is indeed in a band – the most exciting, innovative band to come out of Irish music in years. It's just that time's getting on and they've been kind of sitting on a debut album, in one form or another, for three years. The frustration is beginning to show.

Rhythm & Rhyme is the title of the *magnum opus*, after the lead track from Northern Irish songwriter Eamon McElholm, and Tamalin themselves are proud to be not only from Northern Ireland but from west Belfast – a part of the world given plenty of bad press but surely now, with the rise of both Brian Kennedy and, as far as my money's concerned, Tamalin, beginning to balance up the aura leant by Van Morrison to the east of the city. To play on the notion of austere Protestants and sensual Catholics would be too simple, but Tamalin do share with Van a similar, tough upbringing coloured largely by music – and where one had blues and soul, the other had Irish traditional music. And Tamalin, most especially Tina – at 28 the eldest of the siblings – are just as single-minded and spiritual about the power of music: 'We were brought up in the unemployment culture of west Belfast,' she says, 'and we're playing the music because we love the music. It's a way of life. The Bothy Band brought traditional music to new heights in the Seventies. Planxty, De Danann, Moving Hearts – they all brought a new sound. But after Moving Hearts there was no new sound, just people playing straight, like having a session on stage. We're bringing a new sound to it.'

It's a bold claim, but Tina – a quite exceptional vocalist, a powerful, sensual stage presence and, as the finished version of their album (released this month on Grapevine) confirms, a very fine songwriter – is not one to waste time on false modesty. Neither is she arrogant – indeed there have been times over the past while when her self-confidence has been dangerously low, but such is the way of a true artist. Tamalin, as a unit, have been a rare presence on the Belfast live scene, but always involved individually in other projects. Paul has worked with Brian Kennedy, Liam O'Flynn and Paddy Keenan for instance, while John, at 24, is a piping phenomenon – championed by Donal Lunny and with sessions for Rod Stewart, Gary Kemp, Maura O'Connell and others already under his belt. Tina, likewise, is spoken of in some awe by the local rock 'n' roll fraternity – freely lending her voice to all sorts of demos and localised

Colin Harper · Originally published in *Mojo* (September 1997)

Tamalin, 1997:
(l–r) Tina, Paul, Dod, Jo, John

releases by such people – but is stand-offish about lumping Tamalin in with the likes of Ash and The Divine Comedy as some kind of Ulster renaissance: 'These people are all in the same game really,' she says, diplomatically, 'whereas we're coming down a different road entirely. And there's not too many other people on it.' And is there a living to be made at it? 'I don't know,' she says. 'That's what we're going to find out.'

For reference points, imagine Irish music, Breton music, a dash of East European time signatures, a heavy dose of Plant and Page, The Corrs – at least in the photogeneity department – and you've got Tamalin. Dark, sensual and intoxicating. Compelling versions of Richard Thompson's 'Crazy Man Michael' and Zeppelin's 'Poor Tom' may be a way in to many, but there's so much more to make *Rhythm & Rhyme* a debut-of-the-year contender. John, Paul, Jo and Tina – has a certain ring to it, don't you think?

SECTION 8
LOST &
FOUND!

Cara Dillon,
2003

CARA DILLON
PROLOGUE

Having spent a good two or three years in the mid-Nineties vainly trying to rectify the career impasses of various beleaguered and unsigned Northern Irish musicians, the relationship between the brick wall and my head felt largely unchanged. It's true that a few individuals from that scene, including singer-songwriter Brian Houston, session guitarist Iain Archer, jazz/funk band-leader Linley Hamilton and multi-instrumentalist Steve Jones, did manage to carve their own viability as music professionals (generally as sidemen or in niche markets abroad), but not too many bands or solo artists were able to maintain a career, or the will-power to keep looking for one, past the inevitably self-funded album stage. Two exceptions were Colin Reid and Cara Dillon.

I first met Cara *circa* 1991, in the context of singing and playing second-fiddle (literally) in Paul McLaughlin's newly formed trad quartet, Óige. A canny operator, an easy-going guy and a more than decent guitarist, it would be wrong to say that Paul was a truly vocational musician. Rather, he saw the European demand for Irish music and tapped into it with a part-time band comprising, aside from himself, a trio of gifted pre-school-leaving teenagers from his Dungiven locale.

I thoroughly enjoyed Óige playing live on many occasions, and was vaguely involved in a PR capacity at one point, but mostly I had the uncomplicated joy of being a hanger-on, delighting in the shared adventure of a terrific, fun band. Recordings were never too much of a priority – really, just something to sell at the gigs. I reviewed a 1992 show for *Folk Roots* in which, aside from my unashamedly gushing enthusiasm as a fan, I managed just enough integrity to decry a certain dependency on lifting songs straight off Mary Black albums and suchlike – with the caveat that 'with a singer like Cara Dillon, who not only looks but sounds like a sweeter and younger Máire Brennan, any lack of originality in vocal material hardly seems to matter at this point in time'. Well, it didn't!

Óige made three albums in all: the first (*Inspiration*) a cassette-only local release and the others (*Live In Glasgow* and *Bang On*, this latter with replace-ment vocalist Maranna McCloskey) licensed to Scottish label KRL. Somewhere in the middle, in April 1995, was a live performance recorded at the Warehouse, Belfast for a multi-artist showcase album I pulled together with a load of brinkmanship and financial goodwill from various quarters. Covers of The Bothy Band's haunting 'Maids Of Mitchelstown' instrumental and the Owen Hand (no doubt via Mary Black) whaling lament 'My Donal', with an

Colin Harper

Óige, live at the Warehouse, Belfast, April 1995: Cara Dillon (left), Ruairí Ó Catháin

incredible vocal from Cara, were Óige's contributions. Practically every other band involved were in awe of Cara – and they weren't alone. Around that time she was fielding overtures from people like Phil Coulter and Frankie Gavin. For her *not* to become a professional musician seemed completely wrong. Then again, quiet, shy, seemingly lacking much depth in her listening interests and not yet physically commanding as a stage performer, there were factors that did mitigate against this truly natural talent being able to find a path of her own through the big, bad world of professional music.

When Cara moved to Devon to join the much-heralded folk 'supergroup' Equation, already signed with Warners, the need to find that solitary path was neatly circumvented. And then nothing happened. Then she left to go solo. And still nothing happened.

Several years later I was asked by local PR guru Peter Fleming if I wanted to interview Cara, whose five-year lost weekend as a would-be pop star had just come to a spectacular end with the release of her first, almost wholly traditional, solo album. At last! Reacquainting myself with this incredibly gifted young woman was a revelation – confident, courteous, by now well schooled in the history of music and completely focused on the job in hand, Cara had been through the record-business mill enough times to crush anyone's spirit and had triumphed. Seeing her perform shortly afterwards at the Ulster Hall with passion and presence – and, crikey, standing up as well! – sent any lingering doubts, had any remained, fleeing into the night.

With her partner Sam Lakeman not only a cool-headed fellow-traveller and survivor through the wilderness years but a brilliant piano accompanist and arranger, Cara's long-term future seems assured. The world doesn't owe anyone a living, and especially not the music world. But never believe that Cara Dillon hasn't earned it.

CARA DILLON

'I've been stuck away in studios and in people's houses writing songs with them for *five years* now,' says Cara Dillon, exhausted from a frenzy of recent gigs, radio sessions and an endless round of career *précis*-ing over cappuccinos with people like me. 'So to finally get out and start to do gigs is incredible. It's been a heavy schedule recently but I'm not complaining one bit. I love it and I'm so glad to be out doing the work again. It's what I've been waiting for all this time.'

Born and raised in Dungiven, County Derry, Cara's self-titled album, released in July on long-time champion Geoff Travis' Rough Trade label, will be the first time many people will have heard her voice – and once heard it won't be forgotten. In loosely similar territory to Clannad's Brennan sisters and with a gentle hint of northern lilt and a beautiful, natural quality that eschews any need for soft-focus trickery in the studio, it is the kind of voice that one could imagine luring doomed wayfarers to the Land of Faerie, never to return. Compounding the mystic metaphor Cara herself is the very embodiment of words like 'elfin' and 'sylphlike' – superficially delicate perhaps, but brimming with the measured self-confidence and belief that are crucial in weathering the modern music business and which only come with experience. Of that, Cara – a little like David Gray, who was four albums in before the world beyond Ireland even noticed – has had plenty, and still only 25.

Touring Europe and fronting records during 1990–95 – during school holidays, of course – with part-time traditional group Óige, she was then drafted in to front Warner Music signing Equation, a Devon-based group featuring the brothers Sam, Seth and Sean Lakeman. A career in music seemed ready-made, but the backlash from the English folk community against an act perceived to be a vacuous pop-folk marketing ploy was vicious – let alone those time-honoured 'musical differences': 'Whenever I joined Equation it was really exciting,' says Cara. 'We were all young – I was only nineteen at the time – and we were all totally blown away by the amount of publicity we were getting before we'd even done anything. And the money that was being spent on us . . . We went to Real World Studios and the album *Turn To Me* was recorded there [though, given Cara's decision to leave shortly after, never released], there was a single release, there were videos made, we were on VH1 – everything was going incredibly well. But the problem was there were seven of us in the band, each person incredibly talented and with a lot of ideas. From the very onset Sam Lakeman and myself found we had the same taste in music,

Colin Harper · Originally published in *The Irish Times* (16 August 2001)

same interests, same musical direction. We thought, We're not going to be able to pull this off, because we're not being true to ourselves. Let's go off and try it ourselves – do what we really want to do.'

Sam and Cara left the band and relations are currently civil: 'Because there was such a long build up to it, our leaving wasn't a big deal at the end.' There is a possibility that Rough Trade will license and belatedly release her 'lost' album with the group, which she feels relaxed about: 'It'll show the development of where we're all at today.'

A version of Equation are still going – currently trying to crack America – but within the last four months Sam's brother Seth has also left the family band and joined the two defectors. Should third brother Sean do likewise, there remains the truly bizarre prospect of Cara fronting, once again, Equation in all but name.

Compared to the missing years of 1996–2000, however, the Equation experience was but a picnic. Cara and Sam (currently engaged to be married as well as musical partners) were still signed to Warners and Cara was now 'in development' as a solo artist. Entire future boxed sets' worth of demos – even a finished album, recorded over four months in San Francisco – were recorded and rejected. Nothing was to be released: 'In the end Sam and myself just decided we're never going to give Warners the album they want. Every time we had a song we were happy with they'd say, "Right, back to the drawing board, try and do something more commercial," or they'd introduce us to a producer who'd take the one part of the song we really loved and say, "Right, we'll drop that bit and fiddle about with the music a bit . . ."'

Inevitably, with producers more sheep-like than sheep, the string of people Sam and Cara were teamed up with would identify a vaguely similar successful act and try to mould the Sam and Cara sound in that image: The Corrs, The Cranberries, The Sundays, et al. 'It was fantastic that we were getting all this attention and that they had so much faith that we were able to do it but it was a hell of a lot of pressure – to go to a meeting and play a song and then to have someone say, "We love it, we love it . . . but come back in a couple of weeks with a more jazzed-up version." And we, of course, would have thought that we'd already done the perfect version, got it absolutely right. It was just frustration. I'm sure Warners must have realised at some point that it was never really going to happen. In the end we asked ourselves, "What do we really want to do?" And we wanted to do an album with folk songs and maybe a couple of our own on it and we wanted to do it ourselves.'

Retreating to the Lakeman family studio in Devon, the current album of almost entirely traditional songs was arranged, produced and engineered very largely by Sam, with Sinéad O'Connor associate John Reynolds (a friend of Cara's rather than a record-label place man) finishing things off with a stunningly fresh, airy mix.

Cara sanguinely acknowledges that the whole Warners process was not time wasted but was necessary to steel and refine her for a solo career, and for what

Óige, 1992:
(l–r) Cara Dillon, Murrough Ó Catháin,
Ruairí Ó Catháin, Paul McLaughlin

the real-life, out-there-doing-it music game can throw at one. Though happy to be seen as a 'folk singer', and to bring the traditional songs she loves to a potentially mass audience, her musical tastes – Joni Mitchell, Janis Ian, Talk Talk, Nick Drake – have a breadth and voracious inquisitiveness generally unusual among young folk involved in the folk scenes of either Ireland or England, where she remains based. Refreshingly, Cara Dillon is part of no clique or scene, real or imagined, be it the English 'folk babes' such as Kate Rusby or Eliza Carthy, or the incestuous world of professional Irish trad.

David Kitt is currently remixing two album tracks for a possible single release and, having tested the water with thoroughly successful appearances at the Witness and Cambridge Folk Festivals, September sees Cara's first major Dublin gig at HQ, followed a couple of days later by one for the family at the near-Dungiven Portglenone Festival. Welcome home.

Colin Reid,
moving on in 2004

COLIN REID
PROLOGUE

I could say a lot about Colin Reid and all of it would be good. In fact, I did just that under the guise of a sleeve-note to his first album – a wholly instrumental eponymous effort on a label called Veesik in the Shetlands. Short of doing a tour of Rockall and St Kilda, it doesn't come much more unlikely than that. But then everything about Colin's career has been unlikely.

To quote from that very sleeve-note, written in the latter part of 1998: 'There aren't many world-class practitioners of steel-strung instrumental music kicking around these days who haven't already been doing so, however consummately, for the past 30-odd years. Certainly not in Britain and most definitely not in Northern Ireland. It is a matter of some irony that the slight but delightful tradition of "British fingerstyle" playing seems to be healthier in America today than any place within a hammer-on, trill or legato of the British Isles. It's also remarkable, and refreshingly so, to know that much as Reid now casually admires the holy trinity of Davy Graham, Bert Jansch and John Renbourn (along with the various other people whose names, in his experience, generally follow the words, "Blimey, that last tune you did sounds just like . . .") he is as far removed from being the stereotypical guitar bore as one can imagine . . . The more one hears his recorded work the more clearly every aspect of the man's character appears in the music: a mischievous glance, a witty aside, the generous spirit, the studious cool and the reckless bravado. Most of all, the love of music and the very simplicity of expression that a mastery of technique can offer to those who choose it as a means and not an end in itself. Pundits always assume Northern Ireland's next great export will be another noisy guitar band: The Undertones, Therapy?, Ash . . . Out through the side door, Colin Reid has come forth.'

Three albums and two long-form conceptual pieces in (the latter giving musical wings to the myth of Icarus and Flann O'Brien's *The Third Policeman* respectively) and my opinion remains unchanged: Colin Reid is the exception to every rule there is about success, the music business and Northern Ireland.

I never met Colin during his dues-paying slog around the Belfast pub scene in the early Nineties, as lead guitarist in a band called Charlie Chan – whose prime achievement was apparently coming second in a talent competition – but I've met a hundred and one people in precisely the same position he was in. The only difference being he got out of it. Blissfully unaware of the specialised world of instrumental acoustic-guitar music, Colin left the band, bought a cheap acoustic from an Argos store and went to study music in

Colin Harper

London. I first encountered his name on the side of a cassette demo, discreetly passed on by a mutual acquaintance, and I was stunned at the quality, precision and panache of both the playing and the compositional ideas. I loved the music but I would never in a million years have put money on it finding a market. How lucky it is, then, that my opinion adds up to some way short of a row of beans.

Northern Ireland is full of would-be rock stars who mostly end up burned out and stoic or nursing enormous chips on their shoulders about the people whose fault it supposedly is (and generally isn't) that they're not rich and famous. Fair enough – Colin may not be a household name (except, of course, in his own household) and he's certainly not rich – but he's a generous, genuine, implacably resolved and hugely talented fellow whose international fan base and widespread media support belie the supposedly specialised nature of his art. He has beaten the system, without ever getting hung up on knowing how the system was meant to work in the first place. Long may he continue to do so.

COLIN REID

For seasoned observers of the British folk scene, January 1999 brought something quietly remarkable – on at least two levels. The subject was a low-budget, self-titled, all-instrumental debut album by the largely unknown Colin Reid on the completely unknown Veesik, a record label based (of course) on the Shetland Islands. The first point of interest was that here was an extraordinarily beautiful, exquisitely played record that confirmed the arrival of arguably the first new player of steel-strung guitar of note since the Bert Jansch/John Renbourn generation back in the Sixties – and certainly since the more ghetto-bound Gordon Giltrap/Nic Jones/Martin Simpson refinings of that style in the Seventies. The second point was the quite unprecedented levels of publicity the album received. Broadsheet newspapers, glossy monthlies and the modest organs of the never-say-die folk revival all leapt on Reid's compositional freshness yet seemingly well-rooted style as evidence that the Messiah of that increasingly arcane byway of music known (largely by its legions of earnest American devotees) as 'British fingerstyle', or 'folk-baroque' if you really must, had arrived. And strangely enough, the Messiah spoke with a Belfast accent.

'People need to describe a musician in terms of somebody else,' says Reid, with the breeziness of one to whom the categorisation question is an old favourite. 'So for those people familiar with British fingerstyle, that's what they hear. I had no conception that was what I was doing at all, and consequently sent it off to a whole range of people in the media – and I think that was part of the winning formula. It was naivety, but then again not naivety – I would *still* send anything I did to absolutely everybody I could think of, in the hope that it would click with someone.' Two and a half years down the line, Reid is doing the whole thing again, but who is he, where has he come from and is he not, in fact, closer to a one-man Penguin Café Orchestra than an old-style guitar hero?

Growing up at the leafy end of east Belfast, and currently living with his partner and manager (the managing came first) Kresanna Aigner and their recently born twins in even leafier south Belfast, Reid spent his youth in standard electric-guitar bands before having a road-to-Damascus experience with ragtime music and a cheap acoustic that set him off to music college in London for a year followed by a popular, and periodically ongoing, residency as teacher of guitar classes at Belfast's Crescent Arts Centre, where he also rents an office. Something of a bon viveur around the cosmopolitan coffee houses

Colin Harper · Originally published in *The Irish Times* (6 June 2001)

that abound in this university area of the city, Reid nevertheless puts in the graft and takes music seriously as a business. Talent aside, this very attitude is central in his success to date, in a city swarming with washed-up musical wannabes and whingeing also-rans. Indeed, who would have thought that an unamplified instrumentalist could launch a career of any sort from a place known principally for its angsty guitar bands?

'I suppose in the context of Belfast I am a bit unusual in having done that,' says Reid, over a sunny Sunday cappuccino in one of his regular haunts, 'but at the same time it's always seemed absolutely obvious to me. I've had conversations with the kind of people you're talking about and a paraphrase might run along the lines of "The chairman of Sony hasn't got in touch with me," to which I'd say, "Well, have you actually called him . . .?" About five years ago I realised it was a business and that one had to behave in a businesslike manner. And as soon as I got rid, myself, of any notions of the chairman of Sony arriving with a million quid things started to happen. The word "professional" is quite interesting because it's not quite hand to mouth, but it's certainly month by month. Once you've written the music and done the recording the artistry's over and pragmatism on a business level begins. Can I get to the point where I can feed my family doing this? is a question I've been thinking fairly seriously about recently. It used to be I could work really hard for a month and then take it easier for a couple of months, but since the kids have come along that's changed. Yet the size of the mountain doesn't really interest me, so long as I'm interested in the challenge of climbing it – and because I believe absolutely in what I'm doing in terms of the quality of the work I *have* to believe that there's a market for it.'

One aspect of the challenge is the mischievously, gloriously uncategorisable nature of Reid's new album, *Tilt* – recorded on a relatively sumptuous budget for the venerable English trad label Topic. Boasting a superb ensemble, including Gino Lupari on bodhrán, Brian Connor on piano, Eddi Reader on guest vocals and most pertinently a neither-trad-nor-classical string quartet featuring the likes of Máire Breathnach and Russian gypsy group Loyko's Oleg Ponomarev, the material veers seamlessly between pieces of great cinematic beauty, cartwheeling rumbustiousness and a slightly bizarre slice of pre-war tea-dance pastichery that The Bonzo Dog Band would have sold their granny's greenhouse for. The Penguin Café Orchestra – quirky yet sublime – remains the overall reference point, underlined by Reid's cover of their 'Music For A Found Harmonium'.

'A lot of people think it's a great departure,' says Reid, who clearly delights in confounding those people, 'but I think the clues were all there. If you play the first CD backwards the message, "There will be more strings", is plainly audible! But then one of the things I would like my audiences to expect is something different. I don't mean Belgian nose-flute music, but rather something fresh and exciting and of a certain quality.'

Having toured now quite extensively in Scotland, England and parts of

America, there is a sense in which Reid is an aspirant to European café and neo-classical music but who is generally pigeon-holed as either a Brit-folk guitar hero or a fringe-benefiter of the Celtic scene, within which he has quietly moved for sometime (accompanying on tours, in a previous life, the likes of Niamh Parsons). 'When I write a tune,' he explains, 'I just want it to be the best tune I can make it – not an exercise in writing something that someone can describe as a bit classical, or a bit folky, or whatever else.'

While he has played a number of sell-out solo concerts in his home town, barring odd special-guesting to the likes of Richard Thompson, Anuna and Martin Carthy, the cities of the Republic have thus far eluded him: 'I'm determined to get it,' he says – 'Determined to get viable concerts in the bigger towns. Mind you, myself and everyone I know in the music business are at a loss as to how you achieve that. Do *you* have any ideas?'

Alas, there the coffee and the cassette ran out. Some mountains one must leave to those with an iron will and a better address book than I. I'll gladly write about him when he gets to the top – whether that be via the town halls of Offaly or otherwise – and I'll gladly do so now. Colin Reid: whatever else, he's a touch of class.

SECTION 9
LAST TIME AROUND

Ornette Coleman (far right)
and the 'Belfast Suite'
band, Whitla Hall, Belfast,
November 2000

TOWNES VAN ZANDT, JOHN FAHEY & ORNETTE COLEMAN IRISH SWANSONGS

None of these people are Irish and, so far as we are aware, none have any claim whatsoever upon Irish ancestry – although John Fahey's surname may indeed offer some hope on such a quest. But no, Townes Van Zandt was a Texas country-folk maverick who's way-left-of-Nashville stance defined him as the first of the true believers among the Steve Earles and Nanci Griffithses of the modern world; John Fahey was the father of almost all genres of instrumental guitar music, certainly in America; and Ornette Coleman was and remains an icon of jazz and a rule-book destroyer of J.S. Bach proportions.

Time will tell if Coleman's alternate book of rules – a book that, for the moment, appears to exist only in his head – will ever be understood by anyone else, but all three made rare visits to Ireland, and specifically to Belfast, towards the end of their careers. In Coleman's case, we are making an assumption that given his age and his status (and consequently his fee) it is unlikely he will return. However bizarre, frustrating or challenging Trevor, myself and the Belfast audience in general found their performances, we are surely enriched by having experienced them. Let us not leave them unsung.

On a personal level, the Townes Van Zandt show was the first time I met Trevor – introduced by record distributor Kyle Leitch, who can himself claim a rare degree of responsibility in having made much American singer-song-writer music available to the record buyers of Belfast in the pre-chain-store era of the late Seventies and Eighties. It's a small world, and a smaller town.

My abiding memory of the John Fahey show was sitting round a table in the auditorium having an absurdly intense debate with Trevor and perhaps half a dozen of the other pundits, writers and broadcasters of the city (who had gathered, en masse, for this rare opportunity of sitting at the feet of a legend among legends). It was sometime after the recital – if recital it could be called, for certainly it was no 'show' – had ended and even the most dedicated punters had left, no doubt collecting a prize for endurance on the way out. All around us people were dismantling the stage and PA. Amidst various levels of quizzical doubt about the quality of what we had just been listening to for the previous . . . oh, decade, it felt like, one voice – from a particularly combative member of our clique who, we were all virtually certain, had spent the greater part of Fahey's performance in the bar – was vehemently insisting that the man had given some kind of masterclass, and what a gang of philistines and amateurs we all were if we couldn't grasp it.

While this was going on – and while Trevor, as I recall, was unfortunately

Colin Harper

bearing the brunt of our colleague's booze-fuelled ire – Fahey himself strolled past the table, wearing a big grin and a Sony Walkman. Had the emperor been wearing new clothes? It wouldn't have surprised me if, having taken the rise out of America's po-faced blues fraternity in 1959 with the invention of spurious alter-ego Blind Joe Death, Fahey was now seeing just how far he could do likewise with his entire international fan base, or what was left of it. What, I wondered, was contained in that personal stereo? We shall never know.

Looking back on the Ornette Coleman show, it was clear we were not hearing the work of a charlatan. A visitor from the planet Zog, perhaps, but not a charlatan. At the time I seem to have thrown all the blame on the distinct failure of the fusion (about as fuseable as oil and water, it seemed) on the unfortunate shoulders of the seven traditional musicians. With a bit of retrospect, and the benefit of John McSherry's still wide-eyed recollections of the affair, I admit it: I was wrong. The problem was not in the unyielding rigidity of the traddies, but in the mind-bogglingly all but non-existent nature of Ornette's commissioned canvas. At £70,000 let no one, ever again, say that this man is the father of free jazz!

TOWNES VAN ZANDT
PROLOGUE

Never interview a musician in a crowded dressing room. That was the hard lesson I learned from my encounter with Townes Van Zandt backstage in the Elmwood Hall, Belfast, amidst a madding throng of tossers, dossers, deadbeats and crawlers.

Prior to the interview I had borrowed and listened closely to every album Van Zandt had ever recorded. Trust me: I knew this guy's stuff inside out. But every question I asked was greeted with, at best, snorts of derision from the mob and, at worst, loud jeers and abuse. Every time I asked a follow-up question one angry voice in particular would gulder, 'It's pretty bloody obvious what the man means.' Every mild witticism from Van Zandt was greeted with howls of moronic laughter from the assembled arse-lickers. From time to time a question would even be interrupted by one of these low-lifes elbowing me aside so that they could offer their hero a hit from a hookah or a slug from a bottle of *poitín*.

So far, so bad. But worse, Van Zandt chose to side with the mob. When, for example, I asked him about his spiritual beliefs – a reasonable question because, presumably unbeknownst to the bums who were swigging his complimentary booze, Van Zandt had, years previously, recorded a few explicitly Christian songs – he reacted as if I were some kind of sectarian bigot. And, of course, got a round of applause and a huge cheer, at my expense, for doing so. Well, I guess if you spend long months on the road you have to make your own entertainment, and he's not the first guy in history to go for the easy laugh and play to the gallery.

And, notwithstanding the somewhat bruising experience I had interviewing him, I've no problem acknowledging that there are plenty of people who knew Van Zandt a thousand times better than I did who will tell you what a wonderful guy he was. I'm happy to take their word for that. But I admit that, even now, nine years later, in quiet moments, I sometimes think back to that interview and fantasise about taking the complete works of Townes Van Zandt and ramming them, LP by LP, down the throats of the sleazeballs, scumbags and sycophants who comprised his Elmwood Hall fan club.

Trevor Hodgett

TOWNES VAN ZANDT

Townes Van Zandt is the singer-songwriters' singer-songwriter and the cult artists' cult artist. None of the dozen or so albums he has made since 1968 has sold a damn and yet many a megastar would kill his granny for a fraction of the acclaim from critics and from peers that Van Zandt has received.

The Townes Van Zandt Interview Experience, as sampled after his recent successful gig in Belfast's Elmwood Hall, involves non sequiturs, digressions, put-ons, turn-offs, delightful idiosyncrasy, tedious idiosyncrasy and a measure of squirming embarrassment. Who else but Van Zandt, for example, would answer an inquiry as to whether songwriting becomes more difficult as the years pass, with this explanation: 'I liken it to if you first fall in love and you go into a giant field of daisies. You can just pick whatever daisies you want and take them to your loved one, and you stay in love and you go back to the field and you pick some more daisies. And the longer you stay in love the more daisies you pick, and once you've picked most of these daisies you've got to look around for the daisies to carry your loved one the bouquet!'

Steve Earle famously said that he would 'like to stand on Bob Dylan's coffee table and tell him Van Zandt's a better songwriter'. 'That's a nice thing to say, a fun thing to say. But songwriting's not a competitive sport, so it just doesn't make any sense. Plus, I've met Bob Dylan's bodyguards and if Steve Earle thinks he can jump on Bob Dylan's coffee table in his cowboy boots he'd better be careful! I wouldn't.'

Van Zandt's first album, *For The Sake Of The Song*, was recorded in Nashville in 1968. 'Mickey Newbury ran into me when I was playing in Houston and said, "You got to come to Nashville." I was a cowboy hippy from Texas. All of a sudden I'm in this studio with twelve of the best, top-of-the-line, A-stream musicians, like David Briggs and Charlie McCoy, and I was just awestruck. Caught me by surprise, man, and I listened to it afterwards and I realised that this is not the way. Any deal now, I have veto power.

'When I started,' digresses Van Zandt, 'you could audition on Wednesday and have a job on Friday for twenty bucks, which would last you all week, if you didn't have any bad habits, which I don't, and I still don't to this day. And I don't appreciate you thinking that I do,' he adds bizarrely. 'I don't gamble, I don't lie, I don't cheat, I don't commit adultery and I don't drink.' An impressive declamation, somewhat undermined by the fact that to the untrained observer Van Zandt seems distinctly pissed. But moving briskly on . . .

Van Zandt's second album, *Our Mother The Mountain*, features one of his

Trevor Hodgett · Originally published in *Rock'n'Reel* (July 1994)

greatest songs, the extraordinarily bleak 'Kathleen', recently covered by Tindersticks. A contemporary quote indicated the depression to which Van Zandt was apparently prone: 'There's been a lot of times when depression with me just became physical it hurt so bad. It was wrenching me apart, wrenching my brain apart . . . to the point where I was holding my head and screaming. There's been times when I have the feeling that if I could just chop my hands off then everything would be fine.' So how did Van Zandt manage to come through such depression? 'Perseverance and faith.' Faith in what, Townes? 'The all-powerful, wherever or whoever he or it might be. And in cigarettes and whiskey and gambling!'

Van Zandt's spiritual side is most explicit on his 1971 album *High Low And In Between*, which features two terrific songs of praise – 'Two Hands' and 'When He Offers His Hand'. Had Van Zandt actually been born again, at that time? 'If you're stillborn, you don't have to be born again!' he quips evasively. 'They're just gospel songs. A lot of the time I'm not exactly in charge of writing the songs. Songs write themselves and I write them down.

'You're talking about religion in human terms and that don't get it. That's politics.' No I wasn't, Townes, but go on . . . 'Have you ever hidden in the woods and seen a deer give birth?' he asks, the purpose of this question apparent only – perhaps – to himself. 'I have. I'm an expert hunter and a shot and a fisherman; used to be a pretty good skinner and pretty good tracker. And I made a promise that I will never ever shoot anything that's alive, unless it's attacking me or my family or I have to eat it.'

The Late Great Townes Van Zandt, released in 1973, features the first recordings of Van Zandt's two most famous songs, 'If I Needed You' and 'Pancho And Lefty'. 'If I Needed You' was covered by Doc Watson, amongst others. 'One of the proudest moments of my life. Doc Watson! Wow! I don't know if I ever got any money from it, but it made no difference: it was one of the nicest things that will ever have happened to me – and nice things happen to me almost every minute.'

'Pancho And Lefty' became the most covered of all Van Zandt's songs, being famously recorded by Willie Nelson and Waylon Jennings and countless others. 'Because it's learnable!' asserts Van Zandt. 'There's reports of Eskimos sitting around little ice campfires, singing "Pancho And Lefty" on whale-string guitars! I bet you a dime to a doughnut that somebody, somewhere in the world, is either thinking about it or playing it on the radio or playing it on the guitar. It's learnable.' Apart from the Eskimo version, does Van Zandt have a favourite version of the song? 'The best one I ever heard was me and [guitarist] Philip Donnelly playing it live in Dublin. Second best is the one on my record – the live one. Unless they screwed it up on the CD, which they usually do.' The live album in question is presumably 1977's *Live At The Old Quarter*, which raises a paradox of Van Zandt's career: for someone whose image is of a sombre introvert, he clearly loves playing live. 'I like to meet the people and I like the sound of the microphone. And the only place you can get warm in this country is under the spotlights!'

After 1978's *Flying Shoes* Van Zandt didn't record for nine years. 'I was in the mountains on horseback and in the countryside doing gigs with a band – Townes Van Zandt & The Hemmer Ridge Mountain Boys. All alcoholic lunatics in a motor home. It was like crazy. Our bar tab would be $800 and we're making two beans. It was a terrible period of my life, but during the summer I'd leave them all and go into the mountains on horseback and go into the wilderness by myself. I did that for six to eight years.'

Finally, in 1987, *Live And Obscure* was released on Heartland. 'It was a bootleg,' claims Van Zandt. 'Nobody told me about it. I didn't know it was being recorded. I made a lot of money on it – eight or nine bucks.'

At My Window, on Sugar Hill, confirmed Van Zandt's comeback. 'This is after I came back from the mountain. I decided to come back to Nashville and give it another chance. The reason is my wife had a baby boy and "Pancho And Lefty" went platinum and I felt, Man, I got this family and I'm going crazy in Texas – too much fun in Texas – so we moved to Nashville and made that record and since then I've just been playing.'

Rain On A Conga Drum, released by Exile in 1991, features a surprising cover of The Rolling Stones' 'Dead Flowers'. 'I always loved that song. Sometimes, if there's any kids in the audience, I leave out the line about the needle and spoon and instead I sing, "*I'm in my basement room de da da da da da . . .*" But it usually ain't the case – they don't usually hire me at kindergarten!'

Van Zandt has recently recorded a new album, in Ireland. 'It's called *No Deeper Blue* after one of the lines. It's got a whole Irish feel. I had this dream that said, Come over here and do this with Philip Donnelly, and I called Philip the next morning and he said, "Lovely." And we pulled it off. It's out in August on Veracity.'

Any final thoughts you'd like to impart, Townes? 'Just how much of a pleasure this whole trip has been – I've found the nicest cocktail onions on the roadside that I've ever seen before!'

Postscript: Townes Van Zandt died in 1997, aged 52.

JOHN FAHEY
PROLOGUE

'Hello, John, I'm Trevor Hodgett – I interviewed you yesterday for the *Irish News*.'

'Gnnnnggghhhh.'

'Nice to see you.'

'Urggghhh. Gnnnnggghhhh.'

And the great John Fahey, mere minutes after completing his Irish debut performance, shuffled on past me out into the damp and chilly Belfast autumn air, clad in nought but the T-shirt and shorts, socks and trainers that were rumoured to be the only clothing he had brought with him from his motel home in Oregon.

Well, I certainly didn't mind Fahey not remembering me. In the great cosmic scheme of things a journalist is to a legend as a gnat is to an elephant and that is understood and accepted on both sides. Nor did it bother me that Fahey seemed not to remember that he had even done an interview the day before. To such a creative genius doing an interview must be as trivial and forgettable an experience as being buzzed by a tsetse fly must be to a Rwandan silverback gorilla. I do admit, however, that it did slightly throw me that Fahey seemed only to be dimly aware that at that very moment someone was standing in front of him talking to him. But what the heck – geniuses are allowed to be otherworldly.

And the strangeness of my encounter with Fahey was in keeping with the strangeness of his whole chaotic British tour. Two promoters had joined forces to promote the gigs – and had fallen out spectacularly and catastrophically pretty well immediately after Fahey arrived in the UK. Thus it was that I would get phone calls from Promoter A telling me that the tour had been cancelled and that therefore my projected interview was off, followed by phone calls from Promoter B telling me that the tour was going ahead and that my projected interview was still on. I'm pretty sure I even remember that ten minutes after I had finally interviewed Fahey I got a phone call from Promoter A telling me that Fahey was now actually back in the States. But of course one can accept all such shenanigans and jiggery-pokery as a price worth paying for the chance to experience one of the late twentieth-century's most extraordinary guitarists in action.

Which brings us to our next John Fahey problem: his concert was certainly extraordinary – but not in the way that one might have wished. In fact it was extraordinary because in all my decades of concert going – and, trust me here, during those decades I have seen some of the world's naffest, most abject, most incompetent and most narcotically deranged and deluded bands and solo artists – I have never seen so many people walk out of a performance. The first evacuees made their move after ten minutes. I shuffled uneasily in my seat. How embarrassing – and how bloody typical – that in backward old Belfast a legend should find himself treated with such disrespect, such rudeness. Bloody philistines.

Ten minutes later another half-dozen people walked. By the three-quarters-of-an-hour mark we'd lost twenty more – and before very much longer the exodus began to turn into a stampede. Even worse, I found myself torn between joining the hundreds of punters who were storming the exits, or just nodding off in my chair, so unfocused and so aimless and so unsatisfying was Fahey's music.

Us Hodgetts are hewn from granite, it's often said (although, admittedly, only by ourselves), and so I managed, just, to stay to the end. But I was one of a mere handful of diehards to do so and there were times when the music – which may be too generous a term for the simplistic musical doodling and noodling that Fahey chose to inflict on his audience – was hard to hear for the noise of chairs being scraped back, of stomping footsteps and of doors being opened and shut as punters, variously bemused, bewildered, bored and belligerent, buggered off to the nearest bar.

It would be an exaggeration to say that the handful of punters who stayed to the end subsequently formed a John Fahey Survivors' Support Group but it's certainly true that amongst that hardy band 'The Night John Fahey Played Belfast' remains an entertaining topic of conversation and his performance a sure-fire winner in any 'Weirdest Gig I Ever Saw' competition.

John Fahey,
Elmwood Hall,
Belfast, 1999

JOHN FAHEY

American legend John Fahey, who closes the Moving On Music Festival in Belfast's Elmwood Hall tomorrow, speaks more slowly than anyone I've ever heard in my life. If you ever played a 45 rpm record at 331/3 rpm, you'll have the beginnings of some idea of how impossibly slowly Fahey speaks. The pauses between his sentences last for long, long, long seconds and so, for that matter, do the pauses between the words within a sentence. His first words to me – 'I'm pretty tired' – take so long to utter that by the time he gets to the end of the sentence I'm struggling to remember how it began. But, hey, this is John Fahey, the ultimate guitarists' guitarist, who for 40 years has been making sublime music that has massively influenced musicians as disparate as Leo Kottke, Country Joe and Sonic Youth. So, even if he talks like someone under heavy sedation, meeting him is a genuine thrill.

The earliest records that made Fahey's reputation, like *Blind Joe Death* (privately issued in a limited edition of 100 in 1959, partially re-recorded and reissued in 1964 and entirely re-recorded and reissued in 1967), *Death Chants, Breakdowns And Military Waltzes* (1963), *The Voice Of The Turtle* (1968) and *America* (1970), were beautiful, elegant masterpieces, but the music also contained suggestions of something dark and troubled. Fahey – slowly – agrees. 'That came from inside me. Errrrrrrrrr . . . I made most of those recordings before I went into psychoanalysis, for nine years. Horrible things – physical and sexual abuse by my parents – had happened me as a youth which I had repressed and so I had projected them into the music. I don't play those records anymore. I think they were somewhat dishonest. OK, the dark stuff was honest, but the suggestion of tranquillity and happiness and peace was pure bullshit. You have to put that in a piece for people to like it but to compose a song suggesting things in America were peaceful and tranquil was disingenuous. And if you live in the United States you see it all has disappeared entirely. The place has become hell. It's violent and nobody's interested in anything but money and I hate the place.'

In addition to being revered for the quality of his own work, Fahey is of course revered for the role he played, in the early Sixties, in rediscovering country-blues men of the Thirties, such as Bukka White and Skip James, who had been musically inactive for decades. The story of his rediscovery of White, in 1963, has a legendary quality: Fahey, familiar with White's song 'Aberdeen Mississippi Blues', simply wrote a postcard to 'Bukka White (Old Blues Singer) c/o General Delivery, Aberdeen, Miss.' The card reached White who got in

Trevor Hodgett · Originally published in the *Irish News* (24 September 1999); plus additional material

touch and his career was relaunched. Skip James was tracked down the following year in Tunica County Hospital, Mississippi. 'Bukka was gregarious. He didn't care who he was hanging out with. He just liked to talk to people and make friends, so there was no problem there. But James was some kind of psychopath. A very cruel, sadistic person. Lots of genius but he treated me like shit. He said he was the greatest thing in the world and the universe and everybody else was dreck.'

Mainly associated with blues, Fahey has also recorded hymns and classical pieces. 'I'm not a spiritual or a religious person at all, but classical music has probably been a bigger influence on me than blues, because I tend to think musically in very long segments. To me a piece feels right if it's about 25 minutes long. I don't know how to play three-minute songs. I was influenced by Vaughan Williams, Shostakovich, Stravinsky and Sibelius. In Williams I hear escape from the horror of life on earth; in Shostakovich I hear violence; in Stravinsky I hear suggestions of magical transcendence; and Sibelius is the saddest composer I ever heard.'

In the Sixties Fahey was a hippy hero, his music the soundtrack to many a stoned soirée. 'I didn't want anything to do with those people,' declares Fahey, his voice increasingly reminding me of the sort of voice that could be used for a sad and sleepy bear in a Disney cartoon. 'They were dirty and they took drugs. They were really shallow and took so many drugs they didn't last very long.' Fahey himself claims never to have taken psychedelic drugs. 'I never did, no. People think I did because I compose these long pieces, but that's because I listen to classical music.'

Most of Fahey's contemporaries in the early Sixties' blues boom by and by formed electric bands, but Fahey stuck with solo acoustic music. 'Errrrr . . .,' he groans. 'Errrrrrrrrrrr . . .' – we're talking about thirty-seconds' hesitation here – 'I preferred the sound of an acoustic guitar and I thought what those bands were doing was horrible music, so I didn't want anything to do with it.'

Suggestions that Fahey could be considered the father of new-age music appal him. 'Urggghhhh. I refuse to accept that. It's emotionless; it's stupid; it's mellow . . .' – and Fahey puts a world of disdain into that word – '. . . and mellow is a phony emotion. One I don't experience. To experience mellowness you have to live in California.'

In the Eighties Fahey hit hard times with health problems and, apparently, a drink problem. Reportedly, at one point he was even reduced to living in a hostel, the Union Gospel Mission in Oregon. 'I didn't live in a hostel!' he gasps. 'I kept playing, but I was just recapitulating the early pieces. Every time I tried to do anything new and exciting I'd get put down by the press. But then I discovered there was an audience for new stuff so I started doing it and had a lot of fun and escaped from endless stupid recapitulations.'

His creative momentum regained, Fahey, surprisingly, has switched to electric guitar. 'Because I'm always at the mercy of soundmen and they turn it up and down and distort it and I can't stand that anymore. But I use pre-amplifiers to make the tones that come out [of the electric guitar] pretty round, so it doesn't sound that much different to me.'

Fahey declares that *Womblife*, released in 1997, is the album with which he is most satisfied. 'Yeah, *Womblife*. Listen to *Womblife* and you get a lot of coherence. It just works, it comes together, it sounds great. I like to listen to it. It seems to transcend ideas and things. I can't even tell you what it's about really.'

So, John – and take your time, here – what can we look forward to in Belfast? 'A lot of blues and extended improvisations of blues and bebop and some Latin American and a few old songs. It should be pretty good.'

One final question has to be asked of Fahey, out of pure nosiness. Why does he live permanently in a motel? 'I don't like houses. I got everything I need right there close to me and I don't need to move to another room to do something different,' is the perfectly simple, eccentric answer, from this most singular man.

JOHN FAHEY & HENRY McCULLOUGH
ELMWOOD HALL, BELFAST

Forty years ago John Fahey, who spent his youth tracking down Skip James, Bukka White and the story of Charley Patton, pressed up 100 copies of *Blind Joe Death*. Featuring his alter-ego 'discovery' of that name, and designed to mock the growing band of vintage-blues authorities, the small venture had colossal ramifications. Fahey had invented both the solo acoustic-guitar genre and its industry – achievements which ultimately resulted in the Windham Hill/New Age phenomenon. Fahey, contrary and cantankerous, now dismisses everything he ever did before the Nineties.

Perversely, the support act for the Godfather's first-ever trip to Ireland was making precisely the kind of emotionally 'authentic', instrumentally sinuous and mesmerising country-folk-blues that Fahey would have gone bananas to have discovered from some old delta-shack Negro in the Fifties. No slouch in the 'legendary' stakes himself, Henry McCullough – Northern Ireland's most venerable contributor to the great years of rock – was making this one-off debut as a solo acoustic performer. Melancholy, rage and libido informed his lyrics, with the music an ever-building quest for the lost groove. An impassioned reading of 'Murder In My Heart' was dedicated to British Midlands – to paraphrase Henry, 'a shower of bastards who've just lost the Gibson 335 I've treasured for decades.'

When Fahey emerged, in lurid T-shirt, trainers and Santa Claus beard, there were no such anchors to reality. Relying entirely on a cheap Strat and an irritating delay pedal, he opened with a 25-minute improvisation comprising single-string snapping and twanging with periodic portentous chords. Once concluded – a situation which only one person in the room could know for sure – Fahey put hands on knees and beamed mischievously at his audience. His only utterance being the announcement of an interval, the pattern was repeated thereafter. At least half the audience, Henry McCullough and several of Belfast's arts media failed to last the course. Occasionally, mid-monotony, Fahey would seemingly stumble upon some half-forgotten melody and a structure would appear. But this was music to challenge the will. A rigorous debate on its worth among the remaining journos afterwards was, in truth, infinitely more entertaining than the show. Was this just some old buffer noodling away and winding us all up *à la* Blind Joe Death? Personally, I was not impressed.

Postscript: John Fahey died in 2001. Henry's lost guitar surfaced, as 'Henry McCullough's guitar', on a dubious Internet auction site a couple of years later.

Colin Harper · Concert review originally published in *Mojo* (November 1999)

ORNETTE COLEMAN
WHITLA HALL, BELFAST FESTIVAL

In a thrilling coup the Belfast Festival not only booked Ornette Coleman, for his only European gigs of the year, but enterprisingly commissioned from him an original work, *The Belfast Suite*, and hired seven Irish traditional musicians to perform it with him. But the experiment failed. Bewilderingly, the promised suite didn't materialise and during the 35 minutes for which the Irish musicians augmented Coleman's trio, we only heard familiar Irish tunes. So the much-anticipated *Belfast Suite* by Ornette Coleman turned out to be not a suite and not by Ornette Coleman.

The tunes were certainly played superbly by high-calibre musicians such as piper/whistlers Michael McGoldrick and John McSherry and fiddler Desi Donnelly. But what on earth was the point of having the great Ornette Coleman making very, very minor and often barely audible contributions to a standard set of Irish traditional tunes? The Ornette-freak who afterwards described the music as like a poor man's *Riverdance* may perhaps have been harsh, but, certainly, in no meaningful sense was this a fusion of two traditions. Much more satisfying was the rest of the evening when Ornette, Denardo Coleman (drums) and Charnett Moffett (bass) played on their own, creating music that was adventurous, emotive and often beautiful.

On another night, in another world premiere, Coleman, with his trio and the Ulster Orchestra, recreated the music he originally played on the soundtrack of the film *Naked Lunch*, the performance conducted by the soundtrack's composer, Howard Shore, while the film itself played on a screen suspended behind the players. The film was hallucinogenic, shocking and horrific; the music was dark, disturbing and unnerving – a perfect match.

Trevor Hodgett · Concert review originally published in *Jazzwise* (February 2001) and the *Irish News* (9 November 2000)

Ornette Coleman (second from right) and the 'Belfast Suite' band, Whitla Hall, Belfast, November 2000

ORNETTE COLEMAN
WHITLA HALL, BELFAST FESTIVAL

Playing his only European dates this year in Belfast the very presence of the septuagenarian tenor-sax legend is a real coup for the Belfast Festival's jazz department. The idea of pairing up Coleman and his truly sensational accompanists – Charnett Moffett on bass and son Denardo Coleman on drums – with a squad of Irish trad players, with no more than two days of actual rehearsal scheduled, was an outrageously daring idea and, regardless of outcome, puts the desperately stale programming of the Festival's folk wing to shame.

The evening, however, began with a sterling 90-minute set from Coleman's trio. Although often cited as the father of free jazz, Coleman's music, on this showing, avoids both the cacophony and the call-and-response inevitabilities of those who trade more willingly under that banner. Rather, his ensemble work together, yet separately, around freewheeling melodies, deliciously unfettered to the strictures of resolving chord sequences. In practice this meant that while the rhythm players at least echoed the bebop tradition, Coleman himself was akin to a sweet-toned calypso-ing spider at the centre of the web – almost effortlessly melodic, favouring chromatic freedom to any single major, minor or modal scale. Six improvisations in and a piece boasting an Eastern mode with rock backbeat – perhaps more easily grasped than his more singular work – engendered a heightened response, although everything played was warmly received.

The masses, though, had come to hear *The Belfast Suite* – an advertised premiere of a new fusion piece with trad players. In fact, no such work was debuted: instead, seven traditional players – including the fairly well-regarded Michael McGoldrick, John McSherry and Donald Shaw – came on and played a handful of standard-tune sets around which Coleman's sidemen locked horns with gusto like *Riverdance* regulars, leaving Coleman cruelly exposed as the lone avant-gardist knocking fruitlessly, and with some discordance, at the door of relentlessly unalterable modes and rhythms. The fault for the underachieving lies entirely with either or both the number of Irish players (behaving consequently like sheep) or the sheer inability of the individuals concerned to interact beyond their idiom. Oh, that this exercise had taken place with Martin Hayes instead! As it was, we had something akin to an ill-rehearsed version of Davy Spillane's band. Two songs with Karen Casey were particularly futile. Still, Coleman had willingly made the effort – and the ovation and encores demanded suggested that most of those present appreciated that.

Colin Harper · Concert review commissioned by *The Irish Times* (November 2000) but unpublished

EPILOGUE
JOHN McSHERRY REMEMBERS . . .

'It was a bizarre experience,' says John McSherry, Belfast-born piper and a man not unaccustomed to weird happenings in the wild world of music. 'Ornette was supposed to have written this piece called *The Belfast Suite* and when we turned up at the soundcheck/rehearsal – and it wasn't the two days we'd hoped for, it was the afternoon of the gig – we were all thinking, Oh God, he'll have this mad piece of music and we'll all have to learn it on the day. I mean, I'd already gone out and bought one of his CDs – and it was crazy. So we all arrived, got up on the stage and Ornette says, "I've written this piece of music and I want you to learn it," and he played these five notes, like a hook. So we locked onto that and said, "OK, fine, what's the rest of it?" "That's it." *That was it!*'

Commissioned to the tune of £70,000, it takes a certain amount of chutzpah and a monumental degree of self-confidence in one's art to be able to charge £14,000 per note. They must, one assume, have been bloody good notes: 'Well, I kinda knew where he was coming from,' says John. 'I mean, I don't claim to know exactly what he was at, but the man's been an artist all his life, he can play the music – and if you *can* play the music why limit yourself? Get in there and play what you want to. OK, it's not always pleasant to the ears, but that's not what it's about.'

Pinning down precisely what Coleman, often described (to his own chagrin) as the 'father of free-form', *is* about is a question that's been bothering any number of eminent jazz writers for years. The man has his own rules, his own system – yet nobody seems to know quite what it is. *The Virgin Encyclopaedia of Jazz* (Colin Larkin (ed.), 1999) argues for Coleman's place alongside Louis Armstrong in jazz and Arnold Schoenberg in European classical music as amongst the very few twentieth-century musicians who can be said to have single-handedly kick-started the evolution of a distinct art form. And with Coleman, blissfully mistaking the low C on his sax for an A in his instruction book at the age of fourteen, the seeds of his ideas – later defined by Coleman as the theory of 'harmolodics' – began by accident. For once he had realised his mistake it 'started the process which led to a style based on freely moving melody unhindered by a repetitive harmonic substructure, and, eventually, to the theory of harmolodics'.

Nevertheless, as the *Virgin Encyclopaedia* pithily notes, 'even musicians who have worked with Coleman extensively confess that they do not under-stand what the theory is about'. Consequently, a bunch of Irish traddies hired

Colin Harper · From an interview conducted in Belfast (February 2003); previously unpublished

for an evening, and however accomplished they may have been in their own field, were never going to be anything else than up the creek without a paddle.

With Coleman's notes appearing to have been randomly selected from a number of conventionally non-complementary keys, chordal accompaniment was a particularly insoluble conundrum: 'That was a big confusion for Donald Shaw on the keyboards,' says John. 'What was he gonna do? But Donald handled it fantastically, he got into it. And Mike [McGoldrick] just turned round to me and said, "What the fuck . . .? Let's go for it!" And he started wailing away, going mental – and when we did that in rehearsal Ornette turned round to us and said, "That's it!" Do what you want to do – that was the attitude. Every time we looked over at Ornette he was always very relaxed; any time we looked at the bass player or the drummer they just shrugged their shoulders – they didn't really know what he was up to either! It was like everybody playing "The Fox Chase" – but each one starting in a different place. [When it came to the songs] it would have been very difficult for Karen to sing emotionally and stick to the melody, with all these weird notes going on around her – never mind the audience, *we* were cringing!'

Any time some kind of groove kicked in during the performance of the instrumental material, it seemed to be down to Ornette's rhythm section almost locking on for dear life to the rigidly built escape capsule of the jigs and reels: 'At the rehearsal, after Ornette left,' says John, 'the bass player and the drummer hung on and started jamming away with us, this kind of Irish-jazz fusion. It was still weird, like, but it was working. [During the performance] we [the Irish musicians] would look at each other and at them, and try and click with them. But there *were* odd moments when we'd somehow click with Ornette and he'd get slightly more excited – you could sense that! It was like he was raising his game so we'd raise our game. There were levels of excitement – but you probably couldn't sense that in the audience!'

Yet there were places – albeit perhaps only a few sequential bars here and there – where the fusion almost worked. John McSherry may not, of his own admission, be in Coleman's league, but he can see what it takes to get there: 'You have to have the ability to play loads of notes in the right places,' he says, 'before you can get to that stage where Ornette's at where you're playing so few notes with so much space. You can't be an abstract painter without being able to paint "properly" first. Music is boring – Irish music is boring. You're limited to certain notes, certain structures. If you play it all the time it drives you insane – it certainly drives me insane. With Ornette, we all locked into certain [traditional] tunes, and then locked out of them. Mike would go off on a tangent, I'd follow him, then Desi Donnelly would go off. Poor old Jon Jo Kelly [on bodhrán] had the hardest job, with a drummer behind him crashing around all over the place – what can he do? But looking back, I thoroughly enjoyed it.'

And what about that composition, those exquisitely selected five notes? 'Well, we knew the notes were there . . . we just didn't bother playing them!'

SECTION 10
REUNIONS, REWARDS & A MAN CALLED BOB

Terri Hooley,
onstage in Belfast, 1998

REUNIONS & REWARDS
PROLOGUE

Everyone, apparently, has their fifteen minutes of fame. Me, I just borrowed somebody else's. It was the night of the first *Hot Press* Awards to be televised, sometime in 1997, and the event was taking place at a BBC studio in Belfast. Somehow, I was in possession of two tickets. I can't imagine that I was on anyone's PR priority list so I guess I must have called somebody I knew at the BBC and caught them in a position where they felt too awkward to say, 'No, go away, you're not hip and happening enough.' In any case, I went along with my friend, colleague and sometime chanteuse, Helen McGurk.

Directed towards possibly the least conspicuous table in the studio, bar those occupied by the Tara Records contingent (comprising John Cook and members of his latest, and most incongruous, signings Treehouse Diner), imagine my glee when, minutes from showtime, the floor manager calls for someone, anyone, to occupy two glaringly empty seats at the top table – reserved for U2 envoy Larry Mullen junior and his good lady. Me and Helen – we didn't need to be asked twice.

'So who are *you* then?' I ask breezily of my new-found friends at said table. 'We're Radiohead,' says one of Radiohead.

And so, as 'Mr and Mrs Larry Mullen' for the first half of the broadcast, Helen and I – and I am, of course, in no way implying that the *Belfast Newsletter*'s able and informed business correspondent had failed, as I had so comprehensively, to recognise Britain's coolest musos (though, having said that, she might have . . .) – spend a pleasant half-hour discussing such topics as progressive rock and Fairport Convention with those who shall be known as 'The Future of British Rock'. And very nice they were, too. After a while, of course, Larry and Lady Larry arrive and we are ushered, once more, back to the obscurity from whence we came. Well, it was fun while it lasted.

The following year the awards were back in Belfast and back on TV after what had been judged a thoroughly successful first-time outing. It had been a gamble and everyone involved from the underbelly of Irish rock had known, implicitly or otherwise, that they had to be on best behaviour. Second time around, however, and it was clear that nobody gave a damn anymore. Once again a smattering of celebrities occupied, of course, the best tables, while the majority of the audience, milling hither and thither, seemed to be boozed-up liggers, tossers and second-raters. There was also an air of phoniness about the thing this time – none of the big names, as I recall, had actually released anything or done anything much at all that year (whereas the previous year

Colin Harper

had been, right on cue, a vintage one for Irish rock, pop and trad happenings). And yet one just knew the usual suspects would be getting the lion's share of the awards. They have to, otherwise it's no good for TV.

Given that Something Happens – sadly, at that time, on their last legs as a rock band with realistic long-term aspirations – turned in, typically, the best live performance of the night, this ethos seemed particularly vacuous. People heckled and belched; Bono tried to be funny and wasn't; they tried to keep Terri Hooley out – and they failed miserably. He may be a rough diamond, our Tel, but if ever there was a need for the man's bullshit-free invective this was the time and the place. I made my observations for the *Independent*, and found myself agreeing profoundly with Tom Dunne, wordsmith with Something Happens: 'Why am I here, Colin?' he'd said, wearily. Frankly, I couldn't help him there. Why – at this tarted-up celebration of mediocrity and fake glitz, populated, by and large, by phonies and wasters – would *anyone* with any self-respect be there?

Still, I ended up at one more *Hot Press* Awards do, in Dublin this time, in the good company of Donal Gallagher and Colin Reid, before I decided to seek part-time sanctuary in education. (Actually, one reason for taking a qualification in librarianship in the first place had been an evening spent, towards the end of 1995, in the company of legendary rock svengali and mind-bender Kim Fowley. To cut a long story short, I walked straight into Queen's University the next day and signed up for the most mundane postgraduate course they had – which turned out to be information management. Anything, I reckoned, to be rooted in normality and surrounded by the kind of sensible and wholly reliable people who pursue careers in libraries. Or so I thought.)

For some people – and, by and large, I count myself among them – the rock 'n' roll lifestyle is something best read about in books, its music best heard on remastered discs from the comfort of a sofa and its reunions most rewarding when you simply happen upon them unawares. Would I have travelled to a Planxty reunion? Probably not, but I was certainly glad I was there. 'Next time, the Point!' shouted somebody from the back, in a quiet moment between songs.

A pregnant pause ensued, as everyone looked to Christy Moore for either pithy rebuke or nod of the head. He was mercifully saved from the task as some other punter mumbled, with brilliant timing and just enough volume, 'What's the point?' Ripples of mirth. And nothing more needed saying.

VARIOUS ARTISTS
BELFAST BEAT, MARITIME BLUES

Owen McFadden, one-time drummer with Protex, who enjoyed a string of Good Vibrations and Polydor releases in the wake of The Undertones, is now happily 'retired' as a documentary producer with BBC Radio Ulster. Owen has done much to document the byways of Northern Ireland's music scene through the ages – his professionalism and enthusiasm creating programmes that themselves deserve a wider audience than local radio. Among his works are documentaries on Roger Armstrong, Belfast-born founder of Ace Records, the biggest reissue label in Europe, and an award-winning profile of the city's Maritime Hotel scene of the mid-Sixties, most notable as the birthplace of Van Morrison's Them and, later, as a launch pad for Rory Gallagher.

Now, thanks to McFadden's researches, Ace has released *Belfast Beat: Maritime Blues,* a definitive CD of Northern Ireland's thriving beat scene of 1964–66. The compilation, sourced entirely from original masters, marks the first time on CD for almost all the tracks and includes two numbers from Them (personally sanctioned by Van and including the rare EP track 'Philosophy'), unreleased material by The Mad Lads plus their only Decca 45, as Moses K & The Prophets, and no less than twelve tracks from highly collectable act The Wheels, including three terrific unreleased cuts. Other material, taken from the rare 1966 Ember album *Ireland's Greatest Sounds,* includes The Bats, The Luvin' Kind, The Alleykatz, Just Five and The People – who would later tour America with Jimi Hendrix as psychedelic-soul act Eire Apparent.

'Even when I was in Protex,' says Owen, 'everyone who talked about that whole Maritime scene recalled it as a really fantastic time when Belfast was a vibrant city and was well-known for its music. Van Morrison is the best-known artist from that time, but there were plenty of other bands, too, and I was keen to find out who they were because we didn't hear so much about them in later years. So, really as a result of that Maritime documentary and of a programme I'd made on the career of Roger Armstrong, we came up with this CD. We went in search of original master tapes and finally got enough tracks to warrant a release.

'Through the Maritime programme I'd found out there was a character called Peter Lloyd who'd been really central to recording all the bands at the time. He'd recorded the very first Them tracks in his tiny little studio in Belfast city centre, and through that they got their recording deal with Decca. He was able to supply me with a few unreleased demos by The Mad Lads, whose frontman Kenny McDowell was really the main-man after Van left for England.

Colin Harper · Album feature originally published in *Record Collector* (June 1997)

So it was nice to get those tracks plus the master tapes for their sole single on Decca. Plus, there had been an album made in 1966 on the back of Them's success – a London label called Ember had specially recorded an album, using Peter's studio, featuring some of the other acts that were popular in the North. Roger found that the masters were still sitting on a shelf at Ember, who still exist, and bought them up. Likewise, The Wheels, who cut three singles for Columbia, were a big act here, although their name hasn't endured back home as well as some. But it's apparent that they were a huge attraction in the north of England where they made their base in about '64. Their material especially is much sought after by collectors and so they feature very heavily on the CD. So, finally, we were able to build up a whole album's worth of material.'

Leafing through *Record Collector* magazine's *Rare Record Price Guide* it's clear that anyone who wants mint copies of the three UK Wheels singles, the Moses K single, the Them EP and the Ember LP alone would have to shell out little short of £500. But was there anything else from the period that even Owen couldn't source? 'Well, there was a band called The Interns who were from Magherafelt. Literally busloads of people used to follow them round the country here and, like a lot of these bands, they had their own fan club – and they released a single called "Crying Time". I was very keen to get that on the CD but not even the band members have a copy between them and we couldn't find the masters, so I'm afraid it remains elusive.'

Thanks to the affordability of CD pressings and the DIY attitudes of today's acts in Northern Ireland – still very much the backwater of the UK music industry – when compilations of the great undiscovered acts of the Nineties are made (and either me or Owen will probably be doing it!) there'll be a lot more source material to choose from. But the Ace CD remains a definitive collection of what little remains from Belfast's 'golden era': 'It'd be nice to think about a volume two,' says Owen, 'possibly covering the later Sixties, with early recordings by Rory Gallagher and David McWilliams for instance, but this particular scene had really died by then. I mean, you can be quite specific about it – it was happening between '64 and '66. Music in general changed and the policy of the Maritime changed. They started booking bigger acts from England, and local acts were reduced to playing mere support slots, which is when Belfast developed the reputation it still has as a great place for visiting artists to play.'

Sadly, then, the Troubles kicked in and popular mythology has it that very little happened musically in the North until the legendary Terri Hooley – still a great character on the Belfast scene – launched Good Vibrations and gave focus to the city's punk movement in the late Seventies. But that, as Owen well knows, is another story.

MARITIME REUNION CONCERT
MORRISON'S, BELFAST

Thirty years ago a new blues band debuted on the opening night of a new Belfast club. The band was Them, with Van Morrison, the club was the Maritime – and the Irish music scene changed forever. And so it came to pass that on the 30/31 May 1994, in the aptly named Morrison's, the grey-haired groovers of Belfast gathered to celebrate the anniversary and to pay tribute to the great, the good and the geriatric of the local blues scene.

The Ultimate Blues Band (cocky gits, huh?), led by ex-Aztec Rab Braniff on bass and vocals, rip-roared through 'Messing With The Kid', 'Boom Boom' and 'Stormy Monday', with Robert Braniff jnr. impressing many with his uninhibited guitar playing.

Jim Armstrong (ex-Them), our own resident guitar hero, thrilled with wildly imaginative versions of 'Help The Poor' and 'It Hurts Me Too'.

Henry McCullough (ex-People and ex-Paul McCartney and Wings and, no, I'm not claiming that the Fab One ever played the Maritime) performed with his usual white-hot intensity, with ex-Interns singer Paul De Vito augmenting the band effectively on 'Need Your Love So Bad' and others.

Eric Bell (ex-Deltones, Shades Of Blue, Thin Lizzy) was in mighty form. 'This is an instrumental – you can all sing along with it,' he announced cheerily before unleashing a searing version of 'The Stumble', followed by incendiary versions of 'Shake Your Moneymaker' and 'Hold That Plane'. 'If I was any more relaxed I'd be dead,' mused Eric, adding reflectively, 'If I was any more dead I'd be relaxed.' His wonderfully evocative 'Madame George' was the nicest surprise of the evening – 'For Van Morrison, who basically started the Maritime' – and his version of 'Whiskey In The Jar' one of the most wildly appreciated. 'That song has been paying my rent for twenty years,' he observed.

Students of the bizarre would have relished the extraordinary moment during Bell's version of Them's 'Baby Please Don't Go' when Them's original guitarist Billy Harrison, the creator of the immortal guitar lick that drives the song, elbowed his way through the madding crowd and stood glaring at Bell and sternly wagging his finger at him. Weird, or what? Harrison, having calmed down, later played enjoyable versions of 'House Of The Rising Sun' and the inevitable 'Gloria'. Pianist Jim Daly's set featured deeply satisfying down-home Chicago-style playing on A.C. Reed's 'Going To New York' and others.

Two great gigs, then, that magically mixed magnificent music and nostalgia. But what genius decided to place the stage in an alcove, where the performers were invisible to two-thirds of the audience?

Trevor Hodgett · Concert review originally published in *Blueprint* (July 1994)

MARITIME REUNION CONCERT
MORRISON'S, BELFAST

Not (surprisingly) an all-star jam that's best forgotten in the morning, but a tightly packed, ecstatic evening of blues at its loudest and most exhilarating from some of Belfast's finest sons. It was the first of two nights in celebration of the first gig at the city's late, legendary Maritime Hotel – an early oasis from the ballrooms for the likes of Rory Gallagher's Taste and Van Morrison's Them.

Needless to say, Van and Rory didn't show (were they asked?) but their music and spirit were there in abundance. Only ex-Them men Jim Armstrong (with his own band) and Billy Harrison (mad-eyed and dragged from the backwoods) dared to play 'Gloria', though Eric Bell – over from London and given the welcome of a homecoming hero – practically tore the place apart with 'Baby Please Don't Go'. And followed it with 'Madame George'.

Bell, almost painfully thin and minus the beard of his Thin Lizzy days, all but stole the show. Like Harrison, who followed, he was busking it rightly with organiser Rab Braniff on bass and drummer Joe Trainor from the outrageously named Ultimate Blues Band, who had opened the show with a set of solid Rory-by-numbers. Jim Armstrong, still big on the pub scene, provided an element of modern flash. Henry McCullough, playing with a scratch band and giving ex-Interns man Paul De Vito the vocal mike, took the music right back to the edge of its primitive soul, and wasn't afraid to leap the boundaries of the twelve-bar. His own 'Failed Christian' had more of the blues' real spirit of hope/hopelessness than anything else on the night.

'I wasn't around in them days,' he mumbled, wide-eyed to the first genuine ovation of the night. He was stuck in a showband in Fermanagh. Those were the days.

Colin Harper · Concert review originally published in *The Irish Times* (2 June 1994)

DE DANANN
GALWAY ARTS FESTIVAL

If BBC 2 supremo Alan Yentob threw caution to the wind and commissioned an edition of his channel's *Rock Family Trees* show on the subject of Irish traditional music in the modern era, it would all start with Sweeney's Men in the late Sixties, begetting Planxty in the early Seventies and opening the doors for The Bothy Band, Clannad and De Danann shortly thereafter.

Clannad's ethereal strand of the spectrum had happily stumbled into rock 'n' roll marketing by the middle of the Eighties – around the same time that De Danann had started losing the plot. All the other greats split up at their peak, spawning a perpetuity of semi-legendary solo artists (Christy Moore, Paul Brady and the rest). The trouble with De Danann – named after the *Tuatha Dé Danann*, a tribe of, ahem, god-like beings in Irish mythology – is that they've increasingly been perceived to exist in the same way that The Who exist: nothing for ages, solo projects that nobody's terribly interested in and,

Colin Harper · Concert review originally published in the *Independent* (29 July 1995)

De Dannan, from the sleeve of *Selected Jigs, Reels & Songs*, 1977: (l–r) Alec Finn, Frankie Gavin, Johnny Moynihan, Charlie Piggott, Ringo McDonagh

bang, before you can say 'bandwagon', it's some kind of anniversary.

Two months ago, De Danann fiddler and flag-bearer Frankie Gavin played, at a solo show, to literally 25 people in Galway; this week his band's twenty-first anniversary bash could have sold out the Galway Festival's 1,200-seater marquee thrice over. It was a situation akin to Fairport Convention's annual reunion in Oxfordshire – a current line-up, whatever its own qualities (and with De Danann, vocalist Tommy Fleming is a real find), that is effectively doomed to the looming shadow of its former members' subsequent reputations and left with only the name and the casual, rose-tinted goodwill of an ageing fan base.

Old members trooped on and off the star-filled stage in suitably bemused incongruity – bodhrán king Johnny 'Ringo' McDonagh; Charlie Piggott, with crippled fingers but stroking a banjo for old-times' sake; singers Mary Black and Dolores Keane; accordion wizard Mairtín O'Connor and so on. For all the soundness of the current line-up instrumentally, it took the truly phenomenal interplay of O'Connor and Gavin to really shift proceedings into fourth gear on 'Jewish Reels', 'The Arrival Of The Queen Of Sheba In Galway' and 'Hey Jude' – three sets of idiosyncratic, teasingly fusionistic brilliance, immediately resonant and indicative as to why this group is or was held in such regard.

Mary Black, singing 'Annachie Gordon' for the first time in years, did so with a passion simply absent from her current work; Dolores Keane was on cloud nine throughout; even grim-faced guitarist Alec Finn – Gavin's side-man all these years – looked by the end like he really missed the old days. They were all great musicians making great music once again. There were seven encores – more were deserved. The glory days are over, but if they have a resurrection like this every year, the old gods will always have believers.

Postscript: If you can't beat them, join them: in August 2002 De Danann played at Fairport's annual reunion do in Oxfordshire. The following year they (De Danann) called it a day. Johnny Moynihan, in case you were wondering, was nowhere to be seen.

PLANXTY
WHELAN'S, DUBLIN

Not advertised as anything other than an Andy Irvine gig, this Tuesday night at Dublin's premier roots/rock venue – yet still the preserve of the gig-going cognoscenti – might have expected perhaps a hundred punters. Instead, it's packed to the rafters. Although the situation had only come together organically, by stealth, over the previous couple of days – essentially, Donal Lunny and Christy Moore coming over all nostalgic and finding a free date in their diaries at precisely the right time – the word was out that Planxty were having a reunion. Originally existing for three years in the early Seventies and reuniting

Colin Harper · Concert review originally published in the *Independent* (27 July 2000)

Impromptu Planxty reunion at Whelan's, Dublin, July 2000: (l–r) Donal Lunny, Andy Irvine, Christy Moore

for a couple more albums at the end of that decade, Planxty are now effectively seen as The Beatles of the modern Celtic-music movement. Nobody thought it would ever happen again, but a crowd comprising mostly people, like myself, who would have been in primary school at the time were in for a rare treat indeed.

'This seemed like a good idea until this morning,' mumbled Andy, who handled the burden of expectation admirably during a solo first half that not only held a palpably feverish crowd's attention but grasped the nettle to remind everyone of his skill as an entertainer and as an artist of rare breadth. His repertoire of dustbowl ballads, bawdy sailor songs, the most delicate of Irish laments and the most complex of Balkan dance tunes seemed, in his hands, to be perfect bedfellows. A central figure in Irish music for 40 years, he is nevertheless still a unique artist.

Donal Lunny joined Andy for the second half, generating a huge roar of approval with the opening bars of 'The Plains Of Kildare' – sinuous, dynamic and exploding with energy, the Planxty equivalent of 'Paperback Writer'. The thrill continued through further gleanings from in and around the group's canon: 'My Heart's Tonight In Ireland' (Andy's playfully evocative memoir of the pre-Planxty Sweeney's Men), 'Horo' (from a geographically doomed post-Planxty Irvine/Lunny project with various Bulgarian musicians) and Irvine's traditional show-closer, 'Never Tire Of The Road'.

But far from closing, the fourth gear went into fifth with the brilliantly on-form entrance of Christy Moore, only recently returned from a lengthy performing sabbatical. Andy mumbled something about the shock of re-listening to old Planxty records that very morning; 'I thought they were all dead,' said Christy, drolly setting the tone for a set of gloriously full-scale, no-rehearsal revivals from the old group, held together with splendid badinage – self-deprecating, of course, but tinged with communal pride. Even Andy, who had earlier felt uneasy about the whole thing, was clearly blown away by not only the reception to, but the playing of, the likes of 'Arthur McBride', 'The Blacksmith' and a mesmerising 'Musgrave And Lady Barnard'. By the third encore it was revealed that the fab fourth original member, Liam O'Flynn, had been up for it but simply couldn't get a boat off the Aran Islands in time to make it. But that ramshackle, last-minute spirit was what made the evening so special.

Postscript: The original four-man Planxty line-up reformed for a fabulously successful series of concerts at Dublin's Vicar Street in February 2004. And did I travel to see it? Oh, alright then, I did!

HOT PRESS AWARDS 1998

It's Thursday 9 April 1998: decision day in Northern Ireland. Never mind the politics that were going on up the road, this was the Heineken/*Hot Press* Rock Awards – an annual absurdity sponsored by an organ of popular culture and a bottled beer, bloated to the level of national TV, but whose chief function is, frankly, less to do with who gets what than a colossal excuse for networking, boozing and a bit of mutual back-slapping for those relatively few people on the island who can lay claim to being professionally involved in pop music.

'Just who the hell is Neil Hannon?' raged Garry Bushell to all those *Sun* readers who care, on the recent appearance of someone 'doing' the fellow on *Stars In Their Eyes*. Boorish as it may be, that remark all but defines the lovably quaint idea of an Irish award show for Irish pop music: not necessarily indie enough to be the Irish version of the *NME* Brats awards and not, well, *popular* enough to be the Brits. Of those handful of Irish acts the man in the street – even a street in Ireland – has actually heard of, U2 were there; Sinéad O'Connor was there; Van wasn't: Enya wasn't either and, er, that's it. Shane MacGowan and Morrissey – and Boy George, for goodness' sake – were wheeled in under Irish-football-team rules; the late Phil Lynott's mum and the late Rory Gallagher's brother added a much-needed sense of perspective, presenting awards from 'the hands of history' – a tad lost in the beered-up chaos of the studio, but salvaged in the subsequent broadcast. Somebody from Boyzone sang a duet with Brian Kennedy – 'Love Hurts', actually rather good – and little girls stood in the rain outside to do en masse whatever it is little girls with crushes on pop stars do.

The likes of Neil Hannon (from the admirable if not yet world-conquering Divine Comedy), punky youngsters Ash and fellow-Northerner Kennedy claimed their real moment in history, however parochial that may seem to outsiders, by scooping, for the downtrodden North, most of last year's awards – awards that were held, as a double-first, in Belfast and on camera – in an event charged with celebration and significance. 'The North will rise again,' was always the mantra of one-time Undertones svengali and Belfast's 'godfather of punk' Terri Hooley, and last year he smiled. There was a wonderful, all-in-it-together atmosphere to the event then – sitting at a table with Radiohead discussing Fairport Convention comes to mind like some weird dream. But this time around, even with the same passionate zeal of local BBC jock Mike Edgar and the immaculate head 'n' shoulders of Ulrika Jonsson co-presenting as before, it was a curious affair – verging on the surreal, little quarks of bloated

Colin Harper · Event review originally published in the *Independent* (16 April 1998)

Something Happens, mid-Nineties: (l–r) Ray Harmon, Tom Dunne, Alan Byrne, Eamonn Ryan

self-parody colliding around a regional TV studio absolutely packed to the rafters with essentially ludicrous people, most of whom are at best big fish in a small pond.

The irony had kicked in with the pre-show press conference, over the road in Europe's most-bombed hotel. Bar the endless clicks of photography and a daring young lady from the frivolous bit at the end of a TV news show, no one gathered – awkward looking parade of artists (generally not the ones you'd have heard of) and bemused squad of local hacks, hipsters and hangers-on – knew quite what you were meant to *do* with a press conference. 'The term "freak show" springs to mind,' mumbled someone behind me, clearly expecting no less. Coming from the man who had organised PR for the Belfast Clinton visit – streets teeming for weeks with beefy black men in FBI raincoats trying to look discreet – this was particularly rich. And absolutely right.

Back at the studio, the sanest man in the building – and this, believe me, was a frightening thought – appeared to be Terri Hooley. Friend of the underdog, foe of the capitalist and one of the great Dickensian characters of Irish rock, his famously loose-cannon attitudes seemed to be finding targets like barn-doors at ten paces. It was yet further irony that Hooley, recipient of a previous *Hot Press* 'living legend' type award, hadn't actually been invited to this one, blagged his way in and ended up presenting something to an almost unintelligible Shane MacGowan when it was discovered that a scheduled George Best had failed to show. 'I put on his first gig,' said Hooley (probably true). 'Can't understand a word he says these days, but I'm sure he'll say something outrageous.' He did.

'Well, that'll be edited out,' muttered a grinning fellow from the rival UTV, who seemed to be enjoying himself at the licence-payer's expense.

The irony was not least in the detail – people like Ash and dance-meister David Holmes getting awards when they clearly felt they shouldn't. There was a feeling of déjà vu – of last year having exhausted the novelty of a Northern explosion, pardon the expression, and this year the same old names coming around again for nothing in particular – although Best Male Artist went to someone called Nick Kelly. Bushell would have had a field day. 'I put out his first record,' said Hooley, to anyone who'd listen. 'And it wasn't yesterday.'

U2 scored twice and, first time up, a hooded, red-spectacled Bono made the unwise gesture of trying to be ironic. 'So what's the difference between Ian Paisley and George Michael?' he said languorously between heckles. The room seemed to sigh deflatedly as one, seeing no way out bar the punchline. 'At least George Michael will talk to people.' That one hit the cutting-room floor. Next time around he tried sincerity, and in paying tribute to the late *Hot Press* writer Bill Graham – who effectively created U2's career and whose mother was in attendance – said just about the only worthwhile, genuine thing of the whole evening.

'That was good,' said the guy behind me. The guy who had heckled.

Something Happens, a brilliant but simply unglobally successful bunch of U2 contemporaries who might have been The Who in another life, played out the show and we all trooped over the road to the party in the hotel. Free booze, business cards, loud music, self-mythologising, voyeurs posing for snaps with a near-delirious Shane MacGowan. Over at a quiet corner of the bar I noticed the singer with Something Happens – an affable, soft-spoken man called Tom. Like everyone in Irish rock, I'd met him once or twice before. I gave him a business card. 'Why am I here, Colin?' he said, to me and to no one in particular. 'Why am I here?'

BOB DYLAN
PROLOGUE

'Robert McMillen is in hospital.'

'Dear, dear, I'm sorry to hear that,' I mumbled, wondering why the hell the features editor of the *Irish News* was ringing me at work to give me a medical bulletin about one of her staff.

'And so he can't review tonight's Bob Dylan gig for us,' she continued. 'Would you be interested in doing it?'

'This wouldn't be the Bob Dylan once-in-a-lifetime club gig in Dublin's Vicar Street, for which tickets are changing hands on the black market at £1,000 each, would it?' I asked carefully.

'That's the one. We can let you have two tickets for it. We'll book you into a hotel and you can pick the tickets up at the club. But you must collect them by seven-thirty or the promoter will give them to someone else. And the copy-takers knock off at ten so you must ring in your review before then.'

For a part-time freelance writer, of but modest success, writing mainly about uncommercial music, this was heady stuff. I found myself gleefully punching the air as I accepted the commission. But, almost instantly, a certain troubling reality asserted itself through my euphoria: I couldn't leave work, in Belfast, before three-forty-five; my car, an ancient banger, was at home two miles away; the journey to Dublin would take perhaps three hours; and I had no idea whether my wife Trish would be able to leave work early to join me.

Well, a phone call to her answered the last question. She would rendezvous with me at home and we would then zoom down to Dublin. It looked like the timing might just work out OK.

And it looked like that for most of the journey. Until, in fact, we hit the Dublin rush hour. Bit by bit our plans were downsized. 'I don't think we're going to have time to grab a bite,' I mused at one point. 'I don't think we're going to have time for a shower in the hotel,' was a later re-evaluation. And, by and by, 'Bloody hell, we don't have time to go to the hotel – we'll have to drive straight to the gig.'

Driving straight to the gig, of course, presupposed we knew exactly where Vicar Street was. We didn't. And it was now seven-fifteen. In fifteen minutes our £1,000 tickets would be given away. Panic-stricken, we sped down one street and up another – and, sad to report, back down the first street again and, yes, back up the second street again, trying frantically to locate a landmark or a sign.

We stopped and accosted a pedestrian. Now, I've no wish to caricature here nor would I wish to sneer at the very real and delightful friendliness of Dubliners. But, at seven-twenty, ten minutes before our £1,000 tickets were to be given away, this passer-by really did say, 'Ah, bejasus, sir, would it be the Bob Dylan concert you'd be going to? And, Jesus, Mary and Joseph, would you be after coming the whole way from Belfast? Bejasus, I'd say you'd be a real fan, to be sure.' After I produced my switchblade and held it to his throat he was persuaded to cut the colourful-Dublin-character bollocks and give us directions. We now had five minutes to save our tickets.

A few minutes later we found the street – but it was a one-way street and we were going the wrong way. 'I'll run on and get the tickets – you deal with the car,' I shouted and took to my heels, sprinting up Vicar Street.

As a nearby clock chimed the half-hour, I burst through the door – and was confronted by . . . Robert McMillen, the supposedly hospitalised *Irish News* journo, for whom I was depping. He had a plastic, Royal Victoria Hospital ID bracelet around his wrist. 'I checked myself out because I wanted to see Bob so much,' he said – adding hopefully, 'Are you on your own?' I explained my wife was parking the car. Robert, the *Irish News* staffer, looked at me, the *Irish News* occasional freelance, thoughtfully. Things, it seemed, were about to turn nasty. But Robert was a gentleman. 'Your name is on the tickets,' he said. 'I'll go back to Belfast.' And he shuffled painfully out the door, ticketless and Bobless but honourable, and was last seen dragging his ailing body down Vicar Street, the sound of his demented screaming echoing off the walls.

Our tickets admitted us to the standing area at the back of the balcony. Elvis Costello edged by, Bono was around somewhere and the glitterati of Dublin were here and there and everywhere.

'Wasn't this gig meant to start at seven-forty-five?' I mused, as seven-forty-five came and went. 'Maybe it's an eight o'clock start.' But it wasn't. And it wasn't eight-fifteen and it wasn't eight-thirty or eight-forty-five or nine either. In fact His Bobness didn't hit the stage until nine-twenty. Now, cast your mind back to the beginning of this saga and you will remember that my review needed to be with the copy-takers by ten. This was not good.

Bob began his first song. Disaster. I didn't have a clue what it was. Bob began his second song. Disaster squared. I didn't have a clue what that was either. Nor did I have a clue what his third song was – until towards its end I thought I heard the name Ramona. Didn't he once have a song 'To Ramona'? Could this be it? But it wasn't much to write a review about. In fact it looked like my review in its entirety was going to read: 'Bob's third song might have been "To Ramona".'

He began his fourth song: *'They're selling postcards of the hanging . . .'*. 'Desolation Row'! I was in business. But it was now nine-forty – and I was standing in such pitch blackness that I couldn't see to write. I squeezed through the crowd and out of the room, crouched down by a light at skirting-board height in the darkened corridor, and, still listening to the music, scribbled my review. Then I ran to find a payphone. There was one downstairs. Now, payphones in the Republic of Ireland operate differently to those in Northern Ireland. You don't need to be a genius to work out the difference – but somehow, this time, I just couldn't get through. 'Is there something wrong with this phone?' I shouted over to the barman.

'Yes, it's broken,' he replied.

'Do you have another phone?' I cried desperately.

'No, but there's probably one up the street somewhere.'

I sprinted outside and up the street and at nine-fifty-five I found a payphone – and got through. Now, I had filled my pockets with coins but have you any idea how much it costs to ring Belfast from Dublin from a call box? Well, suffice it to say that *I* do now but I didn't then. Every sentence I dictated seemed to cost another punt. I tried speaking faster and faster. The copy-taker kept telling me to speak slower and slower. My head was throbbing with stress. Sweat was running down my face and down my back. I wasn't going to make it. I put my last coin in the slot – and watched its value evaporate. I shouted to the copy-taker, 'I've no more coins,' and, leaving out a whole chunk of what I'd written so feverishly, while squatting on the floor of the club, I improvised a concluding line.

And then I collapsed on the floor of the phone box sobbing hysterically. Well, not quite, but I was feeling pretty wiped out, I can tell you. Still, at least my work was over for the night and I could go back and enjoy the rest of the gig.

'So just where do you think you're going, sonny?' The bouncer was blocking my way.

'It's all right,' I explained. 'I just stepped out to make a phone call – I was in earlier.'

'I've been on this door all night and you haven't gone past me. Take a hike.'

'Look – here's my ticket.' I proffered the stub of the ticket that I had seized so gratefully from Robert a few hours previously.

'That ticket's not valid. Sling your hook.'

I couldn't believe it. It was a toss-up whether I was going to burst into tears or pass out. But then I glimpsed the barman who had told me the phone was out of order. 'He'll remember me,' I pleaded – and, God bless him, so he did.

'OK,' said the bouncer, 'but don't do it again.'

My head was splitting and I felt weak and dizzy from stress, exhaustion and hunger. But, clutching the banister for support, I made it up the stairs and regained my place in the balcony.

'What kept you?' my wife asked, irritably.

'It's a long story,' I answered, as Bob tore into another unrecognisable classic.

BOB DYLAN
VICAR STREET, DUBLIN

Bob Dylan is indisputably one of the two or three greatest and most influential musicians of the entire rock era. Few, however, of the millions of fans who have revered him over the last four decades have ever had the thrill of experiencing His Bobness' inimitable magic in an intimate club. But last night, extraordinarily, the great man played Vicar Street in Dublin in front of a mere 700 enraptured devotees.

To say the atmosphere was electric would be a mealy mouthed understatement, and the ecstatic shrieks when he ambled on stage surely were as ear-piercing as any that would be heard at a Spice Girls' gig.

Dressed to impress in a black suit, black skinny tie, patterned shirt and a pair of zipped, white leather, winkle-picker boots that were surely a souvenir of his visit to Carnaby Street in 1965, Dylan looked pale and frail. There again, what Sixties rock survivor doesn't?

But the years have not taken their toll on Dylan's talent and he gave an impressive, exciting, focused performance.

To the delight of all he plundered his back-pages for songs like 'To Ramona' and 'Desolation Row', his ominous, apocalyptic masterpiece – a song surely as potent and relevant in the early twenty-first century as it was in the mid-to-late twentieth century. Another revisited, reinvented classic was 'Tangled Up In Blue', sung with extraordinary passion and venom.

Dylan was accompanied by two guitarists and a bassist, who variously played acoustically and electrically, and a drummer. Throughout he proved there's no rock hero like a Sixties rock hero.

Trevor Hodgett · Concert review originally published in the *Irish News* (14 May 2000)

ACKNOWLEDGEMENTS

Given the aeons of time and the pantheon of people who have influenced, helped with and, of course, originally commissioned much of the work which this book encompasses, it would be almost impossible to list – to even remember – everyone who deserves a doff of the hat. So to all those editors who provided the platforms, to the musicians who inspired us and who gave us their time, and to all those others who helped or encouraged us with information, hospitality, kind words and live music: thank you!

Bringing a book from inception to completion is never simple – a view to which our long-suffering wives, Heather and Trish, will attest. Among those who put themselves out for us and to whom we are indebted are James Davis and Mark Case for seemingly endless photo scanning; all those musicians, publicists, friends, fans and professionals who looked for, found and provided us with photographs; Tom Dunne, for such an eloquent foreword; and, most especially, Dominic Carroll, our editor and designer, whose patience and dedication has been absolutely pivotal in bringing the ship to shore. And thanks finally to Seán Body at Helter Skelter and Chris Charlesworth at Omnibus for their input and support.

If any should still, at this farthest-flung outpost of the book, harbour doubts that the true home of rock 'n' roll is in Ireland, I say to you only this: a-ring-dum-a-do-dum-da, whack-fol-the-daddy-o, there's whiskey in the jar-o. Thank you, ladies and gentlemen, goodnight and safe home. The Brush has left the building.

Colin Harper (left), Davy Graham, Ards Guitar Festival, 2000

Henry McCullough (left), Trevor Hodgett, Ards Guitar Festival, 2001

PHOTO CREDITS

INDEX

SELECT DISCOGRAPHY

Rather than seeking to list every record released by every artist featured in the book, we've concentrated on listing and describing recorded works that are easily available, with label details and date of (re)issue. Good hunting . . .

SECTION 1: The Gates Are Opened

SWEENEY'S MEN

The Legend Of Sweeney's Men
(Castle CMDDD 932, 2004)
The complete works: both Pye Ireland singles and both Transatlantic albums, *Sweeney's Men* and *The Tracks Of Sweeney*, plus five Capitol Showband singles sides featuring Sweeney's cameos and a selection of Sweeney-related tracks from Anne Briggs, The Woods Band, Steeleye Span and Andy Irvine. Annotated by Colin Harper. Andy Irvine and Johnny Moynihan can also be heard – along with Christy Moore and Liam O'Flynn – on the 1973 Planxty album, *Cold Blow And The Rainy Night* (Shanachie SHANCD 79011, 1990). And, be assured, practically any album by or featuring Andy Irvine is worth hearing.

ANNE BRIGGS

Anne Briggs: A Collection
(Topic TSCD 504, 1999)
The complete Topic recordings (1962–71) plus the two live tracks featured on Decca's elusive *Edinburgh Folk Festival 1963* LP. This CD supersedes Fellside's 1990 *Classic Anne Briggs* collection of Topic recordings. Annotated by Colin Harper.

The Time Has Come
(Columbia 4916892, 1998)
Mid-price CD issue of the rare 1971 CBS album, previously only available (expensively) on CD in Japan. Annotated by Colin Harper.

Sing A Song For You
(Fledg'ling FLED 3008, 1996)
The previously unreleased third and final LP, recorded with folk-rock band Ragged Robin in 1973. Annotated by Steve Ashley and Anne Briggs.

Also worth finding
Acoustic Routes (Demon/Code 90, 1993), a various artists soundtrack to a BBC documentary on '60s British folkies, includes Anne duetting with Bert Jansch on 'Go Your Way My Love', recorded in Edinburgh, 1992. *Cottonhead* (Vertical Form, 2004), a mesmerising, largely instrumental album by journalist David Sheppard's 'post folk-rock' band State River Widening, includes Anne contributing newly recorded guest vocals on 'Lowlands'. *www.verticalform.com* Additionally, Anne can be glimpsed (sadly, in conversation rather than performance) on the 1966 BBC documentary *Travelling For A Living*, included on DVD in The Watersons box set *Mighty River Of Song* (Topic TSFCD4002, 2004).

DAV(E)Y GRAHAM

The Guitar Player
(Castle CMRCD 622, 2003)
The 1963 LP debut, expanded with tracks licensed in from Rollercoaster's releases (see below) and superseding a previous reissue on See For Miles in 1992 – except that that version is still the only way to find all three tracks from Topic's 1962 *3/4 AD* EP, added there as a bonus. Annotated by Colin Harper.

Folk Routes, New Routes
(Topic TSCD 819, 1999)
The 1964 Decca LP of traditional songs, jointly credited with vocalist Shirley Collins. Annotated by Lawrence Aston.

Folk, Blues & Beyond
(Topic TSCD 820, 1999)
The 1965 Decca LP. Annotated
by Lawrence Aston.

Fire In The Soul
(Topic TSCD 818, 1999)
The third of Topic's trio of Decca-licensed
material, this one being a compilation drawn
from the four 1966–70 LPs *Midnight Man*,
Large As Life And Twice As Natural, *Hat*
and *Holly Kaleidoscope* plus the classic 1962
Topic EP track 'Angi'. None of these LPs
have yet been available individually on CD.
Annotated by Lawrence Aston.

Godington Boundry
(President PRCD 160, 2004)
A remastered reissue of the 1970 President
LP, superseding the 1999 See For Miles
reissue. Annotated by Colin Harper.

After Hours
(Rollercoaster RCCD 3021, 1997)
Davy recorded live on reel-to-reel
at an after-gig party at Hull University,
1967. Atmospheric stuff. Annotated
by John Pilgrim.

All That Moody
(Rollercoaster RCCD 3022, 1999)
The rare 1976 Eron LP, plus six previously
unreleased live/demo tracks from the same
period. Beautifully packaged, as are all
Rollercoaster releases. Also available (like
After Hours) on limited edition heavyweight
10 inch vinyl. Annotated by John Renbourn.

The Complete Guitarist
(Kicking Mule KMCD 3914, 1999)
The entirety of Davy's Irish-influenced
1977 instrumental LP *The Complete
Guitarist* plus bonus tracks from his 1979
Kicking Mule follow-up *Dance For Two
People* and the label's 1980 various artists LP
Blues Guitar Workshop. Released via
Fantasy in the US and Ace in the UK.
Annotated by Duck Baker.

Also worth finding on CD
Acoustic Routes (Demon/Code 90, 1993),
featuring two 1992 tracks recorded for a
BBC documentary; *Playing In Traffic* (Crack
Probe, 1993), a patchy 'comeback' record;
Midnight Magic (2001 fanzine freebie), a
collection of unreleased 1966–2000 amateur
live recordings, made available via the
admirable though short-lived DG fanzine
Midnight Man.

SECTION 2: The Story of Them

THEM

The Story Of Them Featuring Van Morrison
(London 8448132, 1997)
Pretty much the complete works of the Van
Morrison-era Them although, frustratingly,
the much-loved 'Mighty Like A Rose' is
omitted, apparently because Morrison
regards it as a demo which should never have
been released in the first place.

Now And Them
(Rev-Ola CR REV 29, 2003)

Time Out! Time In For Them
(Rev-Ola CR REV 52, 2003)
Hear the 1968 Kenny McDowell-era Them
and hear the sound of rock history being
rewritten as the band venture into the mystic
and prove that there was, in fact, life after
Van. Both albums feature bonus tracks.

Also worth finding
If you particularly want the original Van-era
albums on CD then 1965's *Them* (Deram
844 824–2, 1998) and 1966's *Them Again*
(Deram 8448252, 1998), both bogstandard,
no-expense-incurred reissues, fit the bill. And
if you're a complete Them obsessive and the
medication isn't working then you might be
able to track down *The Happy Tiger Years*
(Synton 1610973, 1997), which compiles
tracks from the Alan Henderson-led Them
that originally appeared on the 1970 *Them*
and 1971 *In Reality* albums, and *Reunion
Concert* (Spalax SPALAXCD 14967, 1996),
which is actually the 1979 studio album *Shut
Your Mouth* in disguise. Finally, the various
artists compilation *Belfast Beat, Maritime
Blues* (Ace/Big Beat CDWIKD 152, 1997) in
addition to featuring a couple of Them
recordings (otherwise available), is the only
place to find on CD recordings of The Mad
Lads/Moses K & The Prophets (featuring
Kenny McDowell on vocals) and The People
(who later became
Eire Apparent).

TRUTH

Of Them And Other Tales
(Epilogue EP1003, 1995)
Listen to these demos and film soundtrack
music, cobbled together 25 years after the
band's demise, relish Kenny McDowell's
masterful and versatile singing, Jim
Armstrong's awesomely imaginative guitar

playing, and, on three tracks, Ray Elliott's extraordinary and inimitable piano and flute playing, and weep at Truth's lost potential.

BELFAST GYPSIES

Them Belfast Gypsies
(Rev-Ola CRREV 49, 2003)
The band's 1967-released album.
Part produced by Kim Fowley, it's way over the top and somewhat mad but only a dullard could resist the band's rowdy, rambunctious, ramshackle charm. Reissued with bonus tracks.

TRADER HORNE

Morning Way
(Castle CMRCD074, 2000)
The original, 1970 classic album plus both sides of a non-album single – the band's entire output. Judy Dyble, having disappeared from the music scene for decades, resurfaced with a perhaps surprisingly impressive solo album *Enchanted Garden* (Talking Elephant, TECD068, 2004), effectively continuing the Trader Horne sound in collaboration with production wizard/multi-instrumentalist Marc Swordfish.

JACKIE MCAULEY

Jackie McAuley ... Plus
(See For Miles SEECD 315, 1991)
McAuley's 1971 solo album – his last album for nearly twenty years – reissued with bonus tracks.

Fretwork
(Road Goes On Forever RGFCD 032, 1996)
A compilation of tracks from *Gael Force*, a 1990 LP by McAuley's band Poor Mouth, and *Headspin*, a 1994 solo album.

Shadowboxing
(Road Goes On Forever RGF/JMCCD 041, 1998)

Bad Day At Blackrock
(A New Day AND CD39, 2000)

KENNY MCDOWELL/RONNIE GREER BLUES BAND

Live At The Island
(no label, 2003)
Absurdly, if we ignore for the moment the posthumous Truth demos-and-soundtrack CD, this is McDowell's first album since *Time Out! Time In For Them* in 1968 -- and he sings magnificently on it. Available from ronlee0@tinyworld.co.uk

Also worth finding
Them drummer John Wilson's albums with Taste – *Taste* (Polydor 8415992, 1992), *On The Boards* (Polydor 8415992, 1993), *Live Taste* (Polydor 8416022, 1994), *Live At The Isle Of Wight* (Polydor 8416012, 1992) – are readily available as is *Best Of Taste* (Polydor 5219992, 2000).

ERIC BELL

Live Tonite ... Plus
(Angel Air SJPCD 084, 2001)

A Blues Night In Dublin
(Voiceprint VP247CD, 2002)
Recorded in Sweden in 1996 and in Dublin in 2002, both provide evidence of Bell's enduring blues prowess.

Also worth finding
Bell's albums with Thin Lizzy – 1971's *Thin Lizzy* (Decca 8205282, 1998), 1972's *Shades Of A Blue Orphanage* (Spectrum 8295272, 2004) and 1973's *Vagabonds Of The Western World* (London 8209692, 1998) – are readily available. Also available are the compilations *Greatest Hits [Enhanced]* (UMTV 9821111, 2004), although this is mainly drawn from the band's post-Bell career, and *Whisky In The Jar* (Spectrum 5520852, 1998). The Noel Redding Band's *Clonakilty Cowboys* (1975) and *Blowin'* (1976), which both feature Bell, have been released on a single CD (BGO BGOCD581, 2003).

SECTION 3: Belfast Blues

OTTILIE PATTERSON

Ottilie Patterson with Chris Barber
(Jazz Colours 8747422, 2000)

Ottilie Patterson with Chris Barber's Jazz Band 1955–1958
(Lake LACD 30, 1993)

Madame Blues And Dr Jazz
(Black Lion BLC 760506, 1991)
Check Ottilie in her gutsy, raunchy prime
and marvel. And then wonder why she isn't a
household name even amongst blues
aficionados.

Also worth finding
Several albums by Chris Barber's Jazz Band
from the '50s and early '60s feature
Patterson here and there, including *In
Barber's Chair* (Lake LACD 185, 2003),
Bandbox No. 1 (Lake LACD 194, 2004) and
*Chris Barber's Blues Book Volume
One/Good Morning Blues* (BGO BGOCD
380, 1997).

SECTION 4: Rock In A Hard Place

HENRY MCCULLOUGH

Unfinished Business
(Head-The-Ball Records HTB CD 002, 2003)
Includes a cover of Paul McCartney's 'Big Barn
Bed' on the original Wings version of which
McCullough played, and versions of classic
McCullough compositions such as 'Belfast To
Boston', 'Failed Christian' and 'I Couldn't
Sleep For Thinking Of Hank Williams'.
Available from *www.henrymccullough.com*

Also worth finding
Blue Sunset (Sell 0030, 1998) and *Belfast To
Boston* (Walk Away WA013, 2001) are other
excellent McCullough albums, mainly
available at gigs.

GREASE BAND

The Grease Band/Amazing Grease
(Line LICD 9011010, 1991)
The two post-Joe Cocker Grease Band
albums – the first from 1971, the second
posthumously released in 1976 – on a single
CD. The self-titled debut album is also
available in its own right (Hux 045, 2003)
with live bonus tracks from a BBC session.

Also worth finding
McCullough plays on many of the tracks on
Joe Cocker's first two albums, 1969's *With A
Little Help From My Friends* (A&M
4904192, 1999) and 1970's *Joe Cocker!*
(A&M 4904202, 1999) and on every track
on *Joe Cocker And The Grease Band On Air*
(Strange Fruit SRSCD036, 1997), which
comprises BBC radio material from 1968 and
1969. He also plays on 1973's *Red Rose
Speedway* (Parlophone CDPMCOL4) by
Paul McCartney and Wings and on some of
the tracks on McCartney's 2002 compilation
Wingspan (Parlophone 5328502).

EIRE APPARENT

Sunrise
(Sequel NEXCD 199, 1992)
1969 Hendrix-produced album. At the time of
writing a new reissue of the album, apparently
with bonus tracks (presumably the 1967 non-
album single 'Follow Me' / 'Here I Go Again'),
has appeared on the Italian label Akarma.

ERNIE GRAHAM

Ernie Graham
(Hux HUX032, 2002)
Graham's 1971 album augmented with his
1978 single, the Phil Lynott-composed
'Romeo And The Lonely Girl' and its B-side.

SKID ROW

Skid Row
(Essential ESMCD913, 2000)
Confusingly (like the Skid Row reissues story
in general), this is actually their first album,
Skid. Annotated by Alan Robinson.

34 Hours
(Columbia 4805252, 1995)
The second album, although this – its most
recent reissue on CD – is unfortunately no
longer available.

Skid Row
(Snapper SMMCD608, 2000)
More confusion: this is in fact the seemingly
untitled third and final album, originally
issued (twenty odd years after the event) by
Castle on vinyl in 1990, in packaging that
suggested their chosen title for it was *Gary
Moore / Brush Shiels / Noel Bridgeman*.
Castle then issued it under the same bets-
hedged title on CD in 1993.

Note: If searching out releases by the Irish Skid Row beware of confusing them with the 1980s/90s American metal band of the same name. At the time of writing contracts had just been signed by Brush, Gary and Noel for the first-time release (title to be decided), on Hux Records, of the group's first four non-album singles sides plus a blistering 33 minute BBC radio concert from 1971 – all that remains of their several session and concert appearances on the BBC. In December 2004 Brush, with his sons Matthew and Jude, delivered a new Skid Row album – at the time of writing, available only at his gigs – seemingly titled (no doubt in deference to the maelstrom of existing confusion) *Skid Row / Brush Shiels* or maybe *Brush Shiels / Skid Row*...

GARY MOORE

Gary has had – and continues to have – such a prolific career, across such a range of bands, solo and collaborative situations, that in the context of this book a representative select discography would be hard to manage and a complete one impossible. His debut solo album, *Grinding Stone*, continues the Skid Row spirit and is available on Essential ESMCD914 (2000). *Back To The Blues* (Sanctuary SANCD072, 2001) is also recommended, as is his 1994 Cream-esque collaboration with Jack Bruce and Ginger Baker, as BBM, *Around The Next Dream* – reissued in 2003 (Virgin MOORECD12) with two bonus live tracks. For those keen on musical arcanery (and if you've bought this book, let us take that for granted), Gary's guest appearances on late '60s albums by Irish contemporaries Dr Strangely Strange (*Heavy Petting*, 1971) and Granny's Intentions (*Honest Injun*, 1969) are currently available on CD. Diehards may also like to seek out the Moore-guesting 1997 'difficult third album' from Dr Strangely Strange, *Alternative Medicine*, which has an advantage over *Heavy Petting* in being in tune throughout.

HORSLIPS

Having won back the rights to their catalogue, Horslips were able to release remastered CDs of their original systematically under license to UK label Edsel in 2000–01. For the uninitiated, the 2-CD compilation *The Best Of...* (also on Edsel) is recommended as are *Happy To Meet* and *The Book Of Invasions*. While none of these

official remasters contain bonus tracks (meaning the non-album late '70s Tooraloora EP remains unavailable), all covers have been tastefully redesigned by Charles O'Connor – which usefully differentiates them from previous CD issues on Outlet and their various licensees (which feature inferior sound and shouldn't be touched with barge-poles). The albums, in chronological order, are as follows:

Happy To Meet, Sorry To Part (1972), *The Táin* (1973), *Dancehall Sweethearts* (1974), *The Unfortunate Cup Of Tea* (1975), *Drive The Cold Winter Away* (1975, an acoustic all-traditional collection), *Live* (1976), *The Book Of Invasions: A Celtic Symphony* (1976), *Tracks From The Vaults* (1977, a collection of the group's non-album releases up to that point), *Aliens* (1977), *The Man Who Built America* (1978), *Short Stories/Tall Tales* (1979), *Belfast Gigs* (1980)

A DVD history, including footage of their Derry one-off reunion, titled *Return Of The Dancehall Sweethearts* is anticipated for release in mid-2005.

RORY GALLAGHER

While some of his work had appeared previously on CD, Rory's back catalogue was comprehensively overhauled and splendidly remastered for systematic reissue – all but *Irish Tour* bolstered by extra tracks – on Donal Gallagher's label Capo via BMG between 1998–2000. At the same time, Donal oversaw the remastering of some of Rory's work with Taste for *The Best Of Taste* (Polydor 521–9992, 2000) – a recommended introduction to the group. The solo albums, in chronological order, are as follows:

Rory Gallagher (1971), *Deuce* (1971), *Live In Europe* (1971), *Blueprint* (1973), *Tattoo* (1973), *Irish Tour* (1974), *Against The Grain* (1975), *Calling Card* (1976), *Photo Finish* (1978), *Top Priority* (1979), *Stage Struck* (1980), *Jinx* (1982), *Defender* (1987), *Fresh Evidence* (1990)

In addition to the original solo albums being reissued a number of posthumous 'new' releases have appeared on Capo/BMG: *The BBC Sessions* (1999) is a fine 2-CD 'best of' drawn from the man's numerous studio and concert sessions for the corporation; *Let's Go To Work* (2001) is a superb, mid-price 4-CD box set comprising beautiful slip cased copies of his three live albums (*Live In Europe*, *Irish Tour* and *Stage Struck*) plus the otherwise unreleased *Meeting With The G-Man*, a stunning bootleg recorded live in 1993 (the set is recommended as a great introduction to Rory, though a longer version of *Meeting With The G-Man* was released as a single CD in 2004); *Wheels Within Wheels* (2003) is a fascinating reconstruction of something approaching the 'acoustic album' Rory was planning in his later years, here assembled from live and demo recordings including collaborations with Martin Carthy, Bert Jansch, Bela Fleck and The Dubliners. For those wishing to Sherlock about on eBay, the withdrawn/unauthorised 1974 LP *In The Beginning*, featuring 1967 demos of Taste Mk1, is worth tracking down. (But you didn't hear it from me ...). A new 2-CD compilation, provisionally entitled *Big Guns*, compiled by Donal Gallagher and featuring Rory's work remixed in 5.1 Surround Sound, is due via Sony/BMG in mid-2005.

A number of Rory appearances on DVD are available, most notably the restored/re-edited Tony Palmer film *Irish Tour* (BMG, 2001) and *Live In Concert* (Wienerworld, 2004) – a collection of three sets for German TV's Rockpalast series spanning 1976–79. Taste can be seen in the Murray Lerner film of the 1970 Isle of Wight Festival, *Message To Love* (Sanctuary, 2005) Further DVDs – of Rory's many BBC *Old Grey Whistle Test* appearances and the full Taste Isle of Wight set – are anticipated.

SECTION 5: Folk In The Seventies

MELLOW CANDLE

Swaddling Songs
(Acme ADCD 1040, 2004)
The 1972 Deram LP remastered plus the elusive 1968 SNB single. Supersedes the early '90's See For Miles CD of the LP only – although curiously that CDs mastering does deliver a notably richer, thicker sound. Annotated by John O'Regan.

The Virgin Prophet
(Kissing Spell KSCD 9520-F, c.1994)
Fascinating collection of professional demos and rehearsal recordings, including five songs never recorded commercially. Annotated by John O'Regan.

Note: New solo albums by both Alison O'Donnell and Clodagh Simonds are expected during 2005.

GAY & TERRY WOODS

The Woods Band
(Edsel EDCD 687, 2001)
The sole 1971 Woods Band LP reissued, albeit from a non-first generation source tape. Annotated by Colin Harper.

Lake Songs From Red Water: The Best Of Gay & Terry Woods
(Hux HUX040, 2003)
Compiled by Gay & Terry from their three 1974–76 Polydor LPs *Backwoods*, *The Time Is Right* and *Renowned*. Annotated by John O'Regan.

Tenderhooks
(Cooking Vinyl GUMBO CD019, 2000)
Straight reissue of the fourth and final Gay & Terry LP (for Mulligan, 1978).

Songs For Echo
(Hux HUX022, 2001)
The only Auto Da Fe CD to date – comprising two 1983 BBC Radio 1 concerts, and including most of their key songs. Phil Lynott contributes bass/backing vocals to one of the concerts. Annotated by Colin Harper.

Also worth finding on CD
Of the many Steeleye Span compilations and reissues which include material from their first album (featuring both Gay & Terry Woods) the best current option is the 2-CD set *The Lark In The Morning* (Castle, 2003) which comprises the group's first three LPs plus stray tracks in their entirety, with annotation by Ashley Hutchings biographer Geoff Wall. Gay's 'Indian Summer' with Steeleye resulted in three studio albums – *Time* (Park, 1996), *Horkstow Grange* (Park, 1998) and *Bedlam Born* (Park, 2000) – and contributions to the (almost-) all-the-line-ups reunion live album *The Journey* (Park, 1999). *Gay & Terry Woods In Concert* (Strange Fruit/Windsong, 1995) is probably out of print but features ten otherwise unavailable live and studio session recordings for the BBC from 1976 and 1978. Alongside periodic reunions with The Pogues, Terry Woods unveiled a new Woods Band in 2002 with the album *Music From The Four Corners Of Hell*, licensed to Market Square Records for the UK, though its direction is closer to that of The Pogues than the original Woods Band.

ARLO GUTHRIE
Last Of The Brooklyn Cowboys
(Koch KOC CD 7952, 1997)

KEVIN BURKE
Sweeney's Dream
(Smithsonian Folkways 40485, 2001)
Kevin B doing the business – on both the above albums, recorded during the same period in the early '70s – prior to his reputation-making involvement in The Bothy Band. Tommy Peoples played violin on the first Bothy Band LP, *1975*, but Kevin can be heard – alongside Paddy Keenan on pipes – fiddling on the subsequent 1976–78 albums *Old Hag You Have Killed Me*, *Out Of The Wind Into The Sun* and *After Hours* (live in Paris) and on the 'posthumous' 1994 Strange Fruit collection *BBC Live In Concert* – all currently available on CD. In the 1990s and beyond he has appeared on numerous albums by Patrick Street, an Irish supergroup also boasting Andy Irvine among its number.

PADDY KEENAN

Na Keen Affair
(Hot Conya HCR 01, 1996)

The Long Grazing Acre
(Compass 743552, 2001)
Na Keen Affair was Paddy's mid-'90s 'comeback' own-label release, made available internationally from 2001. *The Long Grazing Acre* is jointly credited with singer/guitarist Tommy O'Sullivan. Paddy & Tommy tour as a duo – the context in which Paddy currently wants to be heard – and their live shows are purportedly terrific. A number of Paddy's earlier solo (and, with fiddler Paddy Glackin, duo) albums for Gael Linn and Tara are also currently available on CD.

CLANNAD

Where to begin . . . This lot have more 'best ofs' to their name than actual albums, and sometimes – given the dreamy, landscapey sleeve art and similarly blancmangey titles – telling the difference can, even for the determined discographer, be taxing. Nothing new under the Clannad name has appeared for quite some time, although BMG remastered most of their post-'Harry's Game' catalogue in 2003–04, with new (dreamy, landscapey)

sleeve art and annotations from Stuart Bailie. *In A Lifetime: The Best Of Clannad* is the latest anthology, covering only the BMG years, and boasting the chilling thought of a bonus disc of 'chill out mixes'. If you must have a 'best of' go for the John O'Regan-compiled and annotated US release *The Ultimate Collection* (RCA 74321486742, 1998) which brings together material from various labels spanning the '70s to the '90s. Of the standard albums, the two immediate post-'hit single' albums *Macalla* and *Magical Ring* and the later *Anam* (all part of the recent BMG remasters series) best combine the band's singular musicality with some durable songs and the airy studio sound that became their trademark/millstone. Of the '70s albums, those recommended are *Clannad* (Spectrum 5449762, 2002), *Clannad 2* (Gael Linn CEFCD 41, 2004) and *Fuaim* (Tara CD 3008, 2000).

SECTION 6: The High Kings Of Tara

SHAUN DAVEY/RITA CONNOLLY/LIAM O'FLYNN

The Brendan Voyage
(Tara CD 3006, 1992)

The Pilgrim
(Tara CD 3032, 1994)

Granuaille
(Tara CD 3017, 2000)

The Relief Of Derry Symphony
(Tara CD 3024, 1990)
The above four albums – all of them featuring Liam O'Flynn, the latter three also featuring Rita Connolly and *The Relief Of Derry* adding saxophonist Gerard McChrystal to the list – represent the cornerstones of Shaun Davey's career as a composer of major works for orchestra and singular soloists. The dates given above are those of the most recent CD issues of the titles – although, confusingly, the CD packaging invariably maintains dates of original publishing rather than current (re)issue. In the late '90s I (Colin Harper) was commissioned to provide sleevenotes for a new US packaging of *The Brendan Voyage*, although I believe this project was shelved (the album is, however, also available as a book and CD box set, with Tim Severin's account of his re-enactment of St Brendan's legendary trip to America). While the performance on *The Brendan Voyage* album has remained the same since its original 1982 vinyl release, the

discographical history of *The Pilgrim* and *Granuaille* are a little more complex: the mid-'80s vinyl versions of each differing significantly from their '90s CD descendants and (of course) worth seeking out for the Davey diehard. *Granuaille* gets a couple of replaced/improved performances of certain tracks while one track ('The Dismissal') is removed and a new one ('The New Age') added. In 2000 its first CD pressing was replaced with an improved, re-packaged and re-mastered edition (although, in typical Tara style, the catalogue number remains the same). The vinyl version of *The Pilgrim*, meanwhile, was almost entirely replaced by a re-written, re-recorded and substantially expanded version of the work for its CD debut in 1994.

Also worth seeking out

Rita Connolly's two solo albums, *Rita Connolly* (Tara CD 2039, 1992) and *Valparaiso* (Tara CD 3033, 1995), are glorious soft-rock outings with substantial Shaun Davey input as producer, writer and musician. Shaun also provided production and arranging input into Liam O'Flynn's two solo albums of the same period – *Out To An Other Side* [sic] (Tara CD 3031, 1993) and *The Given Note* (Tara CD 3034, 1995). Liam's next solo album, *The Piper's Call*, though without any Davey input this time, continued the lavish productions and roll-call of illustrious musicians and featured guests pioneered by the previous two. An RTÉ film performance of *The Piper's Call* was released on home video in 1998, although it has yet to appear on DVD.

STOCKTON'S WING/MAURICE LENNON

The Stockton's Wing Collection
(Tara 4, 2000)

Letting Go
(Tara CD 3036, 1996)

Brian Boru: High King Of Tara
(Tara CD 3038, 2002)
There are several other Wing albums available on CD from Tara and elsewhere, but the compilation is a perfect introduction for the newcomer of the long-running and celebrated pre-Eamon McElholm version of the band, while *Letting Go* is their glorious swansong of the mid-'90s. What might have been . . . Of course, Maurice's *Brian Boru* remains a pretty epic 'what is'.

ALTAN

Island Angel
(Green Linnet GLCD1137, 1993)

Blackwater
(Virgin CDV2796, 1996)
There have, of course, been many Altan albums before and after the two above – being the last of the Frankie Kennedy era and the first of the major label era – but together they remain the group's mid-career peak. *Island Angel* is by turns serenely beautiful and exhilarating; *Blackwater* introduced new ideas, subtle use of guest musicians (notably Steve Cooney on electric bass) and greater production values, yet built upon the essential sound of the Frankie Kennedy line-up. Subsequent albums have explored new ground, perhaps not always successfully, and are as follows: *Runaway Sunday* (Virgin, 1997), *Another Sky* (Virgin, 2000) and *The Blue Idol* (Venture, 2002). The contractual vagaries of their early career with Green Linnet means there are now, in a depressingly Clannad-ish way, far too many compilations available, most appearing by license on various budget labels. The first of this litany – ironically, Green Linnet's own *The First Ten Years: 1986–1995* – is a good one-disc summary of the period, although some compilations also feature a bonus live disc (a rather muted performance taken from German radio and not used with the band's consent). Now that the band have moved on from Virgin (at least in Europe; they remain associated with the label in the US) there are two post-Frankie era compilations available: The UK release *The Best Of Altan* (Virgin 5930272, 2003) and the US release *The Best Of Altan: The Songs* (Narada, 2003). A new album is released in mid-2005.

MARTIN HAYES

Martin Hayes
(Green Linnet GLCD1127, 1993)

Under The Moon
(Green Linnet GLCD1155, 1995)
The Lonesome Touch
(Green Linnet GLCD1181, 1997)

Live In Seattle
(Green Linnet GLCD1195, 1999)
The last named pair of albums are credited jointly to Martin Hayes and Dennis Cahill, and should be the first for the curious to investigate. *Live In Seattle* is surely the best

of the lot, being a fine representation of (the second half of) a magical evening with Martin and Dennis. The pair have also appeared together and apart on various other albums in recent years. Martin contributes exclusive tracks, for example, to a various artists concert from Cork University, 1995, sampled on record as *The Gathering* (Real World, 1997), and also to the various artists set *Siol/Seed* (Magherabaun Records, 1998) – an album in support of promoting biodiversity, organised by bodhrán player Tommy Hayes. Among Dennis' outside projects is a NAIRD award-winning production credit on the Niamh Parsons' album *The Heart's Desire* (Green Linnet, 2002). Both Martin and Dennis contribute significantly to the film soundtrack album (an album released under vocalist Iarla O'Lionaird's name) *If I Could Read The Sky* (Real World, 2000). The boys also appear, individually, on *The Wildlife Album* (Market Square MSMCD134, 2005).

TAMALIN

Rhythm & Rhyme
(Grapevine GRACD 227, 1997)
Though probably hard to find now, the rights have recently reverted to the band so a re-release is likely. Tina McSherry can also be heard in splendid voice on the various artists charity project *The Wildlife Album* (Market Square MSMCD134, 2005). John McSherry can be heard as guest soloist on far too many albums to name, but the Donal Lunny 'supergroup' album *Coolfin* (Metro Blue 4935422, 1998) and the Michael McGoldrick/John McSherry co-credited *At First Light* (Vertical VERTCD061, 2003) are good starting points for investigation.

CARA DILLON

Cara Dillon
(Rough Trade RTRADECD019, 2001)

Sweet Liberty
(Rough Trade RTRADECD123, 2003)
These are the two career-making Cara Dillon solo albums, though the solo credit disguises the essential partnership with husband/producer Sam Lakeman. Cara can also be heard guesting on the Ashley Hutchings-and-friends album *Street Cries* (Topic TSCD535, 2001) and on *The Wildlife Album* (Market Square MSMCD134, 2005). Those wishing to explore further could try

the 'lost' mid-'90s album by Equation – the folk super group featuring Cara and Sam – which was finally issued as *Return To Me* (Rough Trade RTRADECD083, 2003). The truly committed might endeavour to find the now deleted Óige albums *Inspiration* (cassette-only, own label, 1992) and *Live In Glasgow* (Lochshore/KRL CDLDL1225, 1995), and the 1000-only 2-CD set *Alive In Belfast: The Warehouse Sessions* (local release, 1995) featuring two exclusive Óige live tracks (plus, incidentally, a couple of lengthy workouts by the Henry McCullough band). A new Cara Dillon album is released in 2005.

COLIN REED

Colin Reid
(Veesik VKCD102, 1999)

Tilt
(Topic TSCD530, 2001)

Swim
(Topic TSCD541, 2003)
Impossible to pigeonhole, Colin's eclectic creativity delights on all three of his albums proper, with each one raising his game and widening the palette of sound through careful scoring for a supporting cast of players. Colin can also be heard, solo and (thus far uniquely on record) playing electric guitar behind Tina McSherry on *The Wildlife Album* (Market Square MSMCD134, 2005) and as a backing musician on various Eddi Reader recordings. Those who attend his live shows may be lucky enough to pick up a copy of the limited edition, and self-explanatory, own-label CD *Live*.

MISCELLANEOUS

There are, of course, many 'various artists' compilations of Irish music out there, often with the word 'Celtic' in the title. You pay your money and you take your chance. The most eclectic and all-encompassing compilations – from '60s folk to post millennial rock – are those based on votes from listeners to Tom Dunne's popular and never less than stimulating Today FM show *Pet Sounds*, released as *Tom Dunne's 30 Best Irish Hits Vol.1* and *Vol.2* (Tara, 2003). Tom's show can be heard via the internet: *www.todayfm.com*
There are also, of course, many other artists from the era covered in this anthology who

might well have been included. A couple of delightfully arcane ones that spring to mind are the mid-'70s progressive rock bands Fruupp and Peggy's Leg, both of whom have impressive, recently re-mastered discs available – respectively, *Grinilla* (Kissing Spell, 2002) and *It's All Up Now* (Castle, 2004).

Referred to above, *The Wildlife Album* (Market Square, 2005, available from *www.thewildlifealbum.com*). A charity project organised by one of the authors of this book, Colin Harper, to aid the Ulster Wildlife Trust and the WWF. It includes exclusive tracks involving many of those featured herein – Cara Dillon, Tina McSherry, Martin Hayes, Dennis Cahill, Andy Irvine and Colin Reid. Colin Reid and Martin Hayes also contribute, as does Henry McCullough, to the debut album *The Road To The West* (Market Square, 2004) by Belfast singer Janet Holmes – an album which includes a cover of Sweeney's Men's 'Dreams'. See: *www.janetholmes.com*

A decent six-part RTÉ television series chronicling the history of Irish rock music, *From A Whisper To A Scream*, was released on DVD in America under that title in 2001, and reissued as *Out Of Ireland* in 2003. At the time of writing neither of the authors have had a chance to view these DVDs and consequently can't guarantee that they are as complete as the TV series. All that can be said is that the first two episodes of the TV series covered the development of Irish folk and rock, from the Clancy Brothers and the showbands onwards, pretty impressively, with vintage clips of Skid Row, Planxty, Rory Gallagher, the original Thin Lizzy line-up and Horslips among others. One DVD that can most assuredly be recommended is *Planxty – Live 2004*, capturing the concert reunion of Andy Irvine, Donal Lunny, Christy Moore and Liam O'Flynn splendidly plus a bonus documentary including vintage performance clips and recent interviews.

Finally, one website covering superbly – with information, reminiscences and a vast array of vintage photographs – the Irish showband, beat music and progressive rock worlds of the '60s and early '70s is Francis Kennedy's *www.irishowbands.net* Highly recommended – not least to those for whom this book is simply not long enough!

AVAILABLE ON CD

THEM
Now And Them
CRREV 29

After Van Morrison's bid for solo fame, one half of Them became the Kim Fowley-sponsored Belfast Gypsies, the other half took on Belfast powerhouse vocalist and old mate Kenny McDowell, and headed for California…where with the aid of producer Ray Ruff they signed to Capitol subsidiary Tower. Two overlooked albums resulted, of which this was the first. This album has never before been released on CD and comes complete with the rare single mixes, all from original masters. The sleevenotes contain the full story of Them in California.

Witchdoctor/What's The Matter Baby/Truth Machine/Square Room/You're Just What I Was Looking For Today/Dirty Ol Man (At The Age Of Sixteen)/Nobody Loves You When You're Down And Out /Walking In The Queen's Garden/I'm Happier To Love You/Come To Me

Bonus tracks: Square Room/But It's Alright/Walking In The Queen's Garden/I'm Happier To Love You

BELFAST GYPSIES
Them Belfast Gypsies
CRREV 49

The second part of Cherry Red's Them trilogy details how brothers Jackie and Pat McAuley enlisted a new crew, remaining true to the tough R&B/beat sound of the Them recordings they had contributed to. Meeting maverick producer Kim Fowley, they decided to take this sound forward in a series of blistering recordings which developed the beat sound like psychedelia never happened. This album, put together for the Swedish market where the Gypsies were a legendary live attraction, never saw a proper release outside Sweden but here it is expanded with their mega-rare single 'People, Let's Freak Out' and single mixes of 'Gloria's Dream' and 'Secret Police'. Detailed notes by Jon 'Mojo' Mills of *Shindig!* magazine include an exclusive interview on the album's history with producer Fowley.

Gloria's Dream/The Crazy World Inside Me/Midnight Train/Aria Of The Fallen Angels/Baby Blue/People, Let's Freak Out/Boom Boom/The Last Will and Testament/Portland Town/Hey Gyp, Dig The Slowness/Suicide Song/Secret Police/The Gorilla/Gloria's Dream (single mix)/Secret Police (single mix)

THEM
Time Out! Time In For Them
CRREV 52

The third part of Cherry Red's Them trilogy finds the California-bound edition of the band, having explored pop, psych, full-on garage punk and even their Maritime Club roots on 'Now And Them', plunging full on into the Psychedelic maelstrom they helped create, produced once more by Texas rockabilly maverick Ray Ruff. Released for the first time on CD anywhere, plus bonus non-LP singles in their original mono and extensive liner notes by Jon 'Mojo' Mills of the celebrated *Shindig!* magazine featuring input from band members, this is essential for all fans of quality psychedelia, garage-punk and 1960s psych-pop…the sleeve itself is worth the price of admission!

Time Out For Time In/She Put A Hex On You/Bent Over You/Waltz Of The Flies/Black Widow Spider/We've All Agreed To Help/Market Place/Just One Conception/Young Woman/The Moth

Bonus tracks: But It's Alright/Dirty Old Man/Square Room/We've All Agreed To Help/Waltz Of The Flies/Dark Are The Shadows/Corinna

AVAILABLE FROM THE COLLINS PRESS

Far from the Shamrock Shore
The Story of Irish-American Immigration through Song
MICK MOLONEY

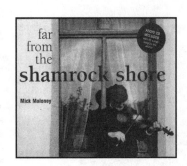

For centuries Irish emigrants expressed their deepest feeling through song. These songs and the stories they tell are captured in a passionately-written illustrated history. The accompanying CD goes beyond the standard compilation. Most of the songs have not been recorded for more than 50 years and make rare and fascinating listening.

ISBN 1-903464-13-7   HB   €25.00

Seán Ó Riada
His Life and Work
TOMÁS Ó CANAINN

Seán Ó Riada is one of the most fascinating and significant characters in twentieth-century Irish artistic life. In this wide-ranging account of his life and work his friend and colleague reveals the complex personality of a unique individual. From schooldays in Clare to student days in Cork city and then working in Dublin and Cork, the author paints a vivid picture of an ambivalent talent.

ISBN 1-903464-40-4   PB   €17.95

A Spring in my Step

JOAN MCDONNELL

FOREWORD BY GAY BYRNE

'I am eight years old and officially declared to be handicapped. I am about to undertake the greatest adventure of my young life. I am going on a long train journey all by myself.' So begins a wonderfully amusing and poignant memoir. Stricken with polio as a baby Joan spends three years in a Dublin hospital. After numerous operations she returns to Limerick walking with the aid of callipers. She must learn to cope with poverty, a housing estate, school and one short, misshapen leg.

ISBN 1-903464-60-9   PB   €12.95

An Irish Navvy

The Diary of an Exile

DONALL MACAMHLAIGH

TRANSLATED FROM IRISH BY VALENTIN IREMONGER

This book is an extraordinarily vivid picture of an Irish navvy's life in the England of the 1950s. Workless days, the hardships of work camps, lonesome partings after trips home, periods of intense isolation and occasional bitterness were all part of the picture. Originally published in Irish to wide acclaim, this translation was first published in 1964.

ISBN 1-903464-36-6   PB   €12.95

The Height of Nonsense
PAUL CLEMENTS

Visit the 32 counties of Ireland with Paul Clements, armed with his own rules of the road, e.g., 'Forsake all twenty-first century Celtic superhighways in favour of boreens'. Faced with some lengthy leave he couldn't afford, Paul travelled the GMRs (Great Mountain Roads) in search of the county tops. He explored remote corners of little-known counties, some very flat, and spent time with the eccentric and quaint. Listen to tales of druids, banshees, high-waymen and loose women.
PS. Why did he find only 28 county tops?

ISBN 1-903464-69-2   PB   €13.95

Dowtcha Boy!
An Anthology of Cork Slang
MORTY MCCARTHY

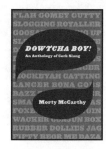

Becoming familiar with Cork 'lingo' isn't easy but *Dowtcha Boy!* aims to make the reader 'crabbit' (cute, wise to) with little effort. It's 'simple out', like! Morty McCarthy, one-time drummer with The Sultans of Ping FC, went out on a mission to record Cork's quirky words and unique expressions and make them available to the public. On his travels around his native city Morty collected over 400 words and phrases voiced by Corkonians. Memories will be jogged and the humorous illustrations by Fergus Keane will surely make it worth a sconce1

ISBN 1-903464-68-4   PB   €7.99

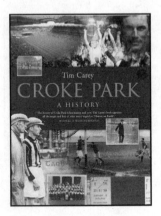

Croke Park
A History
TIM CAREY

Headquarters of our largest sporting and cultural organisation, the GAA, its arena has witnessed many dramas. Thousands have played on its stage while millions have watched. Today it is one of the world's most impressive stadiums – the third largest in Europe – and a symbol of the GAA's strength. This history tells the story of 'Croker' from the late nineteenth century to the present day.

ISBN 1-903464-54-4   HB   €30.00